CLARENDON ANCIENT HISTORY SERIES

General Editors

The aim of the CLARENDON ANCIENT HISTORY SERIES is to provide authoritative translations, introductions, and commentaries to a wide range of Greek and Latin texts studied by ancient historians. The books will be of interest to scholars, graduate students, and advanced undergraduates.

QUINTUS CICERO

A Brief Handbook on Canvassing for Office
COMMENTARIOLUM PETITIONIS

Translated
with Introduction and Commentary by
W. Jeffrey Tatum

OXFORD
UNIVERSITY PRESS

OXFORD
UNIVERSITY PRESS

Great Clarendon Street, Oxford, OX2 6DP,
United Kingdom

Oxford University Press is a department of the University of Oxford.
It furthers the University's objective of excellence in research, scholarship,
and education by publishing worldwide. Oxford is a registered trade mark of
Oxford University Press in the UK and in certain other countries

First Edition published in 2018

Impression: 1

Published in the United States of America by Oxford University Press
198 Madison Avenue, New York, NY 10016, United States of America

British Library Cataloguing in Publication Data
Data available

Library of Congress Control Number: 2018930555

ISBN 978-0-19-815307-8

Printed and bound by
CPI Group (UK) Ltd, Croydon, CR0 4YY

for Diana Burton

Acknowledgements

My work on this commentary, begun some years ago, was interrupted by a personal crisis and would not have been taken up again were it not for the kindness and patience of the editors of this series, especially Miriam Griffin, John Marincola, and Susan Treggiari. Others have also been encouraging, not least Jerzy Linderski and Robert Morstein-Marx. I am grateful to audiences at universities in Australasia, Europe, and America, who listened kindly to my ideas and responded with valuable comments. This commentary also benefited from my participation in workshops organized by Cristina Rosillo López in conjunction with her project, Opinión pública y comunicación política en la República Romana, sponsored by the Spanish government. I enjoyed welcome financial support from the Joint Research Committee and the Joint Leave Committee of the Faculty of Humanities and Social Sciences at Victoria University of Wellington. I also received a very generous Marsden Grant from the New Zealand Royal Society. I want to express my gratitude to the Institute for Advanced Study in the Humanities at the University of Edinburgh and the Institute for Classical Studies at the University of London for providing me with congenial settings in which to work. I could never adequately thank Jon Hall, Chris Pelling, Robin Seager, or Susan Treggiari, each of whom read a draft of the entire commentary. They saved me from numerous errors and offered me suggestions so superb that I avidly seized upon them all. They should not be held responsible for whatever wrongheadedness or blundering remains. I am also grateful to the staff of Oxford University Press, especially Charlotte Loveridge and Georgina Leighton. Rosemary Roberts has done so much to improve this book I hardly know how to begin to thank her. My greatest debt is to Diana Burton. She has never complained when her attentions were distracted again and again from her work on Greek religion, and I have learned a lot from our conversations. And she continues to make life fun. This book is dedicated to her.

Contents

List of Figures

Abbreviations

The abbreviations employed for periodicals are in general those found in *L'Année Philologique*. Abbreviations of ancient authors and their works are those found in *The Oxford Classical Dictionary*, 4th edn. (Oxford, 2012). Asconius' commentary on Cicero's speeches is cited in the edition of A.C. Clark, *Q. Asconii Pediani orationum Ciceronis quinque enarratio* (Oxford, 1907); the Bobbio Scholiast (and other Ciceronian scholia) are cited according to the edition of T. Stangl, *Ciceronis orationum scholiastae* (Hildesheim, 1964). The fragments of Sallust's *Historiae* are cited in reference to P. McGushin, *Sallust: The Histories*, vol. 1 (Oxford, 1992) and vol. 2 (Oxford, 1994).

The following abbreviations are also employed:

AE	*L'Année Epigraphique* (Paris, 1888–).
ANRW	H. Temporini and W. Hasse (eds.), *Aufstieg und Niedergang der römischen Welt* (Berlin, 1972–).
CIL	*Corpus inscriptionum Latinarum* (Berlin, 1863–).
DK	H. Diels and W. Kranz, *Fragmente der Vorsokratiker*, 6th edn. (Berlin, 1952).
FRHist	T.J. Cornell (ed.), *The Fragments of the Roman Historians*, 3 vols. (Oxford, 2013).
ILLRP	A. Degrassi (ed.), *Inscriptiones Latinae liberae rei publicae*, 2nd edn., 2 vols. (Florence, 1965).
ILS	H. Dessau (ed.), *Inscriptiones Latinae selectae*, 2nd edn. (Berlin, 1954).
LHS	M. Leumann, J.B. Hofmann, and A. Szantyr, *Lateinische Grammatik*, 3 vols. (Munich, 1972–9).
LTUR	E.M. Steinby (ed.), *Lexicon topographicum urbis Romae*, 6 vols. (Rome, 1993–2000).
MAMA	*Monumenta Asiae Minoris Antiquae* (Manchester, 1928–).
MMR	T.R.S. Broughton, *Magistrates of the Roman Republic*, vols. 1–2 (New York, 1951–2); vol. 3 (Atlanta, 1986).
OGIS	W. Dittenberger, *Orientis Graeci inscriptiones selectae*, 2 vols. (Leipzig, 1903–5).
OLD	P.G.W. Glare (ed.), *Oxford Latin Dictionary* (Oxford, 1982).
ORF[4]	H. Malcovati, *Oratorum romanorum fragmenta liberae rei publicae*, 4th edn. (Turin, 1967).

RDGE   R.A. Sherk, *Roman Documents from the Greek East* (Baltimore, 1969).

RE   A. Pauly, G. Wissowa, and W. Kroll, *Paulys Real-Encyclopädie der classischen Altertumswissenschaft* (Stuttgart and Munich, 1893–1980).

RRC   M.H. Crawford, *Roman Republican Coinage*, 2 vols. (Cambridge, 1974).

RS   M.H. Crawford (ed.), *Roman Statutes*, 2 vols. (London, 1996).

SIG³   W. Dittenberger, *Sylloge inscriptionum Graecarum*, 4 vols. (Leipzig, 1915–24).

StR   T. Mommsen, *Römisches Staatsrecht*, 3 vols. (Leipzig, 1887–8).

TLL   *Thesaurus Linguae Latinae* (Leipzig, 1900–).

Introduction

I *A BRIEF HANDBOOK ON CANVASSING FOR OFFICE (COMMENTARIOLUM PETITIONIS)*

Some time after the death of Queen Anne on 1 August 1714 and in anticipation of parliamentary elections to be held early in the following year, the radical humanist John Toland (1670–1722) furnished his contemporaries with a fresh English translation of the *Commentariolum petitionis*, which he entitled *The Art of Canvassing at Elections, Perfect in all Respects*.[1] He did so with uncharacteristic wariness. Although his admiration for the work's Latinity was complete, Toland reprehended much of its advice, which he regarded as unsavoury, and uncongenial with his own morality. 'I hope no one will be so unjust as to charge me with approving all the Rules given in this Treatise', he fretted. But the old Roman rules, Toland urged, had not yet gone out of style. Indeed, he insisted, 'the general Rules are still the same'. Hence his translation, the purpose of which, perhaps unexpectedly, was not to counsel ambitious office seekers. Instead, he declared, 'I let the Electors into the secrets of the Candidates'. In this way, he believed, his book might help its readers 'to proceed to the choice of a good Parliament'— once they were capable of peering past the devices of electioneering.[2]

Toland claimed to be the first to read the *Brief Handbook* as a text pertinent to the habits of his own day, not 'purely as a piece of antiquity'.[3]

---

[1] Toland 1714. His was by no means the first vernacular version of the work; an anonymous translator turned the *Commentariolum petitionis* into French in 1583: *Les Offices de Cicéron, avec les traitez de l'Amytié, de Vieillese, de Paradoxes, du Songe de Scipion; plus adjouté de nouveau la Demande du Consulat de Qu. Cicero* (Paris).

[2] Toland 1714, pp. vi–vii. It is perhaps not irrelevant that, when Toland produced his translation, he was out of favour in politics. In espousing views on religion and society that were controversial or even heretical, Toland often turned to classical texts as vehicles for his opinions. On Toland's politics and classicism, see Fox 2007, 274ff.; Fox 2009; Brown 2012; East 2013.

[3] Toland 1714, p. iv.

This is an attitude towards the work that persists.[4] For most readers, however, it is not as a repository for insight into contemporary politics but instead as a guide to ancient Roman electoral practices, and to the attitudes and expectations animating them, that they turn to the *Brief Handbook*. This was true early on. In Book Three of his pathbreaking *Roma triumphans* (1459), the first scholarly attempt to reconstruct accurately and in detail the operations of Roman elections, including canvassing for office, Biondo Flavio relied extensively on information supplied by the *Brief Handbook*.[5]

On its surface, the *Brief Handbook* is a letter from Quintus Tullius Cicero to his elder brother, the famous orator, advising him on the best means of canvassing for the consulship. In doing so, the *Brief Handbook* supplies us with what is by far our fullest account of campaigning for office in republican Rome. Although elections and canvassing were central to Roman civic life (see below, §§II–III), our resources for recovering the Romans' experience of each are less ample than we could desire. This is especially true of canvassing for office. We are fortunate in possessing Cicero's speeches *In Defence of Murena* and *In Defence of Plancius*, both delivered at trials for illegal electioneering, as well as several letters by Cicero, in which he examines in practical terms the likely success or failure of various candidates for office. And, although they are imperial in date, the thousands of campaign notices that survive from Pompeii are illuminating in important ways. These glimpses into canvassing are especially precious because ancient historians and biographers, notwithstanding their habit of reporting the results of elections, do not often describe in detail the contests that preceded them, and when they do so it is usually on account of events that were out of the ordinary.[6] This is why the *Brief Handbook*, which describes quotidian aspects of canvassing in detail and at length, is so valuable a resource.[7] Furthermore, because the *Brief Handbook* closely scrutinizes relationships between different sections of Roman society, modern historians turn to the work again and again for

---

[4] The most recent example in English is Freeman 2012. See, also, the introduction to Fedeli 1987 by Giulio Andreotti. Other translations for a popular audience include Boriaud 1992 and Broderson 2013.

[5] See the detailed discussion by Muecke 2016.

[6] Livy, for instance, rarely extends himself in discussing political campaigns (but see Liv. 22.34.1–35.4; 27.7.11–9.4; 35.10.1–10; 37.57.9–58.2; 39.39.1–15; 39.40.1–41.4). Other historians are comparably selective. Plutarch, too. Still, every scrap of evidence matters. Although Marius' election to a consulship of 107 was untypical, Sallust's account of it (Sall. *Iug.* 64.3–65.5; 73.1–7) remains important. See, further, the sources adduced in §III.

[7] See, for instance, Taylor 1949, 62ff.; Gruen 1974, 138ff.; Tatum 1999, 22ff.; Yakobson 1999, 84ff.; Mouritsen 2001, 90ff.; Lintott 2008, 129ff.; Feig Vishnia 2012, 108ff.

information on a broad range of topics such as group identities, Roman friendship, and civic rituals.[8]

Looking beyond the surface, however, is a good and routine scholarly habit. And students of the *Brief Handbook* have naturally and rightly queried its purpose and its origin. It is not obvious why Quintus would give advice to his more distinguished and experienced brother. For whom, then, was he writing? Nor is the medium of that advice an immediately straightforward specimen of Roman correspondence. Why is the *Brief Handbook* put together in the way it is? Arguments have been advanced that the *Brief Handbook*, on the surface anyway, is too implausible to be what it claims to be and therefore isn't. Attention is drawn to the work's status as a kind of didactic epistle intended, perhaps, not for Cicero, but for a broader audience. Perhaps, it is suggested, the *Brief Handbook* played a role as propaganda in Cicero's campaign. Or perhaps the letter was not composed by Quintus at all and is instead an imperial forgery of some kind, a conclusion that, if true, must affect the uses to which the *Brief Handbook* can be put by modern historians. Each of these matters is taken up in the following sections of this introduction and they recur throughout the notes in the commentary. In some ways, if from a distinctly different perspective, these questions take us back to central aspects of John Toland's early engagement with the *Brief Handbook*. What kind of readership was envisioned by its author? What is the nature of the advice proffered by the work? And what reaction was the work intended to provoke? No historian consulting the *Brief Handbook* can responsibly evade these issues.

The purpose of this volume is to offer readers some aid in their appreciation of the *Brief Handbook* as a literary text, an ideological document, a likely specimen of electoral propaganda, and a resource for recovering various aspects of late republican political and cultural history. With that in mind, this introduction supplies the reader, in §II, with a concise account of the nature and practice of elections in the late republic and, in §III, with a survey of the expectations and habits of canvassing for office. I also rehearse, in §VII, particular aspects of Cicero's career that exhibit his skills as an office seeker and provide the necessary context for understanding his campaign for the consulship in 64, a context that is simply taken for granted in the *Brief Handbook*. Notes in the commentary frequently refer to §VII, where the reader can find, in a fuller and, it is hoped, more comprehensible narrative account, the relevant aspects of events or speeches that the *Brief Handbook* cites only in passing and too

---

[8] Examples include Meier 1980, 179ff.; Brunt 1988, 360f.; Konstan 1997, 128ff.; Miller 1998, 33ff.; Morstein-Marx 1998; Goldbeck 2010; Pani 2010; Robb 2010, 141ff.

succinctly to be meaningful to anyone who is not already very familiar with Cicero's career.

The introduction also examines, in §IV, the literary dimensions of the *Brief Handbook*. This is a facet of the work, as we have seen, that is crucial to its proper interpretation as a historical source. The question of the work's authorship, although nowadays perhaps less central to the study of the *Brief Handbook* than in the past, is considered both in §V and at relevant points in the commentary.

In keeping with the orientation of this series, references to modern scholarship have emphasized works in English whenever doing so was possible or responsible. As a consequence, my citation of work in other languages is uneven. And although this commentary, like every commentary, hopes to offer its readers adequate guidance towards previous and pertinent scholarship, its bibliography is far from exhaustive, even in its treatment of work in English. But it's a good start. And that is what this commentary aims to be. In the zany parallel universe of David Lodge's academic novels, the principal professional passion of the irrepressible Professor Morris Zapp is to complete a series of commentaries on Jane Austen that will shut down all further criticism, thereby leaving all other scholars for all time with 'simply *nothing further to say*'.[9] It will be obvious that that is not a goal of this series—or this commentary.

II ELECTIONS

1 Introduction

Roman government consisted in the official exertions of the senate, the people, and their magistrates. The collective authority of the senate lent it precedence in public affairs, and its membership constituted Rome's aristocracy.[10] Senators were deemed by all to be *optimi*, the best men of the city,[11] a status they asserted largely on the basis of their personal dedication to the civic health of the republic and especially on the basis of their achievements as magistrates: hence the routine description, by modern scholars, of the Roman aristocracy as an 'aristocracy of office' (*Amtsadel*).[12] The occupations of young aspirants to the senatorial order—military or

---

[9] D. Lodge, *Changing Places: A Tale of Two Campuses* (London, 1975), 35.
[10] Polyb. 6.51; Cic. *Rep.* 2.56–7, 59; *Leg.* 2.37; 3.27; see Lintott 1999a, 65ff.; Brennan 2014.
[11] Festus 290L.
[12] *Amtsadel*: Gelzer 1912, 39 (see Gelzer 1969b, 27). Fundamental on the character and normative ethos of the senatorial aristocracy is Hölkeskamp 2011a; see also Earl

diplomatic service, forensic labours in the courts, tendering legal advice, tenure of one of the minor magistracies—all exhibited their fitness for election to high office. In selecting their magistrates, the Roman people did not seek political representatives, as is the case in a modern liberal democracy, but rather leaders: men whose personal superiority made them reliable repositories for enormous responsibilities and powers.[13] In Rome, a magistracy was a *honor*, an honour awarded in recognition of a man's merit (*virtus*) and reputation (*dignitas*).[14] It was through election to office that a man qualified for enrolment in the senate, and all magistracies lay in the gift of the Roman people.[15] Hence the centrality of elections, and the canvassing that preceded them.[16]

2 Magistracies

In Cicero's time, one ordinarily entered the ranks of the senate after serving as one of twenty quaestors.[17] This office was open to plebeian and patrician alike, and the minimum age for standing was apparently 30.[18]

1967, 11ff.; Flower 1996, 91ff.; Rosenstein 2006; Hölkeskamp 2010, 76ff.; Tatum 2015 (each with further bibliography).

[13] Expectations of magisterial superiority: Cic. *Rep.* 1.51; Nippel 1995, 4ff.; Hölkeskamp 2011c; Jehne 2011a; Jehne 2011b; Hölkeskamp 2013, 23ff.; see also Feig Vishnia 2012, 148f. On the Roman people's deference to its magistrates and senate, see Meier 1980, 45ff., 111; Flaig 2003, 164ff.; Hölkeskamp 2010, 45, 52.

[14] *Honor* (or *honos*): Hellegouarc'h 1963, 383ff.; Lendon 1997, 272ff.; Hölkeskamp 2011a, 209ff.; 222ff.; Mouritsen 2017b, 96ff. The association of *honor* and *virtus*, as concepts and as divinities: Clark 2007, 67ff., 111ff.; see ¶1 assiduousness. On *dignitas*, see ¶2 great prestige.

[15] Cic. *Leg. agr.* 2.17: 'it is fitting that all powers, all commands, all commissions are granted by the Roman people'.

[16] Canvassing for office was so distinctive a mark of Roman culture that the Syrian king Antiochus Epiphanes (215–164), a Roman enthusiast, would sometimes circulate through Antioch dressed in the style of a Roman candidate and glad-handing his public—to their astonishment (Polyb. 26.1.5–6).

[17] Election to a tribunate (see pp. 6f.) was also a qualification for the senate in Cicero's day: Wiseman 1971, 98ff.

[18] Roman society divided itself unequally between patricians, a small number of ancient families who prevailed in the government of the early republic, and plebeians, the elite among whom ultimately overcame the patricians' original advantages. Each status was a condition of birth. The patricians' domination of the magistracies was reversed during the Conflict of the Orders, the conclusion of which may be identified with the passage of the *lex Hortensia* of 287; see Drummond 1989b, 212ff.; Cornell 1995, 242ff.; Smith 2006, 251ff. Thereafter, although patrician status carried ample cachet, the crucial elite in Roman society became the nobles, a category that included both patricians and plebeians; see ¶4 nobles.

After relinquishing office, an ex-quaestor entered the senate.[19] His subsequent career in that body required no further popular election: in principle, senators, unless deprived of their civil rights on account of criminal actions, could be ejected only for immorality or personal financial collapse. After Sulla's reforms, the size of the senate, though enlarged from its earlier numbers, probably did not exceed 600 and could regularly have remained well under 500. A sizeable portion of these men will have advanced no further than the quaestorship.[20]

Ambitious senators naturally sought higher offices. The *lex Villia Annalis* of 180, the terms of which were largely preserved in Sulla's *lex annalis* of 81, established a fixed, compulsory *cursus honorum* ('sequence of magistracies') consisting of quaestorship, praetorship, and consulship. Although no one was obliged to go beyond the quaestorship, anyone seeking the consulship had first to serve as praetor. The minimum ages for seeking these magistracies were set at 39 and 42, and between magistracies an interval of two years was compulsory.[21]

Other opportunities for public service, and therefore personal advancement, existed outside the *cursus honorum* by way of the offices of aedile and tribune of the *plebs*. In the late republic there were four aediles in each year: two plebeian aediles and two curule aediles (only the latter position was open to patricians). Aediles looked after the material fabric of the city, supervised the markets (especially the grain trade), and administered the public games beloved of the Roman people. These undertakings, especially the sponsorship of games, entailed considerable personal expense. Still, the resulting celebrity and gratitude were significant in the competition for higher offices.[22] Ten tribunes of the *plebs* were elected each year

[19] Even before their formal enrolment by the censors, ex-quaestors and ex-tribunes enjoyed the right to attend senate meetings and to vote (the *ius sententiae dicendi*, also expressed by the phrase *quibus in senatu sententiam dicere licet*): Festus 454L; Gell. *NA* 3.8; *lex Lat. Bant.* (= RS 193ff.); *lex Tarentina* (= RS 301ff.); Cic. *Clu.* 148; see *StR* 3.858f., 963.

[20] Roman magistracies: Lintott 1999a, 94ff.; Feig Vishnia 2012, 64ff. Minor magistracies: Wiseman 1971, 143ff.; Lintott 1999a, 137ff. Size and character of the senate: Lintott 1999a, 65ff.; Steel 2014. Sulla's reforms: *MRR* 2.74ff.; Steel 2013b, 107ff. Revision of the senate's membership (*lectio senatus*): ¶8 expelled from the senate.

[21] *Cursus honorum*: Astin 1958; Beck 2005; Feig Vishnia 2012, 64ff. Sulla's legislation: *MRR* 2.74ff. Patricians, it seems certain, could stand for the praetorship and consulship two years earlier than could plebeians: Badian 1964, 140ff., but see Sumner 1973, 134ff., for a different view. Because the tribunate was not, properly speaking, a magistracy (Lintott 1999a, 121ff.), it was possible, in the late republic, to hold successive tribunates.

[22] Lavish aedilician games, the point is a recurring one, generated influence (*gratia*) and prestige (*dignitas*): e.g. Cic. *Att.* 14.6.6; *Fam.* 2.6.3; 11.16.3; 11.17.1; see Deniaux 2016. It could apparently be held against a very rich man that he refused to stand for aedile:

(the position was naturally restricted to plebeians). By Cicero's day, a tribune could initiate public legislation, summon the senate, veto senatorial decrees, or forbid passage of a law esteemed detrimental to the interests of the *plebs*. Some tribunes in the late republic flamboyantly exploited their position in order to make themselves into controversial but often formidable political figures. The tenure of most tribunes, however, passed without controversy, its concentration focused on defending the rights of ordinary citizens without provoking the leading magistrates or the senatorial establishment.[23] The aedileship and the tribunate offered abundant possibilities for expanding one's reputation: men with their eyes on the consulship did not fail to compete for one or even both offices.

The praetorship and the consulship represented the highest regular magistracies in Rome. These offices conferred *imperium*, the power which permitted a man to command troops and administer justice in the city and abroad, and *auspicium*, the authority to consult and interpret the will of the gods on behalf of the Roman people. In the late republic, Romans elected eight praetors, who took provincial assignments or presided over Rome's standing courts. The highest executive authority in Rome belonged to the two consuls, at least one of whom must be plebeian. In Cicero's day, the consuls remained in Rome, sharing the chairmanship of the senate and the chief administration of the city. Elevation to the consulship was the supreme achievement of Roman politics, the *summa laus*, the ultimate manifestation of glory, as Cicero describes it.[24]

3 Popular Assemblies

Res publica, even Cicero conceded,[25] could be reformulated as *res populi* ('the people's property'). Neither Rome's officials nor its senate could make law. Instead, all legislation required popular ratification. So, too, did elevation to a magistracy: all offices lay in the gift of the sovereign people.[26]

Cic. *Off.* 2.58 (Mam. Aemilius Lepidus (pr. by 81)); cf. Sulla's excuse for his defeat when he first stood for the praetorship: Plut. *Sull.* 5.2; Val. Max. 7.5.5.

[23] The tribunate: Bleicken 1955; Thommen 1989; cf. Tatum 1999, 9ff.

[24] Cic. *Cat.* 4.21; *Phil.* 2.20, 8.30. The praetorship: Brennan 2000. The consulship: Beck et al. 2011; Pina Polo 2011.

[25] Cic. *Rep.* 1.39.

[26] E.g. Polyb. 6.11; 14–17; Cic. *Leg. agr.* 2.17; *Planc.* 7–12; see Lintott 1999a, 40ff.; Mouritsen 2017a, 96ff. On the still controversial role of the people in Roman politics, see (i.a.) Millar 1998; Yakobson 1999; Mouritsen 2001; Millar 2002, 85ff.; Morstein-Marx 2004; Tatum 2009b; Hölkeskamp 2010, 76ff.; Mouritsen 2017a, 54ff. (each with further bibliography).

Which meant that the political aristocracy of Rome was selected by its subordinates through their agency as voters in the popular assemblies. It was owing to the power of their votes that the people possessed influence (*gratia*) in Roman civic society,[27] and in the view of many Romans it was suffrage that constituted the essential basis of their freedom (*libertas*).[28]

The people could express its will by way of several assemblies, the most important of which, for the purpose of electing officers, were the centuriate assembly (*comitia centuriata*), the tribal assembly (*comitia tributa*), and the assembly of the *plebs* (*concilium plebis*). Fundamental to all of them was the organization of voters into tribes (*tribus*). Roman tribes were not based on kinship ties, but rather were voting districts into which citizens were distributed, originally and ordinarily on the basis of their place of residence. There were four urban tribes and thirty-one rural tribes, which by Cicero's time extended over most of Italy. Many of these were discontinuous: by Cicero's day, some tribes were divided into five or even six separate regions. Cicero's tribe, for instance, the Cornelia, was scattered into no fewer than five separate sections ranging from central Italy to the far south.[29]

In the late republic, the tribal assembly, when electing magistrates (curule aediles, quaestors, and the minor officers), convened under the presidency of a consul or praetor. The plebeian assembly, on the other hand, was summoned by a tribune of the *plebs* or a plebeian aedile. This assembly, closed to patricians, elected tribunes and plebeian aediles. That the two assemblies were distinct cannot be doubted.[30] The method for conducting elections was the same for both assemblies: the thirty-five tribes voted simultaneously. The tribe, not the individual, was the voting unit. For this reason, Romans were not troubled by discrepancies between tribes regarding their respective number of voters. So long as all thirty-five tribes were represented, in whatever quantities, the whole of the Roman people was deemed to be present.[31]

Each tribe cast as many votes as there were offices to be filled. For example, in the case of tribunician elections, inasmuch as there were ten available positions, each tribe cast ten votes. Within every tribe, each indi-

---

[27] Cic. *Leg. agr.* 2.102.

[28] Cic. *Agr.* 2.4; 2.18; *Sest.* 103; *Planc.* 16; *Leg.* 3.34; 3.39; Asc. 78C.

[29] Tribes and their organization: Taylor 1960; see ¶17 **fellow tribesmen**.

[30] On this point, see Lintott 1999a, 53f.

[31] The tribes were in any case unevenly populated: the urban tribes were teeming, as were some rural tribes that covered large and populous sections of Italy; by contrast, a few rural tribes in the vicinity of Rome (e.g. Lemonia and Romilia) were small and poorly populated; see Taylor 1960, 95ff., 157.

vidual cast ten votes and the ten men who secured the most votes within the tribe received that tribe's ten votes. In the case of curule aediles, by contrast, each tribe cast two votes for the two men who gained the most votes from the tribe's electors, each individual casting two votes. A simple majority of eighteen votes sufficed to secure election. Winners were announced as soon as they received the necessary eighteen tribal votes; consequently, the order in which ballots were counted and tribal results were announced was important for the final outcome of any election. After the required number of candidates was returned, the assembly was dismissed.[32]

The centuriate assembly (*comitia centuriata*) was more complicated in organization and operation. Its establishment was attributed to the king Servius Tullius. Whatever the truth of that, it is clear that this assembly originated in the organization of the Roman army and reflected the economic realities of fielding military forces during the early republic. The basic voting unit was the century (*centuria*), of which there were 193 distributed over several property classes. Citizens were assigned to classes and centuries largely on the basis of their wealth, which was assessed at each census.[33]

Cicero, Livy, and Dionysius of Halicarnassus all provide descriptions of the original Servian dispensation.[34] Unfortunately, none offers an account of its late republican manifestation, although each knew that the assembly had been significantly reformed during its history. In the Servian arrangement, all voters were divided into 193 centuries: eighteen centuries were provided by the aristocratic elite, the cavalry (*equites equo publico*; see ¶3 **the equestrian order**); 170 centuries were provided by the infantry, itself divided into further property classes; there were also four centuries of non-combatant military personnel (artisans, trumpeters, musicians, attendants);[35] finally, there was a single century composed of men who, owing to their poverty, were exempt from military service (described variously as *proletarii* or *capite censi*).

The centuries of the infantry were divided into five classes, the minimum property qualifications of which were, in descending order, 100,000 *asses*,

---

[32] Tribal and plebeian assemblies: Taylor 1966, 59ff.; Staveley 1972, 154ff.; Nicolet 1980, 224ff.; Lintott 1999a, 50ff.; Feig Vishnia 2012, 96f.

[33] The centuriate assembly: Taylor 1966, 85ff.; Staveley 1972, 123ff.; Nicolet 1980, 217ff.; Drummond 1989b, 198ff.; Lintott 1999a, 55ff; Feig Vishnia 2012, 94ff.; Mouritsen 2017a, 39ff.

[34] Cic. *Rep.* 2.29–40; Liv. 1.42.5; 1.43.10; Dion. Hal. *Ant. Rom.* 4.19–21.

[35] Livy disagrees with Cicero and Dionysius on the number and identities of the non-combatant military centuries, which Livy believed numbered not four but five (consequently, in his scheme, there are, in total, 194 centuries).

75,000 *asses*, 25,000 *asses*, and 12,500 or 11,000 *asses*. Infantry centuries were also distinguished by age, separating juniors (men aged 17–46) from seniors (men over the age of 46). The resulting organization can be represented as follows:

Rank	Juniors	Seniors	Total centuries
Cavalry			18
Class I	40	40	80
Class II	10	10	20
Class III	10	10	20
Class IV	10	10	20
Class V	15	15	30
Non-combatants			5

At some time after 241 but before 220 there was a major reform of the assembly, the full particulars of which remain uncertain. Romans of the first class, and possibly Romans of all classes, came to be organized by tribes as well as by class and century: in each of the thirty-five tribes, all members of the first class were distributed into two centuries (one of juniors, the other of seniors); consequently, the first class now included a total of seventy centuries, a reduction of ten from the original scheme. This arrangement persisted into the late republic:

Rank	Juniors	Seniors	Total centuries
Cavalry			18
Class I	35	35	70

Inasmuch as the total number of centuries for the assembly continued the same, the ten excess centuries must have been distributed over the remaining four classes. How they were distributed is irrecoverable.[36] It is also unclear whether the centuries in these classes were tribalized along the lines of the first class.

Mommsen believed that they were—a reorganization that should have yielded a total of 280 tribalized centuries for classes II–V. But this figure had to be reconciled with the comprehensive total of 193 voting centuries that survived this reform. Mommsen ingeniously proposed that the newly created tribalized centuries of these classes voted in batches of two or three, the specific combinations within each class being chosen by lot at

---

[36] Mommsen (*StR* 3.274), proposed that, in the reformed centuriate assembly, classes II–V were each allocated twenty-five centuries; Lily Ross Taylor, however, argued that classes II, III, and IV were allocated twenty centuries each and the fifth class was allocated forty centuries: Taylor 1957.

each election, so that, overall, the four lower classes cast 100 century votes in the final tally. This method, owing to its sheer complexity, has seemed implausible to some. However, what is essentially the same method was in fact employed (in the case of newly created elite voting units) during the time of Augustus: the procedure is described in the *Tabula Hebana*, an inscription that was undiscovered when Mommsen advanced his idea.[37] The evidence of the *Tabula Hebana*, though persuasive, falls short of irrefutable proof, and the possibility that tribal coordination did not reach beyond the first class cannot be excluded.[38]

Individual citizens were assigned to their classes during the census. Originally the eighteen equestrian centuries were filled by 2,400 (or perhaps 1,800; see ¶33 **for they are few**) of the richest citizens in Rome, the knights with a public horse (*equites equo publico*).[39] Originally these comprised both knights and senators, but a law of 129 obliged knights with a public horse to surrender it along with their place in the equestrian centuries upon entering the ranks of the senate: senators, then, apparently became members of the first class.[40] The minimum property qualification of a knight (inferred from the *lex Roscia* of 69) was 400,000 sesterces.[41] Members of the senate will have possessed far greater wealth than this (under Augustus the minimum senatorial qualification was 1,000,000 sesterces), which means that the richest members of the first class will often have excelled in wealth those voting in the equestrian centuries.

The minimum property qualifications for the remaining classes are known to us only from the sources' accounts of what they believed to be the Servian dispensation (see above). These minimums are expressed in *asses*, usually taken to represent sextantal *asses*, in which case the minimum requirement for the first class (in the Servian figures) is 40,000 sesterces.[42] By the time of Augustus, however, the minimum for the first class was 100,000 sesterces, and it has been proposed that this was also the figure in the late republic (or perhaps earlier). The question must remain

---

[37] *StR* 3.1.270ff. Text and translation of *Tab. Heb.* (with commentary): *RS* 507ff. Relevance to Mommsen's theory: Tibiletti 1949; Taylor 1960, 89ff.

[38] Mommsen's conclusions are resisted by (i.a.) Staveley 1972, 126ff; Grieve 1985; Lintott 1999a, 59f.

[39] These knights received public funds for the purchase of a horse, which was thereafter maintained by the state through a tax on widows and orphans (Liv. 1.43.9; Ogilvie 1965, 171f.; Nicolet 1974, 25ff.).

[40] This conclusion is not uncontroversial: see ¶33 **centuries of the knights**.

[41] See ¶3 **the equestrian order**; ¶33.

[42] During the Second Punic War, when the silver *denarius* was introduced into Roman coinage, its value was reckoned at 10 bronze *asses*: that is, 10 *asses* weighing 2 ounces or one-sixth of a Roman pound (hence the modern expression sextantal *asses*); see *RRC* 6ff.

open.[43] In any case, there was clearly a very broad range of wealth within the ranks of the first class, all of whom, however, even the most modest, were apparently considered rich, certainly by Romans of the lower orders of society.

The centuriate assembly voted on the Campus Martius in an enclosure known as the Saepta, which, during the late republic, was a modest wooden facility. It consisted of a large rectangular space for the thirty-five separate pens through which the tribalized centuries passed in order to cast their ballots, a great hall in which votes were counted (the Diribitorium), and a forecourt in which voters could gather before entering the pens.[44] The first unit to vote was a century chosen by lot from the first class (possibly selected only from the centuries of juniors), the *centuria praerogativa*. Its votes were tallied and the result announced to the assembly: this result was believed by the Romans to be highly influential.[45] Thereafter, the remainder of the first class voted. One century of non-combatants, the artisans, voted with the first class. Twelve equestrian centuries then voted. These results were tallied and announced. Then the remaining equestrian centuries, the *sex suffragia*, took their turn, and this result was announced. It will be clear how this procedure, through its recurring announcements, could foster something of a 'band wagon' effect, since voters were continually made aware of the contest's leaders and therefore the preferences of elite voters.

After balloting by the knights and the first class was completed, eighty-nine votes had been cast. Because a candidate needed ninety-seven votes to win his magistracy, it was always necessary to summon the second class to vote. If their votes returned the required number of magistrates, the election was concluded. Such unanimity on the part of the elite orders cannot have been frequent, however, and so balloting will usually have extended at least into the third class. Still, our sources insist, it was very rarely the case that the lowest classes were called on to vote.[46] But one could never be certain that what was rare would not occur.

The *lex Gabinia* of 139 replaced oral voting at Roman elections with written ballots, which were cast into voting urns and thereafter tabulated under the watchful eyes of the candidates' representatives. It is widely

---

[43] See the survey in Yakobson 1999, 43ff., who accepts the common view that 40,000 sesterces was the minimum for the first class. Crawford in *RRC*, 621ff., argues for a minimum of 100,000 sesterces, a change he associates with the retariffing of the denarius around 141.

[44] Taylor 1966, 47ff; Mouritsen 2001, 26ff.; *LTUR* 2.17f.

[45] Cic. *Mur.* 38; *Planc.* 49; *Div.* 1.103; 2.83; cf. Liv. 24.7; 26.22; 27.6; see, further, note 71.

[46] Liv. 1.43.11; Dion. *Ant. Rom.* 4.20.5.

accepted that, in an election, each individual cast as many votes as there were magistracies to be filled: two votes in consular elections, eight votes (in Cicero's day) in praetorian ones. In consular elections, then, each century would cast two votes for the two candidates who captured the most votes from its membership. It is uncertain what happened after one of the two consulships had been filled: did voters and centuries continue to cast two votes or did they then cast only one? Complications ensue on either view.[47]

Elections took place exclusively at Rome, and there was no provision made for absentee balloting. In the late republic, elections took place during July (unless, for some reason, they were unavoidably delayed—an occurrence that became increasingly common in the perturbed circumstances of the 50s). There was no prescribed day: elections were announced by the presiding magistrate, after which an interval of three market days, a *trinundinum*, intervened.[48] Elections could be held only on a day designated suitable for assemblies, a *dies comitialis*, and only on a comitial day that did not conflict with a sacred festival (*feria conceptiva*, that is, a moveable feast, or, less likely in the case of elections, *feria imperativa*, an irregular festival proclaimed in reaction to an emergency or in celebration of a military victory) or a designated market day (*nundina*).[49] Nor were elections feasible if held in conflict with the wildly popular *ludi Apollinares* (the Games for Apollo, which took place 6–13 July).[50] Nor could they take place on the *dies Alliensis*, the day commemorating the disastrous fourth-century defeat that resulted in the sack of Rome by the Gauls (18 July).[51] Still, July was furnished with numerous comitial days, especially in the second half of the month (10–14, 17–18, 20, 22, 26–31 July), so, even after discounting market days, the Games for Apollo, and the black day of the Allia, there remained sufficient time for a densely packed schedule of elections.

Consular elections were regularly presided over by a consul.[52] At some point prior to the election, each potential candidate formally presented

[47] Taylor 1966, 98 (number of votes reduced as candidates are elected); Staveley 1972, 183ff. (number of votes remains the same). A case can also be made that individuals (and therefore centuries) cast only one vote; see Hall 1964, 297ff. (who discusses the argument without endorsing it).

[48] Lintott 1999a, 44; a *trinundinum* was, in all probability, at least seventeen days.

[49] *Nundinae* and comitial days: Michaels 1967, 84ff.; Rüpke 2011, 60ff. Comitial days: Michaels 1967, 36ff.; 58ff; Rüpke 2011, 148ff.

[50] Scullard 1981, 159f.

[51] Cic. *Att.* 9.5.2; Gell. *NA* 4.9.5; Festus 348L; see Michaels 1967, 63.

[52] It is not certain how it was determined which of the two consuls should preside over the elections: Linderski 1995, 634ff. If there was no consul in office, elections were conducted by an *interrex*: Staveley 1972, 145; Feig Vishnia 2012, 87.

himself to the presiding magistrate, a procedure known as a *professio*. In practical terms, campaigning for office normally began months or even years in advance.[53] But the *professio* was a formal and public matter, carried out within the *pomerium*, the ritual boundary of the city, and possibly in the forum. At this point, the consul determined whether or not a candidate was in compliance with the regulations governing the *cursus honorum*. If so, he was obliged to accept the candidate's profession. However, the presiding magistrate had the power, when conducting the assembly, to refuse to announce the election of any candidate for office, and on very rare occasions, a consul might give an early indication that he would refuse to announce an objectionable candidate's election: in 100, C. Marius, as consul, rejected the *professio* of C. Servilius Glaucia, on the legal ground that Glaucia was a sitting praetor; in 67, the consul C. Piso made it clear that, if M. Lollius Palicanus should be returned by the people, he would not announce it.

But that was extraordinary, and it was no doubt taken for granted that, unless there was a similar declaration of opposition on the part of the consul, the act of accepting a candidate's *professio* sufficed to eliminate the possibility of a subsequent refusal to announce his election at the assembly. This is why, in 66, the consul L. Volcatius Tullus consulted his advisors before deciding whether he could accept the *professio* of Catilina. The circumstances were unusual: the returned consuls-elect had been condemned for electoral bribery and so new elections had to be held; Catilina had not been a candidate previously, and was himself currently under indictment, so the consul needed to be certain of the correctness of Catilina's timing, and owed it to the candidate to indicate whether he might refuse to name him if he were successful. The disgrace of the consuls-elect will have sharpened standards of correctness and exacerbated moralizing censoriousness at this emergency election. In the event, Catilina decided not to stand.[54]

Once the consul had formally reviewed the candidates, he arranged for a list of their names to be published. That did not necessarily close the matter: it appears that, before the late republic, the consul was free to accept late professions, even on the day of the assembly, and that he could on his own authority put names before the people.[55] Matters became stricter under the Sullan constitution, however: timely profession was legally required and by some point between 63 and 60 it became obligatory

---

[53] See ¶1 **lasting but a few months**; see also §VII.5.
[54] Sall. *Cat.* 18.2–3; Asc. 89C; see Syme 2016, 140; cf. Seager 1964, 338f. and Lewis 2006, 297, for a different view.
[55] Staveley 1972, 146.

to submit one's *professio* in person (even before that, however, candidates were required to be present at the election itself).[56]

On the day of the assembly, after the consul had secured the permission of Jupiter by taking auspices, before sunrise, on the inaugurated tribunal from which he would conduct the elections, he directed a herald to summon the Roman people. An announcement was made in the forum, a red flag was raised on the Janiculum, and trumpets were sounded from the Capitoline and from the city's walls. The centuriate assembly was preceded by an informal assembly, a *contio*, at which the consul offered a prayer to the gods and may have offered some preliminary commentary, including a recitation of the names of the candidates. These men, with their supporters, will have been busy in last-minute canvassing. The consul then dismissed the assembly with the instruction, *discedite, Quirites* ('Citizens, remove yourselves [into your voting units]'). Voting could then commence.

There was apparently no formal method of confirming the eligibility of voters (voters in elite centuries doubtless policed themselves informally). At some point, we do not know when, voters received their ballots (small wooden tablets coated with wax), on which they wrote down their choices for office. At the appropriate opportunity, they proceeded into the pens that led to the bridges (*pontes*) rising up to the tribunal, where they deposited their ballots in a basket (*cista*) under the supervision of an official monitor (*custos*), a person of distinction chosen by the consul, as well as under the scrutiny of monitors (also distinguished men) selected by the candidates themselves.[57] How voters removed themselves from the Saepta is unclear.

After each century had finished voting, the *custodes* counted the ballots and reported the results to the consul. At the prescribed junctures, the consul announced the results. When a candidate received ninety-seven votes, he was declared consul-elect (*renuntiatio*). Voting continued until a second consul had been named, at which time the assembly was dissolved. Voting normally consumed the bulk of the day. Its conduct was noisy, uncomfortable (voting took place under the summer sun), sometimes disorderly, often raucous—and no doubt exciting for all concerned.

---

[56] See Plut. *Mar.* 12. Cic. *Leg. agr.* 2.24 indicates that, as late as early 63, one need not be present in Rome in order to submit one's *professio* (Linderski 1995, 91ff.). On *professio*, see Staveley 1972, 146ff.; Rilinger 1976, 63ff., 635f.; Licandro 1997, 447ff. Levick, 1981, 378ff., argues unpersuasively against the existence of a formal and obligatory *professio*.

[57] The identities of these personnel were recorded and preserved: Cic. *Pis.* 36; *StR*, 2. 547. An image of this voting procedure is supplied by *denarii* minted by P. Licinius Nerva (pr. 104), when he was a moneyer in the late second century: *RRC* 306f.

Irregularities were not infrequently observed, complaints were voiced, with the result that official intervention was often required. Inquiries had to be carried out quickly, however, inasmuch as the assembly was obliged to complete its work before sunset.[58] A separate action on the part of the curiate assembly (a *lex curiata*) confirmed the status of new praetors and consuls.[59]

4 Who Voted?

After the Social War (91–87), Rome's Italian allies became Roman citizens.[60] Because elections took place only at Rome, however, it was incumbent on voters living in the Italian countryside to undertake a lengthy and, for many, expensive visit to the city. The attractions of the games notwithstanding, this was plainly a disincentive for anyone too poor to abandon his livelihood to make an extended and costly journey. Which meant that, outside the vicinity of Rome, only prosperous voters, or voters whose expenses were subsidized by someone else, could attend the annual elections.

Consequently, most of the potential voters at any election were urban dwellers. But a significant proportion of these voters, the majority of whom were men of modest means, were assigned to one of the four urban tribes, which limited their individual and collective efficacy. Now, quite a number of wealthy men who were enrolled in rural tribes were also resident in Rome: Cicero's father, for instance, owned a house in Rome, and Cicero himself remained a member of the rural Cornelian tribe.[61] There were also many urban residents from the lower orders who were members of rural tribes: migration into the city was a constant feature of Italian society, and men who shifted to Rome frequently kept their original tribal affiliation.[62] Put differently, the lower reaches of the urban population were amply supplied with members of the rural tribes, even if, in terms of sheer bulk, the urban tribes preponderated. And this is why the pro-

---

[58] *StR.* 1.180ff.; Staveley 1972, 149ff.; Nicolet 1980, 246ff. No formal method of identifying eligible voters: Mouritsen 2001, 29. An important measure of the pace of elections is an extraordinary consular election held in 45, at which there was only a single candidate whose election was endorsed by the dictator Caesar and so entirely uncontested; it lasted nearly four hours: Cic. *Fam.* 7.30 (with Shackleton Bailey 1977, 434).

[59] Lintott 1999a, 28f.; Humm 2011.

[60] For details of the Social War and its implications for Roman elections, see ¶1 within a single, systematic form and in a logical order.

[61] Cicero's father's house: Plut. *Cic.* 8.6; Cic. *Q. Fr.* 2.3.7. His tribe: Taylor 1960, 260.

[62] Immigration: Purcell 1994, 644ff.; Morley 1996, 44ff.; Kay 2014, 227; 286. Tribal affiliations: Taylor 1960, 280ff.; Lintott 1999a, 204.

ceedings of the tribal and plebeian assemblies, at which the votes of everybody within a single tribe were equal, were ordinarily dominated by the preferences of the urban masses.[63]

In the centuriate assembly, by contrast, the votes of the wealthy, however scanty their attendance, necessarily counted for more than did the votes of the poor. In the first place, owing to the assembly's timocratic design, the wealthy classes simply owned more centuries than did the rest of the electorate. Furthermore, every century in the equestrian order and the first class almost always included far fewer members than those in the lower orders, though that of course depended on how many men from the lower orders actually decided to vote: if they attended in robust numbers, then their centuries will have been teeming. Cicero tells us that a single century of the lower classes contained more citizens that the entirety of the elite centuries.[64] This was almost certainly a personal perception uninformed by any actual statistical knowledge. Still, it provides a relevant if exaggerated comparison of the relative scale of rich and poor centuries.[65] This effect was intentional. As Cicero proudly describes the assembly, it was arranged 'in such a way that the greatest number of votes lies in the power, not of the multitude, but of the rich'.[66] As Livy puts it: 'levels were defined so that no one appeared to be excluded from an election and yet all the clout resided with the leading men'.[67] This does not mean that the wider public did not matter in elections for the consulship or praetorship. But it is obvious that no one could attain these offices if he alienated a majority of Rome's prosperous citizenry.

It is unmistakable how logistical impediments to voting excluded the participation of the majority of Rome's citizens, who remained in the countryside. Unfortunately, for no single election is the number of voters preserved by our sources. Modern estimates, employing varying assumptions and methodologies and reaching different conclusions, nonetheless agree that, in any year, the number of voters was small, perhaps fewer than 50,000 and, perhaps, significantly fewer even than that.[68] Turnout on this modest a scale had significant implications for candidates, not least by increasing the importance of rallying participation on the part of their supporters. A relatively slight advantage over another candidate was

---

[63] Lintott 1999a, 204; Tatum 2009b, 215ff.   [64] Cic. *Rep.* 2.40.
[65] The same view can be found at Dion Hal. *Ant. Rom.* 4.18.12; 7.59.6.
[66] Cic. *Rep.* 2.39.   [67] Liv. 1.43.10.
[68] Taylor 1966, 52ff.; MacMullen 1980; Nicolet 1980, 290f.; Mouritsen 2001, 32ff.; Phillips 2004; Jehne 2006. Cicero's remarks at *Sest.* 109 and *Planc.* 54, each a specimen of tactical hyperbole and each suggesting that, occasionally, fewer than ten and at times no members of a single tribe were present at electoral or legislative assemblies, should not be taken at face value: Kaster 2006, 334. For a different view see Mouritsen 2001, 23f.

potentially of enormous consequence, and because it was difficult to know in advance who would actually be present at the elections in any particular year—it was very likely the case that in different years different voters turned out[69]—a diligent candidate had to solicit as many possible voters as he could: a central task of any campaign, then, lay in motivating voters, especially prosperous voters scattered throughout Italy, to take part in the elections.[70] Vigorous solicitations were all the more necessary during the final weeks of canvassing, when that year's likely voters from the countryside had arrived in Rome, many of whom, we are told, came to Rome as undecided, indeed uninformed, voters.[71]

Nor could a candidate ignore the lower orders—even if their votes counted for less than those of the wealthy and even if it was often the case that they were not summoned to vote at all—because again no one could know in advance whether in any particular year their votes would determine the election's outcome.[72] There were often several plausible candidates, enough to fragment the votes of the elite and therefore leave the final selection with the lower classes. In the elections for 216, for example, only one consul was elected out of six candidates:[73] it must have been the case that none of the others could secure ninety-seven votes although every century cast ballots. A second day of elections was required to fill the vacancy. The elections for 189 exhibit a similar state of affairs, when three patrician candidates so divided the electorate that none could garner enough votes to win office.[74]

Although our sources insist that the lower classes rarely voted in the centuriate assembly, they must have done so often enough to require the attention of serious candidates for office.[75] Let us consider Cicero's election in 64. In a large field of candidates, Cicero came in first, followed by Antonius who only narrowly defeated Catilina, *pauculis centuriis* ('by only a very few centuries') as Asconius puts it.[76] If we take Asconius'

---

[69] Tatum 1999, 29f.

[70] This is a recurring motif in the *Brief Handbook*: ¶¶4, 6, 16–52, 57.

[71] Fest. 290L: 'the *centuria praerogativa* is so called, as we learn from Book Six of Varro's *Antiquities* [*Antiquitates rerum humanarum et divinarum*], because it was summoned to vote first so that Romans from the countryside, who were unfamiliar with the candidates, would be able to make a decision about them more easily.'

[72] Yakobson 1999, 48ff.   [73] Liv. 22.35.1–4.

[74] Liv. 37.47.6–7. A large number of candidates did not always divide voters: the consular elections in 174, for instance, were remarkable and contentious because there were so many competitors and yet there is no indication that a second assembly was necessary (Liv. 41.28.4).

[75] Liv. 1.43.11; Dion. Hal. *Rom. Ant.* 4.20.5 (asserting that voting rarely descended to the fourth class).

[76] Asc. 94C.

pauculis to mean that only two centuries separated them as the balloting proceeded and announcements were made, then it will have been necessary for the fourth class to vote before Antonius could be declared a winner. If the gap between them was greater, and if any of their rivals picked up votes after Cicero was declared consul-elect, the voters' choice may have been postponed until the fifth class had voted.

III CANVASSING

1 Introduction

Elections were the traditional environment for an annual collision between the paired and dynamic principles of republican government: the people's majesty (*maiestas populi Romani*) and the senate's authority (*senatus auctoritas*).[77] Though potentially volatile, this political physics directed itself towards social consensus, especially during the final weeks of any campaign, when candidates occupied themselves with morning assemblies and parades through the forum, meeting and greeting all classes of the electorate.[78] The people's choice remained uncertain until the votes were counted: again and again our sources comment on the unpredictability of elections and record the shock experienced by favoured candidates when they were unexpectedly surpassed. Rejections of individual candidates by the people (*repulsae*) constituted indisputable proof of the people's sovereignty and the voters' independence.[79] This is why candidates had to beg for office: the language of canvassing—*petitio* ('a request'), *petere* ('to importune'), *rogare* ('to entreat'), *servire* ('to be a slave to'), *supplicare* ('to grovel for')—emphasizes the humble posture imposed on a candidate if he hoped to gain power and honour.[80] This

---

[77] *Maiestas populi Romani*: Brunt 1988, 338ff.; cf. Seager 2001; Harries 2007, 72ff. *Senatus auctoritas*: Brunt 1988, 323ff.; Lintott 1999a, 65ff.; ¶53 **a guardian of its authority**.

[78] Tatum 2003–4, 213ff.; Hölkeskamp 2010, 98ff.; Flaig 2013, 355ff. (and pp. 32ff.).

[79] *Repulsae*: Broughton 1991; Konrad 1996, 103ff.; Farney 2004, 246ff. The humiliation of a *repulsa*: Cic. *Off*. 1.71. Unpredictability: e.g. Cic. *Mur*. 35–6; *De or*. 1.2; *Fam*. 8.14; *Att*. 2.52; see §III.13; Mouritsen 2001, 92ff.; Pina Polo 2012. Develin 1979, esp. 309, argues that elections during the middle republic, unlike the late republic, were marked by a high degree of consensus and so were fairly predictable, a view that has been decisively repudiated by Rosenstein 1993.

[80] The language of begging and slavery is a constant in the terminology associated with canvassing (a reality made explicit in Cic. *Planc*. 7–9, 11–12, 24); Cassius Dio uses *therapeuein* ('to serve'), in a patently unflattering sense, to describe canvassing (e.g. 37.37.3; 37.54.3–4); see Linderski 1995, 105ff.; Flaig 2003, 20ff.; Tatum 2007, 112ff.

practice, the Romans believed, was an ancient one, pre-dating even the establishment of the republic.[81]

2 A Plausible Candidate

It was essential for any aspirant to office—and certainly for any candidate for the consulship—that he possess a high degree of personal honour and renown. 'A magistracy', in the words of Scipio Aemilianus, 'has its origins in prestige', that is, in *dignitas*.[82] Elevation through the *cursus honorum* enhanced a man's prestige, and the consulship imbued its holder with *amplissima dignitas* ('the grandest prestige').[83] But to hold a magistracy one must first be worthy of it. This view lies behind the routine expression *dignus honore* ('deserving of office') or some variation of it,[84] and the frequent insistence that election to the consulship depended on a candidate's *dignitas*.[85] Every election was a *contentio dignitatis*, at once a contest for amplified prestige and a conflict between competing claims of superior honour.[86]

Whence came *dignitas* sufficient to stand for office? When our sources register the resources and accomplishments of an outstanding aristocrat, they regularly adduce his wealth, ancestry, martial fame, intelligence, oratory, public service, and private benefactions. The resources of a grand family, an extensive network of loyal friends, and an abundance of dependants are all frequently cited as objects of admiration or envy, and the formulation of these assets is a familiar and recurring one. The nobility (*nobilitas*) boasted ancient splendour and long-standing utility to the republic, and nobles busied themselves reinforcing in the public's sensibilities the endorsement they received from the fame of their ancestors (*commendatio maiorum*).[87] One could almost say that even the dead canvassed on their

---

The vocabulary of supplication pervades the *Brief Handbook*: e.g. ¶8 (*supplicare*); ¶¶4, 5, 19, 21, 44 (*rogare*); ¶¶2, 7, 10, 11, 13, 15, 27, 31, 43, 50–1, 53–4, 56, 58 (*petere*). See, further, §III.4.

[81] So Livy, who says of Tarquinius Priscus that 'he was the first man to canvass [*petisse ambitiose*] for the kingship' (Liv. 1.35.2).

[82] Isid. *Etym.* 2.21.4: *ex dignitate honor*. On *dignitas*, see ¶2 **prestige**.

[83] *Dignitas* amplified through holding offices: Hellegouarc'h 1963, 400ff.; Hölkeskamp 2011a, 212f. The consulship as *amplissima dignitas*: Cic. *Sull.* 30; *Balb.* 10; at *Mil.* 42 it is *honor amplissimus*.

[84] *Dignus honore*: e.g. Cic. *Verr.* 2.2.172; *Leg. agr.* 1.27; *Mur.* 23; *Pis.* 97; *Planc.* 27, 50, 62. Note also the abundant use of *dignus* as a recommendation to office in Pompeian *programmata*: see §III.7.

[85] Cic. *Mur.* 43, 76; *Fam.* 15.12.2; Asc. 86C; [Sall.] *Ad Caes. sen.* 2.7; Suet. *Iul.* 41.2.

[86] Cic. *Mur.* 14; *Planc.* 8; *Off.* 1.38; see Brunt 1988, 35ff.

[87] Cic. *Leg. agr.* 2.100; *Cat.* 1.28; *Planc.* 67; *Brut.* 96; see Hölkeskamp 2010, 88ff.

behalf. Grandees were marked out by the men devoted to them: relations and friends, certainly, but also fellow tribesmen (*tribules*), neighbours (*vicini*), freedmen (*liberti*), clients (*clientes*), and associates from outside Rome (*hospites*).[88] Adherents like these constituted the living proof of an aristocrat's practical potency and thus the basis for his prestige.

But *dignitas* was never stable or static. The accumulation of friends and followers and the maintenance of their loyalty demanded constant—and conspicuous—exertions.[89] It was by doing good to others—the great and the small, the individual and the public—that an aristocrat could shackle them with inevasible debts of gratitude—that is to say, with *gratia*.[90] *Gratia*, in Rome, was influence or clout in its purest form, and it was indispensable in the generation of *dignitas*.[91] Consequently, an aristocrat who was ambitious for high office followed a career defined by its pursuit of gratitude.

Magistrates originated in the equestrian order, and senators were rich men. Although during the republic there was no legally prescribed threshold of wealth for candidates, the requirements of a magisterial career could not be met by anyone whose property was not substantial. A senator's expenditures were considerable,[92] and his daily energies, spent in earning *gratia*, went largely uncompensated in any other currency. This same kind of industry was expected of young men on the make, who put themselves to work on behalf of the public good in the field and in the forum.

In view of the potential responsibilities of all praetors and consuls, it is unsurprising that martial valour was a recommendation in public life. Until the late republic, aspirants to a senatorial career were obliged to serve in as many as ten seasons of military campaigning, and, although military commands became a less common feature of magisterial activity in the first century, young aristocrats continued to seek junior appointments in order to establish their credentials for bravery and leadership.[93]

---

[88] See ¶4 **nobles**; ¶17 **fellow tribesmen; neighbours; clients; freedmen**. Despite the importance of *hospites* for Cicero's support throughout Italy (see Lomas 2004), the word goes unmentioned in the *Brief Handbook* (though Cicero's extensive Italian connections do not: see ¶¶30–1). On the ideological significance of *hospites*, see Gell. *NA* 5.13.1–6.

[89] The performance of power: Bell 2004, 24ff., 151ff; Hölkeskamp 2006; Winterling 2009, 42ff.; Goldbeck 2010, 235ff.; Hölkeskamp 2011b.

[90] E.g. *CIL* I².6, 11; Polyb. 31.23.11–12; 31.25–9; *Rhet. Her.* 1.8; Cic. *Att.* 1.20.7; *Caec.* 57; *Clu.* 94; *Mur.* 22–6, 69; *Parad.* 46; *Part. or.* 87; *Q. Fr.* 1.2.16; *Red. pop.* 3–4; *Red. sen.* 13, 20; *Sest.* 10; *Rep.* 2.11.3; Sall. *Iug.* 85.4; Plin. *NH* 7.139; see Earl 1967, 11ff.; Flower 1996, 91ff.; Tatum 2015. See §III.3.

[91] Hellegouarc'h 1963, 399f.

[92] Shatzman 1975, 84ff., offers a concise but detailed account.

[93] Harris 1979, 10ff.; Blösel 2011.

Often with sensational results: at the age of 15, M. Aemilius Lepidus, who would go on to become consul in 187 and 175, slew an enemy in battle while saving the life of a fellow citizen.[94] Even Cicero, whose temperament was far from bellicose, served as an officer during the Social War, and as proconsul in Cilicia he commanded legions in defence of his province.[95]

'The greatest prestige [*dignitas*] belongs to the men who are most celebrated as warriors', Cicero insists,[96] and it is obvious to us that this sentiment was universal.[97] The prevalence of this view may help to explain why, at elections, voters could be deeply affected by the preferences of the soldiers in their midst: Cicero comments on the 'profound authority exercised over the whole of the Roman people by the voting of soldiers during the election of consuls'.[98] Still, not even *gloria* could guarantee success at the polls: Q. Metellus Macedonicus (cos. 143), notwithstanding a triumph in 146 after his glorious victory in the Fourth Macedonian War, was twice defeated for the consulship owing, apparently, to his unpleasant personality, which offended voters;[99] and in 88 P. Servilius Vatia, although he celebrated a triumph in that year, failed to attain a consulship because he was a close associate of Sulla, whose unpopularity at the time ruined the man's chances.[100]

Straining oneself in forensic application was also an important means of acquiring an attractive reputation. This was a convention of long standing. A young man in Plautus' *Trinummus* is urged to pursue honour by giving aid to his friends in the forum, and Polybius tells us that, when he was resident in Rome, youthful aristocrats were zealously committed to legal affairs and the cultivation of the public, spending all their time in the forum, where trials and other legal business were transacted, in the expectation of gaining popular favour.[101] Roman litigation, especially the complicated and demanding procedures of civil law, relied on the unstint-

---

[94] Val. Max. 3.1.1; see *RRC*, 443.

[95] Cicero during the Social War: Plut. *Cic.* 3.2; Cic. *Lig.* 21; *Div.* 1.72; 2.65; *Phil.* 12.27; Q. *Fr.* 1.1.10. Cicero in Cilicia: *MRR* 2.243, 251f.

[96] Cic. *Mur.* 24.

[97] On Livy's recurring literary treatment of this basic conviction, see Haimson Lushkov 2015, 96ff.

[98] Cic. *Mur.* 38. The influence of soldiers: e.g. Cic. *Mur.* 37–8; *Att.* 4.16.5; Sall. *Iug.* 64–65.5, 73.3 (letters from soldiers); Dio 37.54.3; see Yakobson 1999, 124ff., 221f.

[99] Jer. *De vir. ill.* 61.3; Val. Max. 7.5.4.

[100] Metellus' victory and triumph: *MRR* 1.467. His electoral failures: Broughton 1991, 8f. Servilius' triumph: *MRR* 2.43. Defeat in 88: Broughton 1991, 17. On the implications of military defeat for a candidate's electoral success, see Rosenstein 1990 (with Tatum 1991b).

[101] Plaut. *Trin.* 651: *in foro operam amicis da.* Youthful aristocrats in the forum: Polyb. 31.29.8, with Goldbeck 2010, 193ff.

ing and capable participation of elite citizens, as a consequence of which there were opportunities for earning gratitude through advocacy[102] and by giving legal advice,[103] as well as through informal negotiations as an interested party.[104] Such activity attracted goodwill and exhibited the competence and intelligence Romans expected of their leaders.[105]

At times these exhibitions could be sensational: notable trials, especially criminal cases, were conspicuous events, and some public prosecutions were carried out by men still in their 20s, or even by teenagers.[106] Still, most forensic activity was less than entirely glamorous. Which is not to say that it went unnoticed. Scipio Aemilianus, when not yet 20, bemoaned the bad reputation he had already acquired on account of his unwillingness to plead cases: for that reason, he believed, he was thought by the public to be lazy and an incapable guardian of his household and its interests.[107] Forensic activity remained a reliable means of advancing one's standing at every stage of one's career: after his failure in the aedilician elections for 50, for instance, C. Lucilius Hirrus (tr. pl. 53) turned to taking on cases in the courts, for the first time in his career, in order to regain any lost ground.[108] And in 54, Cicero, aiming at fresh honours, busied himself in the courts (on Quintus' advice), garnering reinforcements of influence (*gratia*) and prestige (*dignitas*).[109]

We are not well informed about Rome's minor magistracies or the advantages that accrued from holding them. These were elected offices, and so at the very least provided an occasion for self-advertisement. And the responsibilities of each office, which were practical and specific in nature, afforded their holders opportunities for engaging with, and possibly winning favour from, more than one segment of the public. There were twenty-six annual positions, informally described as the *vigintisexviri*:

---

[102] See ¶2 **your fame as an orator**; ¶2 **deemed worthy of being patron**; David 1992.

[103] On the importance of jurisprudence, mocked for tactical reasons by Cicero at *Mur.* 23–9, see Frier 1985; Harries 2006; Caprogrossi Colognesi 2014, 126ff.

[104] On the various transactions of Roman legal procedures during the republic, see Kelly 1966, 132ff.; Crook 1967, 73ff.; Lintott 2004, 64ff.

[105] Intelligence an expectation of aristocratic leadership: e.g. Plin. *NH* 7.139–40; *ILS* 1; see Hölkeskamp 2011c; Jehne 2011b.

[106] Youthful prosecutions: Cic. *Acad.* 2.1; Plut. *Luc.* 1.2; Quint. 12.7.3; see David 1992, 497ff. Such prosecutions were important opportunities for publicity for the young: Jehne 2000, 179f. Examples: in 77 Caesar (in his 20s) prosecuted Cn. Cornelius Dolabella (cos. 81); see Alexander 1990, 71; in 56 L. Sempronius Atratinus (cos. 34), a teenager, prosecuted M. Caelius Rufus; see Alexander 1990, 134.

[107] Polyb. 31.23.10–12.   [108] Cic. *Fam.* 8.9.1.

[109] *Q. Fr.* 1.16(15).1–2. On Cicero's likely ambitions, see *Q. Fr.* 1.14(13).1 and 3.5.3 (with Shackleton Bailey 1980, 198, 201).

tresviri capitales, who looked after fire safety and other security matters, often in cooperation with senior magistrates;

tresviri monetales (also denominated *tresviri auro argento aere flando feriundo*), who managed the mint and its production of coinage;

quattuorviri viis in urbem purgandis, who maintained the city's streets;

duoviri viis extra propiusve urbem, who were responsible for Roman roads within a mile of the city;

decemviri stlitibus iudicandis, jurists who oversaw legal challenges to an individual's freedom;

quattuorviri praefecti Capuam Cumas, who represented the praetor in Campania.[110]

There were also occasional offices, established for carrying out specific, short-term tasks.

It would probably be a mistake to discount the value of these positions for men looking forward to a senatorial career. And it is obvious how duties like these, when writ large for more senior officials, helped to propel some men toward the consulship. After holding an extraordinary command in Tarentum, possibly in connection with his quaestorship, T. Quinctius Flamininus won election to a commission responsible for assigning lands to veterans and was subsequently appointed to a board whose assignment was enlarging the colony of Venusia. The enormous goodwill that he earned from these services became clear when, in 198, Flamininus was elected consul—although he was under-age and had held no other magistracy apart from his quaestorship.[111] Flamininus was exceptional but not unique in recognizing the political importance of practical offices: Gaius Gracchus and Julius Caesar likewise recognized their importance, as did others.[112] No situation allowed an aspiring Roman better opportunities for exhibiting his generosity, in ways both practical and sensational, than the aedileship: an aedile's improvements to the city's fabric, which often entailed negotiations with property owners and

---

[110] Lintott 1999a, 137ff.

[111] Special command: *MRR* 3.179f. Settling veterans: *MRR* 1.322. Venusia: *MRR* 1.325f. Consulship: *MRR* 1.330. See Pfeilschifter 2005, 31ff.

[112] C. Gracchus: Plut. *C. Gracch.* 6.7; App. *B.Civ.* 1.23. Caesar: Plut. *Caes.* 5.5. See the remarks of Cicero at *Att.* 1.1.2, and compare the boasts of the so-called Polla *elogium* (*CIL* I².638 = *ILLRP* 454), pertinent whatever the correct identity of its author (see Wiseman 1987, 108ff.). By conducting a favourable levy in Umbria, L. Licinius Murena (cos. 62) won valuable electoral support from that region (Cic. *Mur.* 42).

resident shopkeepers and tradesmen, and especially his production of the annual games, made a lasting impression on likely voters.[113]

Instructive by way of its inversion of the normative aristocratic profile is Cicero's sneering attack on the political deficiencies of his enemy L. Calpurnius Piso (cos. 58). Cicero first (and falsely) impugns the man's family's origins and goes on to allege that, although he has been active in the forum since his youth, Piso has accomplished nothing. Furthermore, he lacks insight (*consilium*), eloquence, military competence, any desire to be personally acquainted with the public, or generosity.[114] This is so severely negative a portrait that it cannot be taken seriously as an accurate representation of Piso. But the specific black marks Cicero isolates are significant: an aristocrat made of the right stuff would possess all the qualities he claims Piso is lacking.

Military, forensic, and administrative exertions, whether on behalf of the community or individuals, were expected to earn lasting debts of gratitude. So, too, constant private transactions carried out in the variegated roles of patron, financial partner, confidant, or friend. We are able to glimpse the delicate negotiations entailed by these often delicate operations in the correspondence of Cicero, who constantly, in his letters to senatorial and equestrian acquaintances, endeavours to nurture his connections with others through favours, compliments, and assurances of faithfulness and goodwill.[115] This continual show of social cooperation was necessary, for Cicero and for everyone else: all Romans were subjected to constant and often conflicting demands for their support, which meant that, in the marketplace of goodwill, everyone, certainly every peer, was a potential competitor.[116] Each political figure was the centre of an intricate and potentially fragile network of varied associations, the totality of which demanded assiduous attention and no part of which could ever be taken for granted—not least because too many members of his coalition were also obliged to others. His hold on the goodwill and loyalty of his fellow Romans, at every register of society, constituted the very essence of a man's political power. And at every election, when advancement to a higher magistracy mattered so much to his public identity, a candidate found himself obliged to put the theoretical basis of his clout to a test in which there was a very real possibility of public failure. Consequently, candidates strained their every resource in asserting their claim to office.[117]

[113] See note 22.   [114] Cic. *Red. sen.* 13.

[115] Verboven 2002; Hall 2009; Bernard 2013; Rollinger 2014. Although their focus is on imperial Rome, there is much that is relevant in Saller 1982; Leunissen 1993.

[116] Meier 1980, 175; see ¶1 **assiduousness**.

[117] Meier 1980, 163ff.; Brunt 1988, 35ff.; Tatum 2015, 263.

3 *Clientela*, Factions, and *Gratia*

Until recently, elections in republican Rome were deemed to have been dominated and determined by the elite and especially by the nobility, apart from terrible exceptions when violence or corruption disturbed normal practices. Powerful figures, it was thought, managed the votes of the lower orders by way of the institution of *clientela*, the bond between patron and client. Thus Syme could explain Cicero's election to the consulship by adducing his domesticated conservatism and its obvious attraction to anxious members of the aristocracy: 'The oligarchy knew their man. They admitted Cicero to shut out Catilina.'[118] The idea that *clientela* was central to the outcome of elections, however, has been demolished by a succession of important studies. This is not to say that grandees did not endeavour to exercise their influence on behalf of candidates they favoured, but rather that, because voters were subjected to a broad array of appeals during a contest, of which the tie between a client and his patron was only one, it was impossible to be sure which appeal would matter most when polling began. Furthermore, since the introduction of the secret ballot in elections, introduced by the *lex Gabinia* of 139,[119] voters were relieved of any intimidating scrutiny on the part of the elite.[120] Which means that, during the late republic, patrons never simply controlled their clients, and even Romans of the lower classes possessed, at elections, a significant degree of independence.[121]

Neither the Roman people, nor their political leaders, organized themselves into anything resembling modern political parties.[122] There were many reasons for this: the political principles held by members of the governing class, though genuine and heartfelt, varied little, and there existed no creditable interest in altering, much less upsetting, the foundations of republican society. Political controversies, when they arose, usually dealt with issues of a very specific and narrowly defined kind, and were animated as much by personal rivalries and personal affiliations as they were by instincts about the wrong or right course of action. The alliances they spawned tended to be ad hoc and short-term, though naturally some politicians were inclined to close associations, or enduring enmi-

---

[118] Syme 1939, 24. [119] *MRR* 1.482.

[120] Quintus complains about this diminution of aristocratic control at Cic. *Leg.* 3.34–9; see Dyck 2004, 527ff.

[121] *Clientela* negligible in deciding the outcome of elections: Brunt 1988, 382ff.; Morstein-Marx 1998; Yakobson 1999, 66ff.; Mouritsen 2001, 67ff.; Mouritsen 2017a, 94ff. See, further, ¶2 **patron**; ¶17 **clients**, and pp. 227f.

[122] Meier 1965, 563; Meier 1980, XXXIIff., 163ff.; Brunt 1988, 35ff.; Mouritsen 2017a, 126ff.

ties, that persisted over time. When Romans employed terms like parties (*partes*) or faction (*factio*), they typically did so in a pejorative sense.[123] Nor did descriptive expressions like *optimates* or *populares* refer to cohesive or even easily identifiable groups.[124] And in any case there existed nothing in the way of a party apparatus, a party's political platform, a party hierarchy, or a party machine designed to ensure the participation of voters or coordinate the political campaigns of multiple members—or to offer members of the public a rubric for their political identity. Politics was a personal endeavour, and competition for office was a contest among individuals and such supporters as they could attract.

Most Romans, we have seen (§II.4), did not vote, nor was it possible to know, even during the final phases of any campaign, which Romans would actually appear at the assembly and cast their ballots. Potential voters were independent operators, and it seems that few of them were deeply knowledgeable about candidates or issues. Consequently, it was incumbent on each candidate to seek out supporters, inspire their enthusiasm, project an attractive and suitable image to the populace at large (after all, even the attitudes of Romans who never intended to vote could influence those who, in the end, did vote),[125] and exhibit his superiority over his rivals. And he must do so in the absence of any party apparatus, in a contentious free-for-all, the results of which clearly mattered most for the candidates, their close associates, and members of the political class. One wonders whether, at the end of the day, the daily lives of most Romans were much affected by the particular identity of the man who was elected praetor or who suffered a disgraceful *repulsa*.[126] It was the job of every candidate to persuade potential voters that it was indeed very important for them that the right man be elevated to high office.

Put differently, politics had to be made personal: that is, individual citizens had to be convinced that each had a personal stake in the process and outcome of any political campaign. Hence the centrality of *gratia* in Roman thinking about elections: canvassing inevitably brought to the fore the past performance of favours and the expectation of future favours, if not from the successful candidate himself then from an important

[123] Seager 1972b; Brunt 1988, 443ff.; Hölkeskamp 2001.

[124] See ¶5 **the best men; champions of popular rights.**

[125] This category includes women, who of course could not vote but could nonetheless express their support for individual candidates; see §III.7.

[126] Although it is probably going too far to describe the results of the elections as irrelevant (*belanglos*) to the mass of voters, it is clear that daily life in Rome was rarely affected by the performance of its elected magistrates in profoundly novel ways, not least owing to formal and informal constraints on the exercise of magisterial power; see Jehne 2010, 22ff.; cf. Beck 2005, 22ff.; Jehne 2009, 500ff.

intermediary of the candidate.[127] And perhaps because this exchange of favours was, in nearly every case, a transaction between men who were not social equals, it was natural for the Romans to associate the candidate's projection of his influence with the ideology of patronage (*patrocinium* or *clientela*), a relationship that, while not exclusively individual, foregrounded individual responsibility on the part of both client and patron. *Clientela* did not determine the outcome of elections in Rome, but feelings and sensibilities pertaining to *clientela*, and especially the very personal moral expectations with which the Romans believed the institution was imbued, animated each candidate's endeavours to satisfy the public— and the public's expectations of a properly conducted canvass.

The Romans believed *clientela* was an ancient institution.[128] Powerful men accumulated dependants, who repaid their patron's aid by placing themselves in his *fides*, his trust—that is, by making a formal gesture of confidence in their patron and by way of offering whatever modest tokens of gratitude they could manage.[129] So pervasive, and so socially significant, was *clientela* that the comic poet Plautus could mock the zeal exhibited by undiscriminating patrons endeavouring to acquire clients in bulk: 'All the so-called best men make this their central preoccupation: they crave clients in quantity, and they couldn't care less whether they're good men or bad men.'[130] *Clientela* on a grand scale was associated with the nobility and was routinely listed among the noble's advantages over his rivals, often as an object of envy on the part of his competitors.[131] Dionysius of Halicarnassus provides our only detailed account of the institution,[132] and it is an idealizing one. In Dionysius' account, patrons compete with one another to win over clients and to keep them: he does not describe *clientela* as a static affair, but rather the focus of continuous hard work on the part of patrons. Success in assembling a vast array of clients, according to Dionysius, brought a man widespread fame because his *clientela* was evidence of his personal virtue (his *aretē*, or, in Latin, *virtus*). *Clientela*, then, was conceived of as an institution that united men who, though unequal, were good men, and it was an institution that demanded heavy

---

[127] 'there are three things that serve as the best incentives for stimulating goodwill and keen electoral support—favours done, the expectation of future favours, and genuine personal affection' (§21); see III.10; §3 **the number and variety of your friends; §4 See to it that ... express their gratitude; §§18, 21.**

[128] See the concise but valuable discussions by Drummond 1989a; Eilers 2002, 1ff.; Deniaux 2006; see §17 **clients.**

[129] Gell. *NA* 5.13.2.   [130] Plaut. *Men.* 572–5.

[131] *Rhet. Her.* 8; Cic. *Clu.* 94; *Part. or.* 87; Sall. *Iug.* 85.4.

[132] Dion. Hal. *Ant. Rom.* 2.10.4.

exertion from the man at the top, whose industry and helpfulness constituted proof of his virtue.[133]

It is not difficult to see how *clientela* became an ideological template for the broader aristocratic practice of exchanging favours, or for the Romans' concentration on *gratia*, especially on obligations of an individual and personal nature, during canvassing. This is evident in the essential rituals of canvassing, to which we shall recur, especially in the morning greeting (*salutatio*), which was crucial to the pageantry of any campaign, and in the determined employment of intermediaries as surrogate candidates, themselves under a debt of gratitude to the candidate and possessing influence over others by dint of their own resources in *gratia*.[134]

4 The Indignities of Canvassing

At the same time, the circumstances of a candidate were radically different from, and more complex than, those of Dionysius' paradigmatic patron. Although he must appear a commanding figure in Roman society, the successful candidate also had to debase himself in begging the public for the honour which, in principle, he already merited. 'If we seek *honores*,' Cicero insists, describing the proper demeanour of a canvassing aristocrat, 'we must not grow weary in begging for them.'[135] References to begging and playing the part of the people's slave constitute the routine discourse for expressing the experience of a candidate for office.[136] Canvassing inverted the natural relationship between the candidate and his public. It was normal, for instance, for members of the elite to be approached and addressed by their inferiors, to whom their response was an expression of aristocratic comity and in itself a benefaction.[137] When canvassing, by contrast, the candidate was obliged to reverse this pattern (§§29–30, 42–3), and the implications of his doing so are obvious.[138] The condition of a candidate, the Romans recognized, was an anxious one, driving the hopeful office seeker to fright, constant solicitude, and

---

[133] On the profound nature of this connection, from the elite perspective, see Gell. *NA* 5.13.1–6.

[134] See, further, pp. 32ff., and §31 **candidates on your behalf**; §35 **morning greeters**. At §36 it is insisted that massive attendance (by anyone, not by clients) furnishes a candidate with *laus* ('glory') and *dignitas* ('prestige').

[135] Cic. *Planc.* 11.   [136] See note 80.   [137] Hall 1998; see §42.

[138] Captured succinctly by Horace: 'this man, of high pedigree [*generosior*], descends to the Campus Martius as a candidate [*petitor*]' (*Carm.* 3.1.10–11); it is not quite right to insist that the literal sense of *petitor* 'undercuts *generosior*' (so Nisbet and Rudd 2004, 11), when, instead, it heightens the normal tension that animates the candidate's social circumstances.

unpleasant punctiliousness in showing courtesy to all and sundry, all while working long hours to win the favour of other, in many cases lesser, men.[139] The aristocracy regarded the experience with distaste.[140] In his *De oratore*, Cicero puts the elite perspective plainly, in lines he attributes to the dialogue's principal figure, M. Licinius Crassus (cos. 95):

> Whenever I canvassed for a magistracy, it was my habit, during the actual glad-handing, to send my friend Scaevola away. I explained to him that I wished to behave unsuitably, for I had to canvass ingratiatingly, and it is a thing that can be done well only if it is done unsuitably.[141]

For 'unsuitably', Cicero uses the words *ineptum* and *inepte*, language that underscores the absurdity and inappropriateness of the business of canvassing, or at least canvassing properly: these words signal canvassing's unnatural fit for an aristocrat.[142]

Horace supplies a vivid sketch:

> If pageantry [*species*] and influence [*gratia*] make a man fortunate, then let's buy a slave who can tell us names, who can elbow us in our left side and make us extend our right hand even when we're crossing the street. 'This man is very important in the Fabian tribe, that one in the Veline. This man can hand the fasces to anyone he takes a fancy to, or, if he's out of temper, snatch the ivory curule chair out from under him.' Best to toss in a hearty 'Brother!' or 'Father!', gracefully adapting your manners to each man's age.[143]

Horace's hapless candidate, desperate to make the right impression and wholly at the mercy of his public (and the recommendation of his servile handler), admittedly meant to be amusing, is not wholly unrealistic, as Cicero's Crassus makes clear.

The potential indignities of canvassing went beyond the awkwardness of social inversions. Petitioning candidates could be ignored, or worse, publicly insulted. At some time, not long before 91, A. Sempronius Musca, whose surname means 'fly', was passing through the forum along with his brother, shaking hands in an effort to win popular favour. When he took the hand of a certain Vargula, the man cried out to his slave, 'Boy, shoo

---

[139] Cic. *Pis.* 55 (punctiliousness); *Mil.* 42 (fright and solicitude); *Att.* 6.2.5 (long hours of work); see ¶1 assiduousness.

[140] The degradations of canvassing, in addition to other passages cited at note 90 and in this discussion: Sall. *Iug.* 85.1; Dion. Hal. 8.31.2; Vell. 2.126.2; Tac. *Ann.* 1.15.1; *Pan. Lat.* 3.16–17; Symm. *Or.* 4.7; Auson. *Grat. act.* 3.13; see also Liv. 3.35.5–6 (the duplicitous pose of Appius Claudius the Decemvir). For a fuller discussion of this point, see Tatum 2007.

[141] Cic. *De or.* 1.112; cf. Val. Max. 4.5.4.

[142] On the essential thrust of these words, see Cic. *De or.* 2.17.

[143] Hor. *Epist.* 1.6.49–55.

away these flies!' (*puer, abige muscas!*).[144] The episode was remembered
a generation later, and for Sempronius it can only have been deeply
humiliating. And yet it was the public's privilege to reject the advances of
any candidate.

Owing to his exposed position, a candidate had to anticipate hostil-
ities not only from his rivals and their supporters, but from enemies
whose only goal was securing his failure. For instance, in 189 the consul
presiding over the elections, M. Fulvius Nobilior, worked vigorously to
guarantee the defeat of his personal enemy M. Aemilius Lepidus (cos.
187). L. Opimius (cos. 121) was defeated by C. Fannius in the consular
elections for 122 on account of Gaius Gracchus (tr. pl. 123), who threw his
support against Opimius. During the aedilician elections for 69, Verres,
whom Cicero was prosecuting, employed bribery agents in an unsuccessful attempt to ruin the orator's chances. And when he was a candidate for the consulship, M. Crassus (cos. 70) worked against Cicero's
election.[145] Such vulnerability can only have exacerbated the indignities
of canvassing.

Not everyone was capable of canvassing properly. Valerius Maximus
records the experience of the noble P. Scipio Nasica, who, when canvassing for the aedileship and pressing the gnarled hand of a farmer, asked the
man whether it was his habit to walk on his hands: the joke offended, and
Nasica's ill-timed remark quickly circulated throughout the city—and
cost him the election.[146] The common people were put off by Nasica's
insolence, and more substantial citizens expected their leaders to be more
skilled in playing the part of a candidate.

We possess two speeches in which Cicero defended clients who were
accused of winning office through illegal electioneering practices.[147] At
each trial, the case for the prosecution was led by a disappointed candidate.
And in each speech, Cicero, for obvious tactical reasons, addresses what
he deems the deficiencies in the failed candidate's canvassing techniques.
In each instance, Cicero asserts, although the personal character of the
defeated candidate was meritorious, his approach to cultivating the voters
was unsound and inadequate.[148] This tactic could be effective because, it
is clear, the Romans assessed a candidate as much by his willingness to

---

[144] Cic. *De or.* 2.247. Nothing more is known of these brothers: Münzer 1923a and
1923b, 1435. Nor of Vargula, who is also mentioned at *De or.* 2.244 (Münzer 1901, 2392).

[145] M. Fulvius Nobilior: Liv. 38.35.1 (with Briscoe 2008, 119); 38.43.1. C. Gracchus:
Plut. *C. Gracch.* 8.2; 11.2–3; Verres: Cic. *Verr.* 1.22–3; 2.1.19. Crassus: Asc. 83C; see
§VII.5.

[146] Val. Max. 7.5.2.

[147] *Pro Murena* (Alexander 1990, 111f.) and *Pro Plancio* (Alexander 1990, 142f.).

[148] *Mur.* 49–53; *Planc.* 7–8, 11.

canvass them appropriately as by his pretensions to dignity and honour. It is notable that in the *Brief Handbook* there is no specific advice on soliciting the public when canvassing in the forum: that facet of canvassing is treated from a very different perspective.[149]

That correct canvassing techniques were crucial is patent in ancient accounts of the campaign of the younger Cato, who was an unsuccessful candidate for the consulship of 51. He fell short because he refused to solicit voters in the traditional, which is to say in the unsuitable, style appropriate to a candidate:

> He preferred to conduct himself in a manner that preserved the dignity of his station instead of winning the dignity of the consulship by working the crowd. Nor would he allow his friends to employ the techniques by means of which the public is captivated and charmed. He failed to win the office.[150]

Cicero criticized Cato for failing the republic simply because he could not be bothered to win over the people by friendly and welcoming exchanges,[151] a reality Cato recognized without regret: 'he knew he had offended the people by his manner, which a man of intelligence, he believed, would not alter in order to win the favour of others'.[152]

5 Canvassing Rituals

Perhaps when he commenced approaching supporters (*prensatio*) or when he formally announced his candidature (*professio*), and certainly during the final weeks of canvassing, a candidate donned a toga, pipe-clayed to a state of conspicuous whiteness, called a *toga candida* (hence his designation as a *candidatus*). Thereafter his candidature remained an obvious feature of his every public action. The origins of this practice remain obscure, as does its significance beyond simply identifying for the public which men were standing for office. There is no reason to regard the *toga candida* as a modest garment: its preparation required both trouble and expense, unavoidably signalling the candidate's wealth.[153] The garment called upon the public to observe and to judge its wearer: the son of Scipio Africanus is said to have tarnished his reputation by appearing as a candiate in a disgracefully stained *toga candida*.[154] According to the

---

[149] See ¶37 third element.   [150] Plut. *Cat. min.* 49.6.
[151] Plut. *Cat. min.* 50.2.
[152] Plut. *Cat. min.* 50.3. Liv. 4.25.12 suggests that in reality canvassing involved menaces as well as solicitations.
[153] Isid. *Etym.* 19.24.6; Polyb. 10.4.8; see Deniaux 2003; Edmondson 2008.
[154] Val. Max. 3.5.1b.

elder Cato, during the early republic candidates wore togas without tunics underneath: Plutarch explains this as an expression of simplicity and therefore humility or (or even, *and*) a means of exhibiting battle scars as proof of martial valour.[155] In view of the number of magistracies to be filled each year and the several contestants for each of them, the *toga candida* cannot have been a rare sight in the weeks preceding elections: still, because it was a garment that concentrated the attention of spectators, it added to the spectacle of public canvassing.[156]

The most obvious, and ostentatious, aspect of canvassing comprised three daily performances which occupied the candidate's final weeks before the election: his morning audience (*salutatio*), a parade from his house to the forum (*deductio*), and his circulation through the forum, during which he solicited public support (*prensatio*).[157] Resplendent in his *toga candida*, any aspiring magistrate, above all a candidate for the consulship, was watched closely and critically by rivals and potential voters alike: how great a crowd did he attract throughout the day, and how confident was his demeanour?[158] This was proof of his influence (*gratia*) and evidence of his prestige (*dignitas*), and a candidate who failed to draw followers in suitable quantities, or somehow blundered in his dealings with the men whose support he sought, soon found his prospects blighted.[159] All his past exertions in winning popular favour, at every social level, led a candidate to this moment in his campaign, when the reality of his appeal was revealed to everyone.

The theatricality of Roman political culture has not gone unobserved by scholars.[160] Again and again, Rome's civic ideology was acted out in a variety of public ceremonies, like aristocratic funerals, magisterial performances at sacred rituals and in popular assemblies, and in rare events like triumphal processions. Even when the cynosure of all eyes was an aristocrat, which was ordinarily the case in such rituals, the people's participation, as observers, remained indispensable. Indeed, it was by way of this brand of collaboration that these public acts became vehicles for sustaining, even celebrating, the Romans' common values, meaningful to

---

[155] Plut. *Mor.* 276c; *Cor.* 14.2; Cato fr. 137 *FRHist*. At *Cor.* 15.1, Plutarch depicts Coriolanus exhibiting his scars while canvassing for the consulship.

[156] Liv. 4.25.12 reports legislation in the early republic that banished the practice of wearing a *toga candida*, an item even he seems not to credit.

[157] ¶¶34–8, 52; see the detailed discussions in the commentary.

[158] E.g. Cic. *Mur.* 44–5; *Fam.* 8.3.1–3.

[159] ¶34 sheer scale; ¶37 a great crowd at all times; ¶52 pageantry.

[160] Fundamental discussions include: Flaig 2003; Bell 2004, 24ff.; 151ff.; Sumi 2005; Hölkeskamp 2006; Winterling 2009, 42ff.; Goldbeck 2010, 235ff.; Hölkeskamp 2010, 107ff.; Hölkeskamp 2011b; Flower 2014; Hall 2014; Russell 2016; Rosillo López 2017, 42ff.

all if not to all alike. The public ideology of Rome was marked by the hierarchical nature of Roman society. Consequently, civic rituals, notwithstanding their urgent inclusion of the public, nevertheless staged the superiority of the governing elite in a visible expression of its capacity for achievement and its exercise of power.

Every civic ritual was a complex affair, incorporating facets of other civic rituals in such a way that it was rendered a distinctive part of Rome's extended system of political and social communication.[161] All aristocrats routinely participated in a *salutatio* and *deductio*, pageants that helped to evoke the ideal virtue of the ideal patron.[162] From that perspective, a candidate's *salutatio* and *deductio* drew attention to his aristocratic superiority, perhaps in an especially marked way inasmuch as his performance in these actions was so keenly observed. And our sources make it clear that a massive retinue was regarded as a good gauge of any candidate's *gratia*. Furthermore, a celebratory *salutatio* and a glorious *deductio* were the opening acts of a new consul's first day in office, moments anticipated in every candidate's daily canvassing.[163] At the same time, as the *Brief Handbook* emphasizes, candidates were obliged to regard attendance largely as a kindness conferred by their supporters and to fall all over themselves in expressing their deep appreciation for it.[164] A similar paradox pervades the *prensatio*. Although it was normal for grand figures to appear in public, where they were approached and addressed by their inferiors, to whom they could exhibit a generous, aristocratic comity, this pattern of behaviour was sharply inverted in the experience of canvassing.[165] Put differently, the rituals of canvassing simultaneously signalled a candidate's elevated status *and* exhibited unmistakable gestures of respect for the voters' independence, which is to say for popular *libertas*.

Magistrates were especially associated with spectacle and ritual,[166] and so it was perhaps natural that the ceremonies of canvassing exposed candidates to a special degree of public scrutiny. The intense competition between rivals for office was, in the end, channelled into familiar, comprehensible performances that allowed voters to compare the electability and soundness of all the candidates through repeated demonstrations of their

---

[161] Hölkeskamp 2011b, 163.   [162] ¶35 **morning greeters**; ¶36 **escort you**.

[163] Hölkeskamp 2011b, 166f.; Pina Polo 2011, 17f.; Flower 2014, 379; Östenberg 2015.

[164] ¶35 **Give unmistakable signs**; ¶36 **you appreciate this more**.

[165] Greeting an aristocrat: Hall 1998. Comity and accessibility: Heuer 1941; Deniaux 1993, 264f. Its inversion: ¶¶19–30, 42–3; see §III.4. Trajan won Pliny's praise for conduct that, although Pliny does not say so explicitly, is very much like that of a republican candidate: Plin. *Pan.* 23.1–3; 24.2–3; see Wallace-Hadrill 1982.

[166] Flower 2014, 379.

popularity. Which is why, in addition to the quality of a candidate's elite supporters, the sheer numbers attending him mattered so strongly. Although both the *Brief Handbook* and Cicero's own works underline the importance of securing attendance by grandees, they chiefly lay stress on a candidate's very present need of retaining a massive following on the part of men from the lower orders.[167]

Our own age, addicted as it is to staged reality in its entertainment but also in its high profile public events, not least political events, is perhaps well suited to appreciate how performances that are known to be contrived and fabricated can never the less be profoundly affecting—often more so than public expressions that are truly spontaneous and authentic. For this reason it will not do to dismiss the Romans' canvassing rituals as mere flummery. Indeed, we probably go too far in watering down their significance whenever we say that *salutatio*, for example, enacts or symbolizes friendship or devotion. Better to say that it *is* friendship or devotion, or certainly a very conspicuous slice of it, and that is why a teeming atrium signalized an aristocrat's traditional, wholesome authority. All the more so when the aristocrat was a candidate. This was a reality that did not require interpretation or unpacking on the public's part. And that is why the game could be gamed. And was. Crowds of followers could not assure anyone of election. But the absence or a crowd, even a detectable deficiency in numbers, spelt doom for anyone seeking high office.

Why this emphasis on the lower orders? Admittedly, their votes were sometimes decisive, but that possibility does not emerge sharply when Cicero or the *Brief Handbook* discuss attendance by the masses. Instead, they focus on the part played by the poor in signalling a candidate's *dignitas* when they accompany him in bulk. Now the *Brief Handbook* describes the ideal candidate as a man the senate believes will champion its authority, the knights and prosperous classes believe will be the guardian of peace and tranquillity, and the multitude believes will not show himself hostile to their entitlements (¶53), a formulation that plainly highlights the centrality of consensus as an ideal in Roman society.[168] And the right man for meeting each criterion in this job description, although he cannot be a demagogue, must be popular with the masses.

The importance of magisterial authority for the practical regulation of Roman society can scarcely be exaggerated. After all, late republican Rome was a densely populated city lacking anything like a modern police

---

[167] ¶¶34–8, 49–50, 52; Cic. *Mur.* 44–5, 70–1.

[168] Consensus in Rome, in Roman rituals, and in Roman elections: Hölkeskamp 2010, 107ff. See also: Lobur 2008; Jehne 2010; Flaig 2013, 351ff.; Jehne 2013b; Arena 2015.

force, which meant that the regulation of public order depended to an extraordinary degree on the respect commanded by the magistrates, not least by the consuls.[169] Their influence was sometimes put to the test. Confronted by a tribune and harassed by a crowd perturbed by the high price of grain, Scipio Nasica (cos. 138) demanded their silence and obedience on the ground that he understood better than they what was best for the republic: the people complied.[170] As consul-designate in 61, Metellus Celer was able to foil an unapproved celebration of the *ludi compitalicii* by the urban masses, in despite of a tribune's interference.[171] A consul, Cicero stresses the point, must possess the *dignitas* requisite to obstruct irresponsible tribunes and deflect popular agitation. Only such a figure could effectively champion the senate and men of property.[172]

Now, it is obvious that the consulship could not be won by a man who had thoroughly alienated the prosperous classes. At the same time, the elite could not sensibly support a candidate who was incompetent in his dealings with the multitude. And this is why grandees and commoners alike were vigilant in inspecting the sheer scale of every candidate's entourage. In the illogicality of pageants and their impressions, a crowd of attendants signified popular favour and lent the candidate who collected such a crowd an aura of soundness: this was a man whom the people could count on (thus the popular inference drawn from a candidate's massive following), and this was a man whose capacity for commanding loyalty and deference among the masses could be relied on to sustain stability (thus the elite inference from a candidate's massive following).[173] This symbolism was so forceful that it seems not to have mattered greatly to most Romans if a candidate's retinue was stimulated by the exertions of a *nomenclator* or hired by way of illegal fees and bribes.[174]

Even a corrupt candidate showed himself capable of managing the masses, even if his version of *gratia* was an unsavoury one. This is an element of Roman canvassing that must not be overlooked, notwithstanding our proper appreciation of the importance of the people in selecting individual magistrates and in exercising, through their assemblies, their sovereign majesty and civic liberty. For the rituals of canvassing, however degrading or injurious to the sensibilities of candidates, were nevertheless pageants which exploited the participation of the poor in such a way that

---

[169] Nippel 1995.   [170] Val. Max. 3.7.3.   [171] Cic. *Pis.* 8; Asc. 7C.
[172] E.g. Cic. *Mur.* 24; see Jehne 2011b; Hölkeskamp 2013.
[173] See, further, Tatum 2003–4; Tatum 2009b.
[174] A *nomenclator* was an assistant (often a slave) who aided an elite Roman in recalling the name of anyone he met. Ban on *nomenclatores*: Plut. *Cat. min.* 8.2, but see Cic. *Mur.* 77; see ¶28 **address them by name**. Legislation against hiring crowds: see ¶37 **a great crowd at all times**. Electoral bribery: ¶¶54–7, with commentary.

their own actions tended to reaffirm their personal subordination. Year after year, they selected their leaders from an array of their superiors, showing their individual support through mass gestures: assembling in the atrium of a great man's house, descending with him to the forum, following him about during the day, and *possibly* casting one of many votes in a teeming century—all in the expectation of preserving their present condition.

6 Tactics: Courting Publicity and Popularity

In ¶¶16–40, the *Brief Handbook* discusses the means through which Cicero can 'gain the support of friends'. These include the traditional canvassing rituals discussed above (§III.5). Cicero is also instructed to win over voters in the city and in the countryside by forging connections and gaining favour with various communities, urban and rural alike (e.g. ¶30 **all the clubs, the boroughs, and the neighbourhoods; ¶30 municipality, colony, prefecture**). In ¶¶41–53, the *Brief Handbook* catalogues techniques for 'dealing with the people'. These Quintus summarizes as 'recognizing people by name, an ingratiating manner, constant effort, generosity, publicity, and civic pageantry' (¶41), and he proceeds to discuss them in detail. Unsurprisingly, a candidate is urged to be unstinting in his attendance on others (¶43),[175] keeping himself accessible to everyone and refusing promises to no one (¶44–8). He must constantly cut a *bella figura* (¶52), showing off his important friends (¶51) and reminding others of his merits (¶50). The importance of negative campaigning, and the correct response whenever one is the object of invective, are also addressed (¶¶7–12, 51, 57). Public banquets are recommended as a suitable means of demonstrating personal generosity (¶44 **in banquets**). Being noticed, for the right reasons, remains paramount. The *Brief Handbook* is also aware of techniques that allow one to be appreciated for the *wrong* reasons. Illegal electioneering, *ambitus*, is addressed at ¶¶55–6 as a tactic likely to be pursued by Cicero's competitors. An examination of each of these canvassing techniques is supplied in the pertinent sections of the commentary.

7 Tactics: Posters

Although nothing remains of them, and although they go unmentioned in our literary sources, it is certain that posters played a part in canvassing

---

[175] See Cic. *Pis.* 55.

in Rome.[176] So too, surely, political graffiti.[177] Thousands of electoral posters, *programmata* as they are called, survive in Pompeii. Our only evidence for their Roman cousins consists of signs warning candidates against posting their advertisements—proof enough of the recurring presence of *programmata* in the capital. These surviving prohibitions were originally deployed in order to protect the integrity of tombs, structures which, for all their sanctity, because they were situated along the roads bringing Italians into the city, were ideal for capturing the attention of rural voters of any class.

At Pompeii, candidates and their supporters painted, on the outsides of houses and shops along the city's most frequented streets, concise appeals for votes. These appeals were not expressed in the candidate's own voice but rather took the form of recommendations by others. However imperfectly Pompeian *programmata* reflect their Roman predecessors, certain similarities to republican canvassing stand out, not least the pervasive language of supplication, so natural and obligatory that it could be abbreviated: for example, *OVF* (*oro vos faciatis*: 'I beg you to elect') or *ROG*, or simply *R* (*rogat* or *rogant*: 'he, or she, or they entreat you'). Typical is: 'Vatia entreats [you to elect] Gaius Julius Polybius *duovir*.'[178]

A candidate's supporters are often individuals, including clients,[179] freedmen, fellow members of a religious fraternity (viz. a *sodalis*)[180]—and supporters who are women.[181] Collective endorsements are also common. These are provided by neighbours, residents of specific neighbourhoods, and practitioners of the same occupations—all groups of the kind Cicero is urged by the *Brief Handbook* to cultivate.[182] And although candidates can be characterized only briefly in such succinct appeals, their merits recall sound republican values: a good candidate is a *vir bonus*, or even an *optimus*; more often he is *dignus* or *dignus rei publicae*; and, most commonly of all, he is *probus* ('capable and upright').[183] Other pertinent qualities appear, like assertions of worthiness owing to past accomplishments,

---

[176] Castrén 1975, 114ff.; Franklin 1980; Mouritsen 1988; Biundo 2003. Helpful introductions include Beard 2008, 188ff. and Weeber 2011.

[177] Morstein-Marx 2012. We are too poorly informed about political graffiti in Rome to be certain of their role in canvassing, but enough suggestive evidence subsists to make it likely that graffiti put in appearances in hotly contested elections; see Baird and Taylor 2011; Keegan 2014; Rosillo López 2017, 144ff.

[178] *CIL* 4.32.   [179] *CIL* 4.822; 4.933; 4.7605.

[180] *CIL* 4.209; 4.221; 4.1105.

[181] E.g. *CIL* 4.368. Mouritsen 1988, 60ff. On women in Pompeian *programmata*, see Savunen 1997, 21ff.

[182] Castrén 1975, 114ff.; Mouritsen 1988, 65ff.; see ¶¶17, 24, 30, 32.

[183] Full references to *programmata* are assembled in the index of vol. 4 of *CIL*: *CIL* 4.1871, 240f. (*dignus* and *dignus rei publicae*, routinely abbreviated *D* and *DRP*), 247

admirable personal morality, even *gloria*.[184] Occasionally slogans offer supplementary recommendations: 'he will preserve our treasury', 'he treats many generously', 'he delivers good bread'.[185]

It appears that, in Pompeii, canvassing by way of posters was administered centrally, by the candidate and his inner circle. Presumably his supporters were approached by the candidate and aided, even guided, by his wishes when they promulgated their endorsements.[186] This was a system that opened the door to a species of sabotage whereby posters were put up which depicted a candidate as the darling of unsavoury characters. A brief sampling includes: 'the pickpockets entreat [you to elect] Vatia aedile'; 'the gamblers entreat you to make Gnaeus Helvius Sabinus aedile'; 'the late night drinkers beg you to elect Marcus Cerrinius aedile'; and 'the assassins beg you to elect Marcus Cerrinius aedile'.[187] The conceit lying behind notices like these is not simply that such figures could find a candidate attractive but furthermore that the candidate has sought them out as supporters. Posters could also express aggression: 'if anyone says no to Quinctius, he can sit with a donkey'.[188] Or they can resort to obscenity: 'I beg you to elect Isidorius aedile: he is unsurpassed at licking cunt'.[189] Now, it is possible that some of these posters are parodies intended only to prompt mirth. But in view of the invective that characterized Roman canvassing (§§7–12, with commentary), many of these must have been designed to undermine the *dignitas* of a rival candidate.

8 Tactics: Letters

Four letters by Cicero are preserved in which the orator appeals for support on behalf of a favoured candidate: one in aid of T. Annius Milo's (ultimately disastrous) campaign for a consulship of 52, and three for L. Aelius Lamia, who stood (successfully) for a praetorship of 42.[190] Both men were past benefactors of Cicero, and in each letter it is Cicero's debt, and his delight in honouring it, that is foregrounded. So, too, the indebtedness Cicero will feel towards each letter's recipient if he takes Cicero's

---

(*virum bonum*, abbreviated *VB*), 244 (*optimus* and *probus*, sometimes abbreviated *P*)—these qualities sometimes appear in combination.

[184] Respectively *CIL* 4.706, 4.768; 4.456, 4.720; 4.7201.

[185] *CIL* 4.3702; 4.7187; 4.499, cf. 4.7925.

[186] Thus *programmata* constituted both endorsements and proof that groups or individuals had repaid a candidate for his past favours to them: Biundo 2003, 55f.

[187] *CIL* 4.581; 4.3885; 4.581; 4.246.   [188] *CIL* 4.2887.   [189] *CIL* 4.1383.

[190] Cic. *Fam.* 2.6 (to C. Curio for Milo); *Fam.* 11.16 (to D. Brutus for Lamia); *Fam.* 11.17 (to M. Brutus for Lamia); *Fam.* 12.29 (to Q. Cornificius for Lamia).

part in the elections. In short, this correspondence teems with sentiments of gratitude, past and future.

Cicero also promotes the advantages of his candidates, in concise but by now familiar terms. Lamia enjoys a fine reputation (*splendor*), ample influence (*gratia*), and prestige (*dignitas*)—and has to his credit brilliant aedilician games. Milo's merits receive finer analysis: prosperous citizens (*boni*) admire him owing to the actions of his tribunate, the masses on account of his games and liberality, and the influential young men of the equestrian order because he has cultivated them diligently. Each letter is addressed to a fellow aristocrat and is elegantly composed.[191] The three letters for Lamia make it obvious how carefully Cicero has suited each letter to its recipient, even when the substance of each letter is more or less identical. Indeed, Cicero is at pains to register his concern with his correspondents' dignity.

The *Brief Handbook* does not comment on this technique, but it is obvious that such letters were commonplace. This is made plain at *Fam.* 12.29.2, where Cicero, flattering his reader as a man of the world, leaves it to him to fill in the blanks:

> I am under no illusion that you are waiting to see just how I formulate the recommendation I am about to put to you. In view of my profound friendship [with Lamia], you know exactly what terms are called for. And you must take it as read that I have used them all.

Canvassing for others by way of correspondence, a practice that during the empire came to be known as *commendatio*, was so widespread that it is rarely mentioned explicitly.[192]

It is doubtful that Cicero relied on either Milo or Lamia for guidance when he circulated letters in support of their candidature. But by then he was a senior consular and a great man. Letters were features of a campaign that were, like electoral posters, often components of a candidate's overall strategy for canvassing. This was certainly true of Gaius Marius' sensationally successful letter-writing campaign for the consulship of 107, instigated by the candidate and executed by Roman soldiers and business-

---

[191] By contrast, when dictator, Caesar's recommendations were entirely formulaic: 'Caesar the dictator to the [fill in the blank] tribe: I recommend the following men to you, so that, owing to your votes on their behalf, each may preserve his prestige [*dignitas*]', Suet. *Iul.* 41.

[192] For instance, when Pompeius supported M. Pupius Piso for a consulship of 61, he recommended him both to his friends and, remarkably, to his enemies—but inasmuch as he was abroad at the time he must have done so by correspondence (Dio 37.44.3); see Hirtius *B.Gall.* 8.50; Cic. *Ad Brut.* 1.6.2. *Commendatio* in the late republic and in imperial practice: Levick 1967.

men in Africa, letters the sentiments of which soon circulated, with striking effect, throughout the city.[193] Marius' tactics reprised an equally brilliant, and successful, letter-writing campaign on the part of Scipio Aemilianus, who, in Spain, stimulated similar enthusiasm in his troops, whose letters soon brought about his election to the consulship (in violation of the *lex Villia Annalis*) in 147.[194]

9 Tactics: Other Written Texts

Other kinds of texts also circulated. During his run for the consulship, it seems clear, Cicero promulgated damaging depositions from Catilina's trial in 65 for provincial extortion.[195] Attention, be it negative or positive, could also be drawn to a man's past orations, if he had published them, or even to speeches, including pseudepigraphic ones, composed specifically for publication during a political campaign.[196] The aedilician prospects of M. Coelius Vinicianus and C. Lucilius Hirrus were scuppered by speeches they had delivered in the senate during their tribunates in 53, as well as by an unwelcome bill promulgated by them during the same year (each of them proposed Pompeius' appointment as dictator, a controversial suggestion that wore badly by the time of their candidature in 51).[197] Even speeches yet to be completed may have played a part: it has been suggested, for instance, that draft passages of invective from L. Lucceius' planned prosecution of Catilina, which took place after the elections of 64, were circulated to Cicero's advantage during the elections.[198] When Quintus was a candidate for the aedileship, a provocative and apparently offensive political poem, attributed to him, was circulated in the city.[199] The deployment of unflattering texts, whether genuine or forged, was, it seems, a routine tactic.[200]

Likewise the spread of invective, in written or oral versions, and the threat of a prosecution, expressed in moralizing as well as insulting terms, in order to blacken a rival's reputation. The former tactic was

---

[193] Sall. *Iug.* 64–65.5; 73.3; cf. Plut. *Mar.* 7.4. See Yakobson 1999, 13ff.

[194] App. *Pun.* 112; see Astin 1967, 63ff. On the likely content of these letters, see App. *Pun.* 104, 109.

[195] Asc. 87C; ¶10 **Read them.**   [196] E.g. Asc. 94C.

[197] Cic. *Fam.* 8.4.3; see Seager 2002, 130f.

[198] Marshall 1985b, 292. On this trial, see Asc. 90–91C; Alexander 1990, 108f.

[199] Cic. *Q. Fr.* 1.3.9.

[200] It is clear from Cic. *Q. Fr.* 1.2.6 and 8–11 that provincials as well as Romans kept unflattering documents in their possession to put to work in threatening or damaging their enemies; this practice will certainly have gone on during electoral campaigns.

traditional.[201] The latter, however, because its consequences were potentially more serious than aspersions or denunciation, was always a risky undertaking for a candidate.[202] Both species of aggression could be, and often were, delegated to surrogates.[203]

Just as posters kept a candidate's name in public view, it was perhaps the case that candidates and their supporters distributed inscribed gifts. Two small bowls, housed in the Museo Archeologico Nazionale in Naples, the authenticity of which remains questionable, appear to attest to this practice.[204] Each bowl may have been filled with something desirable, or perhaps each was a collectable in its own right (Romans did collect inscribed bowls).[205] One of them refers to M. Cato's campaign for the tribunate of 62 and bears the label: 'Marcus Cato who is canvassing to become tribune of the *plebs*'.[206] The other is connected with Catilina's bid for the consulship of 62, and it bears the endorsement of an ally: 'Cassius Longinus who supports the candidature of Catilina'.[207] Although these finds seem too good to be true, they are not certainly fakes, and in any case they may well reflect a republican canvassing technique.

10 Tactics: Surrogates

It is clear how a candidate's success in amassing followers relied, at least in principle, on his previous achievements and services—benefactions the importance of which required constant reinforcement. The necessity of reminding others of his past good works is a steady refrain in the *Brief Handbook*'s advice to Cicero, culminating in the work's instruction on the importance of publicity (*rumor*) at ¶50.[208] Advancing his profile by way of trumpeting his past record and disparaging his competitors was crucial for a candidate, but also difficult in a political culture that discouraged stump speeches or public rallies.[209] Consequently, candidates depended very much on surrogates of various stripes for the publication of their merits and for censure of their rivals.[210]

---

[201] ¶¶7–12 are devoted to invective against Antonius and Catilina; see commentary for a further discussion.
[202] ¶56 already planning to prosecute them.
[203] During Cicero's campaign, L. Lucceius (pr. 67) either indicted or, more likely, made it clear he planned to indict Catilina for murder (Asc. 91C; see Lewis 2006, 299f.), intentions that could only benefit Catilina's rivals; see ¶10 another trial.
[204] Panciera 1980.   [205] Linderski 2007, 452.
[206] AE 1979.64: M. Cato quei petit tribunu plebei.
[207] AE 1979.63: Cassius Longinu quei Catilinae su sufragatur.
[208] ¶¶4, 8, 19, 21, 35–8, 40, 44.   [209] Tatum 2013.
[210] ¶31 candidates on your behalf.

The exertions of family, friends, and followers were certainly indispensable in projecting a candidate's preferred image, exhibiting the scale of his influence, and aiding him in expressions of generosity, be such expressions legal or otherwise.[211] It is in this context that the services of *sodalitates*, electioneering societies, become important: these were organizations equipped with connections and other resources capable of facilitating a candidate's outreach to the voters without removing him from the conspicuous pageantry through which he was obliged to cultivate the public—and, if he was willing to stoop to dishonesty for winning over the people, or turn a blind eye when others did so on his behalf, *sodalitates* offered him a degree of cover and deniability.[212]

11 Tactics: Addressing Political Issues

It is clear from the preceding discussion that, contrary to the habits of modern political campaigns, canvassing in Rome rarely included political speeches. Stump speeches were rare.[213] To some degree, this was because they were difficult to stage: the right to address the people was a prerogative of magistrates; consequently, if he desired to speak publicly, a candidate was obliged to seek an official's invitation to do so. Or he must find a suitable occasion, like a senatorial debate, in which to praise his own merits or denounce the inadequacies of his rivals, something Cicero managed when he delivered his *In toga candida*.[214] But although it was possible to work around the convention against stump speeches, few candidates did so—doubtless out of respect for the convention itself, which existed, at least in part, to focus Roman canvassing on what was deemed by all to be the crucial concern: the extent of a candidate's *gratia*.[215]

It is generally maintained that, apart from a handful of exceptional episodes, elections were apolitical in nature. Owing to the absence in Rome of political parties, or even strongly divergent political ideologies, personal qualities and individual influence remained the central factors in competition for office.[216] And this was deemed a desirable state of

---

[211] The importance of close connections: ¶¶16–17, with commentary; ¶55 **bribery**.

[212] ¶19 **four religious fraternities**.

[213] But not entirely out of the question. The elder Cato's famous campaign for the censorship of 184, for instance, included public speeches: Liv. 39.40–41.4; Plut. *Cat. mai.* 16.5.

[214] See §III.5.   [215] For a fuller discussion, see Tatum 2013.

[216] E.g. Taylor 1949, 8ff.; Staveley 1972, 191f.; Meier 1980, 11ff.; 197; Brunt 1988, 36; Mouritsen 2001, 92ff., with further bibliography. See the nuanced discussion by Morstein-Marx 1998, 263ff. See, also, ¶53 **avoid matters of state**.

affairs: in Rome, a proper election was denominated *gratuita comitia*, an election determined by *gratia*.[217] Objections to this view have been raised,[218] typically and rightly observing how few detailed accounts of actual canvassing are available for modern inspection—which means that scholars are obliged to decide to what extent it is fair to extrapolate patterns of behaviour from such information as subsists. The quality of our evidence renders that decision difficult.

As a candidate for a consulship of 70, to adduce what is perhaps the most famous instance of policy intruding into canvassing, Pompeius promised to restore to the tribunate the rights and powers Sulla had stripped from that office.[219] This action is routinely described as uncustomary. And yet it is clear, even on the current condition of our evidence, that issues of policy make an appearance in several contentious campaigns for office. During the Second Punic War, the best strategy for confronting Hannibal recurs as a concern for voters, though it is usually linked with the military capacities of individual candidates.[220] Likewise, for Gaius Marius, his elevation to the consulship of 107 was based on his claim to know best how to conclude the Jugurthine War.[221] Central to his campaign for the censorship of 184 was the elder Cato's policy for restoring the moral health of the republic.[222] Specific legislative proposals also played a part in the electoral exertions of several candidates, including the brothers Gracchi, Ser. Sulpicius Rufus in 63, L. Domitius Ahenobarbus in 56, and P. Clodius Pulcher in 52.[223] Slogans or props could substitute for substantive debate or exposition. Clodius, it appears, exhibited a *librarium*, a kind of briefcase containing scrolls, to advertise his legislative intentions,[224] and one should perhaps see in Sallust's report that Marius constantly claimed that with only half an army he could have Jugurtha in chains in only a few days a literary elaboration of what was once the slogan of his

---

[217] Cic. *Att.* 4.15.8; *Q. Fr.* 2.15.4.

[218] Most notably Yakobson 1999, 148ff. (with further bibliography); see also Rosillo López 2017, 173ff.

[219] If he made this promise before his election, as App. *B.Civ.* 1.121 indicates; cf. Sall. *Hist.* 4.40 (McGushin); Plut. *Pomp.* 22; Cic. *Verr.* 1.45; Ps.-Asc. 220 (Stangl). For discussion, see Seager 2002, 37ff.

[220] E.g. Liv. 22.34.1–35.4; 24.7.11–9.4; see Erdkamp 1992.

[221] *MRR* 1.550; see Yakobson 1999, 13ff.   [222] Liv. 39.41.1–4; Plut. *Cat. mai.* 16.

[223] Tiberius Gracchus: Plut. *T.Gracch.* 16.1; App. *B.Civ.* 1.14. Gaius Gracchus: Plut. *C.Gracch.* 3.1; 3.11–12; App. *B.Civ.* 1.21–2. Ser. Sulpius Rufus: Cic. *Mur.* 47. Domitius Ahenobarbus: Suet. *Iul.* 24.1; Plut. *Cat. min.* 41.3. Clodius: Cic. *Mil.* 87; *De aere alieno Milonis*, frr. 17–18 (Crawford); Asc. 52C; Schol. Bob. 173 (Stangl); see Tatum 1999, 236ff. See, further, the extensive discussion in Yakobson 1999, 156ff.

[224] Tatum 1999, 237.

campaign.[225] Confronting a contemporary issue or promising a legislative reform, it appears, was always an available electioneering tactic. But it is far from obvious that candidates routinely employed it, and it is almost certainly relevant that, in the *Brief Handbook*, Cicero is admonished to 'avoid matters of state, both in the senate and in public meetings' (¶53). For most candidates, there was nothing to be gained from endorsing a truly contentious proposition.

Which is not to say that Cicero failed to benefit from contemporary political anxieties and the solutions put forward to resolve them. During his campaign, it is clear, Cicero took advantage of the conspicuous hostility felt against men who had profited from the Sullan proscriptions by underscoring Catilina's alleged enormities during that very time (see ¶9 **citizen slaughter**). More effectively, he, or his supporters, so successfully stimulated public concerns over illegal electioneering that a senatorial decree was passed which demanded the postponement of elections and the promulgation of fresh legislation against corrupt campaigning practices. This decree was vetoed, for reasons that may not have been disreputable, but the occasion allowed Cicero both to defame his rivals and to speak out in favour of honest elections.[226] Now this was unquestionably a political issue, a matter of state, but it was hardly a controversial one—no one in Rome championed corruption—nor did it draw attention to any ideological rift on the part of the senatorial order. Instead, it was controversy of a familiar kind and it permitted Cicero to set himself apart from his competitors in the highly conventional terms of Roman moralism. As such, it was, for voters inclined already to see in Cicero a sound and serious candidate, a welcome confirmation of their existing attitude. In Cicero's case, then, although his campaign was not free from any engagement with politics, political issues were not central to his canvassing.

12 Tactics: Exceptional and Exceptionable Means

A successful military commander could advance his standing with the public by spending his spoils (*manubiae*) on public buildings—that is, through manubial construction.[227] The most striking illustration of the payoffs of this investment can be seen in the career of Q. Metellus Macedonicus. After winning a major victory and celebrating a triumph in 146, Metellus twice failed to win election to a consulship owing to his personal unpopularity (see §III.2). He managed to win over the public,

---

[225] Sall. *Iug.* 64.5. See ¶12 **with a single vote, to draw two daggers**.

[226] Asc. 82–94C; see §VII.5.

[227] See the list of likely beneficiaries supplied by Morgan 1973, 222ff.

however, by way of his expenditure on a glamorous portico, which also exhibited Lysippus' famous Granicus Monument, part of Metellus' eastern plunder.[228] Construction on this scale was naturally attractive to equestrian contractors, to urban labourers, and to a populace grateful for so lavish a civic adornment. Metellus was elected consul for 143 and went on to hold a censorship in 131. Still, not every act of manubial construction elevated its builder to high office: the innovative, expensive victory arches of L. Stertinius did nothing to advance him or his descendants to a consulship.[229] Manubial construction was so exceptional a means of self-promotion that it is unsurprising that it goes unmentioned in the *Brief Handbook*.

So, too, stunts of a singular quality. In his account of Scipio Africanus' remarkable election in 210 to an extraordinary Spanish command, Livy refers to the man's well-publicized habit of visiting the temple of Jupiter Greatest and Best before dawn nearly every day, where he meditated in private, as well as his regular show of attributing his actions and decisions to divine inspiration.[230] In 185, the consul, Ap. Claudius Pulcher, after achieving a military victory in Liguria, rushed back to Rome in order to canvass on behalf of his brother. Instead of relying solely on his office and his recently acquired glory, Claudius instead removed his consular regalia and dismissed his lictors, circulating through the forum as if he were a private citizen. This sensational gesture provoked enormous controversy, the pitch of which, however, ultimately escalated into violence (see below, p. 47).[231] L. Hostilius Mancinus was elevated to a consulship of 145 after he installed in the forum a painting depicting his heroics during the Third Punic War, and installed himself next to his painting in order to explain its significance to all and sundry. Not everyone was pleased, but the public were won over by what the elder Pliny regarded as a display of aristocratic affability (*comitas*). It apparently did not matter that Mancinus offered the people a highly revised and inaccurate account of his military achievements.[232] Candidates, according to Cicero, were permitted a degree of fakery and false representation (*candidatorum licentia*),[233] including the adoption of a new *cognomen* in the hope of impressing the electorate. This tactic is ridiculed in the satirical poem *Catalepton* 10, and Cicero jokes

---

[228] Morgan 1971; see, further, *LTUR* 4.130ff.

[229] Liv. 33.27.3–4. On victory arches in republican Rome, see Wallace-Hadrill 1990.

[230] Liv. 26.19.3–9; cf. Gell. *NA* 6.1.6; see Walbank 1985, 120ff.

[231] Liv. 39.32.12–13.

[232] Plin. *NH* 35.23. Mancinus' actual bungling during the war: App. *Pun.* 113–24; Zonar. 9.29. Pliny does not state explicitly that Mancinus' stunt took place when he was canvassing for office, but that is the likeliest context for his account of the incident.

[233] Cic. *Fam.* 15.20.1.

about it in a letter cited above. There must have been something to laugh about, and it is possibly the case that C. Calvisius Sabinus (cos. 39), a new man, was criticized by his enemies as having risen to the praetorship of 46 because he gave himself the *cognomen* Sabinus, which carried virtuous connotations, even though he had no Sabine ancestry.[234] Our knowledge of these stratagems is, unfortunately, very patchy, and it may well be the case that such innovative tactics as these were as rare as our available evidence suggests.

Before the introduction of the secret ballot at elections, established by the *lex Gabinia* of 139, intimidation and menaces were routine features of canvassing that extended even into the operations of the assembly, when votes were being cast.[235] Matters sometimes went beyond imtimidation. Irregular canvassing on his brother's behalf by Ap. Claudius Pulcher, the consul of 185 (see above, p. 46), escalated into violence which, it has been suggested, relied on Appius' employment of personal retainers organized into gangs.[236] Consequently, the elections were postponed more than once. In the end, however, Appius' brother was elected consul. The Gabinian law, however, did not put a stop to violent tactics, which continued to plague Rome until the end of the republic.[237]

Turbulence at electoral assemblies, unlike violence at legislative ones, is poorly documented. Still, it is clear enough that violence was available as a means of halting voting procedures and thereby attempting to influence the ultimate outcome of an election. Tampering with ballots or the urns that housed them often led to disruptions.[238] Enormities also occurred. In the 50s, the deployment of gang violence delayed and marred elections. Pompeius and Crassus were elected consuls for 55 only after protracted violence.[239] Further conflict in the praetorian elections for that year installed P. Vatinius (cos. 47) in office while successfully blighting Cato's

---

[234] On Calvisius, see Syme 1979, 391ff.; *MRR* 3.48f. On the deployment of *cognomina* in the late republic, see Badian 1988. On Roman nomenclature, see Appendix A, pp. 105f.

[235] Liv. 4.25.12–13 (citing the *mixtis precibus minisque*, 'prayers mixed with menaces', of the nobles); Cic. *Leg.* 3.34, describing the influence of the powerful in positive terms as *auctoritatem optimatium*, 'the authority of the best men'. *Lex Gabinia*: Cic. *Leg.* 3.35; *Amic.* 41; Liv. *Per.* 54.

[236] Liv. 39.32.12–13, complaining of the consul's violent tactics (*vi Claudiana*); on this episode, see, further, Lintott 1999b, 75.

[237] Intimidation and disruption are taken for granted as possible, if exceptionable, tactics at Cic. *Pis.* 36; *Planc.* 24–5; see Lintott 1999b, 69ff. Under the empire, violence at republican elections could be cited as evidence of the bad old days before the emperors took charge: *Pan. Lat.* 3.17.

[238] E.g. Varro *Rust.* 3.5.18; Plut. *Cat. min.* 46.3.   [239] *MRR* 2.214f.

candidature.[240] It was after presiding over one such turbulent assembly that Pompeius returned to his home splattered with blood.[241] Violence, however, was by no means a novelty of the 50s. Commotions during canvassing led to the lynching of Ti. Gracchus in 133, and in 100 Saturninus and C. Servilius Glaucia (pr. 100) went so far as to assassinate a rival for office.[242] Violence and death attended the canvassing of 67, and in 66, it was alleged, P. Sulla assembled bands to deploy against his rivals.[243] In his *In toga candida*, Cicero implied that Antonius and Catilina were disposed to turn to violence.[244]

13 The Quantum Mechanics of Canvassing

Apart from the *Brief Handbook*, Cicero's *Defence of Murena*, and his *Defence of Plancius*, canvassing techniques are rarely described by our sources, including our narrative histories, and so their applications remain invisible to us. To take only a single example, Livy, although elections are a recurring feature of his work, usually records only their results, and fierce contests tend to be buried by formulas like 'the competition for office was keen'.[245] For this reason, it is difficult to assess the relative importance of many of the elements of canvassing. Doubtless it was the case that in different years different tactics and electoral attributes mattered more than others. In any case, it appears that it was not easy, even for an astute Roman, to calculate the outcome of the various factors involved in most elections.[246]

This is clear from Cicero's appraisal of the relative advantages and disadvantages of the candidates for the consulships of 53, our fullest account of this kind.[247] According to Cicero, M. Aemilius Scaurus (pr. 56), although under indictment for extortion (a move taken in order to blight his electoral prospects),[248] nonetheless enjoyed enormous popularity on account of his lavish aedilician games, and retained favour in much of Italy owing to the enduring legacy of his father, the consul of 115. Cn. Domitius Calvinus (cos. 53), by contrast, could boast of only

---

[240] *MRR* 2.216.   [241] Plut. *Pomp.* 53; Dio 39.32.2.

[242] Ti. Gracchus: *MRR* 1.494. Assassination in 100: App. *B.Civ.* 1.142; Liv. 69.4; Flor. 2 *Per.* 4.4; Oros. 5.17.5; cf. Cic. *Cat.* 1.4; 4.4.

[243] Events of 67: Dio 36.39.1. Allegations concerning 66: Cic. *Sull.* 68; see Berry 1996, 269f.

[244] Asc. 87–88C.

[245] Livy's very concise references to hotly contested elections: Liv. 25.5.1; 35.24.4; 37.47.6; 41.28.4. His extended accounts: Liv. 35.10.1–10 (consular elections for 192); Liv. 37.57.9–58.2 (censorial elections for 189); Liv. 39.39.1–15 (praetorian elections for 184); 39.40–41.4 (censorial elections for 184).

[246] See note 79.   [247] Cic. *Att.* 4.16.6; cf. *Att.* 4.15.7; *Q. Fr.* 2.15.4; 3.1.16.

[248] Cic. *Scaur.* 35–6; see Dyck 2012, 142ff.

lacklustre games, but had the backing of powerful friends who were active on his behalf. C. Memmius (pr. 58) also had formidable supporters: both Pompeius and Caesar backed him. Caesar even sent soldiers to Rome in support of Memmius' candidature, and Cicero was certain that, should Memmius' prospects wane, a tribune would be found to delay the elections until Caesar could become more centrally involved. Concerning the final candidate, M. Valerius Messalla (cos. 53), Cicero has little to say: his advantages, the orator observes, were well known to all. What Cicero did not know when expressing these views, however, was that a scandal would soon come to light: Domitius and Memmius, and the consuls of 54, were conspiring in electoral bribery, and the revelation of this action threw everything into confusion.[249] Still, we can see that Cicero could not be certain which factors—heritage, public generosity, powerful supporters, the backing of soldiers, the favour of the tribunes—would in the end prevail. And before this campaign could reach its end, the value of each of these variables was drastically altered by unexpected events.[250]

IV THE DESIGN(S) OF THE *BRIEF HANDBOOK*

1 Style

An appreciation of the literary qualities of the *Brief Handbook* is important for any understanding of its contemporary designs. Now, while it may not be unfair to insist that the *Brief Handbook* finds itself on the wrong side of the line separating the most estimable of Latin prose from all the rest, Franz Buecheler went too far when he described the work's style as 'dry, sober, unlovely'. So, too, Friedrich Leo, when he complained that 'there is no trace of rhetorical style in the work'.[251] These critics, as we shall see, were too distracted by the apparent monotony of ¶¶16–53, the most technically didactic section of the *Brief Handbook*, which is discussed in some detail below (see §IV.4). The Latin of the *Brief Handbook* is in fact urbane,

---

[249] *MRR* 2.227f.
[250] At *Att.* 2.52, written in 59, Cicero reviews the electoral prospects of likely candidates for the consulships of 58: even after taking an ambitious survey of public opinion, he entirely overlooks one of the winners (Cn. Calpurnius Piso). Even an astute and interested observer of elections, which Cicero certainly was, could fail to grasp comprehensively the dynamics and possiblities of any election.
[251] Buecheler 1869, 7: 'sicca, sobria, invenusta'; cf. Leo 1895, 447: 'von rhetorischem Stil ist in der Schrift keine Spur'.

sprinkled with literary devices, and enlivened by instances of rhetorical technique—and it is scaffolded throughout by orthodox prose rhythms.[252] There are even moments of wit and charm, and, in its extended invective against Antonius and Catilina, the *Brief Handbook* offers its readers vivid melodrama (¶10: the torture and decapitation of M. Marius Gratidianus) and searing defamation (¶10: Catilina as child molester).[253] The *Brief Handbook* poses as a letter (see §IV.2), and like any proper letter exchanged between aristocrats, because it represents a transaction in cultural capital, displays literary flourishes in part in order to demonstrate its author's and to affirm its recipient's education—and therefore to exhibit the elite status of both.

An unmistakable feature of the *Brief Handbook*'s style, though one impossible to convey in translation, resides in its rhythms.[254] Latin prose often exhibits recurring sequences of heavy and light syllables which, like the metres of verse, contribute significantly to the experience of anyone reading the work aloud or imagining its being read aloud.[255] This is a mannerism originating in oratorical practice, and it was Cicero's view that anyone incapable of appreciating the cadences of oratory suffered from an almost inhuman deficiency in perception.[256] The rhythms of Latin prose, when they are put to use, are far less uniform than poetic metres, and ancient theory and practice tended to concentrate on the patterns,

---

[252] A sampling of the work's rhetorical features includes alliteration (e.g. ¶¶2, 3, 8, 9, 10, 17, 18, 20, 21, 22, 23, 24, 25, 31, 34, 35, 49), anaphora (¶¶8, 10, 11, 12, 16, and elsewhere), antithesis (e.g. ¶¶2, 7, 9, 11, 12), exclamatio (¶9), homoeoteleuton and homoeoptoton (e.g. ¶¶4, 18, 19, 23, 27, 28, 29, 33, 42, 51), paronomasia (e.g. ¶¶8, 10, 12, 31), and synonomia (e.g. ¶3, 20, 23, 36, 42, 55), as well as devices like rhetorical questions (e.g. ¶¶7, 28), sermocinatio (¶9), subiectio (¶8), and the work's strong preference for organizing its material into threefold subdivisions and expressing itself by way of tricola (e.g. ¶¶2, 4, 9, 10, 13, 16, 18, 21, 24, 34, 40).

[253] Doubtless wit and charm lie in the eye of the beholder, but see (e.g.) ¶2, where Quintus' three questions for Cicero to ponder receive their answers in direct discourse by way of a chiastic arrangement and in phrases that are neatly parallel in their prose rhythms, or ¶3, where *recordare* ('to remember') recalls Demosthenes' difficulties in pronouncing the letter *rho*, or ¶4, where, with the words *novum hominem hominum nobilium*, Quintus underlines Cicero's *novitas* through polyptoton, paronomasia, and chiasmus, or (and finally) the description, at ¶47, of C. Cotta as *in ambitione artifex* (on these points, see the relevant commentary). Gripping invective and melodrama in the *Brief Handbook*: ¶¶7–12; contrast the assertion of Balsdon 1963, 243, that the *Brief Handbook* 'hardly even troubles to be interesting'.

[254] Hendrickson 1904, 87ff.; Nardo 1970, 135; Núñez González 1999. On Quintus' epistolary style generally, see Cugusi 1970b.

[255] The topic is complex. Excellent brief introductions to Latin prose rhythm include Nisbet 1990, Berry 1996, 49ff., and Hutchinson 1998, 10ff. (each with further bibliography).

[256] Cic. *Or.* 168.

called *clausulae*, which were felt best suited for marking major pauses within and between sentences. *Clausulae* punctuate, and so lend clarity to, any passage shaped by them, and they often underscore important phrases and therefore important sentiments.[257] We are best informed about Cicero's preferred *clausulae*, but his tastes can hardly have been abnormal and it is in any case obvious that the commonest Ciceronian rhythms were current in Rome before his career began and were also used by his contemporaries, including Caesar.[258] Rhythmic prose, like the other flourishes that adorn the *Brief Handbook*, underscore its highly conventional literariness. This work's readability and its fine but unexceptional, and therefore unexceptionable, style were obviously important to its potential for making an impression on its intended audience, which certainly included elite Roman voters, whose views of Cicero's candidature the *Brief Handbook* was designed to affect.

2 Public Letter

It is unmistakable that the *Brief Handbook* takes the shape of a letter: it commences with an epistolary salutation, its opening lines include gestures characteristic of a letter, and the work closes in an epistolary conceit.[259] Notwithstanding its very personal pose, however, the content and especially the style of the *Brief Handbook*, not least its rhythmic prose, make it clear that this is a public letter.[260] Cicero's private letters, to be

---

[257] As an illustration of this effect, which was marked if not quite emphatic in its quality, consider these lines (chosen more or less at random) from Quintus' instructions on securing a daily escort to the forum (¶36: italics here reflect the presence of *clausulae* even if the English translation does not reflect the Latin's word order or the sentences' major pauses): 'Now, as for those who escort you, inasmuch as their service to you is greater than those who simply greet you in the morning, *you must make it absolutely clear* that you appreciate them even more.... *When a large crowd escorts you to the forum* each day, it makes a great impression on the public and confers great prestige.'

[258] See Suet. *Iul.* 6.

[259] E.g. ¶1 **Although...I nonetheless;** ¶58 **I understand better than you.**

[260] How did a public letter reach its audience? No such thing as publication in its modern sense existed in Rome. A literary text intended for wide circulation was copied by scribes (who ordinarily were slaves) and delivered to friends and connections, who subsequently shared the work with other readers by producing additional copies. Copyright was an unknown concept. There were also bookshops, but little is known of their operation and in any case they do not appear to have been important to the circulation of literary texts among elite readers. See, further, Kenney 1982; Iddeng 2006. Publishing a text, then, was a relatively simple matter for anyone possessing the means to do it. And, owing to the informal nature of publishing in Rome, nearly any document, including private letters not intended for circulation, could be distributed to others (e.g. Cic. *Att.* 10.8A, 10.8B, 10.9A; 14.13A). For this reason, public letters, although

sure, sometimes employ *clausulae*, but not all or even most do. Nor do a majority of his correspondents write to him by way of rhythm.[261] The presence of *clausulae* in any letter drew attention to its formal register, which could indicate a range of epistolary relationships between the letter's author and its recipient: letters intended for public consumption nearly always included prose rhythm as a means of foregrounding their exceptional purpose. Indeed, in a later period, Quintilian regarded the presence of prose rhythms as the hallmark of a public letter.[262] And inasmuch as the content so formally conveyed by the *Brief Handbook* includes political invective, statements of political purpose, and instructions on canvassing the public, it is obvious that the work is a public letter, a kind of document that had become familiar in Roman politics by the second century and pervasive in the late republic.[263]

As early as fifth-century Greece, epistolography had become a richly variegated phenomenon. In addition to their personal and practical uses, letters had become elements in the construction of history (letters are embedded in Herodotus and Thucydides) and of drama (the letter is a favoured device of Euripides).[264] By the fourth century, and increasingly throughout the Hellenistic period, letters could stand alone as independent works, the contents of which included political persuasion (e.g. the letters of Plato and Isocrates), philosophical instruction (e.g. the letters of Epicurus), and, eventually, any academic topic, such as mathematics (e.g. the letters of Archimedes) or literary criticism (e.g. the letters of Dionysius of Halicarnassus). And letters could be composed in verse as well as prose. Many letters were fictitious, whether wholly imaginary or addressed to a historical correspondent under counterfeit circumstances or composed by a literary impersonator. Such letters were not always written for the purpose of fraud, but instead deployed their impersonations in order to affect or enhance their overall effect on readers.[265]

By the first century, Roman society was permeated by a robust culture of letter-writing. A satisfactory epistolary style was a part of any gentle-

---

they were recognized as such, always stimulated something of the feeling of reading the private views of another.

[261] Hutchinson 1998, 10f.

[262] Quint. 9.4.19. *Clausulae* indicate an artful epistolary register: Hutchinson 1998, 13. Public letters by Cicero: e.g. *Att.* 7.17.2; 8.9.1–2; *Fam.* 5.12; *Q. Fr.* 1.1; see Peter 1901, 213ff; Hall 2009, 15ff.; White 2010, 90ff.

[263] At ¶58 the letter finally denominates itself a 'brief handbook' (*commentariolum*). On the implications of this term, see pp. 55ff. Difficulties in classifying letters: Rosenmeyer 2001, 5ff.; Trapp 2003, 1ff.

[264] Rosenmeyer 2001, 45ff., 61ff.

[265] Letters in Greece: Sykutris 1931; Koskenniemi 1956; Thraede 1970; Stowers 1986; Mahlherbe 1988; Stirewalt 1993; Rosenmeyer 2001; Trapp 2003.

man's essential equipment,[266] and, in aristocratic circles certainly, the letter bore much freight as a vehicle for the expression of friendship.[267] Consequently, elite Romans expended enormous energies in sustaining an almost constant and always carefully composed correspondence with others: we spy Cicero writing letters at his morning audience, in the senate, and even at a supper party.[268] The indefatigable Caesar kept multiple secretaries hard at work as he dictated correspondence while on the march in Gaul.[269]

A distinct slice of this activity, and an increasingly important element of Roman political communication, consisted in public letters. This practice first appears to us in a letter composed in Greek by Scipio Africanus and addressed to Philip V of Macedon. In it, the Roman described his capture of New Carthage in 209. This letter's unmistakable purpose was self-glorification on an international scale, but it was also a bold representation of Roman power to the Hellenistic world.[270] Similar is the letter sent 'to a king' (again a Greek letter to a Hellenistic monarch) by P. Cornelius Scipio Nasica Corculum (cos. I 162), Africanus' son-in-law, which included an account of his role at the Battle of Pydna in 168.[271] The letter sent to King Prusias by Africanus and his brother Lucius Scipio when the latter was in command of the war against Antiochus in 190 represents a more diplomatic specimen: by rehearsing the justice of Rome's foreign policy—but at the same listing Rome's sequence of victories—the brothers were able persuade the king to remain a neutral party.[272]

International propaganda led to public letters promulgated for purely domestic political purposes.[273] Metellus Numidicus (cos. 109), exiled in 100 owing to his refusal to swear an oath to observe a law of Saturninus, issued at least one public letter addressed to Gnaeus and Lucius Domitius Ahenobarbus (respectively the consuls of 96 and 94): in this correspondence, Metellus acknowledged the friendship of the brothers Domitius and

---

[266] E.g. Cic. *Att.* 7.17.2; 14.7.2; 15.17.2; 15.16; *Fam.* 2.4.1; 4.13.1; 6.10b; see Hall 2009, 15ff.; Bernard 2013, 165ff.

[267] Letters and friendship: Demetr. *Eloc.* 225, 231; Koskenniemi 1956, 35ff.; Trapp 2003, 40ff.; Hall 2009, 53ff.; White 2010, 24ff.; Wilcox 2012; Bernard 2013, 71ff.; Rollinger 2014, 180ff.; see ¶3 **the number and variety of your friends.**

[268] Respectively Cic. *Ad Brut.* 2.4.1; *Fam.* 12.20; *Q. Fr.* 3.1.19 and *Fam.* 9.26.1.

[269] Plut. *Caes.* 17.7. On the pre-Ciceronian scene in Rome, see Cugusi 1983, 152ff.

[270] Polyb. 10.9.3. On the basis of Cic. *Off.* 3.4, Walbank 1967, 204, concluded that this letter was private. But Cicero is making a different point, observing that Africanus left no public reflections or philosophical compositions despite the intellectual pursuits occupying his leisure time: he is not excluding a document like the letter to Philip.

[271] Plut. *Aem.* 15.5; 21.7.   [272] Polyb. 21.11.

[273] On the Hellenistic background to Roman political correspondence, see Ceccarelli 2013, 160ff.

justified his stance against Saturninus.[274] Earlier than this, the tribune Gaius Gracchus (tr. pl. 123 and 122) published a letter addressed to his friend M. Pomponius, a Roman knight, in which he apparently explained (and justified) his and his brother's careers and policies.[275] More difficult to assess is the letter ascribed to Cornelia, the daughter of Africanus and mother of the Gracchi, addressed to her son Gaius. This letter, fragments of which are preserved in the manuscript tradition of Cornelius Nepos[276]— if genuine—represents a public repudiation by Cornelia of the policies of Tiberius and an entreaty to Gaius not to stand for the tribunate in order to avenge Tiberius' death or to continue his political programme. The letter could well be a later forgery or, more interestingly, contemporary pseudepigrapha. One cannot draw certain conclusions.[277]

Because a letter was a projection of its author's character, as we have seen, and because its sentiments could, at least by an act of disingenuousness on the part of a reader, be regarded as sincere, public correspondence in the guise of a private communication could operate as affecting and effectual propaganda. Hence Metellus' and Gaius Gracchus' recourse to this medium. The practice became common in the late republic. In the immediate aftermath of his invasion of Italy in 49, for instance, Caesar wrote a letter to his close associates C. Oppius and L. Cornelius Balbus (cos. 40), in which he expressed his gratification at their approval of his policy of clemency and reported his continuing exertions in attempting a reconciliation with Pompeius.[278] Balbus duly circulated the letter, and Cicero received a copy, which he passed on to Atticus. Caesar's letter, although it did not induce Cicero to take the invader's part, nonetheless made a highly favourable impression.[279] Which was, of course, its purpose, and Caesar's reputation for clemency quickly became a valuable asset in his contest with Pompeius. Cicero, too, promulgated his political attitudes by way of public correspondence, most famously, perhaps, in a letter to P. Lentulus Spinther (cos. 57) justifying his political realignment following the renewal of the alliance between Caesar, Crassus, and Pompeius in 56.[280]

---

[274] Gell. *NA* 15.13.6; 17.2.7. Metellus' exile: Kelly 2006, 81ff. His correspondence with the Domitii: Cugusi 1970a, 113ff.; Degl'Innocenti Pierini 2000, 249ff.

[275] Cic. *Div.* 1.36; 2.62; Plut. *Ti. Gracch.* 8.7.

[276] Frr. 1 and 2; cf. Cic. *Brut.* 211; Quint. 1.1.6; Plut. *C. Gracch.* 13.1.

[277] The problems associated with this document are complex: Instinsky 1971; Horsfall 1987; Suerbaum 2002, 456ff.; Dixon 2007, 15ff.

[278] Cic. *Att.* 9.7c; cf. *Att.* 8.9a.   [279] Cic. *Att.* 9.7.3.

[280] Cic. *Fam.* 1.9. On the particulars and importance of this moment in Cicero's career, see Lintott 2008, 223ff.

We discover an explicit account of this practice in one of Cicero's letters to Atticus, composed, like Caesar's letter to Oppius and Balbus, in 49: 'you, of course, are already apprised of the response which L. Caesar is taking back from Pompeius, as well as the letter he is carrying from Pompeius to Caesar: indeed, this letter was composed and dispatched so that it could be made public'.[281] In it, Pompeius offered his own terms for an honourable reconciliation between himself and Caesar, a proposition that won popular approval.[282] Examples could be multiplied, but unnecessarily: it will be obvious how ostensibly personal public letters were deployed by members of the senatorial class in order to communicate to a wider public, if often also an elite public, the political stances and values with which they hoped to be associated.[283] Similar purposes animate the *Brief Handbook*, which, because it lays out a view on the proper means whereby Cicero should seek the consulship, inevitably takes a public stand on the virtues reinforcing his candidature and the deficiencies impairing his rivals. The *Brief Handbook*, in other words, can be viewed as something of a manifesto, like other public letters in republican Rome. Naturally its purpose was to recommend Cicero's election to the consulship.

3 Handbook

This public letter, in its concluding lines, identifies itself as a 'brief handbook', or *commentariolum* (¶58). *Commentariolum* is a diminutive derived from the more common expressions *commentarius* and its plural, *commentarii*, terms that describe a range of literary and sub-literary forms, from private memoranda and notes to records of official business to literary and scholarly or technical works[284]—historical narratives too, the best-known of which are Caesar's accounts of his Gallic campaigns and of the civil war.[285] Early *commentarii*, it appears very likely, included *aides-mémoire* and functional instructions for priests and magistrates, a pedigree that sustained the essential Romanness of *commentarii* even in the late republic, when the genre was suffused by the influence of Hellenistic scholarly literature.[286] And we know of republican *commentarii*, or at the

---

[281] Cic. *Att.* 7.17.2.   [282] Cic. *Att.* 7.18.1–2.

[283] See, further, Peter 1901, 213ff.; Nardo 1970, 114ff.; Bernard 2013, 121ff.; Rosillo López 2017, 141ff.

[284] Premerstein 1900; Bömer 1953; Formisano 2001, 141ff. The word is contrasted with 'letter' by Jerome, *Ep.* 42.3.

[285] Cicero composed a *commentarius*, no longer extant, dealing with the events of his consulship: Cic. *Att.* 1.19.10; 1.20.6; see Tatum 2011, 176ff.

[286] *Commentarii* and Romanness: Bömer 1953; see Riggsby 2006, 134ff.

very least of works that by the late republic were retrospectively deemed
to be *commentarii*, dealing with the practicalities and technicalities of
Roman law, Roman religion, and the Roman constitution, all of which
contributed further to the native connotations of any work that designated
itself a *commentarius*.[287] Or *commentariolum*.

The semantic range of *commentariolum* is not far removed from
commentarii: it, too, can refer to personal notebooks[288] as well as handbooks, especially concise handbooks of an introductory or elementary
order.[289] At *De oratore* 1.5, it is obvious that the word is used to indicate
Cicero's *De inventione* (*On Invention*), a technical handbook on rhetoric.
A 'brief handbook' on canvassing aligns its topic with other subjects
suitable for Roman commentaries, like religion or law, and by way of
its genre gestures toward its traditional orientation regarding its native
content.

Now, it does not become obvious to readers that the *Brief Handbook* is
a *commentariolum* until its concluding remarks—closure, however, that
characterizes the work as a whole. The implications of this identification
are important. The *Brief Handbook* aligns itself with traditional commentaries on practical Roman topics even while its author associates himself
with venerable Roman authorities. This effect is made clear by consulting
a passage from Vitruvius:

> Our ancestors acted with wisdom as well as practicality when they estab-
> lished the custom of transmitting their ideas to later generations by
> means of *commentarii*. This way their ideas, which had been published
> in volumes, did not perish but instead were expanded on and gradually,
> over the ages, they reached the most advanced level of learning.[290]

Vitruvius' comment alludes to another aspect of *commentarii*: their ostensibly provisional character.[291] Technical *commentarii*, it appears, represented themselves as functional in such a way as to combine a high degree
of authority with an open acknowledgement that their topics remained
the focus of a continuing tradition of practice and study. It is no accident
that the *Brief Handbook* announces its status as a *commentariolum* in the
same breath in which its seeks Cicero's revision and potential improve-
ment. The *Brief Handbook*, then, although it puts itself forward, as we

---

[287] *Commentarii* explicating Roman civilization: e.g. works on Roman law by Aelius
Paetus Catus (cos. 198) and M. Junius Brutus (pr. 142), see Cic. *De or.* 1.240; 2.224; on
religion by Fabius Pictor, see Varro ap. Non 835L; on the magistracies by C. Sempronius
Tuditanus (cos. 129), see Gell. *NA* 13.15.4; Bömer 1953, 231ff.

[288] E.g. Cic. *Phil.* 1.16.

[289] E.g. Cic. *De or.* 1.5; *Fin.* 4.10; Quint. 1.5.7; see *TLL* 3.1855.

[290] Vitr. De arch. 7 pr. 1.　　　　[291] Seel 1968, xliii; Riggsby 2006, 137f.

shall see, as normative advice on campaigning for office, does not pretend to be the final word, or the only word, on the subject.[292]

4 Didactic Epistle

The *Brief Handbook* is not simply a public letter that denominates itself a handbook: it is also a didactic epistle, an identification made clear by the contents of the whole of the letter and especially by the style and organization of ¶¶16–53, the portion of the work in which Cicero is offered detailed lessons in the matter of canvassing. Putting letters to work as a medium for instruction, resulting in something like an essay or treatise in epistolary form, originates in classical Greece in the writings of Isocrates. His practice was soon taken up by others and became widespread in the Greek world. A central figure in this development was Epicurus, many of whose letters were nothing short of brief handbooks on his philosophical system.[293] But Epicurus was by no means unique in resorting to didactic epistles.

Purists disapproved of the practice, especially when such letters departed too far from the personal and formal expectations of epistolography: 'sometimes we write to cities and kings: admittedly this kind of letter ought to be in some way slightly more elaborate, as one should adapt to the person being written to, but not so elaborate as to become a treatise rather than a letter, as is the case with Aristotle's letters to Alexander and Plato's letter to Dion's friends', complained pseudo-Demetrius.[294] Letters of this ilk, he averred, were not 'letters in the true sense, but treatises prefixed with 'dear so-and-so', which is the case for many of Plato's'.[295] Notwithstanding these reactionary strictures, however, didactic epistolography flourished in the Hellenistic period and, as was the case with Greek public letters generally, soon made a strong impression on Roman literary sensibilities.

---

[292] See also, on the literary characteristics of Caesar's *commentarii*: Batstone and Damon 2006; Riggsby 2006; Grillo 2012.

[293] Importance of Epicurus in Hellenistic epistolography: Peter 1901, 16ff.; Sykutris 1931, 203.

[294] Demetr. *Eloc.* 234.

[295] Demetr. *Eloc.* 228. For the date of pseudo-Demetrius, probably the second or possibly the first century BC, see Innes 1995, 312ff. This sentiment is persistent: e.g. 'if someone were to write about logical problems or questions of natural science, he might indeed write, but it would not be a letter that he was writing' (Demetr. *Eloc.* 231).

But the first appearances of the didactic epistle in Rome remain obscure.[296] It is not even certain whether the elder Cato, who certainly published a public letter to his son and certainly composed didactic works, also furnished Rome with a didactic epistle.[297] In fact, the *Brief Handbook* is our earliest extant Latin specimen. Nevertheless, it is obvious that, by the late republic, the didactic letter was a well-established literary form. Cicero's familiarity with the genre is made clear in his well-known letter to Quintus, advising him on the best practices for governing a province,[298] a letter modelled on Hellenistic didactic epistles on kingship.[299] We can glimpse Cicero's methods of composition, when it comes to didactic epistles, through his correspondence with Atticus describing his attempt to compose, in 45, a public letter of advice to Rome's new master, the victorious Caesar. Cicero found the going difficult, even after consulting Greek models, in this instance letters to Alexander written by Aristotle and Theophrastus.[300] If Shackleton Bailey is correct in suggesting that Cicero refers to the same project at *Epistulae ad Atticum* 13.26.2, we gain an even clearer picture of the creative modelling and careful editorial review that lies behind the composition of an important public letter—even on the part of an author so confident as Cicero.[301]

The author of the *Brief Handbook*, taking similar pains in drafting his didactic epistle, also looked for Greek precedents. Although in view of his specifically Roman subject there was nothing in the way of an apt Greek model for him to rely on,[302] there are unmistakable similarities between the structure and style of the *Brief Handbook* and Epicurus' *Letter to Herodotus*, a didactic epistle providing any neophyte with a concise and uncomplicated account of Epicurus' philosophical system. Each work begins with a conventional epistolary greeting and a direct personal address drawing attention to the difficulty and importance of the letter's topic.

---

[296] Didactic epistolography in Rome: Peter 1901, 15ff.; Sykutris 1931, 202ff.; Cugusi 1979, pp. xvff.; Langslow 2007.

[297] Cato's public correspondence: Cic. *Off.* 1.37; Plut. *Quaest. Rom.* 39; *Cat. mai.* 20.11; Prisc. *Inst.* 2.337.5K. Did Cato compose a didactic epistle? Yes: Schmidt 1972. Maybe, maybe not: Astin 1978, 332ff. See Suerbaum 2002, 412f.

[298] Cic. *Q. Fr.* 1.1.

[299] Rostovtzeff 1941, 1566; Shackleton Bailey 1980, 147. On Cicero's familiarity with Hellenistic didactic epistles, see Hutchinson 1988, 4f.

[300] Cic. *Att.* 12.40.2.

[301] Cic. *Att.* 13.26.2: 'Yesterday I even finished the letter to Caesar—since you liked the project. Writing the letter was not a bad thing, if you think it could prove useful. As things stand now, it is certainly unnecessary to send it. But I will leave that to your judgment. In any case I will send a copy to you.' See Shackleton Bailey 1966, 331.

[302] Buecheler 1869, 7, proposed Theophrastus' lost essay Περὶ φιλοτιμίας as Quintus' model, but too little is known of this work to pursue the suggestion. Quintus was certainly aware of it: Cic. *Att.* 2.3.4.

Each emphasizes the utility of logical organization and explains its appropriate terminology, and each letter stresses memorization. Each letter explicitly refers to itself as a treatise. After a lengthy technical exposition of its subject, each letter draws to its close by means of a summarizing reference to its preceding contents and with a positive assessment of their value (qualified in the case of the *Brief Handbook* by its appeal for Cicero's approval or correction).[303] Now this is by no means to suggest that the *Brief Handbook* is modelled *specifically* on the *Letter to Herodotus*. But Epicurus' didactic epistles were very well known in late republican Rome[304] and exercised a strong influence on Roman epistolography.[305] The similarities between the *Letter to Herodotus* and the *Brief Handbook* suffice to demonstrate the extent to which the latter is self-consciously implicated in the literary tradition of the Hellenistic didactic epistle, a feature of the work that contemporaries could hardly fail to notice.

Another practitioner was M. Terentius Varro, whose *Epistolicae quaestiones* (*Epistolary Inquiries*), a collection of letters addressed to various individuals, dealt with grammatical, constitutional, religious, legal, and antiquarian topics. This collection was assembled after the death of Caesar, but it relied at least to some degree on earlier compositions, one of which is perhaps pertinent to the *Brief Handbook*.[306] Gellius' *Noctes Atticae* (14.7) describes the contents of Varro's *Letter to Oppianus*, which explained senatorial procedures; his account confirms that it was a detailed treatise in the shape of a letter. The *Letter to Oppianus* reprised an earlier work by Varro, his *Eisagogikos* ('Introductory Textbook'), written for

---

[303] Epicurus' *Letter to Herodotus* and the *Brief Handbook*: (i) Greetings and personal address: Epic. *Ep. Hdt.* 35: 'Epicurus to Herodotus, greetings. Some are unable, etc.' (Ἐπίκουρος Ἡροδότῳ χαίρειν. τοῖς μὴ δυναμένοις); see ¶1: 'Quintus Marco fratri S.D. Etsi tibi…' (ii) Organization and terminology: Epic. *Ep. Hdt.* 36: 'fundamental elements and definitions' (στοιχειώματα καὶ φωνὰς); see ¶1: 'ea quae in re dispersa atque infinita viderentur esse ratione et distributione sub uno aspectu ponerentur.' (iii) Letter explicitly a treatise: Epic. *Ep. Hdt.* 37: 'I have prepared for you this epitome, an elementary handbook of all my doctrines' (τοιαύτην τινὰ ἐπιτομὴν ⟨συνέθηκα⟩ καὶ στοιχείωσιν τῶν ὅλων δοξῶν); see ¶58: 'hoc commentariolum petitionis'. (iv) Conclusion: Epic. *Ep. Hdt.* 83: 'These, Herodotus, are the things which are the chief points concerning the science of nature, organized for you in the form of an epitome' (ταῦτά σοι, ὦ Ἡρόδοτε, ἔστι κεφαλαιωδέστατα ὑπὲρ τῆς τῶν ὅλων φύσεως ἐπιτετμημένα); see ¶58: 'Haec sunt quae putavi…me…conligere unum in locum posse et ad te perscripta mittere.'
[304] The currency of Epicurus: Cic. *Fam.* 7.26.2; 15.19.2; e.g. Peter 1901, 15ff.; Sedley 1989; Griffin 1995, 344f.; Trapp 2003, 12f.; McConnell 2014, 16ff.
[305] Epicurus' influence on Roman epistolography: e.g., Inwood 2007, 141ff.; Morrison 2007.
[306] Gell. *NA* 14.7.5 preserves a citation from this work that refers to the *triumviri reipublicae constituendae causa* ('the triumvirs elected for the purpose of restoring the republic'), viz. Antony, Lepidus, and Octavian.

Pompeius on the occasion of his election to the consulship—which office
he had obtained although he had held no previous magistracies and had
never actually been a Roman senator.[307] The premise of the *Eisagogikos*
was that it should explain senatorial procedures to the consul who was,
unprecedentedly, a total stranger to them. But, in fact, the work was far
more extensive than necessary for a simple parliamentary guide: it codi-
fied the (hitherto unrecorded) traditions and customs of the senate, opening the operations of the body to the entirety of Rome's reading pubic.
Furthermore, and perhaps every bit as important for Varro, the *Eisagogikos*
emphasized Pompeius' spectacular and unique achievement even as it
demonstrated his willingness to conform to the traditions of the body he
was entering as its leader. Which is not to overlook the essay's construction of its author: Varro appears at once as Pompeius' friend and as the
ideal student of the institution of the senate. By portraying him in this
way, the *Eisagogikos* revealed to the reading public, what was already
familiar to the senatorial order, an organized description of traditional
senatorial practices—one obvious purpose of which was to promote the
interests of the work's author and its dedicatee. Its relevance to the *Brief
Handbook*, which likewise attempts to codify Roman practice and to
advertise the merits both of its author and of the politician to whom it is
addressed, is obvious. If, as it is often suggested, the *Eisagogikos* took the
shape of a letter, it would be an important precedent, fusing commentary
with didactic epistle. However, in view of *Noctes Atticae* 14.7.10, where
Gellius contrasts 'the book I mentioned above' (*in libro quo supra dixi*)—
viz. the *Eisagogikos*—with 'the letter to Oppianus' (*epistula ad Oppianum
scripta*), that conclusion must be deemed uncertain: it is very possible that
Varro recast his *Eisagogikos* for Pompeius as a letter to Oppianus.[308]

Varro's codification of senatorial procedure on Pompeius' behalf, whether
or not the *Eisagogikos* was a didactic epistle (it was certainly a handbook),
illustrates the Romans' interest in combining cultural work with political
publicity. A similar impulse animates Cicero's letter to his brother, which
was cited above.[309] Although this didactic epistle was superfluous to
Quintus' requirements (he had already been proconsul in Asia for two
years, whereas Cicero had never actually governed a province), it was
nevertheless a highly polished statement of an ideal yet personalized

---

[307] This is the title preserved at Gell. *NA* 14.7.2: 'Pompeius ... rogavit uti commentarium faceret eisagogikon—sic enim Varro ipse appellat' ('Pompeius ... asked him to
compose a *commentarius*, or *Eisagogikos*, for this is what Varro himself entitled it'); see
Bömer 1953, 230 n. 1.

[308] Varro justified his republication of the material he prepared for the *Eisagogikos*
by claiming that work was no longer in circulation: Gell. *NA* 14.7.3.

[309] Cic. *Q. Fr.* 1.1.

Roman approach to managing the complexities of provincial government, another purely Roman phenomenon. In this way, Cicero's letter was able to inscribe, by way of public instruction, Quintus' comprehensive success (despite the occasional slip) in fulfilling the Romans' expectations of an excellent administrator—and this in a document which offered some systematization of sound proconsular conduct at the same time as it advanced the political reputation of the brothers Cicero.

The style of Varro's letters eludes. In the case of Cicero's letter to Quintus, although it is elevated in manner, there is very little about it that one could describe as technical. By contrast, ¶¶16–53 of the *Brief Handbook* is entirely otherwise. Here the text teems with definitions, classifications, and sub-classifications. This is a conspicuously different approach to exposition, and it emphasizes the kind of detailed analysis that Greeks and Romans alike deemed essential in shifting any cultural practice from a knack to a skill or art (an *ars* or, in Greek, *technē*). Put differently, the *Brief Handbook* makes it unmistakable that, in ¶¶16–53, it is introducing a technical form of presentation, the purpose of which discourse is, at least at first blush, to render the cultural practice of canvassing into an art.[310] Applying this degree of intellectual organization to the Romans' electioneering techniques is, in fact, the explicit objective of the *Brief Handbook*: 'My purpose is instead to arrange within a single, systematic form and in a logical order matters which, in actual practice, appear unrelated and indeterminate' (¶1). Here we find an approach that reflects a habit of mind reaching back to the Greek sophists and, in a far more finely developed version, was characteristic of the writings of Plato, Aristotle, and nearly all subsequent philosophers.[311] This is what we may fairly describe as technical writing.

By the second century this very Greek methodology of definition and division had begun to influence exposition in Latin by way of what Elizabeth Rawson has registered as 'the introduction of logical organization in Roman prose literature'.[312] Classification per se became, in Rome, an expression of serious thinking that was indispensable in fashioning an art out of crude, unanalysed experience.[313] Cicero puts this view forward in his rhetorical writings:

---

[310] Nardo 1970, 125ff.; Tatum 2007, 115ff.; Sillett 2016; Prost 2017, 66ff.

[311] Sophists: Fuhrmann 1960, 123ff.; Kerferd 1981. Socrates: Guthrie 1969, 425ff. Plato: Notomi 1999, 115ff. Aristotle and later: Solmsen 1968, 49ff.; Reinhardt 2003, 256ff.

[312] Rawson 1991, 324.

[313] Rawson 1985, 132ff. (fundamental); Rawson 1991, 324ff.; Moatti 1997, 217ff.

almost everything which has now received expression in the form of an
art [*ars*] was once unordered and unorganized...an art...is derived
from the operations of a philosopher, when he renders coherent what
was unordered and unorganized.[314]

Exposition by way of classification along these lines was by no means
limited to didactic epistles, but this analytical approach is very much a
quality of the *Brief Handbook*'s manner of instruction.[315]

Consequently, one finds in ¶¶16–53 of the *Brief Handbook* stylistic features that are entirely appropriate to elevated Latin technical literature,
such as repetitive diction, recurring asyndeton, an abundance of explicit
directions, frequently of the of the *first...then...then...*variety, and,
unsurprisingly, direct commands.[316] In issuing his instructions to his
reader, the author of the *Brief Handbook* ordinarily, if perhaps tediously to
modern tastes, employs second-person imperatives and often resorts to
so-called future imperatives in *-to*. The effect of this insistent sequence of
directives is not always easy to reproduce in English, but a representative
sampling can be extracted from ¶¶29–30:

> The first and obvious thing [*et primum*] is that you must embrace [*complec-
> tere*] the senators and the Roman knights...You must take the greatest
> pains [*elaborato*]...Seek them out yourself [*appetito*]. Send representa-
> tives to win them over [*adlegato*]. Make it plain to them how much you
> are touched by the great favour they do you [*ostendito*]. Then [*postea*]
> take stock of the whole of the city [*habeto*], of all the clubs, the boroughs,
> and the neighbourhoods...After that [*postea*], make sure [*fac ut*]...And,
> finally [*denique*],...

No Roman reader could mistake this brand of didactic prose for anything
other than an attempt at technical instruction.

Intriguingly, in the matter of issuing directions, the habits on display in
the *Brief Handbook* closely resemble those of the elder Cato in what
remains of his didactic and technical writing. And it appears (though it
can hardly be certain) that Cato's brand of imperatival writing was distinctive in Latin technical prose.[317] In any case, on the present state of our

---

[314] Cic. *De or.* 1.187–8, excerpts.

[315] That the *Brief Handbook* includes technical material within the confines of a
didactic epistle has long been recognized: Buecheler 1869, 6; Hendrickson 1904, 78ff.;
Tyrrell and Purser 1904, 119; Bruhn 1908, 259; Sykutris 1931, 202f.; Münzer 1948, 1289;
Henderson 1950, 17ff.; Till 1962, 317; Norden, 1966, 259.

[316] Technical writing and literary style in Rome: Nicolet 1996; Formisano 2001; Horster
and Reitz 2003; Langslow 2007; Fögen 2009; Hutchinson 2009; Taub and Doody 2009.

[317] The elder Cato's instructions: Gibson 1997; Hine 2011 (criticizing important
aspects of Gibson's paper).

understanding, in the conspicuous matter of giving orders to his reader, no text is so similar as the *Brief Handbook* to the writings of the elder Cato. Which draws our attention to its author's effort to adorn his didactic epistle with highly traditional features, derived not only from *commentarii* but also from Catonian prose style—if, that is, his contemporaries noticed his imitation of Cato.[318] At the very least, it should have been clear to any reader that, in managing the difficult task of writing elevated technical literature *as* elevated technical literature, the author of the *Brief Handbook* displayed his literary versatility and his self-conscious inscription into traditional Latin exposition.[319]

The format and style of the *Brief Handbook* inevitably matter to its meaning for the reader. The didactic epistle was at once something elevated and something accessible, and it offered its readers a concise and accurate statement of its topic's fundamental rules and principles.[320] Technical instructions also carried moral implications, as all didactic texts did in Rome. Consequently, a didactic epistle like the *Brief Handbook* promulgated its instructions as normative and paradigmatic, an implicit claim that naturally suggested positive things about its author and its recipient— and its readers.[321] The political aspects of this moral claim were reinforced by Roman sensibilities regarding public letters and their significance for public life. The learned style of the *Brief Handbook*, including its long and technical list of definitions and specific instructions, conformed to contemporary intellectual tastes, which were at the very least informed by the features of Hellenistic erudition.[322] At the same time, the *Brief Handbook* emphasized its native quality in its conspicuous gestures towards the traditions of the Roman *commentarii* and, perhaps, by evoking the old-fashioned learning of the elder Cato. Indeed, the *Brief Handbook* makes it clear that its readers will find within its covers nothing that is new.[323] Members of the established political class could be expected to welcome

---

[318] Unlike Cato, or Varro in his extant treatises, the author of the *Brief Handbook* articulates his technical instruction with rhythmic prose, perhaps to relieve its potential for dryness (Cic. *Or.* 108 and 213–14 stresses the pleasure *clausulae* provide) or to enhance the clarity of these passages.

[319] The difficulties of writing didactic prose: Mayer 2005.

[320] Boscherini 2000; Langslow 2007, 228.

[321] The implications of the didactic texts: Christes 2003; Fögen 2009. Relevance to the *Brief Handbook*: Nardo 1970, 63, 101ff. On the elevated moral posture of the *Brief Handbook*, see, also, Prost 2017, 71ff.

[322] But see Baraz 2012, 15ff., who underlines a lingering Roman suspicion of philosophical writing, even in the late republic.

[323] ¶1: 'Not that you will learn anything new from what follows. My purpose is instead to arrange within a single, systematic form and in a logical order matters which, in actual practice, appear unrelated and indeterminate.'

such a text and to find it reassuring. In the aftermath of the Social War, especially after the census of 70, which saw the final stage of the allies' enfranchisement, the electoral scene in Rome had been transformed: candidates now had to seek out voters in new regions, and it was only by the mid-60s that it was becoming clear to all that the Romans' traditional means of canvassing could succeed in this new political environment.[324] An opportune moment, then, for the *Brief Handbook*, which is a didactic epistle translating the traditional and therefore sound stuff on canvassing into an art.

5 Propaganda

Or is it? The *Brief Handbook*, for all its normative claims as a didactic work, is by no means universal in its application. This point is made explicitly in the work's closing section: 'I have written a work that does not pertain to everyone seeking an office but rather to you in particular and to this specific canvass' (¶58). This handbook, in other words, is specifically a guide to *Cicero's* canvass, not every canvass. But a guide for whom? Not Cicero, as the *Brief Handbook* makes clear more than once. It is instead a work that, by way of offering instruction on the art of canvassing, can help Roman readers to understand the nature and promise of Cicero's canvass. And the dimension of Cicero's candidature, for all its promise, that was most provocative to the Roman electorate was, plainly, his condition as a new man.[325]

That the *Brief Handbook* is neither universal nor comprehensive is patent. It leaves out much of what we know to have been routine in canvassing (see §III), nor is its advice apt for every brand of candidate. Instead, Cicero's status as a new man is central to its construction of the art of canvassing.[326] Much stress is laid on Cicero's distinctly close relationship with the equestrian order[327] as well as on the *gratia* to be gained from oratory.[328] Much, too, on the deficiencies of his rivals, including their likely inclination to resort to bribery in order to win office.[329] The undeniable purchase attaching itself to military achievement, luxurious aedilician games, or noble rank is ignored, presumably because none of these assets belonged

---

[324] For details of the Social War and its implications for Roman elections, see ¶1 **within a single, systematic form and in a logical order.**

[325] Cicero and *novitas*: see ¶2 **new man.**

[326] Emphasis on *novitas* in the *Brief Handbook*: ¶¶2–4, 7, 11, 13, 14; see Prost 2017, 61f.

[327] Cicero's relationship with the knights: see ¶3 **the equestrian order.** Cicero and the equestrian order in the *Brief Handbook*: ¶¶8, 13, 29, 33, 53.

[328] The importance of Cicero's eloquence: see ¶2 **your fame as an orator** Cicero's eloquence in the *Brief Handbook*: ¶¶2–3, 8, 13, 50, 55.

[329] Deficiencies: ¶¶8–12, 28. Bribery: ¶¶55–7.

to Cicero.[330] By contrast, the many respects in which Cicero surpasses the disadvantage of his *novitas* are underscored again and again, all by way of assertions of Cicero's personal excellence, customary social connections, and esteem for the nobility, who, in the *Brief Handbook*, appear as glamorous and influential men who must be cultivated assiduously.[331]

Now, it was not uncommon for didactic texts to organize material around the career of an exemplary practitioner of an art or skill. This was the approach of Varro's (now fragmentary) *De poetis*, as well as Cicero's *De oratore*.[332] And in his *De officiis*, Cicero is not too shy to put himself forward as a model for imitation by the young.[333] Furthermore, it was unusual for any didactic text to be truly comprehensive. Still, it is important to mind the gap between the generalizing tone of at least the didactic exposition of the *Brief Handbook* and the work's clear portrayal of Cicero's canvass as distinctive, even unique.[334] It draws attention to the reality that, in the world of the *Brief Handbook*, Cicero, for all his expertise and self-knowledge, is *not* portrayed as the paradigm of the ideal candidate. Indeed, at ¶47 he is instructed to model his candidature after that of C. Aurelius Cotta (cos. 75), designated there as 'a master in the art of canvassing' (*in ambitione artifex*).[335] In the *Brief Handbook*, then, its combination of traditional and normative instruction, projected to the voters in a public and didactic epistle, serves to depict its Cicero not as *the* paradigm for Roman canvassing but rather as a candidate whose canvass fits suitably *into* the paradigm of Roman electioneering. In this way, it appeals to—and reassures—Cicero's elite contemporaries by foregrounding his political soundness, notwithstanding the potential distraction of his novelty as a new man likely to be elected consul.[336]

Was this means of representing Cicero's candidature helpful to Cicero? Andrew Wallace-Hadrill has stressed the degree to which technical codification in Rome, especially when imposed on topics defined by custom, could compete with the personal authority of the city's nobility as the best grounds for determining what was authentically Roman and so truly traditional. As he puts it, 'social authority and academic learning pull

---

[330] Cicero more or less concedes that his aedilician games were no more than satisfactory: *Off.* 2.58–9; cf. *Mur* 40.   [331] ¶¶4, 6, 50.

[332] On Varro's methods in *De poetis*, see Dahlmann 1963, 5ff. On Cicero's *De oratore*, see, e.g., Mankin 2011, with further bibliography.

[333] See the discussion by Long 1995, 213ff.

[334] E.g. ¶3: 'For what new men have had such a wide range of friends as you enjoy...?'

[335] Cotta as model: ¶47 **master in the art of canvassing**.

[336] Arguments for reading the *Brief Handbook* as electoral propaganda have been put forward by Petersson 1920, 198; Ciaceri 1939, 173f.; Wikarjak 1966, 18ff.; Nardo 1970, 76f.; Bruggisser 1984; McCoy 1987; Duplá 1988; Lucrezi 1998; see, further, §V.6.

in opposite directions'.[337] And one can see, certainly in the development of Roman jurisprudence, a basis for Wallace-Hadrill's claim.[338] At the same time, academic learning, when devoted to Roman topics, could also be viewed as a patriotic assertion of Roman identity within the larger environment of Hellenistic scholarship: that is, as an affirmation of the establishment and not, or at least not exclusively, a challenge to it.[339]

Consider again Varro's *Eisagogikos*. Here was an instance where academic learning served simultaneously to emphasize a plain violation of Roman custom (Pompeius' unique elevation to the consulship) and to assimilate this potential subversion by inscribing the great man's open deference to the conventions of senatorial authority: the work promulgated Pompeius' exceptionalism *and* the senate's traditional values and paramount station. Similarly, the *Brief Handbook* underscores Cicero's circumstances as new man seeking the consulship (admittedly, exceptionalism of a less impressive strain than Pompeius') while endeavouring to make it clear that he represents no threat to the established order because he subscribes to conventions hallowed by time and now elevated by scholarship. Put differently, Cicero's exceptional canvass is rendered unexceptionable by way of inscribing its soundness in a document that formulated Cicero's campaign as an ideal campaign—for a new man.

6 The Attractions of Complexity

The oddity of the *Brief Handbook*, owing to its combination of various if related generic features, cannot be overlooked. Whether this work was a specimen of contemporary electioneering propaganda, as I suggest here, or an imperial fiction (see §V), we must assume its author expected his readers to appreciate his composition's complex literary posture. From this perspective, the work depicts its readership, flatteringly, as intellectually and socially akin to the young aristocrats in Rome who are drawn to Cicero on account of his eloquence (¶4) and culture (¶33), or to readers who, like Cicero, possess erudition sufficient to recognize allusions to Demosthenes (¶3) and Epicharmus (¶39) and are capable of viewing themselves as men who could be Platonists if they wished (¶46). Put differently, the *Brief Handbook*, whatever its other controversies, was clearly written for highly educated readers, whom we must locate within the elite stations of Roman society.

---

[337] Wallace-Hadrill 1997, the quotation is from p. 14; Wallace-Hadrill 2008, 236f.
[338] Jurisprudence and senatorial authority: Frier 1985, 256ff.
[339] Moatti 1997, 109ff., 183ff.; Formisano 2001, 145ff.

V AUTHORSHIP

1 The Problem

The *Brief Handbook* is securely attributed to Quintus Cicero. But did he write it? The question of Quintus' authorship is nowadays less central to studies of the *Brief Handbook* than was once the case, but the matter remains an important one. If, as has been suggested, the work is a specimen of imperial fiction, our appraisal of its value as a guide to republican practices and republican ways of thinking must be affected by that conclusion. The authenticity of the *Brief Handbook* was first challenged by Adam Eussner in 1872, and the controversy persists.[340] The most influential objections to Quintus' authorship have been raised by M.I. Henderson and R.G.M. Nisbet,[341] and there have been numerous responses, the most important of which are by J.P.V.D. Balsdon, Dante Nardo, and a team of French scholars including Jean-Michel David, Ségolène Démougin, Élizabeth Deniaux, Danielle Ferry, Jean-Marc Flambard, and Claude Nicolet.[342]

Although most ancient historians have admired the quality of information conveyed by the *Brief Handbook* and have trusted the accuracy of its analysis of canvassing, that, in itself, is no proof of anything: accuracy can be explained by good sources and intelligent reading at any time. And, in any case, not everyone is persuaded that the *Brief Handbook* supplies reliable information.[343] Still, it is not uncommon in contemporary historical scholarship to see the *Brief Handbook* regarded as a composition by Quintus without reference to the debate over the work's authenticity. More often, however, the work is attributed to Quintus or treated as a contemporary

---

[340] Eussner 1872.

[341] Eussner 1872 argued that the *Brief Handbook* was written during the latter part of the first century BC. Although his claims met with scepticism, the issue of Quintus' authorship was taken up again by Hendrickson 1892 and Hendrickson 1904 in papers that offer a close analysis of the literary texture of the *Brief Handbook*; he maintained that the work was a specimen of imperial pseudepigrapha. Still, the major challenges to Quintus' authorship remain Henderson 1950; Nisbet 1961b; Henderson 1972, both of whom date the *Brief Handbook* to the imperial period. An overview of the arguments against Quintus' authorship is supplied by Waibel 1969. Alexander 2009 offers a new and independent argument against the work's authenticity (see pp. 71ff.); he, too, prefers an imperial date.

[342] Balsdon 1963; Nardo 1970; David et al. 1973. See also McDermott 1970; Richardson 1971; Ramsey 1980b; Lintott 2008, 130ff.; Prost 2017, 52ff. Useful surveys of arguments against and for Quintus' authorship are provided by Fedeli 1987, 14ff.; Duplá et al. 1990, 23ff.; Lucrezi 1998; Laser 2001, 5ff.; Lucrezi 2001, 20ff.; Prost 2017, 45ff.

[343] Henderson 1950; Nisbet 1961b; Henderson 1972; Alexander 2009.

document but flagged by a footnote alerting readers that any approach to the work must remain provisional owing to questions raised regarding its authenticity. A few scholars remain explicitly agnostic, and fewer still reject Quintus' authorship outright.

The primary basis for querying Quintus' authorship resides in what has been deemed the work's unclear purpose. Simply put, why should Quintus write a letter to his brother proffering advice on a subject in which Marcus was so much more experienced? And why should he write it in so highly a didactic a style? And, if the letter was intended for a wider public, why include so many remarks of an ostensibly cynical nature which could potentially damage the reputations of both brothers? Prompted by these questions, scholars turned their attention to other aspects of the work, especially to similarities in expression or idea found in texts by Cicero which appeared later than the dramatic date of the *Brief Handbook*. Anachronisms and errors, too, which would point to the work's later composition, were looked for.

No indisputable proof has been found that the *Brief Handbook* is anything other than what it appears to be, a point that is universally conceded. But controversies over authenticity are difficult to settle, and even the sheer exertion expended in attempting to do so may prove counterproductive. It is all too easy—to filch a phrase from Pope's *Dunciad*—to 'explain a thing till all men doubt it'. And it is formally impossible to prove categorically that any work that goes unmentioned in antiquity is in fact what it claims to be.[344]

In order to aid readers in making up their own minds, a guide to the particulars of the central arguments for and against rejecting Quintus' authorship is provided below (and the topic recurs, when pertinent, in the commentary). It will be obvious to readers of this book that I see no reason not to accept the *Brief Handbook* as a text composed during the election campaign of 64 (see §IV.2–5), and much of this commentary takes that view (without, one hopes, rendering it useless to readers who believe the work is an imperial one). In view of the deployment of pseudepigraphic texts during Roman political campaigns (see §III.9), however, it remains possible that, even if the *Brief Handbook* was composed in 64, Quintus was not its true author.[345]

---

[344] It is unlikely that Cic. *Q. Fr.* 1.1.43, which acknowledges Quintus' contributions to Cicero's success, refers specifically to the *Brief Handbook*. On the silence of antiquity regarding the *Brief Handbook*, see, in the commentary, **A Brief Handbook on Canvassing for Office**.

[345] Very early on it was suggested that Cicero was the actual author of the *Brief Handbook*: Palermus 1583, 241; cf., e.g., Toland 1714, i; Tydeman 1838, 12; and see note 373.

2 Transmission

The *Brief Handbook*, although it takes the shape of a letter from Quintus to Cicero, has not come down to us with Cicero's *Epistulae ad Quintum fratrem* (*Q. Fr.*) but instead is transmitted in conjunction with Cicero's correspondence *ad Familiares* (*Fam.*).[346] In itself this is perhaps not surprising: our sole letter to Cicero by Quintus[347] as well as Quintus' letters to Tiro[348] are preserved in *Fam.* and not in *Q. Fr.* Still, the *Brief Handbook* is not actually a part of *Fam.* and it is missing from the best manuscript that supplies us with a text of *Fam.*[349] This omission has been deemed by some to be a significant sign that the *Brief Handbook* is a spurious work. Furthermore, our earliest manuscripts containing the *Brief Handbook* include it alongside a certainly pseudepigraphical letter from Cicero to Octavian (*Epistula ad Octavianum—Ep. ad Oct.*), and this propinquity has incited suspicions of guilt by association.[350] But the *Ep. ad Oct.* is preserved in several early manuscripts where it is included not with the *Brief Handbook* but with works like *Q. Fr.* and *Epistulae ad Atticum* (*Att.*).[351] Put differently, association with the *Ep. ad Oct.* in our manuscript traditions is not an obvious indicator of anything regarding an ancient or even early perspective on the authorship of the *Brief Handbook*. These works, in every case, were ultimately bundled together because they were epistles in some way linked to Cicero. As for the *Brief Handbook*'s omission from Florence, Laur. 49.9, it is not easy to divine its significance. Laur. 49.9 is the only surviving complete manuscript of *Fam.* When the *Brief Handbook* appears in early manuscripts, it is always in company only with *Fam.* 9–16 in a manuscript tradition that is, in noticeable respects, independent from Laur. 49.9.[352] If the design of Laur. 49.9 centred round supplying a full and superior version of *Fam.*, there was no real reason why it should include the *Brief Handbook*. In any case, the transmission of the *Brief Handbook* is clearly not decisive for the question of Quintus' authorship.

3 Anachronisms and Errors

Even a single anachronism would suffice to show that the composition of the *Brief Handbook* must be later, perhaps much later, than its dramatic

---

[346] Watt 1958a, 79ff.; Watt 1958b. On the transmission of Cic. *Fam.*, see Shackleton Bailey 1977, 3ff.; and Reynolds 1983, 138ff. Occasionally, by way of a slip, the *Brief Handbook* is said to come down with *Q. Fr.*: e.g. Henderson 1950, 8 (corrected at Henderson 1972, 741); Balsdon 1963, 242; David et al. 1973, 248.

[347] Cic. *Fam.* 16.16.   [348] Cic. *Fam.* 16.8; 16.16; 16.26; 16.27.

[349] Florence, Laur. 49.9, or Codex Mediceus 49.9,

[350] Henderson 1950, 8; Nisbet 1961b, 84; Waibel 1969, 100f.; Henderson 1972, 741; Fantham 2013, 197.

[351] Nardo 1970, 31ff.; Reynolds 1983, 137.   [352] Shackleton Bailey 1965, 3ff.

date. So, too, any blunders regarding fundamental facts about late republican Rome. Numerous errors along these lines have been imputed to the work (see the works cited in fn. 341), but none has been substantiated. Some information furnished by the *Brief Handbook*, however, is unattested elsewhere and so cannot be verified: for instance, only the *Brief Handbook* indicates that the Q. Caecilius alleged to be a victim of Catilina during the proscriptions (¶9 and Asc. 84C) was also his brother-in-law, and it has been suggested that this detail is a fabrication.[353] The possibility cannot be excluded, but nor can it be more than a suspicion.[354] The most important of the anachronisms or errors imputed to the *Brief Handbook* are discussed in detail in the commentary: see **¶2 deemed worthy of being patron; ¶3 clubs; ¶10 the tomb; ¶19 Quintus Gallius; ¶33 Now.**

4 Cynicism

The *Brief Handbook* has been criticized for its cynicism even by scholars who do not doubt its authenticity.[355] Concern has been registered over its deployment of invective, and its concentration on winning the favour of Pompeius has been viewed with distaste, not least because the *Brief Handbook* is not shy about emphasizing the sheer instrumentality of Pompeius' mass popularity. Invective, however, was a staple of Roman political discourse (see §VII.5). And Pompeius' support was, in fact, important to Cicero's campaign. As for Cicero's on-again off-again approach to popular principles, this was hardly remarkable on the part of members of Rome's political class.[356]

More serious, however, is the charge that the *Brief Handbook* endorses a dishonest approach to dealing with the Roman public, especially in its discussions of ingratiation (¶42) and generosity (¶¶44–8): in these sections of the work, its author makes it clear that the behaviour he recommends can only compromise Cicero's moral standards, and this advice

[353] Henderson 1950, 10.
[354] And in any case Q. Caecilius may not be the correct reading; see ¶9 **Quintus Caecilius.**
[355] Critics of the work's cynicism: Bruhn 1908, 258ff.; Wiemer 1930, 40; Kroll 1933, 288; Clift 1945, 102f.; Drexler 1966, 240; Lucrezi 2001, 37. Cynicism a mark of inauthenticity: Eussner 1872, 20; Hendrickson 1892, 202; Nisbet 1961b, 84; see, esp., Alexander 2009.
[356] By way of comparison, Cicero's public letter to his brother concerning provincial administration slights Quintus' unnamed quaestor (*Q. Fr.* 1.1.11), admits the possibility of improper conduct on the part of Quintus' Roman staff (*Q. Fr.* 1.1.12), concedes the objectionable behaviour of Roman businessmen and publicans (*Q. Fr.* 1.1.2; 1.1.6–7, 1.1.32–6), criticizes ambitious Greek provincials (*Q. Fr.* 1.1.15–16), and draws attention to Quintus' ill temper (*Q. Fr.* 1.1.37).

appears at odds with the normative claims made for the *Brief Handbook*'s instructions elsewhere in the text (see §IV.4). Still, it is possible to view these sections of the work in terms of the *Brief Handbook*'s effort at reconciling the indignities of canvassing for office with the presumed superior moral fibre of the aristocrats who condescend to seek high offices (see §III.4).[357] Even if one decides that the *Brief Handbook* puts forward exceptional advice in an objectionable way, however, that per se does not render it a later pseudepigraphic work.[358]

Specific and detailed discussions regarding the cynicism of particular passages are offered in the commentary. The sections that have drawn the strongest disapproval from critics are the following: ¶1 (the use of pretence is urged; see ¶1 **Although…nature…pretence is able to defeat nature**); ¶5 (Cicero's speeches addressing popular rights should be treated as a reflex of his effort at winning over Pompeius, a matter also raised at ¶¶14 and 51; see ¶5 **champions of popular rights,** ¶5 **Gnaeus Pompeius,** ¶14 **angry with you…cases you have pleaded**); ¶19 (Cicero is on good terms with *sodalitates* ('religious fraternities'); see ¶16 **religious fraternity**); ¶35 (Cicero is advised to ignore men who are said to be less than entirely loyal to his campaign; see ¶35 **pretend that you have not heard it,** ¶35 **cannot be your friend**); ¶42 (Cicero is advised to be ingratiating; see ¶42 **what you lack by nature**); ¶¶45–7 (Cicero is urged to make false promises; see ¶45 **the next lesson,** ¶47 **master in the art of canvassing**); ¶52 (Cicero is advised to defame his rivals; see ¶8 **But, you will say…Quite the contrary**).

A related and important argument against the authenticity of the *Brief Handbook* is supplied by Michael Alexander, who claims that the work furnishes a version of canvassing for office that is so negative that it can only be a satire, the purpose of which was 'to poke fun at the elections of the Roman republic'.[359] And this satire, he insists, must be imperial. Writers of that period, as Alexander correctly observes, more than once took notice of the unpleasantness, from an aristocratic perspective, of

---

[357] For the argument that the *Brief Handbook* represents Cicero as a candidate of suitably aristocratic sensibilities and yet practical enough to cope with the realities of republican elections (a depiction that is also projected onto the readers of the work), see ¶45 **the next lesson;** ¶46 **a Platonist like yourself;** Nardo 1970, 101ff.; Bruggisser 1984, 121ff.; Tatum 2007; Prost 2017, 57ff., 68ff.

[358] Lucrezi 2001, 37, for instance, argues that, although the *Brief Handbook* was too cynical for wider publication, it circulated among Cicero's supporters. Other scholars have concluded that the work's cynicism rendered it impossible to publish in any sense: e.g. Bruhn 1908, 258ff.; Clift 1945, 102f.; cf. Beltrami 1892, 70f., who argues that, although it could not have been published during Cicero's campaign, it could have been published subsequently.

[359] Alexander 2009, 32.

canvassing for office (so, too, did writers during the republic; see, further, §III.4). Furthermore, the *Brief Handbook*, in Alexander's view, is infused with anti-Ciceronian sentiment of the sort one finds in imperial invectives against Cicero, or the hostile speech the imperial historian Dio composes for Q. Fufius Calenus (cos. 47) at Dio 45.18–47.[360] The *Brief Handbook*, Alexander concludes, is an ironic and witty repudiation both of the indignities of canvassing and its pointlessness. Consequently, according to Alexander's argument, because it is constructed from half-truths, prejudices, and fictions, the *Brief Handbook* is far from a reliable source for recovering anything about republican elections apart from the imperial aristocracy's distaste for them.

Alexander's proposition is ingenious and argued with characteristic erudition. But in justifying his ironic interpretation of various passages he appears to be unduly selective. For instance, as one sign of the *Brief Handbook*'s mockery of republican elections Alexander singles out the work's treatment of friendship, which the *Brief Handbook* extends so widely through the social scale that it constitutes behaviour that would be objectionable outside the confines of a political campaign (e.g. ¶16). Because this utilitarian view of friendship clashes so harshly and so openly with the idealized discussion of friendship in Cicero's *De amicitia*, Alexander's argument runs, it could only be offensive to Cicero, and thus the author of the *Brief Handbook* has introduced into his ostensible advice an irony wrought by this very awkwardness.[361] But the take on electoral friendship one finds in the *Brief Handbook* one also finds in Cicero's correspondence,[362] and in any case the tension between ideal and pragmatic realizations of friendship was a familiar one in Roman literature (see ¶16 **the definition of the word 'friend'**). Which makes it difficult to construe the *Brief Handbook*'s treatment of friendship solely by way of Cicero's proprietary sensibilities regarding *De amicitia*.

As a further example, and another of his 'signs of mockery', Alexander claims that the introduction at ¶47 of C. Aurelius Cotta (cos. 75) as a model for imitation when canvassing must be ironic because Cotta attracted criticism from the nobility regarding his law restoring their old political rights to the tribunes and because he was portrayed by Sallust as something of an intriguer (see ¶47 **master in the art of canvassing**).[363] The abundant evidence for Cicero's admiration of Cotta (see ¶47 **Gaius Cotta**), however, including Cicero's explicit designation of Cotta as 'my friend' (*familiaris meus*),[364] Alexander discounts as largely beside the point. In

---

[360] Alexander 2009, 371ff. [361] Alexander 2009, 46ff.
[362] E.g. Cic. *Att.* 1.1.1; 4.15.7; 4.16.6. [363] Alexander 2009, 53ff.; 394f.
[364] Cic. *Nat. D.* 1.15.

fairness, it can never be easy to make a case for irony that has long gone overlooked. Still, irony does not appear to be a conspicuous feature of the *Brief Handbook*.[365]

5 Literary Borrowings

The *Brief Handbook* exhibits striking literary parallels with Cicero's *Pro Murena*[366] and *In toga candida*,[367] both speeches that were delivered later than the dramatic date of the *Brief Handbook* (the *Mur.* was delivered in 63; *Tog. cand.* was delivered just before the elections of 64; see §VII.5). If the *Brief Handbook* has filched phrases from either speech, then it must be a later work and consequently cannot be what it claims to be.[368]

The similarities between the *Brief Handbook* and *Mur.*, a speech for the defence in a trial for illegal electioneering (see ¶55 bribery), derive mostly from their common topic, viz. canvassing for office. The exception to this is a matter, not of substance, but of technique. At ¶9, the *Brief Handbook* employs the device of imaginary dialogue:

> His nobility does not surpass Antonius', does it? 'No. But he has greater courage [*Non. Sed virtute*].'

This same technique is found at *Mur.* 73:

> The senate does not deem it a crime to go out to meet a candidate, does it? 'No. Only if it does so for pay [*Non. Sed mercede*].' Prove it. To be attended by a multitude? 'No. Only if they were hired [*Non. Sed conductos*].'

Although even Eussner dismissed this similarity as accidental, Nisbet regarded it as important on the grounds that 'the use of *non* to mean "no" is rare in literary Latin'.[369] Rare, perhaps, but even in what subsists of republican literary Latin there are several instances of this phenomenon that predate the *Brief Handbook*.[370] This similarity, like other similarities between the *Brief Handbook* and *Mur.*, appears inconsequential.[371]

---

[365] See Feig Vishnia 2012, 164; Prost 2017, 57f., 62ff.

[366] ¶2~*Mur.* 17; ¶9~*Mur.* 73; ¶17~*Mur.* 69; ¶24~*Mur.* 47; ¶56~*Mur.* 43; see Tyrrell 1877, 53ff.; Nardo 1970, 16ff.; Lucrezi 2001, 31ff.

[367] ¶8~Asc. 74C; ¶10~Asc. 78C; Asc. 80–81C; ¶12~Asc. 83; see Nardo 1970, 37ff.

[368] Eussner 1872, 7f.; 15f.; Hendrickson 1892, 206f.; Hendrickson 1904, 72ff.; Henderson 1950, 9ff.; Nisbet 1961b, 85; Waibel 1969, 11ff. Other literary parallels have been asserted by critics (see Waibel 1969, 11ff.) but unpersuasively and it is the *Brief Handbook*'s relationship with *Mur.* or *Tog. cand.* that continues to play a part in discussions of the work's authenticity.

[369] Nisbet 1961b, 86.

[370] E.g. Plaut. *Merc.* 217; cf. *Cas.* 403; Ter. *Haut.* 1018; Cic. *Div.* 33.

[371] See, further, Nardo 1970, 15.

By contrast, the likenesses between the *Brief Handbook* and *Tog. cand.* are so close in concept and phrasing that they cannot be coincidental. These parallels are all samples of invective against Cicero's rivals, Antonius and Catilina. Only one of three possibilities will explain them: (i) the author of the *Brief Handbook* has cribbed Cicero's speech; (ii) Cicero has borrowed from the *Brief Handbook*; (iii) each work depends on a common source. The question of priority between the two works cannot be decided by comparing their merits. Literary theft is by no means invariably the operation of a weaker writer. In this regard, it is perhaps worth recalling that two of the most memorable phrases of American presidential oratory— 'We have nothing to fear but fear itself' (Franklin D. Roosevelt) and 'Ask not what your country can do for you but what you can do for your country' (John F. Kennedy)—were each of them derived from humble, even pedestrian contexts.[372] Which means it is far from necessary to insist that the *Brief Handbook* has borrowed from Cicero's speech. Though that must remain a possibility.

There is no real reason, however, to think about the relationship between the *Brief Handbook* and *Tog. cand.* in terms of *literary* borrowings. Canvassing at Rome was animated by invective rhetoric (see ¶¶8–10, 52), and political campaigns, it appears, were at least to some degree directed by the candidate and from the centre (see §III.7–10; §VII.5; **¶8 But, you will say…Quite the contrary**). If the *Brief Handbook* was, in fact, designed to be a part of Cicero's campaign, then the abuse it contains is very likely a reflection of the campaign's strategy for going negative in reaction to the coalition against Cicero formed by Antonius and Catilina (see §VII.5). The actual operation of the campaign, then, and not a literary work, is very possibly the common source for the similarities between these two texts.[373] Invective against Antonius and Catilina in 64 hardly appeared for the first time in either the *Brief Handbook* or *Tog. cand.* but was almost certainly voiced early and often—by the candidate and by his surrogates— throughout the campaign. Put differently, it is probably better to view the similarities between the *Brief Handbook* and *Tog. cand.* in terms of modern political talking points and not as specimens of literary intertextuality. Indeed, the admonition in both works not to draw two daggers against the republic, put forward in only slightly different versions at ¶12 and Asc.

---

[372] Roosevelt's line was borrowed from a newspaper advertisement for a department store, Kennedy's from an exhortation delivered by a headmaster at Choate Rosemary Hall; see T. Clarke, *Ask Not: The Inauguration of John F. Kennedy and the Speech that Changed America* (New York, 2004), 78, 106.

[373] Tydeman 1838, 12ff., Wikarjak 1966, 31f., Nardo 1970, 136f., and Lucrezi 2001, 39f. suggest that, in the circumstances of Cicero's campaign, Quintus and his brother collaborated in the composition of the *Brief Handbook*.

83C, sounds very much like a slogan for Cicero's campaign against his two principal competitors.

6 *Raison d'être*

The basic reason for questioning the authenticity of the *Brief Handbook* resides in its unusual nature and uncertain purpose. It is obvious that Cicero did not require the advice contained in the *Brief Handbook*, nor was Quintus a recognized authority in electioneering. And in any case it was easy enough for the two men, both of whom were in Rome at the time of Cicero's canvass, to communicate face to face. Nor is it easy to imagine a pressing need for a manual of instructions on the part of Cicero's supporters or surrogates. This strange, even perplexing quality of the *Brief Handbook* was the point of departure for Eussner's argument against Quintus' authorship, and it is this aspect of the text that sustains any remaining doubts about its genuineness as an artefact of Cicero's campaign for the consulship.[374] Hence the suggestion that it is some kind of fiction.

The routine and sensible response to this concern about the *Brief Handbook* has been to view the work as a specimen of electoral propaganda, composed for circulation during Cicero's campaign as a means of advertising Cicero's attractions as a candidate and drawing hostile attention to the deficiencies of his rivals.[375] After all, when competing for office candidates as well as their supporters ordinarily promulgated letters and texts of other kinds (see §III.8). Nevertheless, the *Brief Handbook* remains an odd and extraordinary contribution to this brand of electioneering bumf, and it is sometimes suggested that, although Quintus wrote the *Brief Handbook*, it was never in any sense allowed to be published.[376] But perhaps it was hoped that, owing to its distinctiveness, it would make an extraordinary impression on readers. That the *Brief Handbook* was designed to further Cicero's candidature, whether or not it was actually circulated in 64, is an approach to the work that is developed in detail in §IV of this introduction.

It should finally be added that the difficulties presented by the literary form of the *Brief Handbook* are not resolved by attributing it to an imperial

---

[374] Eussner 1872, 4ff. See, also, Henderson 1950, 8f.; Nisbet 1961b, 84; Waibel 1969, 56ff.

[375] Petersson 1920, 198; Ciaceri 1939, 173f.; Wikarjak 1966, 18ff.; Nardo 1970, 76f.; Bruggisser 1984; McCoy 1987; Duplá 1988; Lucrezi 1998; Prost 2017, 47ff.; see, further, §IV.5.

[376] E.g. Buecheler 1869, 10; Leo 1895, 448; Till 1962, 316; De Marino 1965, 7f.; Richardson 1971, 439, and see note 358. Concise surveys of earlier scholarship are supplied by Waibel 1969, 63ff.; Nardo 1970, 46ff.

writer.[377] The work remains distinctly dissimilar from any surviving rhetorical showpiece, nor is it anything like any pseudepigraphic letter known to us. As Shackleton Bailey rightly observed, 'it is on a very different level'.[378] Its literary pedigree can be unpacked (see §IV), but in its combination of generic elements the *Brief Handbook* remains an unusual text—however one explains its purpose, be it genuine instruction, electioneering advertisement, or a sophisticated literary impersonation.

VI   QUINTUS TULLIUS CICERO

Quintus Tullius Cicero, like his brother, was born in Arpinum.[379] We do not know the year of his birth. He was close in age to his elder brother, whose magisterial career preceded Quintus' by four years (Quintus was aedile in 65 and praetor in 62). Four years, however, has seemed to some too great a difference to correspond with Cicero's description of his brother as *prope aequalis* ('almost my own age').[380] But Cicero employed this phrase in order to underscore the brothers' closeness at an emotional moment and, in any case, the text of the letter is uncertain.[381] Quintus cannot have been born later than 102, in which case he reached his praetorship at the earliest possible age, but nor can it be excluded that he was born as early as 105.

Both at Rome and abroad, Quintus shared Cicero's extensive education in oratory, law, literature, and philosophy.[382] From 79 through 77 he was with his brother in Greece and Asia. How he was thereafter occupied we do not know. Unlike Cicero, Quintus did not pursue a career in the courts. It has been suggested that he took up military service in this period, which is likely enough but can be no more than a guess.[383] Some time around 70 he married Pomponia, the sister of Cicero's intimate friend Atticus.[384] The match was arranged by Cicero, and it coupled Quintus with a woman who was older than he was, almost certainly previously married, and possibly wealthier.[385] The two did not get along. Still, their marriage lasted about

---

[377] On the cultural situation of imperial fictions, see Peirano 2012.

[378] Shacketon Bailey 2002, 345.

[379] Useful and well-annotated accounts of Quintus' life include Drumann and Groebe 1929, Münzer 1948; Wiemer 1930; McDermott 1971; Mamoojee 1977; Prost 2017, 1ff.

[380] Cic. *Q. Fr.* 1.3.3.   [381] Shackleton Bailey 1980, 166.

[382] Cic. *De or.* 1.1–6; 1.23; 2.1–3, 10; 3.1–4; *Fin.* 5.3; 5.96.

[383] McDermott 1971.   [384] Nep. *Att.* 5.3; 17.1.

[385] On Quintus' finances, see Shatzman 1975, 425ff. The evidence is too incomplete to draw certain conclusions, but it is likely that his circumstances were more solid than his brother's.

twenty-five years, and in 67 a son was born, the only known child of the marriage.

The course of Quintus' career indicates that he possessed bravery and, it appears, integrity. And his administrative talents were not to be despised. His merits, however, were blemished by two glaring personal faults, which Cicero was not too shy to bring to his brother's attention. The man had a temper, and his irritability was often made worse by his tactlessness.[386] Perhaps these were traits that Quintus was disinclined to repudiate. It is clear that, as governor of his province, he took pride in exhibiting old-fashioned severity in the administration of justice.[387] And his political views, if Cicero has depicted his brother accurately, were also old-fashioned, especially in their hard-line advocacy of aristocratic prerogative.[388]

It is not known when Quintus held his quaestorship. Perhaps in 69, in which case he stood for the office somewhat later than was the usual practice of his contemporaries.[389] He attained a plebeian aedileship for 65,[390] doubtless aided by his brother's reputation inasmuch as Cicero was praetor at the time of the elections. Similarly, during the year of Cicero's consulship, he was elected a praetor for 62.[391] Perhaps, however, it is a mistake to view their relationship entirely in terms of its advantages to Quintus. Cicero, in a public letter, openly declares Quintus the partner in all his labours and a chief agent in his own political ascent.[392] As praetor, Quintus crushed the Catilinarian remnant in Bruttium[393] and presided over the trial of the poet Archias conducted before the tribunal established by the *lex Papia* of 65.[394] Afterwards he was proconsul of Asia from 61 until 58, an important post which he held with distinction.[395]

In returning to Rome, Quintus confronted a crisis. Cicero had been driven into exile by his enemy P. Clodius Pulcher (tr. pl. 58), and, in an environment suddenly so toxic for Cicero's family, Quintus could only be vulnerable to prosecution. This threat never materialized.[396] Instead,

---

[386] Temper: Cic. *Q. Fr.* 1.1.37; 1.2.6; cf. *Fam.* 16.27.2. Lack of tact: Cic. *Q. Fr.* 1.1.38–9; 1.2.4.

[387] Cic. *Q. Fr.* 1.2.5.   [388] Cic. *Leg.* 3.17–22; 3.26; 3.34–7.

[389] On the basis of Quintus' long absence from Rome, reported at Cic. *Att.* 1.5.8, his quaestorship is regularly dated to 68. But, if that letter is to be any guide, his quaestorship is correctly dated to 69 (see Shackleton Bailey 1980, 3). Mamoojee 1977, 63f., prefers 71.

[390] *MRR* 2.158.   [391] *MRR* 2.173.   [392] Cic. *Q. Fr.* 1.1.43.

[393] Oros. 6.6.7; Dio 37.41.

[394] Quintus and the trial of Archias: Schol. Bob. 175 (Stangl); Cic. *Arch.* 3, 32. The *lex Papia*: *MRR* 2.158. It has been suggested that Quintus was urban praetor in 62 (e.g. *MRR* 2.62) but this is far from clear (see Brennan 2000, 287, 808).

[395] *MRR* 2.181, 185, 191; 3.209; see Brennan 2000, 566ff.

[396] On the threat of prosecution, see Cic. *Att.* 3.8.3–4; 3.9.1; 3.17.1; *Q. Fr.* 1.3.5; *Sest.* 68.

Quintus devoted himself entirely and energetically to his brother's restoration, taking a leading role and frequently putting himself in the way of personal injury in the violence attending the struggle over Cicero's recall.[397] In the end, the orator's allies were successful and Cicero returned to Rome in September 57. Almost immediately thereafter Quintus became a legate to Pompeius, who had received a special command, endorsed by Cicero, which assigned him the supervision of Rome's grain supply. For several months he served in Sardinia, returning to Rome in June 56.[398]

In 54 and 53 Quintus was a legate to Caesar, with whom he participated in the invasion of Britain. Commander of a camp in Belgium in 54, he heroically defended it against an attack by the Nervii, winning Caesar's commendation for his bravery.[399] During the next year, however, Quintus' forces were nearly routed by an unexpected German assault. For his lack of circumspection in allowing his troops to become vulnerable—Quintus had sent nine cohorts on a foraging mission and it was they who attracted the German attack—Quintus is criticized in Caesar's *Bellum Gallicum*.[400] But the stricture is a slight one, appearing in a larger context acknowledging the unpredictability of warfare. Quintus continued in Caesar's command until the next year, when he departed to join his brother in Cilicia.[401]

In 51 Cicero became proconsul of Cilicia, an assignment he did not desire and for which he was ill prepared.[402] This province, threatened internally by unpacified and still restless tribes and externally by the possibility of Parthian intrusion, required military as well as administrative competence. Cicero, intelligent enough to perceive his deficiencies, appointed as legates his brother Quintus and the able C. Pomptinus (pr. 63), who had celebrated a triumph in 54.[403] Between them they were able to deliver Cicero military victories sufficient for his declaration as *imperator* ('conquering general') by his troops and a decree of thanksgiving by the senate (*supplicatio*).[404] Cicero even hoped to celebrate a triumph.[405] But this expectation was dashed by the outbreak of civil war.

---

[397] Cic. *Att.* 3.18.2; 3.22.1; 4.1.8; Q. *Fr.* 1.3; 1.4; 2.3.7; *Fam.* 5.4.1; *Sest.* 75–7. On the circumstances of Cicero's exile and recall, see Tatum 1999, 150ff., 176ff.

[398] *MRR* 2.205, 213. Pompeius' command: *MRR* 2.203f.

[399] Caes. *B.Gall.* 5.38–52.   [400] Caes. *B.Gall.* 6.35–42.

[401] *MRR* 2.226, 232. Peter Wiseman has suggested that Quintus took part in Caesar's campaign in order to position himself, through the acquisition of plunder and political connections, to stand for the consulship (Wiseman 1987, 34ff.). If so, he soon changed his mind, since he never stood for the office.

[402] *MRR* 2.243, 251.

[403] Pomptinus' triumph, delayed by political opposition, celebrated his crushing of the Allobroges' desperate rebellion in 62 and 61: *MRR* 2.225.

[404] Quintus: *MRR* 2.245, 253. Pomptinus: *MRR* 2.245.

[405] Cic. *Att.* 6.8.5; 7.1.5; 7.2.6; 7.3.2; 7.4.1; 7.7.3–4; *Fam.* 2.12.3; 15.5.2; Plut. *Cic.* 37.

The civil war challenged the loyalties of both brothers, who had established close ties both to Pompeius and to Caesar. In the end, Cicero, Quintus, and their sons joined Pompeius.[406] Early in 49, when the family were making decisions about how to proceed, Cicero informed Atticus that Quintus was joining him mostly out of personal loyalty and in the expectation that Caesar would be furious at his decision.[407] To his credit, Cicero did not deviate from this claim when he was seeking his own pardon from Caesar in late 48.[408] In the aftermath of Pompeius' defeat at Pharsalus, the brothers deserted the republican cause—but each in his own way. Cicero returned to Italy. Quintus and his son travelled east in order to seek Caesar's forgiveness personally.[409] Atticus played a crucial role in their reconciliation.[410]

In the end, both brothers recovered their old status in Caesar's new Rome. In the aftermath of their capitulation, however, the two brothers quarrelled fiercely. Cicero, it seems clear, was willing to bear responsibility for their decision to join Pompeius, but this was evidently not enough for Quintus, who savagely denounced his brother to Caesar and Caesar's associates. Cicero's letters to Atticus, our only source for this breach, make it very clear how bitter and painful the break was for him.[411] Ultimately the rupture was mended. Atticus exerted himself in reconciling the brothers,[412] and by July 47 Quintus was writing to Cicero in an apparently friendly vein.[413] By the next year, they were once again visiting each other's homes.[414] Their renewed relationship is commemorated in Cicero's literary works from the 40s, in which Quintus is a prominent figure, notably in Book 5 of Cicero's *De finibus* (*On Moral Ends*) and especially in *De divinatione* (*On Divination*).[415]

Of Quintus' subsequent career very little is known. By April 44 he had divorced Pomponia and was denying rumours that he intended to marry again.[416] If he played any public role in the aftermath of Caesar's assassination or offered open support for Cicero in his feud with Mark Antony, it goes unmentioned in our sources. But Quintus did not go unnoticed by the triumvirate who seized power in 43. When they published their proscription

---

[406] See esp. Cic. *Att.* 7.18.1; 8.3.5; 10.1.1.   [407] Cic. *Att.* 9.1.4.
[408] Cic. *Att.* 11.12.2.   [409] Cic. *Att.* 11.6.7; 11.7.7; 11.8.2.
[410] Nep. *Att.* 7.3.
[411] Cic. *Att.* 11.5.4; 11.6.7; 11.7.7; 11.8.2; 11.9.2; 11.10.1; 11.11.2; 11.12.1–3; 11.13.2; 11.15.2; 11.16.4–5; 11.21.1; 11.22.1; 11.23.2.
[412] Cic. *Att.* 11.9.2; 11.11.2; 11.13.2; 11.16.4.   [413] Cic. *Att.* 11.23.2.
[414] Cic. *Att.* 12.1.2.
[415] Shackleton Bailey (1971, 179ff.; 1980, 5f.), by way of a close reading of Cicero's correspondence, 'sometimes interlinearly' (Shackleton Bailey 1980, 5), argues that the brothers were never wholly reconciled after their falling out during the civil war.
[416] Cic. *Att.* 14.3.5; 14.17.3.

lists, Quintus and his son, like Cicero, were numbered among their victims. At first, Quintus and Cicero attempted to flee Italy together, but circumstances obliged them to separate. In the end, Quintus was executed together with his son.[417] Quintus shared in his brother's literary enthusiasm if not in his extraordinary talent. Apart from the *Brief Handbook*, Quintus is not known to have undertaken any sort of serious work in prose.[418] He contemplated writing history, a proposition to which Cicero lent his support in a letter dated to 54 BC,[419] but there is no indication that he did so. And in view of Cicero's later complaints about the stylistic deficiencies of Latin historiography, including animadversions in a literary dialogue, one of whose participants is his brother, it must be concluded that Quintus never completed any piece of writing in that line.[420] In a letter of 59, Cicero mentions Quintus' *Annals*, which he had been asked by his brother to revise and promulgate.[421] This, however, was almost certainly a historical epic, although nothing further is known about it.[422]

Indeed, poetry, not history, was Quintus' passion, and Cicero more than once concedes his brother's superior talent in this department of literature.[423] Twenty lines of verse by Quintus survive,[424] preserved, unexpectedly, amid the *Eclogues* of Ausonius. Astronomical phenomena—mostly, but not exclusively, the signs of the zodiac—are their subject, and they adapt the Greek poetry of Aratus by way of influences drawn from Cicero and Lucretius (whom Quintus was enthusiastically reading in 54).[425] Their original context is unknown.[426]

Quintus also composed several tragedies, notoriously completing four in sixteen days while serving under Caesar (though what Cicero tells us is only that the final touches were put on the four works during this period, not that they were written from start to finish in so brief a time).[427] Their

---

[417] Plut. *Cic.* 47.1–4; App. *B.Civ.* 4.83; Dio 47.10.6–7.

[418] On the question of Quintus' authorship, see §V.   [419] Cic. *Q. Fr.* 2.12(11).4.

[420] *Leg.* 1.5–16 (completed after 52), in which discussion Cicero attributes to Quintus the view that Latin historiography remains stylistically defective (Cic. *Leg.* 1.8); cf. *De or.* 2.55 (completed in 55); *Brut.* 288 (completed in 46).

[421] Cic. *Att.* 2.16.4.

[422] So, e.g., Münzer 1948, 1305; Cugusi 1970b, 6f.; *FRHist* 1.648. That Quintus wrote an epic is confirmed by Schol. Bob. 175 (Stangl). This reference, however, is sometimes erroneously folded in with Q. *Fr.* 2.12(11).4 in order to make Quintus into a historian: e.g. Schanz and Hosius 1928, 552; Drumann and Groebe 1929, 665.

[423] Cic. *Q. Fr.* 3.1.11; 3.4.4.   [424] See Courtney 1993, 179ff.

[425] Cic. *Q. Fr.* 2.10(9).3. Aratus and his popularity in Rome: Lewis 1992; Kidd 1998, esp. 41; Hübner 2005. Literary influences on Quintus' verses: Courtney 1993, 179ff.; Dehon 2000; Gee 2007.

[426] Gee 2007, 572ff., challenges the attribution of these lines to Quintus.

[427] Q. *Fr.* 3.5.7.

titles elude. One of them was an *Electra*, doubtless an adaptation of Sophocles' play.[428] Another was possibly a *Troades* (*Trojan Women*), although the transmission of this title is insecure and in any case has been doubted on the grounds that there is no known Sophoclean play of that title. But there is no reason to believe that Quintus was wedded to Sophoclean drama.[429] No other titles can be identified with any degree of confidence.

A disputed passage may reveal another Sophoclean adaptation. At *Q. Fr.* 2.16(15).3, Cicero remarks, 'I don't really approve of Sophocles' *Banqueters*, although I see that you have performed a jolly little play.' It has been proposed that Quintus in fact produced this drama as a diversion for himself and his fellow officers, but that seems highly unlikely. The manuscripts for this letter read *a te actam fabellam…esse festive*, which is translated above, but, by emending *actam* to *factam* we get Cicero referring to literary composition: 'you have written a jolly little play'. *Banqueters* was a satyr play, the indecorous passages of which evidently offended Cicero's sensibilities. Reading *factam* for *actam*, one may conclude that, in Quintus' version of the *Banqueters*, the humour was adjusted to his brother's satisfaction. Still, neither text nor meaning is certain here.[430]

Quintus also composed an *Erigone*, which could be another tragedy (Sophocles wrote an *Erigone*, as did Accius), but this work is never specifically designated a drama by our sources.[431] Inasmuch as her myth was popular among Hellenistic poets, not least the miraculous translation of Erigone and her faithful dog, Maera, into the stars, it is imaginable that what Quintus composed was a miniature and modern epic on the theme.[432]

During the year 54 BC, Quintus urged his brother to write an epic on Caesar's campaign in Britain, as well as other lines on the natural phenomena of the place.[433] There is no evidence that he himself ever entertained the idea of composing a similar epic.[434]

---

[428] On Quintus' fondness for Sophocles, see Cic. *Fin.* 5.3; *Div.* 1.54.

[429] Quintus was also fond of Euripides: Cic. *Fam.* 16.8.2.

[430] On this passage and its difficulties, see Shackleton Bailey 1980, 202.

[431] *Q Fr.* 3.1.13; 3.7(9).6. *Erigone* not obviously a drama: Courtney 1993, 181; Hollis 2007, 216f.

[432] Erigone's catasterism: e.g. Hyginus, *Poet. Astr.* 2.149–209; Nonnus *Dion.* 47.246–9. Erigone and the Hellenistic poets: Call. *Aet.* 178.3–4 Pf.; Erastosthenes' elegiac *Erigone*: Rosokoki 1995. Erigone's dog played a part in Quintus' poem: Cic. *Q. Fr.* 3.7(9).6. Did Quintus, in a flourish of erudition, include in his *Erigone* his lines adapted from Aratus (Erigone was identified with Virgo, though not by Aratus)?

[433] Cic. *Q Fr.* 2.14(13).2; 2.26(15).4; 3.4.4.; 3.5(5–7).4; 3.6(8).3; 3.7(9).6.

[434] It is, however, occasionally but incorrectly remarked in modern discussions of Quintus (or of the passages cited in the note above) that Quintus either commenced or, in fact, completed an epic on Caesar's campaigns in Britain: e.g. Schanz and Hosius 1928, 551; Allen 1955.

One final, and almost entirely obscure, poem remains to be mentioned. In 58 BC, when the exiled Cicero fretted that his brother might be prosecuted for administrative malfeasance while governor in Asia, he advised Quintus to take care that verses attacking a *lex Aurelia* and ascribed to Quintus in the past not be allowed to become part of any proceedings against him.[435] Little can confidently be inferred about this poem. It was, says Cicero, put to use against Quintus during his campaign for the aedileship in 66 BC, so doubtless it was a caustic epigram likely to give offence. But to whom, and why? Perhaps to the average Roman voter, since aediles were elected by the relatively democratic tribal assembly. It is widely agreed that the *lex Aurelia* attacked in these verses was the law of 70 dividing juries into equal groups of senators, knights, and *tribuni aerarii*, and it is easy to see how a complaint against that measure could be deployed effectively in any actual trial.[436] Far more controversial at the time, however, was the *lex Aurelia* of 75, which removed the prohibition on ex-tribunes holding higher offices—and Quintus held strong views against the tribunate.[437] In the political climate of 58 BC, when the tribune Clodius held sway on account of his exploitation of populist sentiments and popular violence, hostility against the tribunate was also unlikely to help any defendant—or, for that matter, the exiled Cicero to win over future tribunes who might help to return him from exile. In any case, it is obvious from Cicero's letter that Quintus was not the author of this epigram, even if its attribution to him indicates what his contemporaries might expect from him.[438]

VII CICERO THE OFFICE SEEKER

1 Quaestor

Cicero's political career was exceptional and, in many respects, unusual for an aspiring new man. Although he had undertaken military service during the Social War, and valour was a high recommendation to public office, especially for a new man, Cicero enjoyed no reputation as a

---

[435] Cic. *Q. Fr.* 1.3.9.   [436] *Lex Aurelia* of 70: MRR 2.127.

[437] *Lex Aurelia* of 75: MRR 2.96. Quintus on the tribunate: Cic. *Leg.* 3.17–22; 3.26. Rotondi 1912, 369f. suggests that Cicero here refers to an otherwise unknown law.

[438] Cic. *Q. Fr.* 1.3.9: 'take care that the attribution is not established by false testimony [*falso testimonio*]'.

soldier.[439] Nor, so far as we know, did he take on any mundane but crucial public chores, such as serving as a moneyer or curator of an important road—employments so valuable in generating grateful connections and a raised profile that even nobles did not despise them.[440] Instead, Cicero ascended to high office on account of the influence (*gratia*) and popular favour (*popularis voluntas*) he accrued from his exertions as a pleader. On oratory's capacity for projecting ability, culture, rectitude, and the qualities of leadership, as well as its usefulness in acquiring precious assets in gratitude, little need be said here: this reality of Roman society is unmistakable.[441] Nor was it overlooked by Cicero, who, early in his praetorship, boasted how theretofore he had expended the whole of his time and talents in rescuing his friends from their perils in the courts.[442]

In 76 Cicero took his first step in the *cursus honorum* when he was elected quaestor for the following year.[443] The importance of this magistracy, and the senatorial status resulting from it, must never be underestimated: senators were by definition distinguished men, even if not all of them were famous men.[444] Although a new man in politics, Cicero was not an entirely unknown quantity. He derived from an old and rich municipal family, a class not unwelcome in Roman civic affairs, and owing to his early brilliance and constant exertions in the law courts, always as an advocate, he was already a familiar and increasingly well-connected figure.[445] He was attractive enough to acquire a wealthy and well-born wife, a reliable indication of his promise in the eyes of Rome's established elite, and his appeal to the general public was made clear enough by his

---

[439] Cicero's early military service: Gelzer 1969a, 5f.; Mitchell 1979, 8f.; Tempest 2011, 27ff. The usefulness of military service for a new man: Wiseman 1971, 176ff., and esp. 143ff.; ¶2 **new man.**

[440] Moneyers: Hahm 1963. *Curatores*: e.g. Cic. *Att.* 1.1.2; see Wiseman 1971, 139; see §III.2

[441] Cicero's *popularis voluntas*: Cic. *Brut.* 321; see ¶16 **goodwill of the people.** *Gratia* and advocacy: Cic. *Off.* 2.51; see David 1992, 591ff.; the essays in Steel and Blom 2013; Blom 2016; Rosillo López 2017, 196ff.; see §III.2; ¶2 **your fame as an orator.**

[442] Cic. *Leg. Man.* 1.

[443] Cic. *Verr.* 2.5.35; *Pis.* 2; see *MRR* 2.98. *Cursus honorum*: see §II.2.

[444] On the quaestorship, see Lintott 1999a, 133ff.

[445] The rise of Gaius Marius (cos. I 107) helped to bring Arpinum's aristocracy to the attention of the Roman elite, a relationship that promoted Arpinate senatorial careers: Badian 1964, 46ff; Wiseman 1971, 30f., 55f. Cicero's extended Arpinate family included Marius and M. Marius Gratidianus, who was twice praetor (see ¶10 **Marcus Marius**). M. Gratidius, Gratidianus' father, was a friend of M. Antonius (cos. 99) (Cic. *Leg.* 3.36; *Brut.* 168; *De or.* 2.2), whose relationship with Cicero was formative: e.g. Blom 2010, 226ff. On Cicero's origins, his civic education in Rome, and his early forensic career, see Gelzer 1969a, 1ff.; Mitchell 1979, 52ff.; Tempest 2011, 19ff. It is worth observing that Cicero's father possessed a house on the Carinae (Plut. *Cic.* 8.6; Cic. *Q. Fr.* 2.3.7) and so was a far from inconspicuous presence in Roman society during Cicero's childhood.

election to this office at the earliest possible age and among the first to be returned.[446]

Although Cicero's reputation, as the *Brief Handbook* correctly observes (e.g. ¶2), resided in his career as an orator, he came to his forensic practice somewhat late.[447] Nonetheless, his ascent into the first rank was as swift as it was notable. With his first published speech, *Pro Quinctio*, delivered in 81 as part of a private suit, Cicero made a display of his legal acumen and, perhaps more significantly, his arrival as a fixture in elite establishment circles. The orator makes it clear how it was through the agency of Sulla's esteemed friend the actor Q. Roscius that he received Quinctius' brief (Roscius was Quinctius' brother-in-law), and Cicero's forensic adversaries (again this is made clear in Cicero's speech) were distinguished figures: Q. Hortensius Hortalus (cos. 69), then Rome's leading orator, and the consular L. Marcius Philippus (cos. 91).[448] In such a contest as this, a good result could have been nothing less than splendid. And even if Cicero failed (the verdict in this case is unknown), the publication of his speech announced his impressive appearance in the forum.

The publication of speeches by Roman political figures originated in the exhibitionism of the venerable M. Porcius Cato (cos. 195), the grand new man deemed exemplary by Cicero and a figure whose capacities for self-interested self-fashioning remained unsurpassed before the first century.[449] Although the practice of publishing speeches remained inconsistent in aristocratic circles, it was seized upon avidly by Cicero, who rarely missed a chance to write himself up.[450] Even before the publication of *Pro Quinctio*, Cicero had composed and perhaps promulgated his first rhetorical essay, *De inventione rhetorica* (*On Rhetorical Invention*), a precocious composition displaying learning and eloquence, whatever its deficiencies in the judgment of the mature orator.[451] Owing to oratory's sheer power in Roman society, opportunities for speechifying were

---

[446] On Terentia, see Treggiari 2007. Cicero's place in the polls in 76: Cic. *Pis.* 2 (*in primis*).

[447] Cicero had begun pleading cases by 81, when he was 25 (*Pro Quinctio* was not Cicero's first case: *Quinct.* 4). He later insisted that his late start was motivated by a desire to commence his career fully prepared for pleading: *Brut.* 311.

[448] Role of Q. Roscius: Cic. *Quinct.* 77–9. Cicero's adversaries: *Quinct.* 1–2, 72. On this speech, see Lintott 2008, 43ff.; Tempest 2011, 32ff.

[449] Astin 1978 remains fundamental; see, further, Sciarrino 2011. Cicero and Cato: Blom 2010, 42.

[450] The importance of Cicero's publications in advancing his contemporary public and political standing has frequently been observed: e.g. Dugan 2005; Steel 2006, 25ff.; Gildenhard 2011 (each with further bibliography).

[451] Cic. *De or.* 1.5, Cicero's expression *pueris et adulescentulis*, could date *Inv. rhet.* to his later teenage years, though nothing prevents its being assigned to his 20s.

limited by convention: the courts, however, offered aspiring speakers welcome venues for proving themselves, occasions that Cicero publicized widely and unflaggingly.[452] From the start, he exerted himself not simply in acquiring gratitude and connections and in achieving successes but also in amplifying his accomplishments by way of their literary advertisement— publications which, in the light of Cato's precedent, signalled a traditional brand of personal ambition. In resorting to literature as a medium for putting himself forward, Cicero reflected his times, but his talent and industry shone brighter than those of his contemporaries.

His reputation was advanced still further by his success in the criminal trial (Cicero's first) of Sextus Roscius, a defence in which the orator sensationally, and certainly courageously, challenged the influence of Sulla's sinister freedman Chrysogonus, and after which he was recognized by everyone as a speaker capable of handling any case.[453] The political significance of this trial has often been exaggerated, but its importance to Cicero's career has not, and in securing Roscius' acquittal Cicero gained for himself the gratitude of Roscius' noble patrons, not least the Metelli, Servilii, and Cornelii Scipiones.[454] And there were other early triumphs, the publicity and impact of which we can scarcely now gauge. In a private suit in 79, for instance, Cicero joined with C. Aurelius Cotta (cos. 75) in pleading against C. Scribonius Curio (cos. 76). This was, once again, grand company, and Cicero remained proud of his performance in this trial and so confident of its renown that, in the 40s, he could expect his readers still to be aware of it.[455] Not yet a famous man, perhaps, Cicero was nonetheless more than distinguished enough to assume a place in the Roman senate.

Cicero served his quaestorship in Sicily, where he endeavoured to favour the interests of the nobility and, it is natural to assume, look after the fortunes of equestrian investors.[456] Returned to Rome, he again devoted his energies to forensic oratory.[457] Which is not to say that Cicero did not

---

[452] Limited opportunities for young speakers: Jehne 2000.

[453] Cic. *Brut.* 312.   [454] Cic. *Rosc. Am.* 15. Berry 2004; Dyck 2010.

[455] Cic. *Brut.* 217; *Orat.* 129. Tatum 1991a; Rosillo López 2013. Cicero tells us that, while aiming at the quaestorship, he participated in celebrated cases (*causas nobilis egimus*: *Brut.* 318).

[456] Sources: *MRR* 2.98. His exertions on behalf of the nobility: Plut. *Cic.* 6.2; see Crawford 1984, 39ff. On behalf of the *publicani*: Cic. *Verr.* 2.2.181; see §3 publicans. Cicero's quaestorship: Gelzer 1969a, 29; Mitchell 1979, 99f.; Tempest 2011, 38ff.

[457] Although we know of very few cases, Cicero informs us that, in the five years preceding his election as aedile, he was involved in many important trials (Cic. *Brut.* 318). In 72 Cicero defended C. Mustius (a *publicanus*: *Verr.* 2.1.139; Ps.-Asc. 252 (Stangl)); in 72, Sthenius of Thermae (a distinguished Sicilian: *Verr.* 2.2.100); in 71, M. Tullius (denominated a friend at *Tull.* 4 but otherwise unknown; this speech merited publication).

also play a responsible role in senatorial affairs: in 73 he served on a select committee advising the consuls on a dispute between the Greek city of Oropus and Roman tax-farmers; the *publicani* had a weak case, but it was advanced by the young noble L. Domitius Ahenobarbus, the future consul of 54; in the end, however, the committee sided with Oropus.[458] We cannot, of course, know what position Cicero took during these deliberations— in the immediately subsequent years he was as friendly with Domitius Ahenobarbus as he was with the publicans[459]—but this episode suffices to make it clear that Cicero was by no means inactive in the senate.

2 Aedile

In 70 Cicero decided to stand for the aedileship.[460] The tribunate did not attract, not even after its full restoration in the same year: Cicero was not naturally disposed to the office, nor could its opportunities for exhibiting eloquence or offering aid and assistance add much to his achievements in the courts.[461] By contrast, election to an aedileship, because it was more exclusive than the tribunate, represented a more impressive achievement. And the aedileship entailed duties, like the sponsorship of games, which won popular gratitude without attracting demagogic imputations.[462] All in all, here was an office capable of lending a new man the appearance of being on the rise. Cicero cunningly combined his ambitions for the aedileship with his sensational prosecution of Verres, a tactic that kept him at the centre of public attention.[463] Once again, he was successful at the polls, and, once again, at the earliest possible age.[464] His electoral success was punctuated by his decisive victory, as aedile-elect, over Hortensius,

---

[458] *RDGE* 133ff.; Cicero refers to this matter at *Nat. D.* 3.49.

[459] Cic. *Att.* 1.1.3.

[460] On the office, see Lintott 1999a, 129ff. Its appeal to ambitious new men: Wiseman 1971, 158ff.; Gruen 1974, 178ff. One of Cicero's colleagues in 69 was M. Caesonius, also a new man.

[461] On the tribunate, see Lintott 1999a, 121ff. Its potential for acquiring publicity and gratitude: Gruen 1974, 23ff.; Thommen 1989, 21ff.; Morstein-Marx 2004, 38, 266ff. Cicero did not fundamentally disapprove of the office: *Rep.* 2.59; *Leg.* 3.28. According to Dio 36.43.5, Cicero preferred the aedileship to the tribunate because he hoped that by doing so he could enhance his appeal to the better classes. When Cicero appears to elevate the tribunate over the aedileship at *Planc.* 13, his purpose is purely tactical.

[462] Cic. *Off.* 2.57–8. See ¶44 **generosity**. On the importance of the games to candidates for higher offices, see §II.2 note 11; §III.2.

[463] Tatum 2013, 138ff. It was perhaps at this point that Cicero published the valedictory speech he delivered at the conclusion of his quaestorship (Crawford 1994, 19ff.) in order to advertise the depth of his relationship with Sicily and his soundness as a provincial administrator.

[464] Cic. *Pis.* 2.

by then consul-elect, at Verres' trial.[465] Behind the scenes, by contrast, and after the verdict, Cicero showed himself willing to make significant concessions in the matter of any penalty to be exacted from the condemned Verres, a wily display of cooperation that can only have attracted approval from his senatorial peers.[466]

By his own admission, Cicero did not excel expectations in carrying out his aedilician responsibilities.[467] Nor did he speak out on public matters in the assemblies or, so it seems, in the senate, not while in office or thereafter—not even during the controversies of 67.[468] Instead, he persisted unrelentingly in his work as an advocate: looking back as praetor in 66 Cicero described his forensic labours as occupying nearly every day of his civic life.[469] Cicero's aedileship was the year of his *Pro Fonteio (Defence of Fonteius)* and his *Pro P. Oppio (Defence of P. Oppius)*, each a case in which Cicero could put himself forward as a champion of equestrian interests.[470] In his *Pro Caecina (Speech in Behalf of Caecina)*, the orator flaunted his profound legal learning, and he exhibited his close personal connections with the Etruscan aristocracy of Volaterrae.[471] He could also claim, for this case, something of a landmark victory, since his success played an undeniable role in the restoration of citizen rights to the people of Volaterrae and Arretium, who had been deprived of their civic standing by a vengeful Sulla.[472] Industry of this kind continued to predominate in Cicero's occupations during the two years preceding his praetorship, even if only one case from that period is recorded.[473]

Outside the courts, Cicero was actively acquiring villas in the Italian countryside, thereby extending his neighbourly relationships throughout

---

[465] Cicero later described their confrontation as the greatest contest of his early career: Cic. *Brut.* 319. See, further, Frazel 2009; Tempest 2011, 45ff.

[466] Plut. *Cic.* 8.1.

[467] Cic. *Off.* 2.58–9; cf. *Mur* 40. Cicero's aedileship: Gelzer 1969a, 51ff.; Mitchell 1979, 150; Tempest 2011, 59ff.

[468] The year 67 witnessed debate over the *lex Gabinia* and perturbations associated with the legislative programme of the tribune C. Cornelius. Events of 67: *MRR* 2.142ff.; see Steel 2013b, 144ff. Cicero's first *contio* was his speech *Pro lege Manilia*, delivered during his praetorship (*Leg. Man.* 1–3).

[469] Cic. *Leg. Man.* 2; cf. *Brut.* 321.

[470] On the central issues of *Pro Fonteio*, see Lintott 2008, 101ff.; Dyck 2012. Its equestrian connection: Bleicken 1995, 21. On *Pro P. Oppio*, see Crawford 1994, 23ff. Its equestrian connection: Quint. 5.13.2.

[471] On *Pro Caecina*, see Lintott 2008, 73ff. Cicero's valuable links with Volaterrae: Lomas 2004, 106ff. Volaterrae's influence over its tribe (the Sabitina): Wiseman 1971, 140.

[472] Harris 1971, 271ff.; Santangelo 2007, 174ff.

[473] This was not a trial but rather Cicero's assistance to D. Matrinius, who faced formal and public scrutiny when he endeavoured to become a scribe: see Brennan 2000, 449; Crawford 1984, 58ff.; this hearing probably took place in 67.

the various tribes.[474] His appeal remained undiminished: in the praetorian elections of 67 he was elected ahead of all his competitors,[475] who included nobles like C. Antonius, L. Cassius Longinus, and P. Sulpicius Galba. Indeed, owing to procedural delays, fresh votes had to be taken on three different days, and on each occasion Cicero was returned at the top of the poll.[476] By the end of the year, Cicero's daughter was betrothed to the noble C. Calpurnius Piso Frugi.[477]

3 Praetor

Although Cicero firmly rejected the idea that his election to the consulship in any way owed itself to the inferior quality of his competition,[478] this imputation persists.[479] Its first suggestion, in fact, resides in the *Brief Handbook*, which strains itself in making it clear that Cicero's noble opposition was abnormal in their failure to exhibit the best qualities of their class (¶¶7, 11, 27). Was Cicero elected *faute de mieux*, a candidate who, in a mediocre field, was at least good enough to be preferred over his inadequate rivals? In reality, it is nearly always difficult for us to assess the relative advantages and disadvantages of contending candidates: only rarely is it obvious or are we told what it was that rendered one candidate more appealing than another. This is not to say that we are unaware, in general terms, of features (like noble birth or military glory) that voters tended to find attractive. It is rather that we can almost never be certain which combination of attractive attributes won the day on the day. Nor, in many instances, could the Romans, who (as we have seen) repeatedly emphasized the sheer unpredictability of their elections (see §III.1).

A quick survey of Cicero's rivals, potential and actual, can help in furnishing at least something in the way of an awareness of the human obstacles he confronted. It is, however, difficult, on the present condition of our evidence, to recover in anything like full detail the cohort amid which Cicero contended for high office. Of his colleagues in the praetorship, four are securely attested: C. Antonius (cos. 63; see ¶8), C. Aquillius Gallus,

---

[474] Cic. *Att.* 1.4.3; 1.5.7; 1.6.2; Plin. *NH* 22.12. Cicero's villas: Shatzman 1975, 404ff.; Mitchell 1979, 102ff.; Ioannatou 2006, 212ff. On the value of neighbourliness (*vicinitas*) in Roman elections, see ¶17 **your neighbours**.

[475] Cic. *Leg. Man.* 2; *Pis.* 2; *Brut.* 321; *Off.* 2.59; Asc. 85C.

[476] Cic. *Leg. Man.* 2.

[477] Cic. *Att.* 1.3.3. Cicero's praetorship: Gelzer 1969a, 55ff.; Mitchell 1979, 156ff.; Tempest 2011, 71ff.

[478] Cic. *Leg. agr.* 2.3.

[479] Sall. *Cat.* 23.6; Plut. *Cic.* 10–11; App. *B.Civ.* 2.2; see Gruen 1974, 137; Taylor 1949, 65, 118; Brunt 1988, 428f.; Wiseman 1994, 347f.; Tempest 2011, 81; Syme 2016, 140ff.

L. Cassius Longinus (see ¶7), and C. Orchivius (see ¶19).[480] To these we may confidently add M. Caesonius.[481] For the remaining two praetorships of 66, three credible candidates remain: Q. Cornificius, P. Sulpicius Galba (see ¶7), and P. Varinius. Each had certainly served as praetor by 66. Antonius, Cassius Longinus, and Sulpicius Galba were noble. Aquillius derived from praetorian stock. The residue, however, were of scarcely more distinguished birth than was Cicero: Orchivius, Caesonius, and Varinius were new men, and Cornificius was the son of a new man.[482]

We must not overlook men who were slightly ahead of Cicero in the *cursus* but who had not yet, by 64, attained a consulship. Out of our defective evidence emerge the names of notables whose subsequent disappearance we can no longer explain, be the cause an early death, personal misadventure, or want of ambition. One of Cicero's fellow quaestors was P. Cornelius Lentulus Marcellinus, a patrician who enjoyed early senatorial favour: he was sent to Cyrene in 75 as *quaestor pro praetore*, a signal honour.[483] Thereafter he vanishes from the record. Another of Cicero's colleagues in the quaestorship was P. Autronius Paetus (cos. desig. 65), by no means noble and possibly even a new man: late in arriving at the quaestorship, he was elected consul for 65 but subsequently condemned for *ambitus*.[484] M. Caecilius Metellus was praetor in 69, the same year in which his brother, Metellus Creticus, was consul.[485] P. Cornelius Dolabella and C. Licinius Macer were praetors in 69 or 68.[486] Neither of these Metelli nor Dolabella is attested afterwards. Macer, we know, died in 66. Among the praetors of 67 was the noble M. Junius, another evanescent presence in the *fasti*.[487]

In the year prior to Cicero's candidature, there were three noble aspirants to the consulship—L. Julius Caesar, C. Marcius Figulus, and D. Junius Silanus—as well as a new man, L. Turius (pr. 75).[488] In July of 65, Caesar's

---

[480] *MRR* 2.151–2.

[481] Because Caesonius was Cicero's colleague as plebeian aedile in 69, after which a *biennium* was required before he could hold the praetorship (so, correctly, Taylor 1939; *contra* StR 1.534–5), and, like Cicero, a legitimate candidate for the consulship in 63, he can only have been praetor, along with Cicero, in 66.

[482] Orchivius: Wiseman 1971, 247; Caesonius: Wiseman 1971, 219; Varinius: Wiseman 1971, 270; Cornificius the son of a new man: Wiseman 1971, 227.

[483] *MRR* 2.97; see Brennan 2000, 408–9.

[484] *MRR* 2.97, 157; Wiseman 1971, 105.   [485] *MRR* 2.131–2.

[486] Dolabella: *MRR* 2.132; 3.65. Macer: *MRR* 2.138. Macer's death: Val. Max. 9.12.7; Plut. *Cic.* 9.1–2.

[487] Brennan 2000, 449.

[488] Cic. *Att.* 1.1.2. That the Thermus referred to in Cicero's letter was in fact C. Marcius Figulus is by now generally agreed: see, e.g., Shackleton Bailey 1965, 292; Broughton 1991, 9–10; Ryan 1995, 307–8.

election seemed certain to Cicero, and he very much hoped that Marcius would also be returned since, if he were again a candidate in 64, he would be a formidable rival. No one, Cicero informed Atticus, believed Turius had a chance. In the end, Caesar was elected, as Cicero foresaw, along with Marcius. But, for all his advantages, Marcius was very nearly pipped to the post by the new man.[489] Despite this good showing, however, Turius did not stand again. Nor did Silanus stand again in 64 (he went on, however, to hold the consulship in 62). More names could doubtless be recovered, but this suffices to make it plain how advantageous it was to Cicero that, during his canvass, more than a few distinguished men were no longer on the scene as rivals for the consulship.

This degree of good fortune, however, should not distract from the reality that, after his brilliant success in the praetorian elections of 66, Cicero was unquestionably a front-runner in the race for a consulship in 63.[490] If not quite the cynosure of all eyes, he was now, by virtue of his office, a major figure in public affairs and bound to be an object of intense scrutiny. And the ambitious Cicero was determined to make the most of his new stature. For his province, he was assigned the *quaestio de repetundis*, the standing court that dealt with extortion by Roman magistrates and promagistrates, a welcome appointment that permitted Cicero to reside in Rome and continue to keep himself before the public.[491]

Early in 66, Cicero delivered his first public address (*contio*) in support of the proposal by C. Manilius (tr. pl. 66) to install Pompeius as supreme commander in the war against Mithridates.[492] Unlike the *lex Gabinia* of the previous year, which, in furnishing Pompeius with a special command against Mediterranean piracy, ignited fierce controversy,[493] Manilius' bill, though it met with token resistance, was certain to be carried. Consequently, for Cicero there was little chance of embarrassment in supporting it[494] and the debate offered him an opportunity to render public his very real desire to associate himself with the great man. Although not yet at the peak of his authority, Pompeius was already a glorious and glamorous figure in Roman society—and a politician possessed of enor-

---

[489] *MRR* 2.261. Turius' narrow loss: Cic. *Brut.* 237.

[490] Cic. *Mur.* 35 indicates that, in the view of many Romans, whoever topped the polls in the praetorian elections was deemed a likely success when he stood for consul.

[491] Cicero's province: *MRR* 2.152. *Quaestio de repetundis*: Cloud 1994, 505ff.; Lintott 1999a, 158ff.; Harries 2007, 61ff.; Capogrossi Colognesi 2014, 208ff.

[492] Manilius' proposal: *MRR* 2.153. Its military and political circumstances: Seager 2002, 49ff.; Steel 2013b, 147ff. Cicero's oration: Steel 2001, 114ff.; Lintott 2008, 427ff.

[493] *MRR* 2.144–5; Seager 2002, 40ff.; Steel 2013b, 147ff.

[494] The *contio* was a conspicuous gauge of popular favour (and so carried a very real risk of public failure): Morstein-Marx 2004, 120ff.

mous reserves of influence.[495] Many amid the nobility had already attached themselves to Pompeius' career, and so Cicero's effort to leap aboard this bandwagon, however obvious, was hardly exceptionable.[496] Which is not to say that Cicero could avoid giving at least some offence in making his case on Pompeius' behalf: although he was gracious to L. Licinius Lucullus (cos. 74), whom Pompeius was destined to replace under Manilius' measure, and Q. Lutatius Catulus (cos. 78), who led such opposition as the *lex Manilia* provoked, Cicero cannot have overlooked the reality that Pompeius' advancement came at a cost to others—and presumably he expected Pompeius to appreciate Cicero's willingness to risk their enmity on his behalf.[497] In his speech, Cicero also underlined how attractive Manilius' proposal was to equestrian interests, not least to the *publicani*, arrogating to himself the role of their spokesman in the matter.[498] So pleased was Cicero with his oration that he published it, promptly documenting the indebtedness of all parties who had a stake in Pompeius' eastern command.

It was an issue of a very different nature that prompted a second *contio* from Cicero.[499] Faustus Sulla, son of the dictator, was charged with peculation by an unknown tribune in a belated attempt to recover public wealth that had been misappropriated by the man's father. Resentment over the injustices of Sulla's regime, not least the horror of the proscriptions, remained heightened in the 60s, and it is obvious how this prosecution was intended to advance a programme of redress and retribution.[500] For many in the senatorial elite, whose primacy derived at least in part from the settlements of Sulla's dictatorship, such restorative justice was unappealing, nor was the programme's potential for destabilization attractive to every member of the propertied classes. In his speech, Cicero recognized the legitimacy of the concerns relevant to the tribune's action, but insisted that the time was not yet ripe for dispassionate justice—a delicate balance. The jury before whom Faustus Sulla's case was presented

---

[495] See ¶6 Gnaeus Pompeius.

[496] Public supporters of Manilius' bill included P. Servilius Vatia (cos. 79), C. Scribonius Curio (cos. 76), C. Cassius Longinus (cos. 73), and Cn. Lentulus Clodianus (cos. 72). Noble attachments to Pompeius' command against the pirates: Seager 2002, 47.

[497] In addition to Lucullus and Catulus, Cicero's posture threatened to put him at odds with Hortensius, Q. Marcius Rex (cos. 68), M'. Acilius Glabrio (cos. 67), and Q. Metellus Creticus (cos. 69); see Seager 2002, 50–1. See also ¶14 **angry with you…cases you have pleaded**.

[498] See esp. Cic. *Leg. Man.* 4, 11, 14–19.

[499] Asc. 73C; see Crawford 1984, 61ff.; Mitchell 1979, 156f.; Gelzer 1969a, 59; Tempest 2011, 88f.

[500] Redress and retribution: see ¶9 **citizen slaughter**.

agreed: they refused to hear it.[501] This episode thus illustrated Cicero's soundness—he championed the status quo but without alienating a less than entirely satisfied public—and could be adduced as evidence of his very real influence with the classes of men who dominated Rome's juries.[502]

It was vital for Cicero's prospects that he remain calculating, a disposition he reveals to us in his correspondence with Atticus. As president of the *quaestio de repetundis*, Cicero presided over the trial of the orator and historian C. Licinius Macer (pr. 68), who, despite a robust defence, was convicted (and thereafter died, probably by suicide).[503] From Cicero's perspective, however, this grim outcome was not a wholly unwelcome result:

> As for me here at Rome, my management of C. Macer's trial has won the public's approval—indeed incredibly and extraordinarily so. Although I treated him favourably, still, in terms of the goodwill of the people, I gained a far greater advantage from his conviction than I should have gained from his gratitude had he been acquitted.[504]

Now, as tribune in 73, Macer had championed the restoration of the tribunate, advocacy that ought to have attracted the goodwill of the people: Sallust provides Macer with an oration in which he savages the domination of the senate's oligarchs and claims Pompeius as his ally.[505] Through his even-handedness, however, Cicero avoided giving offence to any sections of the populace who continued to hold Macer's tribunate in high regard or who viewed him as a friend of Pompeius. At the same time, the result of the trial meant that, although he had earned a share of popular favour, he could not thereafter be associated with Macer's hostility towards the nobility (a danger for Cicero if somehow he came to be credited, or blamed, for Macer's acquittal).

Cicero did not, as praetor, ignore his forensic practice. His only certain case[506] in this year was his defence of A. Cluentius, a rich equestrian from Larinum. It was a sensational and lurid affair, featuring accusations of illicit sex and multiple murders in the remote Italian countryside and judicial corruption in Rome. Moreover, this trial's sordid background

---

[501] Cic. *Clu.* 94.

[502] See ¶8 classes that constitute the juries.

[503] On Macer, see *FRHist*, 1.320ff. His death: Val. Max. 9.12.7 (suicide); Plut. *Cic.* 9.1–2 (shock on learning that he had been convicted).

[504] Cic. *Att.* 1.4.2.

[505] Macer's tribunate: *MRR* 2.110. His speech in Sallust: Sall. *Hist.* 3.34 (McGushin). Macer's association with Pompeius may be no more than his own invention: Seager 2002, 35.

[506] The date of Cicero's defence of C. Fundanius (it was either 66 or 65) is uncertain: see ¶19 Gaius Fundanius. Similarly, it remains uncertain whether Cicero defended Q. Gallius in 66 or 63; see ¶19 Quintus Gallius.

threw up past instances of tribunician prosecutions and censorial disapprobation. All in all, these were proceedings too alluring to fail to seize the public's attention—and Cicero's speech was a spectacular success.[507] One of the orator's tactics in this case was his accumulation of delegations not merely from Larinum but from several districts surrounding it, Italian dignitaries whom Cicero displayed before the court by inviting them to stand while their testimonials were read aloud (a manner of presentation unparalleled in our sources).[508] There is no possibility of missing the forensic advantage of this striking novelty, but we should not overlook how the presence of these same delegations signalled the wide extent of Cicero's engagement in the world of municipal elites, important Italians from several different rural tribes.[509]

During the summer of 66, Cicero's brother won election to an aedileship for 65,[510] a proud accomplishment reflecting Cicero's continued popularity. Near the end of his year in office, however, and perhaps for the first time in his career, Cicero blundered. The tribune C. Manilius, immediately after laying down his office in early December, was charged with extortion, in reaction to which he asked the court for an adjournment of ten days. The request was routine, but Cicero allowed Manilius only one day's delay, apparently intending to initiate proceedings as soon as possible and thereby insulate himself from Manilius' defence either by rushing the case through or at least leaving its conduct in others' hands. This action, however, provoked popular outrage.[511]

Now, Manilius was an unsavoury figure, whose tribunate had been marred by constitutional irregularities and violence so extreme that the nobility, in the person of L. Domitius Ahenobarbus, had taken up arms against him, and the senate had declared one of his laws invalid.[512] However keen Cicero was about joining his name to Pompeius' cause, he calculated that there was little advantage to be got now from aiding Manilius, whom he deemed expendable. By contrast, Cicero had long been busy cultivating a close political relationship with the young but influential Domitius.[513] The public, however, saw matters otherwise: in their view, Manilius was Pompeius' friend and ally and his prosecution was an attack on Pompeius' reputation; consequently, Cicero was obliged

---

[507] Kirby 1990; Alexander 2002, 173ff.; Patimo 2009.

[508] The tactic: Cic. *Clu.* 197–8. Its novelty: Hall 2014, 87.

[509] Mitchell 1979, 103; Lomas 2004; Tempest 2011, 74ff.   [510] Cic. *Att.* 1.4.1.

[511] Plut. *Cic.* 9.4–7; Dio 36.44.1–2. For detailed discussion, see Phillips 1970; Ramsey 1980a; Crawford 1994, 33ff.; Lintott 2013, 146–7 (each with further bibliography).

[512] *MRR* 2.153. Conflict with L. Domitius Ahenobarbus (who was then quaestor): Asc. 45C.

[513] E.g. Cic. *Verr.* 2.1.139; *Att.* 1.1.3.

to exhibit his support for Pompeius by offering Manilius his every assistance.[514] These sentiments were put forward forcefully at an assembly summoned by the new tribunes,[515] at which Cicero endeavoured to explain away his treatment of Manilius, expressed his disapproval of the charges against the man, and promised to defend him in the coming year. It is not absolutely certain that he did so, however, owing to our inadequate accounts of Manilius' eventual trial in 65: the episode was marked by disorder so violent that it led to senatorial intervention and strict supervision by both consuls—all resulting in Manilius' condemnation.[516] What is certain is that, when he was confronted by Manilius' supporters in 66, Cicero gave a speech vigorously denouncing Pompeius' enemies.[517] And it is almost a certainty that Cicero published this speech,[518] so important was his public relationship with Pompeius, and hoped that by doing so he could make it plain to Manilius' senatorial adversaries where his true sympathies lay: not with the former tribune but with Rome's commander in the east.

4 Praetorian

Cicero found a far more congenial defendant in another ex-tribune hounded by Pompeius' enemies, C. Cornelius (tr. pl. 67).[519] He had once been Pompeius' quaestor and so remained closely associated with the great man. As tribune, he had been a genuine reformer, some of whose measures will have appealed to broad swaths of the propertied classes, not least Romans in the municipalities. But these same measures diminished the personal clout of the senatorial elite and so naturally were resented and even resisted by some in their number, men described by Asconius as *potentissimi*.[520] In one instance, Cornelius ignored a colleague's veto at an assembly that subsequently degenerated into violence, and although the issue between Cornelius and his senatorial opponents was ultimately settled by way of compromise, his action at the time was unquestionably

---

[514] Although Pompeius appears to have done little on Manilius' behalf (see Seager 2002, 64), it is clear that the Roman public expected Pompeius' allies to lend him their support.

[515] Cicero was also approached on Manilius' behalf by the praetor C. Attius Celsus (Asc. 65C), but it is unknown whether Celsus was praetor in 66 or 65.

[516] Dio 36.44.2; Asc. 60C, 66C; Schol. Bob. 119 (Stangl).   [517] Plut. *Cic.* 9.7.

[518] The arguments of Ramsey 1980a seem decisive, but Crawford 1994, 37–8, takes a different view; see, further, ¶51 **taken up the case of Manilius**.

[519] Cornelius' tribunate and his trial for *maiestas*: MRR 2.144; Griffin 1973; Crawford 1994, 67ff.; Seager 2002, 64f.; Lewis 2006, 261ff. See also ¶19 **Gaius Cornelius**.

[520] Asc. 58C.

actionable. Consequently, it was taken up by men hostile to Pompeius. Cornelius was prosecuted for treason (*maiestas*) in 66, but the hearing was so disrupted by gangs that the president of the court did not appear, the prosecutors fled, and order was restored only by the consuls—who were present on Cornelius' behalf. Thereafter the prosecutors let the matter drop. In the aftermath of Manilius' conviction, however, these same prosecutors revived their case against Cornelius, now defended by Cicero, who doubtless intended to burnish his credentials with Pompeius, Pompeius' admirers, and Romans who valued responsible tribunician reform. Indeed, Cicero turned his defence of Cornelius into a vindication of the very institution of the tribunate.

Little is actually known of Cornelius, but he was certainly a member of a *sodalitas* that possessed influence at Roman elections.[521] In other words, although never himself destined for high office, Cornelius was a figure who could, through his network of associations, offer consequential support—or opposition—to the electoral ambitions of others. Cicero, then, had more than one good reason to accept Cornelius' case.

The prosecution was backed by Pompeius' most powerful enemies, Hortensius, Q. Catulus, Metellus Pius (cos. 80), and Mam. Aemilius Lepidus (cos. 77). But Cornelius benefited from a vast array of sympathizers: the ex-tribunes of 67, including the man whose veto Cornelius had ignored; the consuls of 66 (again); the equestrian members of the jury; and such senators on the jury who were not obliged to the faction prosecuting Cornelius.[522] Asconius explains this degree of support largely in terms of Cornelius' ties to Pompeius, but one should not discount a genuine appreciation for Cornelius' service as tribune.

The trial lasted four days, attracted large crowds, and, although the case was well argued on both sides,[523] Cicero's victory was overwhelming:[524] his oratory was answered by storms of applause on the part of the public.[525] He will not have been unduly worried that, in scoring this triumph, he had unavoidably upset some of Pompeius' enemies.[526]

Now it is sometimes alleged that, in his forensic oratory, Cicero promulgated his position on current issues and, in doing so, even if he had little influence on political events, managed nonetheless to fashion a recognizable political identity.[527] But this view is hard to sustain. It is true that, in defending an otherwise unknown woman from Arretium, Cicero argued—

---

[521] See ¶19 Gaius Cornelius; ¶19 religious fraternities.   [522] Asc. 61C.
[523] One of Cornelius' prosecutors also published a speech from this trial: Asc. 61C.
[524] Asc. 81C.   [525] Quint. 8.3.3–5.
[526] Cic. *Vat.* 5–6; see ¶14 angry with you…cases you have pleaded.
[527] E.g. Vasaly 2009; Vasaly 2013.

during Sulla's lifetime—against the legality of Sulla's disenfranchisement of that city, just as he would later, in his defence of Caecina, challenge the dictator's treatment of Volaterrae. In these speeches, Cicero involved himself in a very real political controversy. In each of these cases, however, Sulla's legislation was pertinent to Cicero's defence and was therefore a topic he could hardly escape addressing. In his *Pro Sexto Roscio Amerino* (*Defence of Sextus Roscius*), Cicero asserted explicitly that he would speak *de re publica*,[528] but, in reality, he didn't, and this speech's loud complaints about the iniquities of the Sullan regime are almost certainly the result of later revision.[529] Not even in his prosecution of Verres, neither in the speech he delivered nor in the extended fiction of his Second Action, can one detect anything in the way of political self-definition, apart from the orator's unsurprising preference for honest juries and probity in provincial administration. Naturally enough, Cicero seized every opportunity to advertise his personal importance and his soundness: again and again, Cicero identifies his cases with serious matters—the proscriptions, the rights of citizens, imperial responsibilities—and exhibits himself as an ardent champion of normative values, nothing of which constituted a political manifesto.[530] Quite the contrary: Roman audiences appreciated the tactical requirements of forensic oratory. After all, whereas political speeches were intended to sway the public or the senate to take action, speeches in the courtroom sought the conviction or acquittal of an individual, no less but also no more.[531]

This is not to insist that Cicero held no political views or held himself aloof from senatorial deliberations. As an ex-praetor and consequently a leading man in the senate, he could not avoid expressing opinions on important matters and taking sides in senatorial divisions. One might, however, get a very different impression from Cicero himself. In his speech *Pro Sulla* (*Defence of Sulla*), which Cicero delivered in 62, he described the priorities of his praetorship in this way: 'I was not at the time immersed in political affairs because I had not yet attained the goal of high office I had set myself, because my ambition for office and my forensic labours kept

---

[528] Cic. *Rosc. Am.* 2.   [529] Berry 2003.

[530] Hölkeskamp 2011c; Steel 2013a; See the balanced discussion by Riggsby 1999, 151ff. Cicero's own distinction between politics per se and civic exertion by way of the courts is illuminating. Writing to Atticus in 59, a time when he felt menaced by Clodius, Cicero describes his efforts at increasing his popular support in this way: 'I take no part in politics and instead devote all my energies to my cases and pleading them in the forum, which I believe is the best means for winning favour not only from those who benefit from my services but also the wider public' (*Att.* 2.22.3).

[531] See the important discussion by Jehne 2000, 173ff.

me from thinking about any matters of state.'[532] Here Cicero appears to confess that, before his election to the consulship, he was too preoccupied with his own elevation to be bothered with issues of state. But this is to take the passage out of its context, where, as D.H. Berry has demonstrated, it is a specimen of irony.[533] Certainly, in 65 Cicero rose in the senate to speak against the plans of no less a figure than M. Crassus, who was censor in that year and who hoped to persuade the senate to annex Egypt. Crassus' designs disintegrated, and Cicero advertised his part in foiling Crassus' ambitions by immediately publishing his speech.[534] These were hardly the actions of a senator aloof from the affairs of state.

5 Candidate

By 65 Cicero was busy bending his mind and energies toward his campaign for the consulship. A letter written to Atticus not long before 17 July 65 affords a precious glimpse into his early preparations.[535] By this point, although several individuals, including, of course, Cicero, had made clear their interest in standing for the consulship of 63, only one had begun an earnest solicitation of voters—what the Romans denominated as *prensatio* ('glad-handing'): this was the noble P. Servilius Galba (pr. by 66). Cicero relishes reporting the rebuffs he experienced, unvarnished rejections that were unexpected in view of the man's status, even if his family's best days were behind it. There was nothing objectionable about Galba: he is in fact described in highly positive terms by Cicero and Asconius;[536] he held a priesthood and enjoyed the cachet of patrician status. Plainly, however, he was deficient in *something*—lineage was not everything[537]—and in Cicero's later estimation what Galba lacked was *gratia*,[538] whereas the *Brief Handbook* criticizes him for a lack of vigour (¶8). Or perhaps he was being penalized for bungling: Cicero describes Galba's exertions as a *praepropera prensatio*, 'premature glad-handing'.[539]

Galba's importunate campaigning, however, was a positive fillip to Cicero's prospects because so many who declined to endorse Galba did so on the grounds that they were obligated not to Catilina, his patrician rival, but instead to Cicero.[540] This answer may have been disingenuous, since

---

[532] Cic. *Sull.* 11.   [533] Berry 1996, 153f.

[534] Testimonia and discussion in Crawford 1994, 43ff.   [535] Cic. *Att.* 1.1.

[536] Cic. *Mur.* 17; Asc. 82C.   [537] See Cic. *Planc.* 18.   [538] Cic. *Mur.* 17.

[539] Cic. *Att.* 1.1.1. Although there were no explicit regulations, there was clearly an expectation that candidates would commence campaigning neither too early nor too late: Cic. *Fam.* 10.25.2.

[540] The *lex Licinia Sextia* of 367 stipulated that no more than one of the two consuls elected each year could be a patrician; see Liv. 6.35.5; *MRR* 1.109, 114; Oakley 1997, 652ff.

there was nothing to prevent anyone from supporting two candidates—or no candidates—for the consulship, but in any case Cicero took it as a promising sign: 'I hope to gain some advantage as it becomes widely known how many friends of mine there are to be found'.[541] Even before launching himself a candidate, then, Cicero could see distinctly positive signs for his candidature. Cicero decided to commence his own *prensatio* at the tribunician elections on 17 July, by which time, presumably, voters could be expected to have made up their minds about the current elections, leaving it clear and fair for the next year's slate of candidates to initiate their solicitations. Cicero goes on to tell Atticus that he will exhibit all due diligence in carrying out a candidate's every responsibility (*nos in omni munere candidatorio fungendo summam adhibebimus diligentiam*).[542] Everything to form, then, and nothing taken for granted. Exactly the correct posture for a new man who had apparently already surpassed one noble rival.

Cicero admitted to Atticus that nothing now mattered more to him than his canvass, during which he was determined to expand his already ample supply of *gratia*.[543] With that in mind, he was soon fretting about certain antagonistic nobles with whom he hoped Atticus had influence that could be put to work on his behalf.[544] This is not to suggest that Cicero was unstocked with noble supporters: C. Calpurnius Piso (cos. 67), for instance, then governor of Cisalpine Gaul, offered Cicero a legateship so that he could (doubtless with Piso's endorsement) solicit supporters there.[545] And Cicero emphasizes the enthusiasm displayed for him by the influential young noble, L. Domitius Ahenobarbus (cos. 54).[546] One noble whose support Cicero constantly trumpeted throughout his campaign, even to the point of exaggeration, was Pompeius.[547] Pompeius' backing had been assiduously cultivated by Cicero, as we have seen, even if doing so had entailed some political risks, as we have also seen (see §VII.3). One of the reasons for the prominence Cicero accords Domitius' support, it has been suggested, lay in the fact that he was not a friend or ally of

---

[541] *Att.* 1.1.1. See ¶16 the definition of the word 'friend'. The difficulties afflicting one candidate's canvass did not automatically work to the advantage of other candidates: Cic. *Fam.* 8.3.1.

[542] Cic. *Att.* 1.1.2. On *diligentia* and its importance in the *Brief Handbook*, see ¶1 assiduousness.

[543] Cic. *Att.* 1.1.4.   [544] Cic. *Att.* 1.1.2; 1.2.2.

[545] Cic. *Att.* 1.1.2. Cisalpine Gaul, in which multiple tribes were represented, was apparently teeming with citizens substantial enough to travel to Rome for the elections (Cic. *Q. Fr.* 2.3.4; *Phil.* 2.76; Hirtius *B.Gall.* 8.50); it appears from Cic. *Phil.* 2.76 that Cicero did, in fact, take Piso up on his offer, nor was he the last to canvass profitably in this region; see Taylor 1960, 126ff.

[546] Cic. *Att.* 1.1.3–4.   [547] ¶5 Gnaeus Pompeius; ¶¶14, 51; see §VII.3–4.

Pompeius. Quite the reverse. For this reason, his endorsement of Cicero's candidature can only have enhanced Cicero's appeal, even to members of the nobility who were displeased by his past exertions on Pompeius' behalf.[548] In the end, Cicero's campaign was successful: the nobility supported him.[549]

At this stage, Cicero was confident that, in addition to the unfortunate Galba, he would also face C. Antonius Hybrida (cos. 63) and Q. Cornificius (pr. by 66). Catilina, too. Other names had also been raised—M. Caesonius, C. Aquillius Gallus (pr. 66), T. Aufidius (pr. 67 or 66), and M. Lollius Palicanus (pr. 69)—but Cicero had a low estimation of their prospects.[550] Now, Cornificius derived from a family that was new to the senate, and only a little grander than Cicero's.[551] He was an upright figure,[552] but Cicero expects Atticus to agree with him that Cornificius has little chance of securing election. M. Caesonius was very probably a new man; Palicanus and Aufidius were certainly new men.[553] None of these stimulates wariness on Cicero's part. Aquillius, by contrast, was of praetorian stock and a distinguished jurist, but he had already begun to make it clear he would not stand.[554] It is perhaps remarkable that so many new men felt it worthwhile to test the waters in 64. Still, in despising their chances of winning, Cicero affirms the reality of the electorate's prejudice against new men.

Aquillius, Aufidius, Caesonius, and Palicanus all dropped out. Galba and Cornificius persisted in a field that was enlarged by the candidatures of L. Cassius Longinus (pr. by 66) and C. Licinius Sacerdos (pr. 75). Like Cornificius, Sacerdos came from a family of recent senatorial standing.[555] And, like Cornificius, he is described by Asconius in complimentary terms.[556] It is far from obvious why, quite late in his career and a decade after his praetorship, he elected to stand for a consulship.[557] Perhaps during his recent service in Crete as a legate to Metellus Creticus (cos. 69) he had won some distinction by which he hoped to profit. We know that Sacerdos was with Metellus in 68 and 67: did he remain to return to Rome

---

[548] On this point, see Seager 2002, 66f.   [549] Sall. *Cat.* 23.6.

[550] Cic. *Att.* 1.1.1. See, further, ¶8 **Antonius**; ¶8 **Catilina**. Cornificius, Caesonius, Aquillius, Aufidius, and Lollius Palicanus go unmentioned in the *Brief Handbook*.

[551] Wiseman 1971, 227.   [552] Asc. 82C.

[553] Wiseman 1971, 219 (Caesonius); 237–8 (Palicanus). On Aufidius, see Nicolet 1974, 794–5 (Wiseman omits him but collects his brother, M. Vergilius (tr. pl. 87)); cf. Wiseman 1971, 272.

[554] Aquillius descended from L. Aquillius Gallus (pr. 176). His eminence as a jurist: Frier 1985, 140ff.

[555] Wiseman 1971, 237.   [556] Asc. 82C.

[557] His decision was not without parallel: e.g. L. Gellius Publicola, praetor in 94, was elected consul for 72; Serv. Sulpicius Rufus, praetor in 65, became consul in 51.

with Metellus (in 65 or 64)? Or did he hope to take advantage of the presence of Metellus' troops, on whose support he believed he could rely, upon their return to the city? Years later, speaking of Sacerdos as legate in Crete, Cicero described him, admittedly for tactical purposes, in admirable terms (*in ea provincia fuit C. Sacerdos: qua virtute, qua constantia vir!*).[558] Whatever spurred his ambition in 64, he did not emerge as a serious contender (he is overlooked in the *Brief Handbook*). As for Longinus, his nobility was splendid and consequently he could only be deemed a real threat, even if he was fat[559] and stupid.[560] Nonetheless, in all this crowded field, the rivals to Cicero who appeared most dangerous were Antonius and Catilina, as the *Brief Handbook* observed (§8).[561]

Antonius was the son of a great man, whom Cicero much admired: M. Antonius celebrated a triumph in 100, was consul in 99, and censor in 97. He was also a distinguished orator who plays a central role in Cicero's *De oratore*.[562] It was this man who ennobled the Antonii, and his son inherited his father's splendour. Not, however, his talent, and in 70 Gaius Antonius, in what was admittedly a severe census, was ejected from the senate. He returned to public life as tribune of the *plebs* in 68 and in 66 was elected praetor—with Cicero's endorsement. As *praetor urbanus* Antonius produced lavish games that brought him abundant, even, according to Cicero, intimidating popularity.[563] Catilina, unlike Antonius, derived from an ancient, though in recent generations undistinguished, family. He was a man of profound personal charm and real ability, as even Cicero conceded,[564] and he profited from his extensive circle of influential friends. His career was proof of his military courage, even if it was mostly exhibited under the baleful conditions of civil war. In his administration of Africa, however, Catilina blotted his record: in 65 he was tried for extortion but acquitted owing to the exertions of his eminent allies. His disrepute was by no means dispelled, however, and in 64 a fresh prosecution was brought. Again, he was acquitted, again owing to his consular connections.[565]

Both men were formidable rivals, not least Antonius, who very likely belonged to the same tribe as Cicero, a circumstance that could only

---

[558] Cic. *Planc.* 27.   [559] Cic. *Cat.* 3.16.

[560] Asc. 82C. See §7 **Lucius Cassius**.   [561] See Asc. 82–83C.

[562] Scholz 1963. The evidence for Antonius' career, forensic and political, is assembled at *ORF*⁴ 221–37; *MRR* 1.563, 539, 576, 568, 572; 2.16–17; 3.19. Cicero's admiration: Blom 2010, 226–30.

[563] *MRR* 2.126–7, 141, 151–2; see, further, §8.   [564] Cic. *Cael.* 10–14.

[565] *MRR* 2.72, 138, 147, 155. Catilina on trial: Alexander 1990, 106, 108–9, 111, 178. For a concise and useful summary of Catilina's life and career, see Levick 2015. See also §8.

intensify their competition for supporters.[566] Which is why, when Catilina was indicted in 65, Cicero came very close to defending him, in the hope that the patrician might thereafter show himself accommodating, even cooperative, during Cicero's canvass.[567] This scheme fell through, however, and in the end Catilina joined with Antonius in an electoral alliance (what Romans called a *coitio*) against Cicero,[568] a tactic that in retrospect reveals Cicero's real advantages in this race but which, at the time, the orator can only have viewed as a steep obstacle.[569]

Asconius tells us that Crassus and Caesar also worked against Cicero's interests, information that he discovered in Cicero's *Expositio consiliorum suorum*, a late and bitter work, keener on settling old scores than furnishing an accurate account of Cicero's career.[570] Nevertheless, Crassus had good reasons for opposing Cicero's candidature: his Egyptian policy had been stymied in the senate by Ciceronian oratory, and Cicero was in any case positioning himself as an ally of Crassus' chief rival, Pompeius. Crassus' influence was substantial, and, if he campaigned against Cicero, it is very possible that so, too, did his young friend Caesar.[571] They will not have been the only aristocrats who preferred Catilina or Antonius to Cicero, and the contest between these three men, its narrow result makes clear, was a close one.

Whatever positive claims they put forward during their campaigning— Antonius' supporters surely touted his praetorian games, while Catilina's celebrated his courage (see ¶9 **greater courage**)—Cicero's rivals cannot have surprised anyone by emphasizing their nobility at the expense of his *novitas*.[572] However unimaginative this contrast, it was a potent one: hence the lengthy disquisition on Cicero's condition as a (remarkable) new man in the *Brief Handbook* (¶¶2–7, 11–15). It was not enough, then, for Cicero to remind voters of his past services and present excellence:

---

[566] Mark Antony belonged, like Cicero, to the Cornelian tribe: *MAMA* 6.104; it is highly likely, though not a certainty, that C. Antonius was also a member of the Cornelian tribe.

[567] Cic. *Att.* 1.2.1; see Asc. 85C.   [568] Asc. 83C.

[569] *Coitio*, although not an illegal practice (Cic. Q. *Fr.* 3.1.16; Hall 1964, 301–2), was certainly an exceptionable one (e.g. Cic. *Parad.* 46; see Meier 1980, 178–80; Bauerle 1990, 93–100; Feig Vishnia 2012, 117–19). Antonius' and Catilina's combination came about as a consequence of Cicero's position as a front-runner.

[570] Asc. 83C; see Lewis 2006, 292; Tatum 2011, 180–1; *FRHist* 1.376–9.

[571] If so, at least in terms of canvassing within his own tribe, the Fabian, Caesar will have had to contend with the pro-Ciceronian endeavours of Domitius Ahenobarbus, who was a member of the same tribe. Crassus was closely connected with electoral *sodalitates*: Dio 37.54.3.

[572] Asc. 86C, 93–94C; App. *B.Civ.* 2.2; Sall. *Cat.* 35.2; Quint. 9.3.94; Schol. Bob. 80 (Stangl). They may also have attempted to portray Cicero as a new man who was also an extreme *popularis*: see ¶5 **champions of popular rights**.

he was obliged, like his competitors, to go negative. The *Brief Handbook*, like Cicero's speech *In toga candida*, teems with invective, vicious and vitriolic—but mostly conventional (¶¶8–10; Asc. 83–93C). At the same time, Cicero was able to fold into the abuse of his rivals cunning accusations that did more than degrade or embarrass them: Cicero activated certain very real anxieties permeating the city in 64.

We turn, then, to the political circumstances in which Cicero operated as a candidate. It was a disquieting time, not least on account of economic difficulties both in the city itself and throughout Italy.[573] Credit had become scarce, and indebtedness, already severe, was worsened—to the point that, in 63, there were tribunician demands for debt reform and land distributions, insurrection in Etruria, worrisome instability elsewhere in Italy, and, infamously, the Catilinarian conspiracy in Rome, all fuelled by economic embarrassment. Indeed, Catilina and his confederates went so far that year as to incite rebellion on the part of ruined men in the province of Transalpine Gaul.[574] That, too, took place in 63, but these ills had long been festering.[575]

The urban poor were also dissatisfied and, as a consequence, susceptible, in the view of their betters, to manipulation by unsavoury members of the political elite. Hence in 64 the senate's suppression of numerous *collegia*, deemed potential media for corruption or violence, even if this expression of senatorial authority offended the city's masses.[576] Public confidence had been shaken in 66, when the consuls-designate were sensationally condemned on charges of electoral bribery. Nor had public confidence been bolstered in 65, when quarrelling censors failed to complete their work, or in the subsequent year when contentiousness between censors and tribunes led to the same unsatisfactory result.[577] The conditions of Cicero's canvass, unmistakably, were disturbing, and in such an atmosphere it was only natural that questions of integrity and competence should be brought to the fore. These were concerns that put Cicero in his best light, which meant that there were advantages for him in exacerbating Rome's anxieties—if he could put them to work in eroding the voters' faith in the soundness or suitability of Catilina or Antonius.

In his forensic oratory, Cicero routinely favoured the fabrication of invisible but influential forces scheming against justice, by which he

---

[573] Frederiksen 1966; Kay 2014, 257–9.

[574] Wiseman, 1994, 346ff.; Dyck 2008, 4ff.; Lintott 2008, 136ff.; Steel 2013b, 150ff. (each with further bibliography).

[575] See Cic. *Leg. agr.* 2.8 on the disturbing conditions in Rome at the beginning of 63, significant even if exaggerated.

[576] Cic. *Pis.* 8; Asc. 7C; Tatum 1999, 117ff.; Lewis 2006, 200. See ¶3 clubs.

[577] *MRR* 2.157, 161.

meant scheming against Cicero.[578] This device was apt to his purposes as a candidate. In his *In toga candida* Cicero imputed to his rivals, in vague but unmistakable terms, involvement in various intrigues against the established order: in the case of Catilina, Cicero declared that he had once plotted to murder Rome's leading men (*caedem optimatum facere voluisti*)[579]—perhaps the earliest installation in the sequence of stories that later yielded the fictitious First Catilinarian Conspiracy. Subversion was in fact the last thing desired or intended by either Catilina or Antonius in 64, but uncertain circumstances invite conspiracy theories, an invitation Cicero was disinclined to disappoint.[580] That Catilina was a dangerous man was a point Cicero and the *Brief Handbook* hammered home by reminding voters of his past participation in the Sullan proscriptions.[581] There is no reason to suppose that Cicero's insinuations along these lines originated in his speech: doubtless they were continually voiced, in the manner of modern talking points, by the candidate and his supporters.

In the same way, Cicero's campaign insinuated that Catilina and Antonius were engaging in illicit bribery, an accusation to which any *coitio* was vulnerable owing to the association Romans tended to make between electoral alliances and *ambitus*.[582] And yet it was a bold claim on Cicero's part: new men, not nobles, were frequent targets of accusations of *ambitus*, especially when a noble was defeated by a new man.[583] But Cicero was somehow able, by exploiting contemporary fretting over corruption and conspiracy, to incite the Roman senate's natural moralizing tendencies, which in turn led to fresh demands for legislation *de ambitu*. In view of his reputation for probity, Cicero doubtless hoped that these demands might serve to underline and lend credibility to his attacks on his rivals, especially if Antonius and Catilina challenged the idea of new measures against electoral bribery. And this is what happened. The controversy over *ambitus* gained traction, and only a few days before the election the senate attempted to clear the way for the promulgation of a law on electoral bribery.

---

[578] Cic. *Off.* 2.51.   [579] Asc. 92C.

[580] Asc. 92C; ¶10: 'the fear he provokes'. On the origins of the fiction of the First Catilinarian conspiracy, see Seager 1964 (with full testimonia); Levick 2015, 35ff.

[581] ¶9 **citizen slaughter**.

[582] ¶¶54–7; Asc. 83, 88C. *Coitio* and *ambitus*: Staveley 1972, 205f.; Bauerle 1990, 93ff. On accusations of corruption and their deployment in Roman politics, see Mouritsen 2001, 93; Rosillo López 2016.

[583] More than one noble argued that only criminal activity could explain his electoral defeat by a new man: e.g. Cic. *Mur.* 15; *Planc.* 6, 12, 14–15, 17, and *passim*. At *Clu.* 69, Cicero insinuates that the new man C. Staienus (q. 77) needed large sums of money in order to succeed in winning election to the aedileship.

Now, in fact, this was a technical and far from straightforward matter. In order to put forward a bill on *ambitus*, the senate had first to postpone the elections, for a matter of weeks, and such postponements, which affected all candidates for all offices, inevitably posed difficulties for everyone involved in the elections. It was almost certainly on this basis that the senate's decree was vetoed by the tribune Q. Mucius Orestinus.[584] Orestinus, however, was almost certainly a relation of Catilina and was without question his partisan and an opponent of Cicero.[585] This was the occasion of Cicero's *In toga candida*, a speech the searing moralizing of which evaporated any nuances advanced by the orator's opponents, whom he savaged with blistering invective. Cicero's speech was by no means spontaneous, and it was instantly made available to the Roman public, who could relish Cicero's denunciation of the dark and subversive forces behind Orestinus' repudiation of the senate's will.[586] Orestinus' veto, and all that it could be meant to signal to the voters, will also have been seized upon by all Cicero's supporters in order to sully his opponents' reputations even further during the crucial last days before polling took place. Both the *Brief Handbook* and *In toga candida* warn voters against, in one vote, drawing two daggers against the republic (¶13),[587] which must have been the veritable slogan of Cicero's campaign: in this way, Cicero managed to concentrate his invective against his opponents—much of it typical abuse along the lines of personal immorality, past political malfeasance, violence, greed, and financial ruin—into negatives of a different order, vices that fed into contemporary fears over social stability. It would be a mistake to exaggerate the effectiveness of Cicero's inculpations—after all, Antonius was elected and Catilina only just fell short—but it is clear that, during his canvass, Cicero found methods that effectively neutralized the efficacy of the public's prejudice against *novitas*.

It was not Cicero's negative campaigning that made him consul. His final success was the culmination of a career marked by brilliant oratory, sound political opinions, genuine if not uncompromising rectitude, and the assiduous accumulation of gratitude at every opportunity. Still, the canvass, because it was the last stage of any campaign for office, remained the crucial stage. Cicero prepared for his consular canvass at the very least from the moment he was elected praetor. His progress from praetor to consul was not flawless, but it was nimble and adroit—and characterized

---

[584] On these matters, see, more fully, Tatum 2013, 148f.

[585] Orestinus was probably related to Catilina's wife: Shackleton Bailey 1976, 122–3. His veto was motivated by his support of Catilina (Asc. 86C).

[586] On the importance of this speech in Cicero's campaign, see, further, Tatum 2013, 147ff.

[587] Asc. 93C.

by an insightful apprehension of his immediate political circumstances and their immediate requirements. His achievement—he was the first new man to reach the consulship in at least twenty years and the first to do so *suo anno* since Q. Pompeius in 141—was an undeniably glorious one.[588]

VIII TEXT AND TRANSLATION

The Latin text is that supplied by Watt 1958a, who cites prior editions; the translation is based solely on this text. Any doubts or disagreements concerning Watt's text are expressed in the commentary, where alternative translations are furnished. Since the publication of Watt's edition, Nardo 1972, Shackleton Bailey 1988, and Shackleton Bailey 2002 (with English translation) have appeared. Each is a useful critical edition. The best and most concise discussion of the manuscript tradition of the *Brief Handbook* remains Watt 1958b, though Watt 1958a, 79ff. is also important. Nardo 1972, 7ff. is helpful in furnishing details missing from Watt 1958a and 1958b; he also includes a very full bibliography of prior work on the text of the *Brief Handbook*.

For readers who will make use of Watt's Latin text, I have supplied, in Appendix B an explanation of the abbreviations and references employed by him in his critical apparatus. I have introduced one important change. In his apparatus, Watt routinely made cross-references to other passages in the *Brief Handbook* by citing the page numbers in his edition. Because those page numbers will mean nothing in this edition, I have replaced them with specific chapter references. For example, instead of Watt's '*cf. p.* 193.11', which indicates line 11 on page 193 of his edition, the reader will now find '*cf.* ¶3.11', which indicates ¶3 of the *Brief Handbook*, line 11 on the page of the pertinent Latin text.

APPENDIX A: ROMAN NOMENCLATURE

During the republic, Roman personal names, in their fullest expression, included as many as six elements. M. Cicero was, when denominated fully and officially, M. Tullius M. f. M. n. Cor. Cicero (Marcus Tullius, son of Marcus, grandson of Marcus, of the tribe Cornelia, Cicero): 'Marcus', the first name (*praenomen*) corresponds with our category of given names;

---

[588] On new men in the consulship prior to Cicero, see ¶11 **Gaius Coelius**.

'Tullius' is the *nomen*, or hereditary name of Cicero's clan (*gens*); 'M. f.' abbreviates 'son of Marcus', which indicates the *praenomen* of Cicero's father (the remainder of whose name can then be inferred from his son's name); similarly, 'M. n.' abbreviates 'grandson of Marcus'; 'Cornelia' indicates to which of Rome's thirty-five tribes Cicero belonged; 'Cicero' is Cicero's *cognomen* which was originally an unofficial nickname given to an individual that some families (Cicero's is an example) elected to preserve (see Plut. *Cic.* 1.3–5 for the origins of Cicero's *cognomen*). Quintus' complete name was Q. Tullius M. f. M. n. Cor. Cicero. The habits of Roman nomenclature, never entirely static, changed in important ways during the imperial period (see Salway 1994, 124ff.).

Reference to another Roman by a single name can indicate informality, familiarity, or contempt (see Adams 1978, 145f., 161; Dickey 2002, 36ff.). An example of this is Cic. *Phil.* 13.22, where Cicero castigates Mark Antony for omitting his addressees' offices—Antony had written simply 'Antony to Hirtius and Caesar'—in a public letter in which he clearly intended to convey contempt. Quintus' salutation to Cicero at the commencement of the *Brief Handbook* obviously indicates informality and familiarity. At ¶8, however, Antonius, Catilina, Sabidius, and Panthera are each of them referred to by a single name, probably in order to register contempt. The reference to L. Cornelius Sulla (on whom see ¶9 **Sulla**) is a different matter. Quintus conforms to Ciceronian practice by referring to Sulla by this single name only: in his correspondence, Cicero refers only to 'Sulla', although, in his essays, he sometimes prefers 'Lucius Sulla' (*Off.* 1.43, 109; 3.87; *Brut.* 179, 227). Sulla's singular stature in the decades after his dictatorship renders him a special case.

Outside formal contexts that require the *nomen*, the regular Ciceronian practice (which can be assumed to be typical of republican practices) is to refer to living members of the nobility by *praenomen* and *cognomen*, the individual's distinguished *nomen* being too obvious to require mention (see Syme 1979, 361ff.). There is no clearly consistent practice for families outside the nobility (see Shackleton Bailey 1995, 2ff.). Quintus adheres to the same practices as Cicero: see, e.g., the names expressed at ¶¶5 and 7.

APPENDIX B: ABBREVIATIONS AND REFERENCES IN WATT'S CRITICAL APPARATUS

The following list of abbreviations and references is furnished for readers who wish to consult the critical apparatus of Watt's Latin text. Any texts that also appear in the Bibliography of this commentary (pp. 291ff.) are

cited here solely by author and year of publication; others are cited by way
of the short form that appears in the List of Abbreviations (pp. xiiif.).

Angelius	Angelius, N. 1515. *Orationes M. Tulli Ciceronis.* Lyon, fols. 423–30.
Baehrens[1]	Baehrens, E. 1872. 'Kritische Satura', *Neue Jahrbücher für Philologie* 105: 45–6.
Baehrens[2]	Baehrens 1878, 27.
Baiter[1]	see Or.[2] below
Baiter[2]	Baiter, J.G. 1860–9. *M. Tulli Ciceronis opera quae supersunt.* Leipzig.
Buech.	Buecheler 1869.
Constans	Constans, L.A. 1934–6. *Cicéron, Correspondance,* 3 vols. Paris.
Constans[1]	Constans, L.A. 1933. 'Tulliana: Observations critiques sur quelques letters de Cicéron', *REL* 11: 129–52.
Corradus[2]	Corradus, S. 1555. *Egnatius sive Quaestura.* Bologna.
Ernesti	Ernesti, J.A. 1774–7. *M. Tulli Ciceronis opera omnia.* Halle.
Eussner	Eussner 1872.
Facciolati	Facciolati 1732.
Gesner	Gesner, J.M. 1745. *Enchiridion.* Göttingen, 28–57.
Gruter	Gruter, J. 1618.
Gulielmius	Gulielmius, I., emendations recorded in Gruter.
Hendrickson	Hendrickson 1904.
Hoffa	Hoffa, J. 1837. *De petitione consulatus ad M. Tullium fratrem liber.* Leipzig.
Kaibel, Com. Graec. Fragm.	Kaibel, G. 1899. *Comicorum Graecorum Fragmenta.* Berlin.
Klotz	Klotz, R. 1853–4/1869–70. *M. Tulli Ciceronis scripta quae manserunt omnia.* Leipzig.
Koch[1]	Koch, H.A. 1868. *Coniectanea Tulliana.* Naumburg, 33–5.
Koch[2]	Koch, H.A. 1863. *Philologische Anzeiger* 5: 162.
Lamb.	Lambinus, D. 1565–6. *M. Tulli Ciceronis opera omnia quae exstant.* Paris.
L.–H.	*LHS.*

Malaespina	Malaespina, L. 1564. *In epistolas ad Atticum, Brutum, et Q. fratrem emendationes ac suspiciones.* Venice.
Man.	Manutius, P. 1541. *Ciceronis De philosophia*, vol. 2. Venice, 205–14.
Mommsen, *Röm. Staatsr.* iii	*StR.*
Mueller[1]	Mueller, C.F.W. 1860. *Coniecturae Tullianae.* Königsberg.
Muretus	Muretus, M.A. 1559. *Variae lectiones.* Venice.
Or.[1]	Orelli, J.C. 1826–31. *Tulli Ciceronis opera omnia quae supersunt.* Zurich.
Or.[2]	Orelli, J.C., Baiter, J.G., and Halm, C. 1845–63. *M. Tulli Ciceronis opera omnia quae supersunt.* Zürich.
Palermus	Palermus, V. 1583. *In M. Tullii Ciceronis De Philosophia volumen secundum Aldi Mannuccii commentarius, In Q. Ciceronis de petitione consulatus ad M. Tullium fratrem librum Valerii Palermi Veronensis commentarius.* Verona.
Petreius	Petreius, R. 1564. *Epistulae duae.* Paris.
Purser	Purser, L.C. 1902. *M. Tulli Ciceronis Epistulae,* vol 3. Oxford.
Puteanus	Puteanus, C., emendations recorded in Gruter.
Rom.	1471. *Ciceronis philosophicorum editio Romana.* Rome.
Schoell	Schoell, F. 1918. *Ciceronis orationum deperditarum fragmenta.* Leipzig.
Schültz	Schültz, C.G. 1809–10. *M. Tulli Ciceronis Epistolae ad Atticum, ad Quintum fratrem, et quae vulgo ad familiares, dicuntur.* Halle.
Schwarz	Schwarz 1720.
Sedgwick	Sedgwick, W.B. (personal correspondence with W.S. Watt)
Sj.	Sjögren, H. 1914. *M. Tulli Ciceronis scripta quae manserunt omnia*, fasc. 38. Leipzig.
Sj.[1]	Sjögren 1913.
Squ.	Squarzaficus, J. 1485. *Ciceronis Rhetorica.* Venice, fols. 188–91.
Stangl	Stangl, T. 1912. *Ciceronis orationum scholiastae.* Vienna and Leipzig.

Sternkopf	Sternkopf, W. 1904. *Berliner philologische Wochenschrift* 24: 299–301.
T.L.L.	*TLL.*
Turnebus	Turnebus, A. 1565. *Adversaria*, vol. 2. Paris, lib. xvi, cap. 8: Turnebus, A. 1573 *Adversaria*, vol. 3. Paris, lib. xxv, cap. 3.
Tydeman	Tydeman 1838.
Vahlen	Vahlen, J. 1882. 'Varia', *Hermes* 17: 595 [=Vahlen, J. 1923. *Gesammelte philologische Schriften*, vol. 2. Leipzig and Berlin, 795].
Verburgius	Verburgius, I. 1724. *M. Tulli Ciceronis opera quae supersunt omnia*. Amsterdam.
Wes.	Wesenberg, A.S. 1872–3. *M. Tulli Ciceronis Epistulae*. Leipzig. Wesenberg, A.S. 1873.
*	Watt 1958b.

MANUSCRIPTS

H = Harleianus 2682 (11th century).

F = Berolinensis Lat. fol. 252 (12th or 13th century).

D = Palatinus Lat. 598 (15th century).

V = Parisinus Lat. 14761 (15th century).

B = Canonicianus Class. Lat. 210 (15th century).

X = consensus of the manuscripts HFDV(B).

Corrections in the manuscripts are noted in the following way:

H^1, F^1, D^1, etc., indicate the original hand of the manuscript.

H^2, F^2, D^2, etc., indicate a correction introduced by a second hand.

H^C, G^C, D^C, etc., indicate a correction introduced by an undetermined hand.

A Brief Handbook on Canvassing for Office

COMMENTARIOLUM PETITIONIS

Text

Commentariolum petitionis

QUINTUS MARCO FRATRI S. D.

(1) Etsi tibi omnia suppetunt ea quae consequi ingenio aut
usu homines aut diligentia possunt, tamen amore nostro   5
non sum alienum arbitratus ad te perscribere ea quae mihi
veniebant in mentem dies ac noctes de petitione tua cogitanti,
non ut aliquid ex his novi addisceres, sed ut ea quae in re
dispersa atque infinita viderentur esse ratione et distributione
sub uno aspectu ponerentur. Quamquam plurimum natura   10
valet, tamen videtur in paucorum mensum negotio posse
simulatio naturam vincere.

(2) Civitas quae sit cogita, quid petas, qui sis. Prope cottidie
tibi hoc ad forum descendenti meditandum est: 'Novus sum,
consulatum peto, Roma est.'   15

Nominis novitatem dicendi gloria maxime sublevabis. Semper ea res plurimum dignitatis habuit; non potest qui dignus
habetur patronus consularium indignus consulatu putari.
Quam ob rem quoniam ab hac laude proficisceris et quicquid

---

1 cf. ¶58.14–15: commentarium consulatus petitionis *X praeter F, in quo titulus
deest*: Q. Cicero de petitione consulatus ad M. Tullium fratrem [*vel* Q. Ciceronis…
fratrem liber] *dett.*   3 *sic, vel sic fere, X*   *5 aut diligentia *DB*:
ad diligenciam *V*: aut intellig[-leg- *H*]entia *HF*   7 ac *FDVB*: et *H*
8 addisceres *Lamb.*: -rem *X*   10–12 quamquam…vincere *in* §42
(¶42.16, *post* videare) *transpos. Puteanus* [*cf. Constans* 1.278]   12 naturam
Rom.: -rarum *X*   13 prope] proinde *Baehrens*[1]: propterea *coni.*
Constans 1.81: nempe *coni. Buech.*: quippe *Eussner* 37: *fort.* prorsus [*cf.* ¶18.17]
13–14 *cf.* ¶54.2   14 est *Tydeman*: sit *X*

Translation

A Brief Handbook on Canvassing for Office

QUINTUS SENDS GREETINGS TO HIS BROTHER MARCUS

(1) Although you are furnished with all that men can acquire through talent, application, and assiduousness, I nonetheless thought it consistent with our mutual affection that I compose for you a detailed account of my reflections as I think day and night about your political campaign. Not that you will learn anything new from what follows. My purpose is instead to arrange within a single, systematic form and in a logical order matters which, in actual practice, appear unrelated and indeterminate. Although the strength of nature is indeed powerful, still, in an undertaking lasting but a few months, it seems clear that pretence is able to defeat nature.

(2) Consider what state this is, what office you are seeking, who you are. Almost every day, as you go down to the forum, you must say to yourself, 'I am a new man. I seek the consulship. This is Rome.'

Your name is a new one, but you will decidedly decrease its unfamiliarity by virtue of your fame as an orator. Eloquence has always possessed great prestige. The man deemed worthy of being patron to ex-consuls can hardly be judged unworthy of the consulship. Consequently, since you are launching your candidature on the basis of your reputation for eloquence—and since it is owing to this reputation that you are whatever

es ex hoc es, ita paratus ad dicendum venito quasi in singulis
causis iudicium de omni ingenio futurum sit. (3) Eius facultatis
adiumenta, quae tibi scio esse seposita, ut parata ac prompta
sint cura, et saepe quae ⟨de⟩ Demosthenis studio et exercita-
tione scripsit Demetrius recordare. Deinde ⟨fac⟩ ut amico-   5
rum et multitudo et genera appareant; habes enim ea quae
⟨qui⟩ novi habuerunt?—omnis publicanos, totum fere equestrem ordinem, multa propria municipia, multos abs te defen-
sos homines cuiusque ordinis, aliquot conlegia, praeterea studio
dicendi conciliatos plurimos adulescentulos, cottidianam ami-   10
corum adsiduitatem et frequentiam. (4) Haec cura ut teneas
commonendo et rogando et omni ratione efficiendo ut intellegant qui debent tua causa, referendae gratiae, qui volunt,
obligandi tui tempus sibi aliud nullum fore. Etiam hoc multum videtur adiuvare posse novum hominem, hominum   15
nobilium voluntas et maxime consularium; prodest, quorum
in locum ac numerum pervenire velis, ab iis ipsis illo loco ac
numero dignum putari. (5) Ii rogandi omnes sunt diligenter et ad
eos adlegandum est persuadendumque est iis nos semper cum
optimatibus de re publica sensisse, minime popularis fuisse;   20
si quid locuti populariter videamur, id nos eo consilio fecisse
ut nobis Cn. Pompeium adiungeremus, ut eum qui plurimum
posset aut amicum in nostra petitione haberemus aut certe
non adversarium. (6) Praeterea adulescentis nobilis elabora ut
habeas, vel ut teneas studiosos quos habes; multum dignitatis   25

2 ingenio ⟨tuo⟩ *Wes.*   3 scio *DVB*: socio *F*: sotio *H*   4 de *add. Squ.*
5 fac *addend. coni. Buech.* [*cf.* ¶20.12, ¶22.2, ¶30.13, ¶44.10, ¶55.17 *et* 19]:
⟨vide⟩ *Baehrens*[1]   7 qui *add. Sedgwick*: ⟨non multi homines⟩ *Baiter*[2]
ex Fam. 5.18.1   omnes *B*: -nibus *HFDV*   7–8 equestrem *FDB*: -rum *HV*
12 commonendo *Koch*[1] *ex* ¶19.6: commendo *VB*: commendando *HFD*
18 num- dig- *VB*: dignum- *HFD*   ii] hi(i) *DVB*: hic *HF*   19 -gandum
VB: -gendum *HFD*   est [*ante* pers-] *HFB*: *om. DV* est [*ante* iis] *HDVB*: *om. F*
23 posset *FDVB*: -sit *H*   25 vel = vel potius [*cf. Mueller*[1] 4–5]   studiosos.
Quos habes, multum *Buech.*

it is you are—you must be well prepared for every speech you deliver, as if in each and every case a judgment were to be rendered on every dimension of your talent. (3) Take care that the aids to this skill, aids that I know you keep in reserve, remain ready and at hand. And often remind yourself what Demetrius has left in writing about the exertions and application of Demosthenes.

Then, you must exhibit to the public the number and variety of your friends. For what new men have had such a wide range of friends as you enjoy—all the publicans, nearly the whole of the equestrian order, the many municipalities that are devoted exclusively to you, many men of every rank whom you have defended in the courts, several clubs, as well as large numbers of young men who have been drawn to you by their study of oratory, and a constant crowd of friends in daily attendance? (4) See to it that you keep your hold on these supporters by resorting to forceful reminders and solicitations and every other means of making it clear that, so far as you are concerned, there will never be another opportunity for those indebted to you to express their gratitude, or for those who desire to do so to put you under an obligation.

This, too, can be immensely helpful to a new man: the goodwill of the nobles and, especially, of the ex-consuls. It is an advantage if those men whose station and society you hope to join should judge you worthy of that station and society. (5) These men must be solicited assiduously. You must send your connections to speak with them in your behalf. They must be persuaded that our political opinions have always coincided with those of the best men and that we have by no means been champions of popular rights. They must be convinced that, if we gave any speech that appeared to support popular rights, we did so solely to attach Gnaeus Pompeius to ourselves, so that, in our campaign for the consulship, we might have this most powerful of men either as a friend or at least not as an opponent.

(6) Furthermore, take pains to secure the support of young nobles and to sustain the enthusiasm of the young nobles you have already won over. They will bring you considerable prestige. You have many attachments of

adferent. Plurimos habes; perfice ut sciant quantum in iis putes esse. Si adduxeris ut ii qui non nolunt cupiant, plurimum proderunt.

(7) Ac multum etiam novitatem tuam adiuvat quod eius modi nobiles tecum petunt ut nemo sit qui audeat dicere plus illis nobilitatem quam tibi virtutem prodesse oportere. Nam P. Galbam et L. Cassium summo loco natos quis est qui petere consulatum putet? Vides igitur amplissimis ex familiis homines, quod sine nervis sint, tibi paris non esse. (8) At Antonius et Catilina molesti sunt. Immo homini navo, industrio, innocenti, diserto, gratioso apud eos qui res iudicant, optandi competitores ambo a pueritia sicarii, ambo libidinosi, ambo egentes. Eorum alterius bona proscripta vidimus, vocem denique audivimus iurantis se Romae iudicio aequo cum homine Graeco certare non posse, ex senatu eiectum scimus optimorum censorum existimatione, in praetura competitorem habuimus amico Sabidio et Panthera, cum ad tabulam quos poneret non haberet (quo tamen in magistratu amicam quam domi palam haberet de machinis emit); in petitione autem consulatus caupones omnis compilare per turpissimam legationem maluit quam adesse et populo Romano supplicare. (9) Alter vero, di boni! quo splendore est? Primum nobilitate eadem qua †Catilina†. Num maiore? Non. Sed virtute.

5

10

15

20

---

1 -ferent *DVB*: -ferrent *HF*   2 non *DVB*: *om. HF* [*cf.* ¶14.18, ¶32.2]
3 proderit *coni.* Facciolati [*cf.* ¶4.16, ¶16.6, ¶43.2]   4 adiuvat *VB*: -ant
HFD   quod *B*: atque *HFDV*   6 nam *Corradus*[2] 323: iam *X* [*cf.* ¶33.17]
9 sint *HDVB*: sunt *F*   9–10 Ant- et Cat- *HDVB*: Cat- et Ant- *F*
10 navo *Puteanus*: novo *X*   13–15 *cf.* Schoell 427.1–2; Stangl 65.12–13
16 optimorum *Eussner* 37 [*conl.* Pro Clu. 120]: -ma vero *X*: -ma [vero] *coni.*
Hoffa: -ma verorum *Baehrens*[2]   17 cum *Lamb.*: quam *HFDV*: quod [*et*
habebat] *B*: quom iam *Constans* 1.83   ⟨alios⟩ ad *Wes.*   *20 caupones[-is
D] *H*[c]*D*: compones *V*: caupadoces *H*[1]*F*: Cappadoces *Buech.* [*cf.* Sj.[1] 120]
23 qua Cat- *del.* Muretus 7.11: qua C. Antonius *Manutius ap.* Palermum
[Cat- *gloss. ad* alter (v. 22) *puto*]

this kind. See to it that they know how important you think they are. If you succeed in convincing those who are already well disposed towards you to become passionate in their favour, they will be immensely valuable to you.

(7) Your condition as a new man is also ameliorated by the fact that the nobles contending against you are of such a quality that no one would dare suggest that their nobility ought to be a greater advantage to them than your merit is to you. For who is there who would believe that Publius Galba and Lucius Cassius are standing for the consulship, though both are men of distinguished birth? You see, then, that there are men from the greatest families who are not your equals because they lack vigour.

(8) But, you will say, Antonius and Catilina are the dangerous rivals. Quite the contrary. For a man who is industrious, hard-working, blameless, eloquent, and influential with the classes that constitute the juries, they are the very competitors to be hoped for! Both have been cut-throats since their childhood, both are wanton, both are deeply in debt. We have seen the property of one of these men sold at auction. We have heard him swear an oath that in Rome he could not compete, in an impartial trial, with a Greek. We know that he was expelled from the senate by the verdict of estimable censors. He was one of our competitors when we stood for the praetorship, when Sabidius and Panthera were his friends, when he owned no slaves that he could offer at auction—although once he became praetor he bought a girl from the stands at the slave markets so that he could keep her at home, indiscreetly, as his lover. And although a candidate for the consulship, instead of remaining in Rome and imploring the Roman people for its votes, he preferred to plunder all the innkeepers by taking advantage of a sleazy foreign mission.

(9) As for the other one—good gods! What distinction sets him apart? 'In the first place, he possesses the same nobility [†as Catilina†].' His nobility does not surpass Antonius', does it? 'No. But he has greater

Quam ob rem? Quod Antonius umbram suam metuit, hic
ne leges quidem, natus in patris egestate, educatus in sororiis
stupris, corroboratus in caede civium, cuius primus ad rem
publicam aditus in equitibus R. occidendis fuit (nam illis
quos meminimus Gallis, qui tum Titiniorum ac Nanneiorum   5
ac Tanusiorum capita demetebant, Sulla unum Catilinam
praefecerat); in quibus ille hominem optimum, Q. Caecilium,
sororis suae virum, equitem Romanum, nullarum partium,
cum semper natura tum etiam aetate iam quietum, suis
manibus occidit. (10) Quid ego nunc dicam petere eum tecum   10
consulatum qui hominem carissimum populo Romano, M.
Marium, inspectante populo Romano vitibus per totam urbem ceciderit, ad bustum egerit, ibi omni cruciatu lacerarit,
vivo stanti collum gladio sua dextera secuerit, cum sinistra
capillum eius a vertice teneret, caput sua manu tulerit, cum   15
inter digitos eius rivi sanguinis fluerent; qui postea cum
histrionibus et cum gladiatoribus ita vixit ut alteros libidinis,
alteros facinoris adiutores haberet; qui nullum in locum tam
sanctum ac tam religiosum accessit in quo non, etiam si in
aliis culpa non esset, tamen ex sua nequitia dedecoris suspi-   20
cionem relinqueret; qui ex curia Curios et Annios, ab atriis
Sapalas et Carvilios, ex equestri ordine Pompilios et Vettios

---

1 Antonius *Corradus*[2] 327 [*sed is* C. Ant-]: manius *HFV*: inanius *D*: ille [anius
ex gloss. An⟨ton⟩ius *or tum ratus*] *coni. Or.*[1]   2 ne leges *Anon. ap. Petreium*:
nec leges *HFD*: negleges *V*   *sororiis *scripsi*: sorore *H*[1]*DV*: sororis *B*: sororum
H[c]*F*   5 nanniorum [*cf. Att.* 1.16.5 Nanneianis] *HDVB*: mannorum *F*:
Manliorum *Buech.*   6 demetebant *Verburgius*: demebant *X* [*cf. T.L.L.*
1.483.61–71, 496.25]   Catilinam *DVB*: -na *HF*   7 Q. *cod. Turnebi*: -que
X Caecilium *Man.*: cauc- *HFDB*: conc- *V*   10 tecum *VB*: *om. HFD*
[*cf.* ¶7.5, ¶27.14]   10–16 *cf. Schoell* 429.9–10, 431.3–5; *Stangl* 68.5–6,
69.27–8   14 stanti] spiranti *Puteanus*   16 fluerent *VB*: fluerunt *D*:
fluxerunt *HF*   17 cum *FDVB*: *om.* H   18–21 *cf. Schoell* 432.3–5;
Stangl 70.25–7   19–20 in aliis *B*: mali is *D*: malus *V*: aliis *HF*
22 Sapalas *nomen ignotum*: Scapulas *Puteanus*   Vettios *Lamb.*: vectios *D*:
nectios *V*: vit(t)ias *HF*: Vit(t)ios *coni. Sj.*

courage'. Why? Because whereas Antonius is afraid of his own shadow, Catilina does not even fear the law? Born into his father's poverty, reared in debauchery with his sister, grown to manhood in the thick of citizen slaughter, he first made his way into public life by murdering Roman knights. For Sulla had put Catilina in sole charge of those Gauls—whom we still remember—who at that time were mowing off the heads of men like Titinius and Nanneius and Tanusius. He also took part, and, with his own hands, cut down Quintus Caecilius, his own sister's husband, an excellent man, a Roman knight, a man who was uninvolved in politics, a man who was always retiring by nature and, by that time, owing to his age as well. (10) Why should I go on to mention that your rival for the consulship is the man who had Marcus Marius, who was beloved of the Roman people, flogged through the entire city—in the full view of the Roman people? He led him to the tomb. There he mangled him with every torture. As Marius stood there, still alive, he took a sword in his right hand, grabbed the hair of Marius' head with his left, cut through the man's neck and, carried the head in his own hand, while streams of blood flowed between his fingers.

Afterwards he lived among actors and gladiators: the former he kept as partners in debauchery, the latter as his accomplices in crime. However sacred or holy the place, and however innocent any others who were present there, such was his wickedness that, should he but enter, he invariably left behind opprobrium and the suspicion of scandal. He procured himself intimate friends in the senate like Curius and Annius, like Sapala and Carvilius in the auction halls, like Pompilius and Vettius in the equestrian

sibi amicissimos comparavit; qui tantum habet audaciae,
tantum nequitiae, tantum denique in libidine artis et effi-
cacitatis, ut prope in parentum gremiis praetextatos liberos
constuprarit? Quid ego nunc tibi de Africa, quid de testium
dictis scribam? Nota sunt, et ea tu saepius legito; sed tamen   5
hoc mihi non praetermittendum videtur, quod primum ex eo
iudicio tam egens discessit quam quidam iudices eius ante
illud iudicium fuerunt, deinde tam invidiosus ut aliud in eum
iudicium cottidie flagitetur. Hic se sic habet ut magis timeant,
etiam si quierit, quam ut contemnant, si quid commoverit.   10
(11) Quanto melior tibi fortuna petitionis data est quam nuper
homini novo, C. Coelio! ille cum duobus hominibus ita
nobilissimis petebat ut tamen in iis omnia pluris essent quam
ipsa nobilitas, summa ingenia, summus pudor, plurima beneficia, summa ratio ac diligentia petendi; ac tamen eorum   15
alterum Coelius, cum multo inferior esset genere, superior
nulla re paene, superavit. (12) Qua re tibi, si facies ea quae natura
et studia quibus semper usus es largiuntur, quae temporis
tui ratio desiderat, quae potes, quae debes, non erit difficile
certamen cum iis competitoribus qui nequaquam sunt tam   20
genere insignes quam vitiis nobiles; quis enim reperiri potest
tam improbus civis qui velit uno suffragio duas in rem public-
cam sicas destringere?

(13) Quoniam quae subsidia novitatis haberes et habere posses

1 comparavit *Squ.*: -pararit *X*   4 tibi *DVB*: *om. HF*   8 illud *B*:
illum *DV*: illud in eum *HF*   fuerunt *DB*: -re *V*: *om. HF*: -rant *Wes.*
9–10 timeant... contemnant *Tydeman*: -at... -at *X*   12 C(a)elio *X*
16 Coelius *HD*: Cel- *FVB*   17 re paene nulla *Buech.*: *malim* nulla
paene re   19 erit *VB*: *om. HFD*   21 insignes *secl. Buech.*: nobiles
Vahlen   nobiles] insignes *Vahlen*   22–3 *cf. Schoell* 433.9; *Stangl* 72. 8–9
23 destringere *D*: dis- *HFV*   24 posses *FDVB*: -sis *H*

order. He has such brazenness, such wickedness, such facility and skill in acts of lewdness that he has violated children when they were virtually in the laps of their parents. Why should I now write to you about Africa and about the statements of the witnesses? They are well known. Read them for yourself—frequently. Nevertheless, I must not fail to make two points: first, he left that trial as impoverished as some of the jurors had been before it began; second, he remains so hated that every day another trial is clamoured for. The reality is that, however much contempt men feel for him whenever he undertakes any action, this pales in comparison to the fear he provokes whenever he retires from public view.

(11) Far better luck has come your way in canvassing for office than was the case for Gaius Coelius, another new man, not so long ago. He was competing against two men of surpassingly noble birth. And yet their other assets were of greater value than their actual nobility: matchless talent, matchless probity, an excellent record of favours to others, and matchless technique and assiduousness in conducting a political campaign. Nevertheless, Coelius, though he was far inferior in birth, superior in hardly anything, defeated one of these men. (12) Consequently, if you will take advantage of what nature and the studies that you have always practised furnish you, if you will apply the methodology required by your present situation, if you will do what you can and should do, then it will be an easy contest against these competitors, who are by no means so distinguished for their birth as they are notable for their vices. Indeed, can a citizen be found who is so wicked that he would want, with a single vote, to draw two daggers against the state?

(13) Inasmuch as I have explained the means that you have or could

exposui, nunc de magnitudine petitionis dicendum videtur.
Consulatum petis, quo honore nemo est quin te dignum
arbitretur, sed multi qui invideant; petis enim homo ex
equestri loco summum locum civitatis, atque ita summum ut
forti homini, diserto, innocenti multo idem ille honos plus   5
amplitudinis quam ceteris adferat. Noli putare eos qui sunt
eo honore usi non videre, tu cum idem sis adeptus, quid dignitatis habiturus sis. Eos vero qui consularibus familiis nati
locum maiorum consecuti non sunt suspicor tibi, nisi si qui
admodum te amant, invidere. Etiam novos homines prae-   10
torios existimo, nisi qui tuo beneficio vincti sunt, nolle abs
te se honore superari. (14) Iam in populo quam multi invidi sint,
quam multi consuetudine horum annorum ab hominibus
novis alienati, venire tibi in mentem certo scio; esse etiam
non nullos tibi iratos ex iis causis quas egisti necesse est. Iam   15
illud tute circumspicito, quod ad Cn. Pompei gloriam au-
gendam tanto studio te dedisti, num quos tibi putes ob eam
causam esse ⟨non⟩ amicos. (15) Quam ob rem cum et summum
locum civitatis petas et videas esse studia quae tibi adversen-
tur, adhibeas necesse est omnem rationem et curam et labo-   20
rem et diligentiam.
(16) Et petitio magistratuum divisa est in duarum rationum
diligentiam, quarum altera in amicorum studiis, altera in
populari voluntate ponenda est. Amicorum studia beneficiis
et officiis et vetustate et facilitate ac iucunditate naturae   25
parta esse oportet. Sed hoc nomen amicorum in petitione

9 sunt *HFV*: sint *DB*   si *HFD*: om. *VB* [*cf.* ¶26.6]   11 vincti (?*F*)*DB*:
iuncti*H*(?*F*)*V*   12–13 invidi multi sint, quam cons- *Sedgwick*   12 sint
DV: sunt *HFB*   13 quam multi *VB*: quam *HFD*   hominibus *Squ.*:
honoribus *X*   14 certo *HFD*: -te *VB*   17 dedisti *Rom.*: edid- *X*:
dedid- [*cf.* ¶35.11] *codd. Palermi*   *18 esse ⟨non⟩ am- [*cf.* ¶6.2] *Lamb.*:
⟨non⟩ esse am- *Turnebus*: esse inim- [*cf.* ¶25.2] *coni. Petreius*   19 tibi *VB*: om.
HFD   22 et *HFVB*: om. *D*   petitio *DB*: -onem *HFV*   magistratuum *B*:
-tum   *D*: a -tu *V*: -tus *HF*

have at your disposal for palliating your condition as a new man, it now seems the right moment to discuss the sheer gravity of your campaign for office. You are seeking the consulship. There is no one who does not judge you worthy of that office, but there are many who are resentful of you. This is because, although you are a man whose original station was that of a Roman knight, you are now seeking the state's highest station—so much the highest that this office confers far greater dignity on a man who is brave, eloquent, and blameless than it does on all others. Do not think that those who have held this office fail to recognize how great your prestige will be once you have attained the same office. I very much suspect that men from consular families who have not attained the station of their ancestors are envious of you, except for those who are closely attached to you in friendship. I suppose that even the new men who have reached the praetorship, except for those who are obligated to you by a previous favour, hope that they will not be surpassed in office by you. (14) Now, I know full well that it occurs to you how many, even among the public, share this envy, how many, in the fashion of recent years, are averse to new men.

It must also be the case that some have become angry with you on account of the cases you have pleaded. Now, ponder this point carefully: do you think certain men are hostile to you because you have devoted yourself with such enormous zeal to increasing the glory of Gnaeus Pompeius? (15) Therefore, since you are seeking the state's highest station, and since you recognize what interests are arrayed against you, you must bring to this undertaking all your reason, care, industry, and assiduousness.

(16) Now, a campaign for high office divides itself into assiduousness of two types, one directed at gaining the support of friends, the other at gaining the goodwill of the people.

The support of friends ought to be obtained by means of favours and the reciprocation of favours, the proper observance of one's own responsibilities, long-standing familiarity, and an accommodating and agreeable nature. During an election campaign, however, the definition of the word

latius patet quam in cetera vita; quisquis est enim qui osten-
dat aliquid in te voluntatis, qui colat, qui domum ventitet, is
in amicorum numero est habendus. Sed tamen qui sunt amici
ex causa iustiore cognationis aut adfinitatis aut sodalitatis aut
alicuius necessitudinis, iis carum et iucundum esse maxime   5
prodest. (17) Deinde ut quisque est intimus ac maxime domesticus, ut is amet ⟨et⟩ quam amplissimum esse te cupiat valde
elaborandum est, tum ut tribules, ut vicini, ut clientes, ut
denique liberti, postremo etiam servi tui; nam fere omnis
sermo ad forensem famam a domesticis emanat auctoribus.   10
(18) Deinde sunt instituendi cuiusque generis amici: ad speciem,
homines inlustres honore ac nomine (qui, etiam si suffragandi
studia non navant, tamen adferunt petitori aliquid dignitatis);
ad ius obtinendum, magistratus (ex quibus maxime consules,
deinde tribuni pl.); ad conficiendas centurias, homines ex-   15
cellenti gratia. Qui abs te tribum aut centuriam aut aliquod
beneficium aut habeant aut ut habeant sperent, eos prorsus
magno opere et compara et confirma; nam per hos annos
homines ambitiosi vehementer omni studio atque opera elaborarunt ut possent a tribulibus suis ea quae peterent im-   20
petrare; hos tu homines, quibuscumque poteris rationibus,
ut ex animo atque [ex illa] summa voluntate tui studiosi sint
elaborato. (19) Quod si satis grati homines essent, haec tibi omnia
parata esse debebant, sicuti parata esse confido. Nam hoc

3 in *HDVB*: *om. F*   4 cognationis *VB*: cognit- *HFD*   6 quisque
FD: -quis *HVB* [*cf. Sj.*[1] 116, *L.-H.* 487]   7 et quam *cod.*(?) *Turnebi,*
Petreius: quod *HFDV* [*cf. Att.* 10.8A.2]   8 tum *HFD*: tu *V*: *om. codd.*
Palermi   11 deinde *cf.* ¶33.11–12   14 ius *HFD*: iustitiam [*fort.*
ex ius tuum *or* tum] *VB*   consules *Squ.*: -ul *X*   16 tribum *FDV*: -bunatum
H   17 aut [*sed* ut *H*ᶜ] habeant *H*ᶜ*DV*: *om. H*¹*F*   ut habeant *HFDB*:
habere *V*: *secl. R. Klotz* [*cf. Sj.*[1] 118, *L.-H.* 764]   prorsus *HDVB*: rursus *F*
19 opera *V* [*a ex e mutato*]: -re *X*   19–20 elaborarunt *Turnebus ap.*
Lamb.: laborarunt *DVB*: laborant *HF*   20 possent *DVB*: -sint *HF*
*22 ex illa *seclusi*   illa *FDVB*: illo *H*   24 debebant *DV*: debeant *HFB*

'friend' is broader than it is in the rest of life. Indeed, if anyone shows you any goodwill, seeks your company, or makes a habit of visiting your home, that man should be counted as one of your friends. Nevertheless, it is also very helpful to stay on affectionate and agreeable terms with those who are more legitimately regarded as friends—that is, those connected to you by blood or by marriage or by fellowship in a religious fraternity or by any other close tie. (17) You must also take special pains to ensure that all the most intimate members of your household love you and want you to be as great a man as possible. You must do the same with your fellow tribesmen, your neighbours, your clients, your freedmen, and, finally, even your slaves. For nearly every item of gossip that affects one's public reputation originates from sources within one's own household.

(18) Next, you must deploy your friends, whatever their category, each to their own purpose: for sheer pageantry, men distinguished by office and by lineage—who, even if they do not devote themselves enthusiastically to a campaign, nevertheless confer on a candidate a degree of prestige; for guaranteeing your legal rights, the magistrates, of whom the consuls are the most important, then the tribunes of the people; for delivering the votes of the centuries, men of exceptional influence. It is imperative that you recruit and retain those men who, on account of you, have, or expect to have, control over a tribe or a century, or some other advantage. For, in recent years, men eager for advancement have worked very hard, with unreserved eagerness and energy, to be able to get what they want from their fellow tribesmen. For your part, you must work, through whatever means lie at your disposal, to make these men your sincere and zealous supporters.

(19) Admittedly, if men were sufficiently grateful, all of this should already be arranged for you—just as I am confident that it has been

biennio quattuor sodalitates hominum ad ambitionem gratio-
sissimorum tibi obligasti, C. Fundani, Q. Galli, C. Corneli, C.
Orchivi; horum in causis ad te deferendis quid tibi eorum
sodales receperint et confirmarint scio, nam interfui; qua re
hoc tibi faciendum est, hoc tempore ut ab his quod debent   5
exigas saepe commonendo, rogando, confirmando, curando ut
intellegant nullum se umquam aliud tempus habituros referendae gratiae; profecto homines et spe reliquorum tuorum
officiorum et[iam] recentibus beneficiis ad studium navandum
excitabuntur. (20) Et omnino, quoniam eo genere amicitiarum   10
petitio tua maxime munita est quod ex causarum defensioni-
bus adeptus es, fac ut plane iis omnibus quos devinctos tenes
discriptum ac dispositum suum cuique munus sit; et quem ad
modum nemini illorum molestus nulla in re umquam fuisti,
sic cura ut intellegant omnia te quae ab illis tibi deberi putaris   15
ad hoc tempus reservasse. (21) Sed quoniam tribus rebus homines
maxime ad benevolentiam atque haec suffragandi studia
ducuntur, beneficio, spe, adiunctione animi ac voluntate,
animadvertendum est quem ad modum cuique horum generi
sit inserviendum. Minimis beneficiis homines adducuntur ut   20
satis causae putent esse ad studium suffragationis, nedum ii
quibus saluti fuisti, quos tu habes plurimos, non intellegant,
si hoc tuo tempore tibi non satis fecerint, se probatos nemini
umquam fore; quod cum ita sit, tamen rogandi sunt atque
etiam in hanc opinionem adducendi ut, qui adhuc nobis   25
obligati fuerint, iis vicissim nos obligari posse videamur. (22) Qui

2 Fundanique gal(l)ii *X*   C. Cornelii *VB: om. HFD*   2–3 C. Orchivi]
corchivii *D:* corthini *V:* cho(r)civii *HF*   5 est *HDVB: om. F*
8 homines] hi omnes *Buech.*   9 iam *del. Rom.:* tam *coni. Purser*
12 omnibus *V:* homin- *HFD* [*cf.* ¶50.4]   13 discriptum *V:* des- *HFDB*
14 nemini *H¹* [*bis scriptum*]: mem- *HᶜFDVB*   ulla *Muretus* 7.12
16 homines *HDVB: om. F* [*cf.* ¶55.14]   18 adducuntur *Lamb., fort.*
recte [*cf. vv.* 20, 25, ¶6.2, ¶40.1]   adiunctione *DVB:* -ni *HF*   voluntatis *Lamb.*
25 etiam *B:* et *HFDV* [*cf. T.L.L.* 2.910.52]

arranged. For, during the past two years, you have put under an obligation to yourself four religious fraternities, whose memberships include men of immense influence in elections: Gaius Fundanius, Quintus Gallius, Gaius Cornelius, and Gaius Orchivius. I know what these men's fellow members pledged and promised to you when they brought you their cases, for I was there. Consequently, you must now demand that they meet their obligations; by frequent admonitions, entreaties, and assurances, you must make certain that they understand that they will have no other opportunity to express their gratitude. Indeed, people will be stirred to action on your behalf by the expectation of reciprocity on your part as well as by recent favours.

(20) This is the chief point: since your campaign is stoutly fortified by the kind of friendships you have acquired by defending others in court, see to it that there is a clearly defined and specific duty for each of those whom you hold under an obligation. Since you have never imposed on any of them in any matter, do take care that they realize how you have kept in reserve for this particular moment what you regard as their entire debt of gratitude to you.

(21) Now, inasmuch as there are three things that serve as the best incentives for stimulating goodwill and keen electoral support—favours done, the expectation of future favours, and genuine personal affection—it must be a matter of your highest consideration how best to attend to each of these matters. Now, it is owing to the most trivial of favours that men are led to believe they have a satisfactory reason to support a canvass. All the more, then, will those whom you have actually saved from ruin—and there are many such men—realize that no one will ever respect them if they do not do their duty by you during this vital time. Even so, these men must still be solicited for their support, and, although they are already under an obligation to us, we must bring them to the view that we, in our turn, may become obligated to them.

(22) As for those who are attached to you by the expectation of future favours—a category of person even more assiduous and dutiful—make it

autem spe tenentur, quod genus hominum multo etiam est
diligentius atque officiosius, iis fac ut propositum ac paratum
auxilium tuum esse videatur, denique ut spectatorem te suorum officiorum esse intellegant diligentem, ut videre te plane
atque animadvertere quantum a quoque proficiscatur ap-   5
pareat. (23) Tertium illud genus est studiorum voluntarium, quod
agendis gratiis, accommodandis sermonibus ad eas rationes
propter quas quisque studiosus tui esse videbitur, significanda
erga illos pari voluntate, adducenda amicitia in spem familia-
ritatis et consuetudinis confirmari oportebit. Atque in his   10
omnibus generibus iudicato et perpendito quantum quisque
possit, ut scias et quem ad modum cuique inservias et quid a
quoque exspectes ac postules. (24) Sunt enim quidam homines in
suis vicinitatibus et municipiis gratiosi, sunt diligentes et
copiosi qui, etiam si antea non studuerunt huic gratiae, tamen   15
ex tempore elaborare eius causa cui debent aut volunt facile
possunt; his hominum generibus sic inserviendum est ut ipsi
intellegant te videre quid a quoque exspectes, sentire quid
accipias, meminisse quid acceperis. Sunt autem alii qui aut
nihil possunt aut etiam odio sunt tribulibus suis nec habent   20
tantum animi ac facultatis ut enitantur ex tempore; hos
ut internoscas videto, ne spe in aliquo maiore posita praesidi
parum comparetur.
(25) Et quamquam partis ac fundatis amicitiis fretum ac munitum esse oportet, tamen in ipsa petitione amicitiae permultae   25
ac perutiles comparantur; nam in ceteris molestiis habet hoc

1 etiam est *Gruter*: etiam si *HFDV*: est *B*   2 propositum] promptum
coni. Ernesti [*cf.* ¶3.3]   3–4 suorum *DVB*: *om. HF*   5 pro[per- *B*]-
ficiscatur *HDVB*: proficiatur *F*: perficiatur [*cf.* ¶50.2] *Buech.*   6 illud
FDVB: id *H*   studio⟨so⟩rum *Koch*[2]: *secl. Buech.* [*cf. Sj.*[1] 125]   8 significanda *Man.*: -do *X*: *fort.* -do…pari ⟨studio ac⟩ [*cf.* ¶40.2–4]   12 et quem
HDVB: quem *F*   17 hominum *HDVB*: omnium *F*   22 ut *FD*: *om.*
HVB   internos casui deto ne *D*: internos eas videto ne *V*: inter noscas et videto
ne *B*: inter nos calumniatores *HF*   26 comparantur *HDV*:- rentur *FB*

appear that your help and protection are ever ready and at their disposal. And make sure they perceive how attentively you are keeping an eye on their services to you. Make it obvious that you are observant and paying close attention to each individual's actual exertions on your behalf. (23) The third category is that of voluntary supporters. You will need to encourage their loyalty by showing them your gratitude, by adapting your conversation with each individual to the particular motives that lie behind his support for you, by displaying how your goodwill towards them is as strong as theirs towards you, and by leading them to expect that their friendship with you will lead to real intimacy. In the case of each of these categories, you must assess and weigh the capacities of each individual in order to decide how best to cultivate him and what exactly you can expect and demand from him.

(24) Now, there are certain men who are influential in their neighbour-hoods and municipalities, industrious and prosperous men who, even if they have exhibited no previous inclination to exercise their influence, are nevertheless in a strong position to give opportune support to the candi-dature of a man to whom they are indebted or whom they like. You must so cultivate such men that they realize you know just what you expect from each of them, you notice what you get, and you remember what you got. There are other men, however, who are ineffectual or even odious to their fellow tribesmen and lack the character or skill to be relied on in a pinch. See that you recognize these men for what they are, lest you repose too great a hope in someone only to get too little assistance in return.

(25) It is necessary, to be sure, for you to rely on and be reinforced by well-established, long-standing friendships. Nonetheless, during the actual course of a political campaign, numerous—and very useful—new friendships are formed. This is because, despite all its other encumbrances,

tamen petitio commodi: potes honeste, quod in cetera vita
non queas, quoscumque velis adiungere ad amicitiam, quibus-
cum si alio tempore agas ut te utantur, absurde facere videare,
in petitione autem nisi id agas et cum multis et diligenter,
nullus petitor esse videare. (26) Ego autem tibi hoc confirmo, esse   5
neminem, nisi si aliqua necessitudine competitorum alicui
tuorum sit adiunctus, a quo non facile si contenderis im-
petrare possis ut suo beneficio promereatur se ut ames et sibi
ut debeas, modo ut intellegat te magni se aestimare, ex animo
agere, bene se ponere, fore ex eo non brevem et suffragatoriam   10
sed firmam et perpetuam amicitiam. (27) Nemo erit, mihi crede,
in quo modo aliquid sit, qui hoc tempus sibi oblatum amicitiae tecum constituendae praetermittat, praesertim cum tibi
hoc casus adferat, ut ii tecum petant quorum amicitia aut
contemnenda aut fugienda sit, et qui hoc quod ego te hor-   15
tor non modo adsequi sed ne incipere quidem possint. (28) Nam
qui incipiat Antonius homines adiungere atque invitare ad
amicitiam quos per se suo nomine appellare non possit?
mihi quidem nihil stultius videtur quam existimare esse eum
studiosum tui quem non noris. Eximiam quandam gloriam   20
et dignitatem ac rerum gestarum magnitudinem esse oportet
in eo quem homines ignoti nullis suffragantibus honore ad-
ficiant; ut quidem homo nequam, iners, sine officio, sine
ingenio, cum infamia, nullis amicis, hominem plurimorum

---

1 petitio *VB*: noticio *HF*: notitia *D*   potes *HF*: potest *D*: possis *VB*: ut possis *dett.*
2 amicitiam *VB*: inim- *HFD*   3 alio *HDVB*: aliquo *F*   ut te utantur *VB*:
om. HFD   5 nullus *Rom.*: nullius *X*   6 si *DVB*: *om. HF* [*cf.* ¶13.9]:
qui *vel* si qui *Wes.*   7 contenderis *HF*: -it *DVB*   9 magni se aestimare
Koch[2]: -nis est- [*cf.* ¶31.24] *H*[1]: -ne exist- *F*: -ni exist- *D*: -ni est- *H*[c]*VB*
12 qui *F*[c] [d *partim eraso*] *B*: quid *HF*[1]*DV*   14 ut ii *Muretus* 7.13: uti *X*
17 qui *coni. Gesner*: quid *X*   22 quem *DVB*: *om. HF*   23 homo
nequam *Gulielmius*: homine(m) quam *HFDV*   24 cum] summa *coni.*
Schütz[1]   *infamia *VB*: -ma *H*[c]*FD*: -mis *H*[1]

standing for office offers this one expedience: you can honourably do something that in your ordinary life you cannot do—that is to say, you can make friends with whomever you like. If at any other time you found yourself on intimate terms with certain people, you would appear ridiculous. However, when you are canvassing, unless you act that way—and do so assiduously and with lots of people—you would hardly appear to be a candidate at all.

(26) For my part, I assure you of this: there is nobody, unless he is attached to one of your rivals by some personal connection, whom you could not easily convince, if you but made the effort, that by his doing you a favour he could gain your friendship and put you under an obligation to him—provided he was made to understand that you hold him in high esteem, that you are sincere, that he is making a good investment for himself, and that out of this will come a friendship that is secure and lasting instead of one that is temporary and sought only for the purpose of winning his vote. (27) Believe me, no one, provided he has any sense, will let slip this opportunity of gaining your friendship, especially since this stroke of luck has come your way: your competitors in this election are men whose friendship must be despised or shunned, and who could not begin to undertake, let alone carry out, what I am recommending to you. (28) For how could Antonius begin to attach men to himself or invite them to become his friends when he cannot, on his own, address them by name? Indeed, nothing seems stupider to me than believing that a man whom you do not even know favours your candidature. Nothing short of supreme glory, prestige, and a record of grand accomplishments is demanded before strangers, unsolicited by a candidate or his supporters, will confer a magistracy on him. A man who is useless, lazy, ungrateful, without talent, disgraced, and friendless cannot outpace someone who is

studio atque omnium bona existimatione munitum praecur-
rat, sine magna culpa neglegentiae fieri non potest. (29) Quam ob
rem omnis centurias multis et variis amicitiis cura ut confirmatas habeas. Et primum, id quod ante oculos est, sena-
tores equitesque Romanos, ceterorum ⟨ordinum⟩ omnium   5
navos homines et gratiosos complectere. Multi homines ur-
bani industrii, multi libertini in foro gratiosi navique versantur; quos per te, quos per communis amicos poteris, summa
cura ut cupidi tui sint elaborato, appetito, adlegato, summo
beneficio te adfici ostendito. (30) Deinde habeto rationem urbis   10
totius, conlegiorum omnium, pagorum, vicinitatum; ex his
principes ad amicitiam tuam si adiunxeris, per eos reliquam
multitudinem facile tenebis. Postea totam Italiam fac ut in
animo ac memoria tributim discriptam comprensamque habeas, ne quod municipium, coloniam, praefecturam, locum deni-   15
que Italiae ne quem esse patiare in quo non habeas firmamenti
(31) quod satis esse possit, perquiras et investiges homines ex omni
regione, eos cognoscas, appetas, confirmes, cures ut in suis
vicinitatibus tibi petant et tua causa quasi candidati sint.
Volent te amicum, si suam a te amicitiam expeti videbunt;   20
id ut intellegant, oratione ea quae ad eam rationem pertinet
habenda consequere. Homines municipales ac rusticani, si
nomine nobis noti sunt, in amicitia se esse arbitrantur; si vero
etiam praesidi se aliquid sibi constituere putant, non amittunt
occasionem promerendi. Hos ceteri et maxime tui competi-   25
tores ne norunt quidem, tu et nosti et facile cognosces, sine

5 ⟨ordinum⟩ omnium *Buech.* [*conl.* ¶24.17 *et Pro Rab. perd. r.* 27]: hominum
X: ordinum *coni. Petreius*   10 habeto rat- *D*: habet orat- *HFV*
11 omnium] montium *Mommsen, Röm. Staatsr.* 3.114. *adn.* 5 [*conl. De Domo*
74]   14 discriptam *Mueller.*[1]   11: des- *HFD*: districtam *V*   17 et
HFDV: etiam et *B*   22 municipales *DVB*: -piales *HF*   23 nom- nobis
DV: nom- vobis *H*: nobis nom- *F*   23 se esse *HDVB*: esse se *F*
24 praesidii se aliquid *B*: -sidisse alii quid *DV*: -sidis alii quid *H*: -sides alii *F*

reinforced by the devotion of most people and the good opinion of everyone—unless monumental negligence is to blame.

(29) Consequently, see to it that you have a secure hold on all the centuries by means of multiple and varied friendships. The first and obvious thing is that you must embrace the senators and the Roman knights, as well as men of all the other orders who are industrious and influential. There are many hard-working men living in the city, many freedmen, who are industrious and influential in the forum. You must take the greatest pains, on your own behalf and through common friends, to make as many of these men as you can into your eager partisans. Seek them out yourself. Send representatives to win them over. Make it plain to them how much you are touched by the great favour they do you.

(30) Then take stock of the whole of the city, of all the clubs, the boroughs, and the neighbourhoods. If you succeed in making the leaders of these organizations your friends, then, through their agency, you will easily hold the rest of the multitude. After that, make sure that you know and can recall how the whole of Italy is divided into tribes and districts. And, finally, make sure there is not a single municipality, colony, prefecture—not even a single locality in Italy—where you do not enjoy a satisfactory measure of support. (31) Seek out and find men from every region. Get to know them, visit them personally, encourage their loyalty. See to it that they campaign for you in their own neighbourhoods, and that they become, so to speak, candidates on your behalf.

These men will want you as a friend, if they perceive that their friendship is sought by you. Make them understand this by conversing with them in a manner that suits just this purpose. Now, men from the municipalities and from the countryside consider themselves our friends if they are simply known to us by name. If, in addition, they believe they are acquiring a bit of protection for themselves, they do not lose any opportunity of making themselves worthy of it. Other candidates, and especially your rivals, do not even know who these men are, whereas you both know

quo amicitia esse non potest. (32) Neque id tamen satis est,
tametsi magnum est, si non sequitur spes utilitatis atque
amicitiae, ne nomenclator solum sed amicus etiam bonus esse
videare. Ita cum et hos ipsos, propter suam ambitionem qui
apud tribulis suos plurimum gratia possunt, studiosos in   5
centuriis habebis et ceteros qui apud aliquam partem tribulium propter municipi aut vicinitatis aut conlegi rationem
valent cupidos tui constitueris, in optima spe esse debebis.
(33) Iam equitum centuriae multo facilius mihi diligentia posse
teneri videntur: primum ⟨oportet⟩ cognosci equites (pauci   10
enim sunt), deinde appeti (multo enim facilius illa adulescentulorum ad amicitiam aetas adiungitur). Deinde habes
tecum ex iuventute optimum quemque et studiosissimum
humanitatis; tum autem, quod equester ordo tuus est, sequentur illi auctoritatem ordinis, si abs te adhibebitur ea diligentia   15
ut non ordinis solum voluntate sed etiam singulorum amicitiis
eas centurias confirmatas habeas. Nam studia adulescentulorum in suffragando, in obeundo, in nuntiando, in adsectando mirifice et magna et honesta sunt.
(34) Et, quoniam adsectationis mentio facta est, id quoque   20
curandum est ut cottidiana cuiusque generis et ordinis et
aetatis utare; nam ex ea ipsa copia coniectura fieri poterit

---

2 si non *D*: non se *V*: sed *HF* [*cf.* ¶6.2]: sed ut *B*   sequitur *HFD*: consequatur
VB, fort. recte   3 nomenculator *B*: nomendator *V*: nomine dator *D*:
commendator *HF*   5 possunt *Palermus*: -sint *X*   6–7 tribulium
Angelius: -lum *X*   7 vicinit- *Petreius*: civit- *X*   *10 oportet *addidi*
cognosci *HFDV*: -cendi sunt *B*: -ce *vel* -cito *coni. Or.²*   11 ap(p)eti *HFD*:
adepti *V*: adipiscendi *B*: appete *vel* -tito *coni. Or.²*   12 deinde *cf.* ¶6.6 *et*
¶7.11   habes *HFDV*: -bebis *B*: -beto *Eussner* 40   14 autem *cod. Turnebi*:
aut emi *DV*: autem emi *HF*   14–15 sequentur *HᶜDV*: sequuntur *H¹*:
secuntur autem *F*   15 illi *sunt qui v.* 13 *designantur* [*cf. Sternkopf* 300]:
alii *Hendrickson* 23   adhibebitur *HDVB*: adhibetur *F*   17 nam *Wes.*:
iam *X* [*cf.* ¶6.6]   18 obeundo *DV*: ob(o)ediendo *HFB*   22 utare
nam *B*: ut arenam *HFDV*: utare frequentia. nam *codd. Palermi* [*cf.* ¶3.11,
¶37.24, ¶50.22, ¶50.1]

them and recognize them easily whenever you meet. Without this degree of familiarity, friendship is impossible. (32) However, familiarity alone, though important, is insufficient unless it entails the expectation of a friendship that is truly advantageous. So you must appear to be a friend of genuine value and not merely a slave with a good head for names.

To sum up, when your supporters in the centuries are those men who, because of their experience of elections, know how to exert their influence over their fellow tribesmen, and when your partisans include others who carry weight with some part of their tribe owing to their municipality or neighbourhood or club, then you ought to have very high hopes.

(33) Now, as for the centuries of the knights, these, I think, can be secured even more easily—if you are assiduous. First you must get to know the knights (for they are few). Then visit them personally (for young men are at an age when it is very easy to win their friendship). I should add that you already enjoy the support of the best of our youth, who are distinguished by their enthusiasm for high culture. Furthermore, because the whole of the equestrian order is devoted to you, these young knights will respect the authority of their order, so long as you make the effort to secure those centuries not only by way of the general goodwill of the order but also by way of personal friendships with its individual members. For the zeal of the young in canvassing on your behalf, in meeting voters, in reporting information, and in offering you their attendance all redounds quite marvellously to your credit.

(34) Since I have just mentioned attendance, this, too, is something requiring your attention. You must have daily attendance by supporters of every sort, of every rank, of every age, for its sheer scale will be a good indication of the magnitude of your backing on election day. Now, attendance

quantum sis in ipso campo virium ac facultatis habiturus.
Huius autem rei tres partes sunt: una salutatorum [cum
domum veniunt], altera deductorum, tertia adsectatorum.
(35) In salutatoribus, qui magis vulgares sunt et hac consuetudine
quae nunc est ⟨ad⟩ pluris veniunt, hoc efficiendum est ut hoc   5
ipsum minimum officium eorum tibi gratissimum esse videatur; qui domum tuam venient, iis significato te animadvertere
(eorum amicis qui illis renuntient ostendito, saepe ipsis dicito);
sic homines saepe, cum obeunt pluris competitores et vident
unum esse aliquem qui haec officia maxime animadvertat, ei   10
se dedunt, deserunt ceteros, minutatim ex communibus pro-
prii, ex fucosis firmi suffragatores evadunt. Iam illud teneto
diligenter, si eum qui tibi promiserit audieris fucum, ut dici-
tur, facere aut senseris, ut te id audisse aut scire dissimules,
si qui tibi se purgare volet quod suspectum esse arbitretur,   15
adfirmes te de illius voluntate numquam dubitasse nec debere
dubitare; is enim qui se non putat satis facere amicus esse
nullo modo potest. Scire autem oportet quo quisque animo
sit, ut et quantum cuique confidas constituere possis. (36) Iam
deductorum officium quo maius est quam salutatorum, hoc   20
gratius tibi esse significato atque ostendito, et, quod eius
fieri poterit, certis temporibus descendito; magnam adfert
opinionem, magnam dignitatem cottidiana in deducendo
frequentia. (37) Tertia est ex hoc genere adsidua adsectatorum
copia. In ea quos voluntarios habebis, curato ut intellegant   25

---

1 sis in *B*: si sint *HFDV*   2–3 cum domum veniunt *damnavit Or.*[1], *def.*
Sj.[1] 126   4 hac consuetudine *HFD* [*cf.* ¶14.13]: [ad *B*] hanc -inem *VB*
*5 ad *addidi*   pluris *X*: -res [*nom.*] *Squ. vulg.*   7 venient his *B*: -enti *DV*:
-ent *HᶜF*: *om. H*[1]   8 dicito *Rom.*: dicto *B*: digito *HFDV*   9 obeunt
DVB: obediunt *HF*   12 teneto *FDVB*: -eo *H*   14 aut [*prius*] *vulg.*:
ut *DV*: aut ut *HF*: vel *B*   id *DVB*: vel *HF*   dissimules *DB*: -miles *HFV*
15 esse ⟨se⟩ *Schwarz*   16 illius *DVB*: illis *HF*   17–18 esse n- m-
pot- *HDVB*: n- m- pot- esse *F*   19 et *HDVB*: *om. F*   24 assect- *B*:
a(d)- (s)spect- *HFDV*   25 curato *HFD*: -rate *V*: -ra *B*

is a subject that can be separated into three parts: the first is concerned with those who greet you in the morning [when they come to your home]; the second with those who escort you from your home to the forum; the third with those who make up your entourage throughout the day.

(35) Most morning greeters are common folk, and they practise the modern custom of visiting several houses. Make it clear that this very simple service of theirs is exceedingly gratifying to you. Give unmistakable signs that you notice who visits your home. Make your gratitude known to their friends, who will repeat it to them. Tell them yourself—often. It frequently happens that, when men greet several candidates and realize that one of them pays greater attention to their services than the others do, they devote themselves to that one candidate, forsake the others, and soon become his loyal supporters instead of merely joining everyone's morning audience: they become genuine partisans instead of sham ones.

Now, keep this carefully in mind: if you hear that anyone who has committed himself to you is playing you false, as they say, or even if you see it for yourself, pretend that you have not heard it or are unaware. If anyone thinks that you suspect him and wishes to clear himself, assure him that you have never doubted his intentions and that it would be wrong for you to do so. For the man who believes that he is letting you down cannot be your friend. Still, you should find out how each man is truly disposed towards you, so that you can come to some conclusion as to how much you may trust him.

(36) Now, as for those who escort you, inasmuch as their service to you is greater than those who simply greet you in the morning, you must make it absolutely clear that you appreciate them even more. And, to the extent that you can, go down to the forum at fixed times. When a large crowd escorts you to the forum each day, it makes a great impression on the public and confers great prestige.

(37) There is a third element in this category: a steady supply of constant attendants. Some will perform this favour voluntarily. See that they know how this very great kindness on their part puts you forever in their

te sibi in perpetuum summo beneficio obligari; qui autem tibi
debent, ab iis plane hoc munus exigito, qui per aetatem ac
negotium poterunt, ipsi tecum ut adsidui sint, qui ipsi sectari
non poterunt, suos necessarios in hoc munere constituant.
Valde ego te volo et ad rem pertinere arbitror semper cum   5
multitudine esse. (38) Praeterea magnam adfert laudem et summam dignitatem, si ii tecum erunt qui a te defensi et qui per
te servati ac iudiciis liberati sunt; haec tu plane ab his postu-
lato ut, quoniam nulla impensa per te alii rem, alii honestatem,
alii salutem ac fortunas omnis obtinuerint, nec aliud ullum   10
tempus futurum sit ubi tibi referre gratiam possint, hoc te
officio remunerentur.
(39) Et quoniam in amicorum studiis haec omnis oratio versatur, qui locus in hoc genere cavendus sit praetermittendum
non videtur. Fraudis atque insidiarum et perfidiae plena   15
sunt omnia. Non est huius temporis perpetua illa de hoc
genere disputatio, quibus rebus benevolus et simulator diiudi-
cari possit; tantum est huius temporis admonere. Summa tua
virtus eosdem homines et simulare tibi se esse amicos et invidere coegit. Quam ob rem Ἐπιχάρμειον illud teneto, nervos   20
atque artus esse sapientiae non temere credere, (40) et, cum
tuorum amicorum studia constitueris, tum etiam obtrecta-
torum atque adversariorum rationes et genera cognoscito.
Haec tria sunt: unum quos laesisti, alterum qui sine causa
non amant, tertium qui competitorum valde amici sunt.   25
Quos laesisti, cum contra eos pro amico diceres, iis te plane

2 exigito *coni. Or.*[1]: -gitur *HFD*: -git *V*: -ge *B*   4 ⟨ut⟩ suos *coni. Buech.*
6 adferet *Wes.* [*cf. Sj.*[1] 136]   8 haec] hoc *cod. nescioquis ap. Or.*[1]
9 honestatem *HD*: honestam *VB*: honorem *F*   10 obtinuerint *Mueller*:
-runt *X*   11 futurumst *Buech.*   13 oratio *HDVB*: ratio *F* [*cf.* ¶49.19]
14 sit *HDVB*: est *F*   20 *cf. Att.* 1.19.8; *Kaibel, Com. Graec. Fragm.* 137
teneto *FDVB*: -eo *H*   21 esse *VB*: sese *HFD*   24 unum *DV*: unum
ex his *B*: *om. HF*   26 diceres hic te *B*: -ere [-eres *D*] si iste *DV*: -ere *HF*

debt. As for those who owe you a favour, from these you must demand this service in plain terms: all for whom neither age nor business is an impediment should be in constant personal attendance; if there are any who cannot accompany you personally, these should appoint their personal connections to the task. I very much want you to be attended by a great crowd at all times. In my opinion, this is crucial to a political campaign.

(38) One further point. It will bring you high renown and great prestige if those whom you have defended, who, owing to your exertions, have been preserved and rescued from condemnation, join your retinue. You must make this request of them in no uncertain terms. Since it was through your energies and at no cost to themselves that some of these men preserved their property, others their respectability, still others their standing as citizens and the whole of their fortunes—and since there will be no other opportunity for them to show you the gratitude they owe you—they should repay you with this service.

(39) Now, inasmuch as my entire discussion is here concerned with encouraging the support of your friends, I must not fail to mention, under this heading, an issue that requires caution on your part. All the matters I have been reviewing are vulnerable to deceit, treachery, and faithlessness. This is not the time to rehearse that eternal debate over the means by which a sincere friend can be distinguished from a false one. This is the time for a warning only. Your matchless virtue goads the same men both to pretend that they are your friends and to envy you. Therefore, hold fast to that apophthegm of Epicharmus, that the sinews and bone of wisdom consist in not trusting rashly.

(40) After you have organized the support of your friends, take pains to understand the general characteristics of your detractors and enemies. These come in three types: first, those whom you have offended; second, those who dislike you for no reason; third, those who are close friends of your rivals. As for those whom you have offended when speaking against them on behalf of a friend, from them you must win a full pardon. Remind

purgato, necessitudines commemorato, in spem adducito te in
eorum rebus, si se in amicitiam contulerint, pari studio atque
officio futurum. Qui sine causa non amant, eos aut beneficio
aut spe aut significando tuo erga illos studio dato operam ut
de illa animi pravitate deducas. Quorum voluntas erit abs te   5
propter competitorum amicitias alienior, iis quoque eadem
inservito ratione qua superioribus et, si probare poteris, te in
eos ipsos competitores tuos benevolo esse animo ostendito.
(41) Quoniam de amicitiis constituendis satis dictum est, dicendum est de illa altera parte petitionis quae in populari   10
ratione versatur. Ea desiderat nomenclationem, blanditiam,
adsiduitatem, benignitatem, rumorem, speciem in re publica.
(42) Primum id quod facis, ut homines noris, significa ut appareat,
et auge ut cottidie melius fiat; nihil mihi tam populare neque
tam gratum videtur. Deinde id quod natura non habes induc   15
in animum ita simulandum esse ut natura facere videare;
nam comitas tibi non deest ea quae bono ac suavi homine
digna est, sed opus est magno opere blanditia, quae, etiam
si vitiosa est et turpis in cetera vita, tamen in petitione
necessaria est; etenim cum deteriorem aliquem adsentando   20
facit, tum improba est, cum amiciorem, non tam vituperanda,
petitori vero necessaria est, cuius et frons et vultus et sermo
ad eorum quoscumque convenerit sensum et voluntatem

1 purgato *DVB*: -tio *HF*   in [*ante* spem] *FDVB*: ad *H*   2 amic-
⟨tuam⟩ *Mueller*[1] 14   [*cf. Sj.*[1] 130]   4 tuo…studio *HFD*: tua…-ia *VB*
7 inservito ratione *cod. Turnebi*: -vi [*sed* -unt *V*] *orat- X*   11 nomen
clat- *B*: nomen dat- *V*: nomen elat- *HFD*   12 rumorem *Rom.*: -rum *X*
speciem *Lamb.* [*cf.* ¶18.11, ¶52.12–14; *Hendrickson* 24]: spem *X*   re p. *FDVB*:
rem p. *H*: publico *Hendrickson* [*conl. Tac. Dial.* 6.4]   13 id *DVB*: *om. HF*
16 videare *cf. adnot. ad* ¶1.10   17 comitas *FD*: commit(t)as *HVB*
19 turpis in *DVB*: inturpi *HF*   20 necessaria est *D*[1]: -arias *V*: -aria
HFD^cB   etenim *coni. Petreius*: te enim *HFDV*: ea enim *Buech.*   assentando
cod. Turnebi: adsectando *H*[1]*DVB*: adsectatio *Hc*: assectatio sectando *F*
22 et frons *DVB*: frons *HF*

them of the obligations of friendship, and lead them to expect that you will be equally zealous and dutiful in looking after their interests, if they become your friends. As for those who dislike you for no reason, endeavour to turn them away from this vicious attitude by means of a favour or the expectation of a favour or by exhibiting your zeal on their behalf. As for those who are estranged from you on account of their friendship with your rivals, treat these men to the same courtesies as the previous types. And, if you can manage to convince them, indicate that you are, in fact, well disposed towards your rivals.

(41) Enough has now been said about fostering friendships. It is time to turn to the other part of a political campaign: the correct method for dealing with the people. This requires recognizing people by name, an ingratiating manner, constant effort, generosity, publicity, and civic pageantry.

(42) First, show off the fact that you can recognize people by name, and extend your familiarity with others' names so that it improves every day. In my opinion, nothing else is so gratifying to the public.

Then, make up your mind that what you lack by nature you should simulate so effectively that you actually seem to be acting in accordance with your nature. For you do not lack that affability proper in a distinguished and refined gentleman. But you very much need an ingratiating manner, which, however base and sordid in the rest of life, is nevertheless crucial when canvassing. To be sure, whenever ingratiation corrupts someone through flattery, it is immoral. But when instead its effect is that someone becomes friendlier to you, then it is less to be censured. And it is truly indispensable to a candidate, whose expression and looks and conversation must be adapted and accommodated to the mood and disposition of everyone he meets.

commutandus et accommodandus est. (43) Iam adsiduitatis nullum est praeceptum, verbum ipsum docet quae res sit; prodest quidem vehementer nusquam discedere, sed tamen hic
fructus est adsiduitatis, non solum esse Romae atque in foro
sed adsidue petere, saepe eosdem appellare, non committere   5
ut quisquam possit dicere, quod eius consequi possis, se abs
te non [sit] rogatum et valde ac diligenter rogatum. (44) Benignitas autem late patet: [et] est in re familiari, quae quamquam
ad multitudinem pervenire non potest, tamen ab amicis ⟨si⟩
laudatur, multitudini grata est; est in conviviis, quae fac ut   10
et abs te et ab amicis tuis concelebrentur et passim et tributim; est etiam in opera, quam pervulga et communica,
curaque ut aditus ad te diurni nocturnique pateant, neque
solum foribus aedium tuarum sed etiam vultu ac fronte, quae
est animi ianua; quae si significat voluntatem abditam esse   15
ac retrusam, parvi refert patere ostium. Homines enim non
modo promitti sibi, praesertim quod a candidato petant, sed
etiam large atque honorifice promitti volunt. (45) Qua re hoc quidem facile praeceptum est, ut quod facturus sis id significes
te studiose ac libenter esse facturum; illud difficilius et magis   20
ad tempus quam ad naturam accommodatum tuam, quod
facere non possis, ut id aut iucunde ⟨neges aut etiam non⟩
neges; quorum alterum est tamen boni viri, alterum boni

3 discedere *HFD*: dicere *VB*   4 atque *FDVB*: aut *H*   6 se *Lamb.*:
si *X* [*cf.* ¶32.2]   7 sit *seclusi*: esse *Lamb.*   8 et *del. Baiter*[1]
9 si *add. Koch*[1] [*cf. v.* 15]   10 grata *Rom.*: -tia *X*   10–11 fac ut
et *cod. Lambini*: facete *HFDB*: fac et *V*   11 ab am- *HF*: am- *DVB*
14 ac *HFD*: et *VB*   15 si *DVB*: *om. HF*   abditam *H*[c] [*ut videtur, super
ac scripto* l' *ab*] *Rom.*: abid- *B*: add- *HFV*: ad- *D*   17 a condidato [*sic*]
B: aquãdidato *V*: aquandi dato *D*: equandum dato *HF*   18 large *VB*:
longe *HFD*   19 facturus *V*[1] [*ut videtur, sed prima littera erasa] Baiter*[2]:
iact- *B*: act- *HFDV*[c]   21 accommodatum *VB*: -tum tu(m) *HFD*
22 id aut *DV*: id *HFB supplevi idem fere quod Purser et Constans: sententiam
iuc-* neges aut adeo simulate promittas *desiderat Buech.*   23 tamen
HFDV: *om. B*: *ante* boni [*posterius*] *transponend. coni. Purser*

(43) Now, no lesson is required when it comes to constant effort: the very expression is instruction enough. It is certainly advantageous never to withdraw from the city. But the real profit of constant effort comes not only from being present in Rome and in the forum, but from campaigning unceasingly, from calling on the same men frequently, from making it impossible, so far as you can, for anyone to say that he was not solicited by you—and solicited thoroughly and assiduously.

(44) Generosity, by contrast, covers a wide field. One can exhibit generosity in one's private affairs. Although this does not affect the common people directly, it influences them nonetheless when your generosity is praised by your friends. Generosity is manifested in banquets: see to it that banquets, both for all and sundry and for individual tribes, are celebrated both by you and by your friends. Generosity finds expression especially through services to others, services that you must advertise widely and make available to all. Every means of approaching you must lie open, both day and night. By this I mean not only the entrance to your house but also the look on your face, which is the doorway to your mind. If your facial expression suggests that your true feelings are concealed and hidden from view, then it hardly matters that your front door is open. For men do not simply want to receive promises—particularly when they are asking a candidate for something—they want to be made these promises with a courtesy nothing short of lavish.

(45) Hence this easy lesson: whenever you agree to do something for anyone, show him how keen and how pleased about it you are. The next lesson is harder and better suited to your situation than to your nature: whenever something is asked of you that you cannot agree to do, you must manage to be agreeable in saying no—or, better, do *not* say no. Although the former action is characteristic of a good man, the latter is characteristic

petitoris. Nam cum id petitur quod honeste aut sine detri-
mento nostro promittere non possumus, quo modo si qui
roget ut contra amicum aliquem causam recipiamus, belle
negandum est, ut ostendas necessitudinem, demonstres quam
moleste feras, aliis te id rebus exsarturum esse persuadeas. 5
(46) Audivi hoc dicere quendam de quibusdam oratoribus, ad
quos causam suam detulisset, gratiorem sibi orationem ⟨eius⟩
fuisse qui negasset quam illius qui recepisset; sic homines
fronte et oratione magis quam ipso beneficio reque capiuntur.
Verum hoc probabile est, illud alterum subdurum tibi homini 10
Platonico suadere, sed tamen tempori tuo consulam. Quibus
enim te propter aliquod officium necessitudinis adfuturum
negaris, tamen ii possunt abs te placati aequique discedere;
quibus autem idcirco negaris, quod te impeditum esse dixeris
aut amicorum hominum negotiis aut gravioribus causis aut 15
ante susceptis, inimici discedunt omnesque hoc animo sunt ut
sibi te mentiri malint quam negare. (47) C. Cotta, in ambitione
artifex, dicere solebat se operam suam, quod non contra
officium rogaretur, polliceri solere omnibus, impertire iis
apud quos optime poni arbitraretur; ideo se nemini negare, 20
quod saepe accideret causa cur is cui pollicitus esset non
uteretur, saepe ut ipse magis esset vacuus quam putasset;
neque posse eius domum compleri qui tantum modo reci-
peret quantum videret se obire posse; casu fieri ut agantur
ea quae non putaris, illa quae credideris in manibus esse 25
ut aliqua de causa non agantur; deinde esse extremum ut

1 honeste *X, sed in H* l' honestum est *superscriptum*   1–2 aut non
sine det- est nostro F [*cf. Sj.*¹ 120]   5 exsarturum *Lamb.*: exauct- *DV*:
exact- *HFB*   6 audivi *HF*: -dii *DVB*   7 eius *B* [*sed post* fuisse]:
om. HFDV   11 tuo *DVB*: *om. HF*   13 equique *B*: et quique *V*:
(a)que *HFD*   15 amiciorum *Eussner* 41 [*conl.* ⸿42.21, ⸿49.6]   hominum
HFD:*om. VB*   16 ⟨i⟩ inim- *coni. Buech.*   sunt *DVB*:sint *HF*   17 sibi
Rom.: tibi *X*   18 quod] quoad *Lamb.*   21 quod *Rom.*: quo *X*
24 casu *DVB*: causa *HF*

of a good candidate. Let me explain. Whenever anyone asks us to undertake anything that we cannot do without doing damage to our honour or our interests—for instance, if anyone should ask us to accept a legal case against a friend—that request must be declined, but it should be declined graciously. You must draw his attention to the obligations entailed by friendship; you must show him that you regret turning him down; you must convince him that you will make up for your refusal on a different occasion. (46) I once heard someone say, regarding certain orators to whom he had offered his case, that he was more gratified by the words of the one who turned it down than by those of the one who accepted it. Thus you see how men are won over more by looks and by words than by an actual favour.

But you will find nothing exceptionable in this. It is far more difficult, however, to make an argument to a Platonist like yourself that convinces you of the alternative option. Nevertheless, I shall shape my advice to your present situation. Now, there are some men who are able to go on their way appeased and unruffled when you make it clear that there is a personal obligation preventing you from helping them. Others, however, depart as your enemies, even after you explain that you have no choice but to say no, owing to the business of your friends or to weightier cases or to cases you have previously accepted. And all of them are left feeling it would have been better had you lied to them instead of turning them down.

(47) Gaius Cotta, a master in the art of canvassing, used to say that he routinely promised his help to anyone, so long as doing so did not conflict with his duty to others, but gave it only to those in whom he reckoned he was making the best investment. Consequently, he refused no one, because, as he explained, it was frequently the case that men to whom he had promised his help did not in the end avail themselves of his offer, or that he found himself less busy than he had expected. It was impossible, he insisted, for an orator to fill his house with supporters if he accepted only so many cases as he was certain he could see through to their conclusion. By chance it happens that cases must be argued which you did not anticipate going to trial or that those which you believed required your immediate attention are for some reason never argued. The worst thing that could happen, he pointed out, was anger on the part of the man to

irascatur is cui mendacium dixeris. (48) Id, si promittas, et incer-
tum est et in diem et in paucioribus; sin autem [id] neges, et
certe abalienes et statim et pluris; plures enim multo sunt
qui rogant ut uti liceat opera alterius quam qui utuntur.
Qua re satius est ex his aliquos aliquando in foro tibi irasci   5
quam omnis continuo domi, praesertim cum multo magis
irascantur iis qui negent quam ei quem videant ea ex causa
impeditum ut facere quod promisit cupiat si ullo modo possit. (49) Ac ne videar aberrasse a distributione mea, qui haec in
hac populari parte petitionis disputem, hoc sequor, haec   10
omnia non tam ad amicorum studia quam ad popularem
famam pertinere: esti inest aliquid ex illo genere, benigne
respondere, studiose inservire negotiis ac periculis amicorum,
tamen hoc loco ea dico quibus multitudinem capere possis,
ut de nocte domus compleatur, ut multi spe tui praesidi   15
teneantur, ut amiciores abs te discedant quam accesserint, ut
quam plurimorum aures optimo sermone compleantur.
(50) Sequitur enim ut de rumore dicendum sit, cui maxime ser-
viendum est. Sed quae dicta sunt omni superiore oratione,
eadem ad rumorem concelebrandum valent, dicendi laus,   20
studia publicanorum et equestris ordinis, hominum nobilium
voluntas, adulescentulorum frequentia, eorum qui abs te defensi sunt adsiduitas, ex municipiis multitudo eorum quos tua
causa venisse appareat, bene ⟨te⟩ ut homines nosse, comiter
appellare, adsidue ac diligenter petere, benignum ac libera-   25
lem esse loquantur et existiment, domus ut multa nocte

2 id *del. Puteanus*   4 utuntur *HF*: utan- *DVB*   7 his *HF*: hi(i)
DVB   ei*Corradus*[2]336:hi(i)*X*   quemvid-*H*:quiinvid-*VB*:quivid-*FD*   ea ex
[*cf. T.L.L.* 2.1104.72] *HF*: ea *DVB*: iusta [*cf.* ¶16.4] *Lamb.*   12 aliquid
F: -quod *HDV*   13 studio- se *DVB*: -so *HF*   19 oratione *VB*: rat-
HFD   20 concel- *HFD*: cel- *VB*   24 te *add. Schütz*[1] comiter *VB*:
-tes *HFD*   25 ac [*ante* diligenter] *DVB*: *om. HF*   26 ⟨et⟩ loqu- *Wes.*
⟨de⟩ nocte *Malaespina ad Att.* 8.6.1

whom you lied. (48) But this man's anger, if you do make him a promise, is by no means an inevitable occurrence, and in any event it happens later and in relatively few instances.

On the other hand, should you refuse anyone, you are sure to give offence to more people and to do so from the very beginning. This is because the number of men who seek to have another's services at their disposal is far greater than of those who actually employ them. Therefore, it is better if some of these people are occasionally angry with you in the forum than if all of them are always angry with you in your house—especially since men are far angrier with those who refuse them than they are with anyone whom they see prevented from keeping his promise by circumstances so urgent that it is plain how much he would like to keep his promise if he could.

(49) Now, lest I appear to have departed from my own system of classification by examining these matters in my discussion of the correct method for dealing with the people, this is the organizing principle that I am following: everything in this section has less to do with gaining the support of one's friends than it does with enhancing one's reputation with the public at large. Admittedly, the two categories are not entirely unrelated. In supporting one's friends one must naturally give gracious replies and must offer them the most zealous service when it comes to hazardous affairs. Nevertheless, here I am discussing the means by which you may win over the masses, so that your house may be filled before dawn, so that many may be won over to you by their expectation of your protection, so that when men leave your company they feel even friendlier to you than they did when approaching you, so that the ears of as many men as possible ring with excellent reports about you.

(50) It follows, then, that the next topic for discussion must be publicity, to which you must be slavishly devoted. But everything discussed so far in this work is acutely fitted to magnifying your publicity: your reputation for eloquence; the devotion of the publicans and the equestrian order; the goodwill of the nobles; attendance by constant crowds of young men and of those whom you have defended in court; the presence of multitudes from the municipalities, who, it is obvious, have come to the city for your sake; the fact that men say—and believe—that you are familiar with the public and address them courteously; the fact that you canvass constantly and assiduously, that you are generous and munificent, that your house is

compleatur, omnium generum frequentia adsit, satis fiat oratione omnibus, re operaque multis, perficiatur id quod fieri
potest labore et arte ac diligentia, non ut ad populum ab
his hominibus fama perveniat sed ut in his studiis populus
ipse versetur. (51) Iam urbanam illam multitudinem et eorum
studia qui contiones tenent adeptus es in Pompeio ornando,
Manili causa recipienda, Cornelio defendendo; excitanda
nobis sunt quae adhuc habuit nemo quin idem splendidorum
hominum voluntates haberet. Efficiendum etiam illud est ut
sciant omnes Cn. Pompei summam esse erga te voluntatem
et vehementer ad illius rationes te id adsequi quod petis
pertinere. (52) Postremo tota petitio cura ut pompae plena sit,
ut inlustris, ut splendida, ut popularis sit, ut habeat summam
speciem ac dignitatem, ut etiam, si qua possit ⟨ratio⟩ne,
competitoribus tuis exsistat aut sceleris aut libidinis aut lar-
gitionis accommodata ad eorum mores infamia. (53) Atque etiam
in hac petitione maxime videndum est ut spes rei publicae
bona de te sit et honesta opinio; nec tamen in petendo res
publica capessenda est neque in senatu neque in contione.
Sed haec tibi sunt retinenda: ut senatus te existimet ex eo
quod ita vixeris defensorem auctoritatis suae fore, equites
R. et viri boni ac locupletes ex vita acta te studiosum oti
ac rerum tranquillarum, multitudo ex eo quod dumtaxat
oratione in contionibus ac iudicio popularis fuisti te a suis
commodis non alienum futurum.

5

10

15

20

25

---

1 compleatur *DVB*: -antur *HF*   2 perfic- *DV*: profic- *HFB*   4 hominibus
DVB: omn- *HF* [*cf.* ¶19.12, ¶24.17]   *6 adeptus *HF*: quae ad- *DVB*
7 manilii *DVB*: manlii *HF*   8 quin idem *Man.*: qui idem *HFDB*:
quidem *V*   splendidorum *H^fD*: -ndorum *H^1F*: -ndorem *VB*   10 Cn. *D*:
C. *VB*: G. *HF*   14 qua *Palermus*: qu(a)e *HFDV*: quid *B*   possit *V*:
posset *B*: poscit [*sed* -cis *F*] *HFD*   *ratione *scripsi*: ne *X*: re *Sternkopf* 299: in
Palermus: nova *coni. Buech.*   17 hac petitione *HF*: hanc -onem *DVB*

filled long before dawn, that you are attended by a crowd drawn from every sort, that you satisfy all in what you say, many in what you actually do; and especially the fact that you are doing everything that can be done through industry, skill, and assiduousness to bring about not only the spread of your reputation among the public by these supporters of yours but also the commitment of the public itself to your cause.

(51) You have already won over the urban masses and the men who dominate public meetings because you have glorified Pompeius, taken up the case of Manilius, and defended Cornelius. We must now mobilize that popularity which to this day no one has ever enjoyed if he lacked the goodwill of the distinguished classes. You must also make sure everyone knows that Pompeius' goodwill towards you is total and that your success in this election is entirely in keeping with that great man's plans.

(52) Finally, see to it that your entire campaign is full of pageantry, that it is brilliant, distinguished, and appealing to the masses—that it is carried out with the utmost display and prestige. Furthermore, if it is at all feasible, see to it that each of your competitors is traduced by a smear fitting his character, whether it is defamation for wickedness or lust or bribery.

(53) This above all else: throughout this campaign you must make it absolutely clear that the republic reposes high hopes in you and that your reputation remains sound. However, during your canvass, you must avoid matters of state, both in the senate and in public meetings. Instead, let these be your aims: that, on the basis of your life's conduct, the senate deems you a guardian of its authority; that, on account of your past actions, the knights and prosperous classes believe you are a man devoted to tranquillity and stability; that the masses accept that you will be favourably disposed to their entitlements, because, at least in your speeches in public meetings and in court, you have championed their interests.

(54) Haec mihi veniebant in mentem de duabus illis commen-
tationibus matutinis, quod tibi cottidie ad forum descendenti
meditandum esse dixeram: 'Novus sum, consulatum peto'.
Tertium restat: 'Roma est', civitas ex nationum conventu
constituta, in qua multae insidiae, multa fallacia, multa in　　　5
omni genere vitia versantur, multorum adrogantia, multorum contumacia, multorum malevolentia, multorum superbia,
multorum odium ac molestia perferenda est. Video esse magni
consili atque artis in tot hominum cuiusque modi vitiis
tantisque versantem vitare offensionem, vitare fabulam, vitare　　　10
insidias, esse unum hominem accommodatum ad tantam
morum ac sermonum ac voluntatum varietatem. (55) Qua re
etiam atque etiam perge tenere istam viam quam institisti,
excelle dicendo; hoc et tenentur Romae homines et adliciun-
tur et ab impediendo ac laedendo repelluntur. Et quoniam in　　　15
hoc vel maxime est vitiosa civitas, quod largitione interposita
virtutis ac dignitatis oblivisci solet, in hoc fac ut te bene noris,
id est ut intellegas eum esse te qui iudici ac periculi metum
maximum competitoribus adferre possis. Fac ut se abs te
custodiri atque observari sciant; cum diligentiam tuam, cum　　　20
auctoritatem vimque dicendi, tum profecto equestris ordinis
erga te studium pertimescent. (56) Atque haec ita te nolo illis
proponere ut videare accusationem iam meditari, sed ut hoc
terrore facilius hoc ipsum quod agis consequare. Et plane sic
contende omnibus nervis ac facultatibus ut adipiscamur quod　　　25
petimus. Video nulla esse comitia tam inquinata largitione

1　mihi ven- *DVB*: ven- mihi *HF*　　　1–2　commentat- *Palermus*: commonit-
VB: commot- *HFD*　　　2　quod *Lamb*.: quo *X*: quas *Facciolati*　　　3　novus
sum *DVB*: novissimum *HF*　　　5　multae fallaciae *Lamb*.　　　8　odium
FDVB: odia *H*　　perferenda *VB*: prof- *HFD*　　　13　institisti *coni. Gruter*:
instituisti *X*　　　14　homines *DVB*: *om. HF* [*cf*. ¶20.16, ¶35.9]
22　pertimescent *HFVB*: -cant *D*　　te nolo *scripsi*: te volo *DVB Lamb*.: volo te
HF: nolo te *Buech*.　　　23　⟨non⟩ ut vid- *Lamb*.　　iam *Lamb*. [*ante* accus-]:
tam *HFDV*: non *B*

(54) So much, then, for my reflections on the first two of the morning lessons that I admonished you to repeat to yourself each day when going down to the forum: 'I am a new man. I seek the consulship.' The third lesson remains: 'This is Rome'—a state formed of a confluence of nations, a state in which there is much treachery, much deception, and many vices of every sort, a state in which one must endure the insolence of many, the contumacy of many, the spitefulness of many, the arrogance of many, the tiresomeness and the vexatiousness of many. I recognize how wise and skilful a man has to be, in this milieu so marked by numerous and wide-spread vices, to escape animosity, gossip, or treachery—indeed, to continue to be one and the same man even as he adapts himself to so profound a diversity in character, conversation, and disposition.

(55) Therefore, continue unwaveringly on that path that you have chosen: be the best at oratory. It is through oratory that men at Rome are influenced and charmed—or warded off, should they want to hamper or harm you. For our state is especially depraved in this respect: when bribery enters the picture, it is apt to ignore merit and prestige. In view of this reality, you must remember who it is you are. By this I mean that you must see how you are just the man to instil in your rivals an acute fear of the dangers of being brought to trial. Let them know how closely they are being watched and monitored by you, and they will stand in fear not only of your assiduousness, your authority, and the forcefulness of your eloquence, but also of the equestrian order's devotion to you. (56) Now, I do not want you to exhibit this readiness in such a way that you give your competitors the impression that you are already planning to prosecute them, but rather so that, owing to their fear of prosecution, you can more easily achieve your objective. Strive, then, with your every fibre and faculty to achieve the aim of this canvass of ours. For it is clear to me that no election is so debased by bribery that there are not at least some centuries

quibus non gratis aliquae centuriae renuntient suos magno
opere necessarios. (57) Qua re si advigilamus pro rei dignitate, et
si nostros ad summum studium benevolos excitamus, et si
hominibus studiosis nostri gratiosisque suum cuique munus
discribimus, et si competitoribus iudicium proponimus, se-   5
questribus metum inicimus, divisores ratione aliqua coerce-
mus, perfici potest ut largitio nulla fiat aut nihil valeat.

(58) Haec sunt quae putavi non melius scire me quam te sed facilius his tuis occupationibus conligere unum in locum posse
et ad te perscripta mittere. Quae tametsi scripta ita sunt ut   10
non ad omnis qui honores petant sed ad te proprie et ad
hanc petitionem tuam valeant, tamen tu, si quid mutandum
esse videbitur aut omnino tollendum, aut si quid erit praeter-
itum, velim hoc mihi dicas; volo enim hoc commentariolum
petitionis haberi omni ratione perfectum.   15

---

3 benevolos *secl. Buech.* [*cf. Sj.*[1] 124]   4 studiosis *DVB*: -diis *HF*: gratiosis
coni. Petreius   nostri grat- *coni. Gesner*: grat- nostri *X*: [grat-] nostri *Buech.*:
studiosisque nostri *coni. Petreius*   5 discribimus *H*: dissc- *V*: distribuimus
D[1]: describimus *FD*[c] (*in marg.*)   5–6 sequestribus *HF*: si equ- *DB*:
etequ- *V*   7 ⟨aut⟩ nulla *Lamb.*   fiat *H*[c]*DVB*: fit *H*[1]*F*: sit *Buech.*   9 his]
istis *Lamb.*   10 scripta ita sunt *HDV*: ita sunt sc- *F*: ita sc- sunt *B*
12, 13 tu *et* esse *FDVB*: *om. H*

which, without receiving payments, return those candidates to whom they have strong ties. (57) Therefore, if we remain vigilant, as is fitting when one's objective is a matter of great prestige, and if we rouse to the keenest condition of zeal those who are already well disposed to us, and if we assign the right task to each of our enthusiastic and influential supporters, and if we set before our rivals the possibility of a prosecution, strike fear into dishonest electioneers, and find a means of intimidating bribery agents, then we can be sure that this election takes place without corruption, or, if corruption obtrudes, it has no bearing on the result.

(58) Here, then, are matters that I by no means believe I understand better than you but which, on account of your current preoccupations, I am better able to collect into a single account and send to you in writing. I have written a work that does not pertain to everyone seeking an office but rather to you in particular and to this specific canvass. Still, I should like you to tell me if anything strikes you as requiring revision or even outright expunging. For I desire this brief handbook on canvassing for office to be esteemed perfect in every respect.

Commentary

Throughout this commentary, 'Cicero' refers to M. Tullius Cicero (cos. 63); 'Quintus' refers to Q. Tullius Cicero (pr. 65). All dates are BC unless otherwise indicated.

A Brief Handbook on Canvassing for Office. There is no indication that the *Brief Handbook* ever carried a formal title (Nardo 1970, 3 n. 1), though matters must remain unclear inasmuch as no ancient author refers to the work explicitly (Palmer 1971, 387, is wrong to detect a reference to the *Brief Handbook* at Cic. *De or.* 1.5, nor does *Pan. Lat.* 3.16–17 reflect any acquaintance with the *Brief Handbook*, *pace* Nixon and Rodgers 1994, 419). In manuscripts the work is routinely designated as the *Handbook on Canvassing for the Consulship* (*commentarium consulatus petitionis*), which aptly describes its contents. The conventional title adopted by modern editors derives from the work's final sentence: 'I desire this brief handbook on canvassing for office [*commentariolum petitionis*] to be esteemed perfect in every respect' (¶58). That with these words the author meant to indicate the title by which his work should be known is urged by Facciolati 1732, p. ii; Buecheler 1869, 2; and Tyrrell 1877, 40; cf. Tyrrell and Purser 1904, 116. If, however, the work's chief purpose lay in contributing to Cicero's election (see §IV.5), the question of its formal title may be an irrelevance. In any case, the reader only encounters the expression 'brief handbook' when coming to the conclusion of the *Brief Handbook*: the work, significantly, commences as a 'letter' (see next note). On the *Brief Handbook*'s status as a *commentariolum* and the implications of that aspect of the work, see §IV.3.

QUINTUS SENDS GREETINGS TO HIS BROTHER MARCUS. This work instantly identifies itself as a letter, a medium that signals friendship and candour (Demetr. *Eloc.* 225, 231; Koskenniemi 1956, 35ff.; Trapp 2003, 40ff.; Hall 2009, 53ff.; White 2010, 24ff.; Wilcox 2012; Bernard 2013, 71ff.; Rollinger 2014, 180ff.)—even in a letter that, like this one, was intended for public consumption (see §IV.2). Public letters, especially public letters promulgated for the purpose of expressing political views or political solidarity, were familiar features of Roman society: readers of the *Brief Handbook*, then, would expect to find in what follows, because it is a letter from one brother to another (see ¶1 **our mutual affection**), a highly favourable characterization of Cicero, his public standing, his views and habits, and (inasmuch as this letter portrays itself as circulating while Cicero is canvassing) his approach to the central political enterprise of standing for the consulship. At the same time, readers would be keenly interested in, and presumably influenced by, the basis of this letter's positive characterization: just how Cicero is constructed as an attractive candidate for office was crucial to this work's effectiveness in winning over voters who were not already supporters (and for preserving the enthusiasm of partisans); or, if the letter is a later work, its characterization of Cicero and his campaign must be central to its purposes. Even during the canvassing of 64, readers of the *Brief Handbook* would be aware that Quintus might not be the actual author of this letter, inasmuch as political campaigns spawned pseudepigraphical works; see §III.9. On the epistolary dimensions of the *Brief Handbook* and their importance for understanding the piece as a whole, see §IV.2.

Salutations in Roman letters, expressed in the third person, tend to be so formulaic that, as here, they can be expressed with abbreviations ('sends greetings' is S. D. = *salutem dicit*). Formulaic, but not without social implications that never passed unobserved (e.g. Cic. *Fam.* 7.32.1; 16.18.1; see White 2010, 67ff.; Bernard 2013, 133ff.), and it was always possible to make a social blunder even in a public letter (e.g. Cic. *Phil.* 13.22). Quintus' greeting is casual and intimate, as one should expect in correspondence between brothers, and here he employs the simple style of salutation found in all the letters between Marcus and Quintus (on its distinctiveness, see White 2010, 68; Bernard 2013, 135f.), including Cicero's formal and public letter to Quintus on provincial administration (*Q. Fr.* 1.1.1, on which see §IV.4; Quintus' only surviving letter to Cicero, apart from the *Brief Handbook*, is *Fam.* 16.16). It appears that at least some of the greetings in the surviving Ciceronian correspondence are spurious (Constans 1940, 46ff.), and Shackleton Bailey, expressing concern over the uniformity in the headings of the letters in the collection *Ad Quintum fratrem*, raised doubts about the genuineness of its salutations (Shackleton Bailey 1995, 142), probably unnecessarily; in any case, the *Brief Handbook* is not a part of that collection (see §V.2). On Roman nomenclature and Roman habits in referring to one another, see Appendix A.

¶1 Although…I nonetheless. Roman letters, public and private, frequently proffer advice. The matter was a delicate one, especially among the senatorial order, because conferring advice on a fellow aristocrat was freighted with the possibility of giving offence (Hall 2009, 118ff.; White 2010, 117ff.). Here Quintus employs a common introductory formula for letters of advice (*etsi...tamen*: Nardo 1970, 25, accumulates 33 examples, including the introduction of Cic. *Q. Fr.* 1.1), the purpose of which, by suggesting that the addressee has no real need for the counsel that follows, is to nullify any suggestion that the author is asserting, in any degree, his superiority. Quintus soon goes further in underlining Cicero's superior competence as a candidate for office (see below, **anything new**).

Although the *Brief Handbook* opens by way of this common epistolary feature, it does not, here or at its conclusion, exhibit any of the personal touches, such as wishes for good health or acknowledgement of previous correspondence, that were characteristic of ordinary letters (see Trapp 2003, 35f.; Bernard 2013, 138ff.). By way of contrast, Cicero's public letter to Quintus (*Q. Fr.* 1.1) opens and closes in the manner of private correspondence.

talent. Quintus begins with a reference to Cicero's *ingenium*, a word that can refer to character and talent alike (see *TLL* 7.1423–4). Although the word occasionally occurs in company with aristocratic concepts, and of course no one in Rome, including the aristocracy, would fail to claim native talent, nevertheless, because *ingenium* was susceptible to varying and sometimes ignoble actualizations, the word never obtained 'a precise place in the aristocratic ideal' (Earl 1967, 52f.; Tatum 1988, 254f.). Still, *ingenium* carried important contemporary political associations. Lucretius can describe the hurly-burly of political competition with the line *certare ingenio, contendere nobilitate* ('[they] vie with one another in talent, they compete in nobility'; Lucr. 2.11), and *ingenium* was central to the rhetoric of the new man (see ¶2 **new man**).

On Cicero's natural capacities, see Plut. *Cic.* 2.2–6, discussing his *euphuia* ('natural talent'), which Cicero possessed in greater abundance than Demosthenes, the subject of the parallel *Life*; see *Dem.* 8.3.

assiduousness. Cicero works hard: the point is made here, and hard work is a recurring motif of this work. Cicero's personal industry is again cited at ¶¶15 and 50. Assiduousness (*diligentia*) is regularly demanded of a candidate by Quintus (see ¶¶11, 15, 16, 33, 50, 55). So, too, labour (*labor*; see ¶¶15, 50; cf. Cic. *Sull.* 73) and industry (*cura*, a rough synonym for *diligentia* in republican political discourse; see ¶15; Hellegouarc'h 1963, 252f.). A candidate must also be hard-working (*industrius*; see ¶¶8, 29; cf. Sall. *Iug.* 4.3: canvassing is *maxuma industria*) and industrious (*navus*; see ¶8), qualities also required of his supporters: ¶¶18, 19, 29 (where industry is linked to influence). *Diligentia* is one of the subdivisions of Quintus' analysis of a political campaign (¶16) and as such it is the focus of ¶¶16–53, where Quintus discusses the actual practices required in canvassing. This emphasis is not unique to the *Brief Handbook*: Cicero also stresses the necessity of *diligentia* in winning elections (Cic. *Planc.* 7; cf. *Planc.* 11, 66–7). In describing to Atticus his long hours and hard work as governor of Cilicia, Cicero claims that his exertions are as exacting as they were 'back in the days when I was a candidate' (*ut olim candidatus*: *Att.* 6.2.5); cf. *Pis.* 55 (*officiosissima...natione candidatorum*: 'the tribe of candidates, unsurpassed in the scrupulous performance of every courtesy').

Sustaining one's political standing in Rome did in fact demand constant exertion (Meier 1980, 175; Hopkins and Burton 1983; Tatum 2015, 259ff.; §III.2), and hard work was a crucial constituent in the Roman concept of excellence (*virtus*), the fundamental quality of an aristocrat (Hellegouarc'h 1963, 248ff.; Lau 1975, 26ff.; McDonnell 2006, 335ff.). Cicero makes this point in his public letter to Quintus on provincial administration (*Q. Fr.* 1.1.4: success requires *diligentia*). Hence the disgrace associated with sloth: Cic. *Off.* 2.36; see Earl 1967, 23. The vocabulary of industry, owing to its relationship with *virtus*, played a prominent role in the rhetoric of the new man (see ¶2 **new man**).

Diligentia, industria, and *labor* were also deemed the qualities of a successful orator (Cic. *De or.* 2.147–50; see Leeman, Pinkster, and Rabbie 1989, 85ff.; see further David 1992, 87ff.; Wisse 2013): Cicero's reputation for eloquence, a topic raised for the first time in the next section (¶2), stands as proof of his superior industry as well as his talent. Quintus' courteous gesture in his opening sentence, then, is at the same time an advertisement for Cicero's merits and his qualifications as a sound candidate.

our mutual affection. Quintus does not cite patriotism or political ideology as motives either for this essay or for his support of Cicero's campaign, nor would his contemporaries have expected him to do so. He instead advertises his brotherly devotion. Affection (*amor*) was a dimension of *pietas*, the loyalty felt toward one another by members of the same family (see Saller 1994, 105ff.). And one's family, for a political figure, remained a vital source of his influence (see ¶16 **by blood or by marriage**). Brothers, it was assumed, would support one another in public as well as private life: 'who is more bound by the bonds of friendship than brother with brother' (Sall. *Iug.* 10.5; see Bannon 1997, 91ff., esp. 101ff. on Quintus and Cicero). In his public letter to Quintus, Cicero declares himself motivated to write by his profound affection (*propter singularem amorem*), on account of which he is avid for Quintus' glory (Cic. *Q. Fr.* 1.1.45).

day and night. Quintus, too, is assiduous in his support of Cicero's candidature, the ostensible motive for his composition. In this way he identifies his own with his brother's virtue. The assertion of long nights spent in literary labour was a routine boast on the part of authors advertising their learning (e.g. Cic. *Parad.* 5; Plin. *NH* 18 praef.; see Janson 1964, 97f.). Thus Quintus underlines the seriousness and thoughtfulness of the work that follows.

your political campaign. The word is *petitio*, its first appearance in the letter. It means 'importuning' and reflects the humbling language used to describe canvassing in Rome: see, further, §§III.1, III.4. Although *petitio* refers to the process of campaigning for *any* magistracy and not exclusively for the consulship, it was normal Latin to employ the verb *petere* absolutely in the sense of 'to canvass for the consulship' (Leeman and Pinkster 1981, 206), and in any case all is made clear in ¶2 ('I seek the consulship').

anything new. Quintus makes it absolutely clear that Cicero will learn nothing new from the *Brief Handbook*. In other words, its purpose is not to *teach* Cicero, but, at least ostensibly, to transform the Roman practice of canvassing for office into a systematized art, a transformation that requires analysis and classification (see next note). Because the *Brief Handbook* now reveals itself as a didactic epistle (see §III.4), and because it was natural for didactic epistles to be addressed to an individual in need of instruction (a figure sometimes described by scholars as 'the didactic fool'; see Mitsis 1993, 124; Morrison 2007, 125), it is vital for Quintus' representation of Cicero here that he close down any possible implication that Cicero is anything other than an ideal candidate: hence Quintus' care in making it clear that Cicero has not requested the *Brief Handbook* (contrast the introductions provided at *Rhet. Her.* 1.1; Cic. *De or.* 1.1; *Orat.* 1.1; see Janson 1964, 2). Nor does he need it. Similarly, when Cicero composed for Quintus his public letter on provincial administration, he insisted 'but you do not need exhortations and instructions from me or from anybody... I have not written these things to instruct you... but writing this allowed me the pleasure of dwelling on your excellence [*virtus*]' (*Q. Fr.* 1.1.36). In each letter, the advice contained within constitutes an expatiation on the excellence of its recipient. On Cicero's care in adapting the subject matter of his letters to the personality of his correspondent, doubtless a general Roman practice, see Morello 2013 (who adduces previous scholarship).

Quintus' formulation here, 'nothing new' (*non...aliquid...novi*), also emphasizes the conventional and traditional quality of the instruction to follow: there is nothing innovative here. Instead, Cicero's canvassing, the implication is clear, reflects normative Roman expectations of the behaviour of candidates for the consulship (see §IV.4). In this way, the *Brief*

Handbook, from the start, allays anxieties about Cicero's standing as new man, a central concern of the entire work (see ¶2 **new man**).

within a single, systematic form and in a logical order. Here Quintus makes the bold claim that, by way of his detailed analysis and classification, he is transforming the traditional Roman practice of canvassing into an art or skill (*ars*). On the implications of this literary move, especially its importance as an assertion of the normative quality of Quintus' instructions to Cicero and as a means of representing Cicero as a sound, in some ways paradigmatic, candidate, see §IV.4.

Quintus' approach to the techniques of canvassing should have found a receptive audience in the sixties. Roman traditions governing canvassing had been put to the test on account of the Social War (91–87), when Roman citizenship was extended to the allies, and nearly the whole of Italy, in all its diversity (Dench 2005, 130ff.; Farney 2007, 179ff.), was transformed into the Roman electorate (on the profound nature of this transformation, see Dench 2013). Members of the senatorial order, and certainly Rome's nobility, could not be certain that past methods for securing electoral success would subsist, and as a consequence the disposition of Rome's new citizens as voters became so controversial that, in 88, conflicts over the way forward led first to sedition and then to Sulla's first march on the city (Badian 1958, 230f.; Seager 1994; Konrad 2006; Steel 2013b, 87ff.; Tatum forthcoming a). It was not until the census of 70 that the matter was finally resolved (on the constitutional circumstances of Rome's new citizens, see Sherwin White 1973, 134ff.; Brunt 1988, 93ff.; Bispham 2007, 161ff.). In the event, electioneering techniques in Rome did not require radical readjustment, even if candidates now had to cultivate voters up and down the peninsula. And although municipal aristocrats were able to find places in the senate, the nobility continued its domination of the consulship (Badian 1990). Still, even in the late sixties, Quintus could expect an interest on the part of the propertied classes and especially on the part of the aristocracy in the idea of canvassing as an art. By then, because it was clear that the aristocracy's traditional approach to canvassing remained robust and effective, its elevation to the status of an art could be viewed as, if not celebratory, then at least reassuring. In putting Cicero the new man (see ¶2 **new man**) forward as a modern paradigm of the old order, Quintus must have believed, he enhanced his appeal to members of the aristocracy, not least the nobility, with an abiding stake in continuity.

Quintus' theoretical approach to canvassing in the *Brief Handbook* may seem at odds with Cic. *De or.* 1.5, where Quintus is represented as believing that eloquence is achieved *simply* by means of the right combination of talent (*ingenium*) and practice (*exercitatio*) and does not require theoretical training. However, what Quintus rejects at *De or.* 1.5 is the proposition that oratory requires profound and extensive philosophical learning (*artes eruditissimorum hominum*), which is not at all the same thing as a rejection of the *ars* appropriate to oratory (a foundation that tends to be taken for granted in *De or.*) (Leeman and Pinkster 1981, 21ff.; *contra* Waibel 1969, 80f.).

in a logical order. By way of hendiadys (*ratione et distributione*), Quintus stresses the importance of strict classification and therefore didacticism in the *Brief Handbook* (see §IV.4). *Ratio* ('logic' or 'method') recurs whenever Quintus emphasizes electioneering methodology: 'matchless technique... in conducting a political campaign' (¶11: *summa ratio... petendi*); 'the correct method for dealing with the people' (¶41: *in populari ratione*, a discussion that continues through ¶53). Cicero, too, in advising Quintus on provincial administration, points out the importance of combining *ratio* with assiduousness (*Q. Fr.* 1.1.4). *Distributio* is any division into parts, but is especially common as a technical term in rhetoric (e.g. Cic. *Inv.* 1.32) and philosophy (e.g. Cic. *Part.* 33). Quintus defends the consistency of his *distributio* at ¶49 ('lest I appear to have departed from my own *distributio*'). Quintus' employment of analysis by way of a highly technical, didactic syle (see §IV.1), although perhaps the most conspicuous feature of the work, is mostly limited to ¶¶13–53, his instruction on canvassing for the consulship: he expresses himself differently when addressing Cicero's condition as a new man (¶†2–12) or the perils of electoral corruption (¶¶54–6).

Although... nature... pretence is able to defeat nature. This is the most perplexing sentence in the whole of the *Brief Handbook*, nor can the problems it raises be said to be resolved—which matters because this sentence, in its transmitted form and context, tends to characterize the *Brief Handbook* as a guide towards dishonest and unsavoury practices and not as normative instruction in traditional electioneering techniques; the complaint that the *Brief Handbook* is excessively cynical in its exposition has been raised by more than one scholar and figures in challenges to the work's authenticity (see §V.4).

The contrast presented here between 'pretence' (*simulatio*) and the nature it conquers is stark (note the word order of the Latin: *simulatio naturam vincere*). But Quintus has thus far said nothing about pretence, and its introduction here is jarring. Furthermore, and more importantly, *simulatio* is a profoundly disreputable word in political and philosophical contexts alike. For Cicero it suggested an unacceptable means for social advancement (*Q. Fr.* 1.1.15; *Off.* 2.43) and it was ordinarily linked by him to the idea of *false* friendship (*Planc.* 22; *Amic.* 92; *Off.* 3.60–1; see Merguet 1884, 507; Merguet 1894, 542ff.; *OLD* 1767). The word carries a neutral connotation only when it translates the Greek term *eironeia*, either in the sense of Socratic dissimulation (e.g. Cic. *Off.* 1.108; *Ac.* 2.5.15; *Amic.* 15; see Vlastos, 1991, 33ff.) or rhetorical irony (Lausberg 1990, 302ff., 446ff.), neither of which is pertinent here. And yet, because in the next section Quintus turns to actual instruction, this sentence, as it stands, seems to characterize Quintus' treatment of canvassing as an essay not on a venerable Roman institution but rather on the art of shifty behaviour.

Misgivings arose early: Gruter 1618 reports that Puteanus (Errijek de Rut (1574–1646)) transferred this sentence to ¶42, a section of the *Brief Handbook* dealing with 'an ingratiating manner' (*blanditia*), a quality necessary for canvassing the general public and especially the lower orders:

> Then, make up your mind that what you lack by nature [*natura*] you should simulate so effectively [*ita simulandum*] that you actually seem to be acting in accordance with your nature [*natura*]. Although the strength of nature is indeed powerful, still, in an undertaking lasting but a few months, it seems clear that pretence [*simulatio*] is able to defeat nature. For you do not lack that affability proper in a distinguished and refined gentleman.

The presence of *simulatio* in this context is not inappropriate: *blanditia* is a potentially morally compromising aspect of canvassing and is registered as such in Quintus' treatment of it (at ¶42; see Tatum 2007, 123ff.).

Puteanus' transposition offers an attractive solution and was accepted by many subsequent editors of the *Brief Handbook* (with the exceptions of Baiter and Kayser 1866 and Wesenberg 1872, each of whom simply deleted the sentence). Constans, however, making a case that this sentence disrupts the sequence of ideas in ¶42 (see Constans 1940, 278), restored the sentence to ¶1 (though, because he recognized how suddenly it introduces a new thought in ¶1, he posited a hiatus immediately preceeding it), and most modern editors and translators have been persuaded by Constans (e.g. Watt 1958a; Nardo 1970, 1972; Henderson 1972; Fedeli 1987; Shackleton Bailey 1988, 2002; Fatás in Duplá, Fatás, and Pina Polo 1990; Boriaud 1992; Laser 2001; Lucrezi 2001; Puteanus' transposition is accepted by Broderson 2013).

But Constans's restoration takes us back to the original problem thrown up by *simulatio*. Nardo proposes that, in view of the importance in ¶1 of the balance between talent and instruction, 'pretence' is here meant to serve as a kind of technical term equivalent to *ars* or *ratio* ('training' or 'logical method'; Nardo 1970, 125). This gloss on the word 'pretence' (*simulatio*) can also be found in several modern translations of the *Brief Handbook* (e.g. Fedeli 1987; Fatás in Duplá, Fatás, and Pina Polo 1990;

Boriaud 1992). John Toland, it is clear, perceived this same problem and discovered the same solution; in his translation we find 'I am of the opinion, that Art may get the better of Nature' (Toland 1714). It is not obvious, however, that the sense of *simulatio* can be stretched so far, nor does Nardo address the word's unsavoriness (why use *simulatio* when *ars* or *ratio* is available and neither is freighted with the negative connotations of *simulatio*?). Fedeli 1987, taking a tack not dissimilar from Nardo's, translates *simulatio* (without explanation) as *tattiche ben orchestrate* ('well-orchestrated tactics'). Laser 2001, 101f., thinking, apparently, of the art of rhetoric, associates Quintus' sentiment here with the persuasive tactics required by oratory, when a speaker must sometimes strike a pose or utter falsehoods in order to win over his audience; but rhetoric is not the obvious topic in this sentence, and the techniques of persuasion can be justified in more elevated language than what the reader finds here (e.g. Cic. *Off.* 2.51; cf. Quint. 2.17.26; 12.1.36). Sillett 2016, 187, proposes that *simulatio* here means something like 'following a philosophical position', a sense suggested to him by Cicero's use of *simulare* at *Nat. D.* 2.168; there, too, however, *simulare* appears to register something unattractive. Finally, Prost 2017, 2, renders *simulatio* as *une attitude étudiée* ('a disciplined approach'), which he, too, refers to Quintus' instruction in the *Brief Handbook*.

A different solution is offered by Cooley, Murrell, Taylor, and Thorpe 2009, who translate *simulatio* as 'fraud' and see in it a reference to illegal electioneering (*ambitus*), the topic of ¶55–7. Now it is difficult to make *simulatio* mean *ambitus*. Still, basic to their proposal is the intriguing idea of viewing Quintus' introduction of *simulatio* here as a reference to the likely practices of Cicero's rivals. In this way, the *Brief Handbook* becomes Cicero's defence against his opponents' *simulatio*. Although this approach must remain a legitimate possibility, its construction of the passage can only be described as strained.

Another solution is possible. Pasoli 1975 proposes that the presence of *simulatio* here owes itself to corruption and, furthermore, that the word disguised by the manuscripts' *simulatio* must be *ratio*. His complete restoration is *simul <adhibita r>atio*, a correction that yields the translation: 'Although the strength of nature is indeed powerful, still, in an undertaking lasting but a few months, it seems clear that logical method, when once it has been applied, is able to defeat nature.' That is, the application of art gives a talented man an advantage even over other talented men (see **¶54 how wise and skilful a man has to be**). This provides excellent sense, and Pasoli's neat emendation is very attractive. That one's natural capacities could be improved through training, including theoretical training based on an *ars* (or, in Greek, *technē*), was an intellectual commonplace going back to fifth-century Greek literature and still robust in the late republic (e.g. Cic. *Inv.* 1.5; see e.g. Shorey 1909; Brink 1971, 394ff.; Rawson 1985, 132ff.) Here Quintus rounds off his sole claim for originality—that is, his organization of canvassing into an art—by way of what had long been viewed as the principal utility of theoretical analysis. Although Pasoli's emendation is a more elegant solution to the problems of this sentence than Puteanus', the latter is still worth considering, even if the reason for such a transposition is less than obvious.

lasting but a few months. This phrase raises the question of the date, real or dramatic, of the *Brief Handbook's* composition. Although consular campaigns commenced early, we learn from *Att.* 1.1.1 that in July 65 Cicero had not yet begun canvassing; in the same letter (*Att.* 1.1.2), Cicero indicates that in September 65 he may join the staff of C. Calpurnius Piso (cos. 67), then the governor of Transalpine and Cisalpine Gaul, in order to court the voters in those regions (see §VII.5). This has been proposed as a possible dramatic date for Quintus' letter (Beltrami 1892, 25). However, although the *Brief Handbook* takes the form of a letter, it is a public letter (see §IV.2) and there is therefore no compelling reason to seek out a situation in which Quintus could communicate with Cicero only by way of correspondence. Quintus contrasts Cicero's busy schedule with his own free time for contemplation and composition (¶58): inasmuch as Quintus was aedile in 65, such a contrast could have been appropriate only after he had left office and was again a private citizen. The idea that an aristocrat ought to employ his leisure time in providing services to the Roman state, including literary services, goes back to the elder Cato (Cic. *Planc.* 66; cf. Sall. *Cat.* 4.1; *Iug.* 2.4; Cic. *De or.* 1.1–4; *Leg.* 1.9–14). This sentiment animates Quintus' public letter to his brother (on the relationship between leisure and literary composition, see Stroup 2010, 37ff.). Consequently, it is probably better to date the *Brief Handbook* to 64. Since consular elections could be expected to take place in July (see §II.3), the work was composed (or depicts itself as having been composed) at some point during the first half of the year.

¶2 consider what…what…who. First by posing, in indirect discourse, then by answering, in reverse order and in direct discourse, three questions, Quintus indicates the three fundamental divisions of the *Brief Handbook*, which subsequently are dealt with in the order of Quintus' answers rather than the questions: (i) Cicero's identity as a new man and the consequences of that for his candidature (¶¶2–12); (ii) the nature of the magistracy he seeks and the best techniques for attaining it (¶¶13–53); and (iii) the nature of the political environment in which he campaigns (¶54–7). Hereafter, the reader will be aware of the work's central concerns, the first and most important of which is Cicero's condition as a new man (see below **new man**), a reality that colours everything that follows it in this work. In asking Cicero to consider who he is and what he is aiming at, Quintus underlines the difficulty of Cicero's undertaking (see Cic. *Div. Caec.* 37). The conceit of question and answer was a pleasing one for the Romans (Quint. 9.2.14; see Lausberg 1990, 381ff.) and, at least during the imperial period, was commonly employed by teachers in the instruction of their pupils (Kaster 1988, 160), a didactic approach that doubtless obtained in the republic as well. It has been suggested that *commentarii* ('handbooks') like the *Brief Handbook* were inclined to adopt a tripartite structure (Rüpke 1992, 213ff.), but this claim remains controversial (Riggsby 2006, 138ff.). A technique similar to the one employed here is used by Plutarch in his treatise *Political Precepts* (*Mor.* 798–825): at *Mor.* 813de, the addressee is urged to recall the advice Pericles routinely gave himself ('take care, Pericles; you are governing free men; you are governing Greeks, citizens of Athens'); this lesson, and others, Plutrach instructs his addressee to call to mind in direct discourse.

Almost every day. Editors regularly print the reading of the manuscripts, viz. *prope* ('almost'). Many, however, reject it in their apparatus, inasmuch as, when Quintus recurs to this sentiment at ¶54, he reminds Cicero that he has been admonished to contemplate these three points 'every day'. In addition, Quintus repeatedly urges Cicero to circulate daily (¶¶3, 34, 36). Beltrami 1892, 29 n. 2, defends the manuscripts' reading but does so by taking *prope* with *meditandum est* (the sense being, in his view, something like: 'every day…you must repeat to yourself almost constantly'). It is better to emend. A sampling of rectifying conjectures includes: *nempe* ('indeed', Buecheler 1869); *porro* ('henceforth', Tyrrell and Purser 1904); *propterea* ('consequently', Constans 1940); *prosus* ('indeed', Watt 1958a). It is the habit of modern translations to print and translate *prope*, sometimes without comment (e.g. Henderson 1972; Fedeli 1987; Duplá, Fatás, and Pina Polo 1990; Laser 2001; Lucrezi 2001; Shackleton Bailey 2002; Cooley, Murrell, Taylor, and Thorpe 2009).

go down to the forum. The forum (*forum Romanum*), located at the foot of the Capitoline and Palatine hills, was the centre of public life in Rome (Richardson 1992, 170ff.; *LTUR* 2.325ff.; Carandini 2017, 143ff.). It was a crucial duty for every candidate that, accompanied by an escort, he descend to the forum from his house in the hills (*deductio*) and circulate through the forum glad-handing potential voters (*prensatio*): see further ¶¶34–8, especially ¶36 **escort you** and ¶37 **third element**, and §III.5. On the ideological importance of the forum and its role in civic rituals in Rome, see Russell 2016, 43ff.; Rosillo López 2017, 43ff.; §III.5.

At the time of his candidature, Cicero occupied a house on the Carinae, which he had inherited from his father; in 62, when he purchased a house on the more glamorous Palatine, Cicero handed his property on the Carinae over to Quintus (Plut. *Cic.* 8.3; Cic. *Q. Fr.* 2.3.7; *Har. resp.* 31). Of Cicero's serious rivals in the election of 64, Catilina seems to have possessed a house on the Palatine (Suet. *Gramm.* 17); the location of Antonius' house, mentioned at ¶8, is unknown.

new man. The expression 'new man' (*novus homo* or, as here, simply *novus*) most commonly refers to a man who is the first of his line to enter the senate. In a traditional society like Rome's, newness was never an unqualified good thing, and the expression *novus homo* undoubtedly originated in social prejudice. Cicero, who derived from the municipality of Arpinum, was of equestrian origin (see ¶3 **the equestrian order**) and the first of his family to enter the senate. Roman voters preferred men of noble stock (see ¶4 **nobles**) and exhibited a clear bias against new men (see the evidence assembled by Badian 1990). Before Cicero's election, the most recent new men to attain the consulship were C. Coelius Caldus (cos. 94) and (probably) C. Norbanus (cos. 83) (see ¶11 **Gaius Coelius**). On new men and *novitas* ('newness'), see Syme 1958, 566ff.; Wiseman 1971; Dondin-Payne 1981; Brunt 1982; Shackleton Bailey 1986; Vanderbroeck 1986; Dugan 2005; Blom 2010; Yakobson 2014.

Cicero's status as a new man is a major theme of the *Brief Handbook* and the preoccupation of ¶¶2–14. Cicero's *novitas* is fundamental to his identity in the work: even Cicero's standing as an orator, his principal claim to fame, is here subordinated to it (see below **your fame as an orator**). This is hardly surprising inasmuch as Cicero's *novitas* represented his candidature's most conspicuous liability and the central point of attack on the part of his noble rivals and their supporters (Asc. 86C, 93–4C; App. *B.Civ.* 2.2; Sall. *Cat.* 35.2; Quint. 9.3.94; Schol. Bob. 80 (Stangl)). At *Clu.* 69, Cicero describes, in matter-of-fact fashion, a new man competing against nobles as likely to incur envy (*invidia*) and give offence (*offensio*). Neutralizing these attacks was central to Cicero's campaign strategy (see §VII.5), and the *Brief Handbook* plays its part in this strategy (see §IV.5).

New men, in putting themselves forward in opposition to nobles and their influence, sometimes emphasized their personal excellence (*virtus*) and especially their native talent (*ingenium*: see ¶1 **talent**) along with their superior industry (see ¶1 **assiduousness**)—in contrast to the indolence and moral decay of the nobility (e.g. Cic. *Verr.* 2.5.180; *Pis.* 1–2; Sall. *Iug.* 63.7; 85; *Cat.* 23.6; Asc. 23C; see Syme, 1958, 566ff.; Earl 1961, 8ff., 31ff., 105; Earl 1967, 44ff.; Wiseman 1971, 107ff.; Dugan 2005; McDonnell 2006, 320ff.; Blom 2010, 35ff.; Yakobson 2014). Cicero deployed this tactic in his prosecution of Verres (*Verr.* 2.3.7; 2.4.81; 2.5.180–2) and recurred to these sentiments throughout his career both in his oratory (e.g. *Leg. agr.* 2.3, delivered in the opening days of his consulship; *Mur.* 17; *Sull.* 22–5; *Planc.* 58; *Har. resp.* 17; *Sest.* 136; *Balb.* 51; see Blom 2010, 50f.) and correspondence (e.g. Cic. *Att.* 1.16.10; *Fam.* 1.7.8; 3. 7. 4–5; 5.1; 5.2.2). In the case of his Verrine orations, it is probably true that Cicero's appeal to the rhetoric of *novitas* was intended as a means of attracting support from new Italian voters (Dench 2013, 130ff.; cf. Dugan 2005, 6ff.): after all, in 70 no one could have been confident that the nobility's long-standing hold on elections could persist (Mouritsen 1998, 110ff.; Bispham 2007, 161ff.; **¶1 within a single, systematic form and in a logical order**). By 64, however, it was as obvious to the Romans as it is to us that the nobility had entirely mastered their new electoral circumstances, which meant that Cicero's well-publicized denunciation of the nobility in his *Verrines* had become a potential public relations problem that threatened to exacerbate his difficult situation as a new man seeking the consulship.

Hence the extended treatment of Cicero's *novitas* in the *Brief Handbook*, whose take on the matter is very different from the aggressive tone in Cicero's *Verrines* or the orator's later speeches and letters (*pace* Dugan 2005, 6; Blom 2010, 51; Dench 2013, 130f.). Instead, Quintus acknowledges the difficulties confronting a *novus* without attributing them to the opposition or the envy of the nobility: envy, in the *Brief Handbook*, belongs to anyone who is surpassed in politics, noble or new man (¶13), and the electorate's aversion to new men in the consulship is attributed to the Roman people's instincts, not the nobility's hostility (¶14). Indeed, the paramount value to Cicero of the nobility's support is strongly emphasized, and the nobility are respectfully distinguished from other levels of Roman society (¶¶3–4). Quintus observes explicitly that it is the society of the nobility Cicero seeks to join (¶4). When Quintus adduces C. Coelius Caldus, the new man who was consul in 94 and one of Cicero's favourite role models (Blom 2010, 158ff.), he makes it clear that the man was *not* superior to his noble rivals (¶11). Indeed, the true exemplar of electioneering in the *Brief Handbook* is a noble, C. Aurelius Cotta (cos. 75) (¶47). The point is made more than once that sound nobles know how to canvass, as indeed every candidate must (see ¶¶11, 47; cf. Liv. 4.25.12; Morstein-Marx 1998, 278f.). Even in his invective against Cicero's noble rivals, Antonius and Catilina, Quintus depicts them as disappointments to their class, not typical specimens of it (¶7): it is in fact Cicero's good luck that his rivals fall short of the quality one expects of the nobility (see ¶¶11, 27). In short, Quintus' Cicero is a new man who possesses a share in the superiority of the nobility, acknowledges their social preeminence, and endeavours to canvass in a style that will satisfy their expectations. By depicting Cicero's candidature in this way, the *Brief Handbook* seeks to reassure all elite voters of Cicero's soundness and to deflect criticisms of his *novitas* on the part of his rivals for office.

your fame as an orator. Fame (*gloria*) was freighted with attractive aristocratic associations (see Hellegouarc'h 1963, 369ff.) and was a concept intimately connected with elections: Cic. *Off.* 2.31–8, drawing on his (lost) *De gloria*, relates how 'the peak and perfection of fame' (*summa... et perfecta gloria*) depends on the affection of the multitude, their confidence, and their opinion that one merits high office (see Dyck 1996, 409ff.). 'Fame as an orator' (*dicendi gloria*) was a traditional aristocratic accomplishment (Liv. 30. 1.5; Plin. *NH* 7.139.3), not least because oratory was instrumental in sustaining political order in Roman society (see (i.a.) Morstein-Marx 2004; David 2006; Steel 2006, 3ff.; Rosenstein 2006, 368f.; Steel 2013a; Steel and Blom 2013; Blom 2016). Oratory was also a recognized means of rising from (relative) obscurity to glory (Cic. *Off.* 2.45), and speaking for the defence (see below **deemed worthy of being patron**) was deemed a brilliant method for acquiring fame and influence (*gratia*) (Cic. *Off.* 2.51; see David 1992, 591ff.; Alexander 2007; §§III.2, VII.1). At *Mur.* 24, Cicero insists that eloquence, like military glory, was a vehicle for elevating new men to the consulship. Here Cicero's undeniable primacy in oratory is adduced by Quintus as compensation for *novitas* (see above **new man**), a move that allows Quintus to showcase Cicero's brilliance by way of an expression of respect for Rome's traditional hierarchy. At ¶55, Quintus will return to Cicero's eloquence and adduce it as his best weapon against the corruption of his rivals: see ¶55 **through oratory**.

Cicero's rise to high political station was achieved through his eloquence, just as other new men were aided by their expertise in jurisprudence or their military abilities (see Liv. 39.40.5; Cic. *Mur.* 30; Wiseman 1971, 118ff., 143ff.). But Cicero's rise, it is worth observing, was possible only because he enjoyed, as a knight (see ¶3 **the equestrian order**), a high social station in the first place. Advocacy was practised at many levels of Roman society and was by no means a universally accessible means of social advancement (see Crook 1995, 44).

great prestige. 'Prestige' (*dignitas*) was a concept of vital significance to the political life of the Roman republic, especially of the late republic (Wegehaupt 1932; Alföldi 1956; Balsdon 1960; Drexler 1966; Rilinger 2007, 95ff.). *Dignitas* was at once rank, prestige, and personal honour—and influence. It was sustained by fame (*gloria*; see Hellegouarc'h 1963, 400) and was demonstrated when recognized by the people—that is, through expressions of popular esteem and especially through election to high office. For this reason, every election was a 'struggle for prestige' (*contentio* *dignitatis*; see Cic. *Mur.* 14; *Planc.* 8; *Off.* 1.38). Winning office rewarded and enhanced prestige (Hellegouarc'h 1963, 400ff.; Hölkeskamp 2011a, 212f.), and the consulship represented *dignitas* of the highest order (Cic. *Sull.* 30; *Balb.* 10). At the same time, prestige was deemed necessary for winning office in the first place (Isid. *Etym.* 2.21.4; cf. Cic. *Verr.* 2.2.172; *Agr.* 1.27; *Mur.* 23; *Pis.* 97; *Planc.* 27, 50, 62), especially for winning the consulship (Cic. *Mur.* 43, 76; *Fam.* 15.12.2; Asc. 86C; [Sall.] *Ad Caes. sen.* 2.7; Suet. *Iul.* 41.2.); see §III.2. New men had to confront the complaint that they lacked the *dignitas* appropriate to the consulship (e.g. Sall. *Cat.* 23.6; 35.3; *Iug.* 63.7), which helps to explain why Quintus here insists on Cicero's possessing the traditional prestige associated with excellence in oratory.

deemed worthy of being patron. Patronage in Rome was a multifarious phenomenon. Simply put, men of station entered into a voluntary relationship of unequal reciprocity with lesser men, a relationship based on good faith (*fides*) rather than law; the patron (*patronus*) aided his client (*cliens*) through favours, and the client responded with gratitude and deference. Acting as a traditional patron implied virtue and was deemed an advantage of the nobility (see the detailed discussion in §III.3; ¶17 **clients**). Here, however, Quintus refers to Cicero's career as a pleader in the courts, in which venue the same concept of aid in exchange for gratitude operated: an advocate was his defendant's patron (Rouland 1979, 275ff.; David 1992, 49ff.; Lintott 2004). Patrons in the courts were forbidden to accept fees (by the *lex Cincia* of 204: sources assembled at *MRR* 1.307; see Kaser 1971, 602ff.; *RS* 741ff.), and instead received their client's gratitude as well as wide public appreciation for their service (Cic. *Off.* 2.51), all of which, an aspiring politician could hope, would result in electoral support.

Elite defendants loathed being described as clients (Cic. *Off.* 2.69) and avoided referring to their advocate as 'patron'. To do so was a rare gesture of courtesy (e.g. Cic. *Fam.* 6.7.4; 7.29.2) and might signal friendship as well as gratitude (Saller 1989, 53ff.; Tatum 1997, 486ff.). This delicate relationship animates Quintus' description of Cicero, whose worthiness to be numbered among Roman consulars is underlined (on the social distinction attaching itself to the word 'patron' even when used in a forensic sense, see Gelzer 1969a, 70ff.); at the same time, Quintus is careful in avoiding any formulation that might offend aristocratic sensibilities.

Still, although Cicero may have been deemed worthy to defend ex-consuls, he had not, so far as we know, done so by 64 (Powell and Paterson 2004, 417ff.). It is possible that, by the time he was a candidate, Cicero had undertaken to defend C. Calpurnius Piso (cos. 67), whose trial took place in 63 (Cic. *Flacc.* 98; see Alexander 1990, 112), but that must remain uncertain (the argument put forward in support of this view by McDermott 1970 is fantasy, but the basic claim, that Cicero had, by early 64, agreed to take Piso's case, is not implausible). Nardo 1970, 10, suggests that Quintus has in mind Cicero's speech in support of the Manilian law, which was delivered on behalf of Pompeius' interests (see §VII.3), but that is clearly not what is suggested by *patronus* here. It is worth noting that Cicero, over the whole of his career, defended few ex-consuls: Piso, C. Antonius (cos. 63; see Alexander 1990, 119f.); A. Gabinius (cos. 58; see Alexander 1990, 148, 178). He may also have defended C. Marcius Figulus (cos. 64; see Alexander 1990, 121), but that is far from certain. In view of these facts, Nisbet 1961b, 84f., argued that this item in the *Brief Handbook* is an anachronism and evidence of its later composition by an author other than Quintus.

But Quintus does not here claim that Cicero has, in fact, defended an ex-consul. As Buecheler 1869, 26, observed, Quintus 'did not write *est* [which would give us: 'who *is* the patron of ex-consuls'] because, in fact, so far as we know, Marcus had not yet defended in court an ex-consul'. Quintus' language, then, is precise—and more affecting than informative. Its purpose is to associate Cicero with the dignity of consular figures by drawing attention to his forensic talents.

ex-consuls. Ex-consuls spoke first in any senatorial debate (Lintott 1999a, 78), a privilege that accorded them exceptional influence in that body and consequently in the direction of politics in republican Rome (Syme 1939, 20ff.; Jehne 2011b; Yakobson 2017). Ex-consuls are often described as the 'foremost men of the state' (*principes civitatis*: the evidence is assembled by Gelzer 1969b, 44ff.). In his oratory, from early in his career until its very end, Cicero consistently addresses ex-consuls with a striking degree of deference (e.g. Cic. *Verr.* 2.3.209–11; *Rab. Perd.* 21–2; *Red. Sen.* 17; *Phil.* 8.17; 14.4).

unworthy of the consulship. That is, *indignus consulatu*. On the importance of *dignitas* in securing election to office and the frequency of phrases like 'worthy of office' (*dignus honore*), see §§III.2, III.7, and, above **great prestige.** Cicero's rivals in 64 denounced him explicitly as unworthy of the consulship (Asc. 86C).

for every speech. Cicero's only known court case in 64 was the trial of Q. Gallius (see Alexander 1990, 107; ¶19). He also delivered *In toga candida* (*Tog. cand.*) in the senate shortly before the elections.

¶3 aids to this skill. Buecheler 1869, 26, saw here a reference to Cicero's library (the verb *seponere*, 'keep in reserve', tends to refer to tangible things), but Quintus is more likely to have in mind Cicero's constant alertness, practice, and application; hence the immediately following reference to Demosthenes' work ethic.

remind yourself. A possible witticism. At *Div.* 2.96, Cicero relates the story, told by Demetrius of Phalerum (see next note), that Demosthenes, originally unable to pronounce the Greek letter *rho*, learned to do so perfectly by practice (*exercitatio*). Perhaps this is the evidence of Demosthenes' hard work that Quintus had in mind here and perhaps Quintus' word choice, *recordare*, was intended to recall Demosthenes' difficulty: although the *Brief Handbook* frequently deploys terms referring to memory and recollection, this is the only occurrence in the text of any form of *recordari*.

Demetrius. Demetrius of Phalerum (*c.*360–280) combined in one life careers as a peripatetic philosopher (a pupil of Theophrastus, he was a philosophical author in his own right), a statesman (he was *strategos* in Athens, and Cassander installed him as sole ruler of Athens, which he governed from 317 until 307, when he was ejected by Demetrius Poliorcetes), and orator (he is complimented by Cicero at *Brut.* 37f. and *Or.* 94, where he is the exemplar of the middle style; see Quint. 10.1.80). Cicero admired him on account of these multiple accomplishments (*Leg.* 3.14). After he fled Athens, Demetrius settled in Alexandria, became an advisor to Ptolemy I, but died in disfavour under Ptolemy's successor, Ptolemy II Philadelphus (see Green 1990, 36ff.; O'Sullivan 2009).

the exertions and application of Demosthenes. Demosthenes (384–322) is generally regarded as the greatest of the Attic orators (see, i.a., MacDowell 2009; Worthington 2013; Lintott 2013). He is frequently cited by Cicero as the best of all orators (e.g. *Brut.* 35, 141–2, 282; cf. Plut. *Cic.* 24.6), and, in his *Orator*, Cicero repeatedly emphasizes Demosthenes' comprehensive superiority (esp. *Or.* 104) (see, i.a., Wooten 1997; May 2007). Although it is impossible to tell what specific story about Demosthenes Quintus alludes to here (see above **remind yourself**), Demosthenes was famed in antiquity for his habit of coming to every speech thoroughly prepared (e.g. Plut. *Dem.* 9.2). For Demetrius' assessment of Demosthenes' delivery (he was not a fan), see Fortenbaugh and Schütrumpf 2000, 239ff.

exhibit to the public. Public actions were essential to aristocratic self-fashioning and to electoral success, and oratory played an important role in this self-fashioning: for instance, in 54, when Cicero's political career was at an ebb, Quintus urged Cicero to busy himself in the courts in order to amplify his influence (*gratia*) and prestige (*dignitas*) (*Q. Fr.* 1.16(15).1–2). The importance to any aspiring politician of living in the public eye is stressed by Cicero when he lectures M. Juventius Laterensis (pr. 51) on how to be a successful candidate (*Planc.* 66–7; the trial took place in 54). See further **¶43 being present in Rome; ¶50 publicity; ¶52 full of pageantry; §§III.2, III. 5–12.**

the number and variety of your friends. Quintus deals with 'gaining the support of friends' at ¶¶16–40. Here he anticipates that discussion by trumpeting the expansive network of friendships enjoyed by Cicero, associations that are here represented as deriving from his brilliance as an orator. Cicero was delighted, at the outset of his campaign, when he discovered how many friends—by which he meant political supporters—he already enjoyed (*Att.* 1.1.1); in appraising the electoral prospects of Domitius Ahenobarbus (cos. 54) during the summer of 54, Cicero observed that he was formidably equipped with friends (*Att.* 4.16.6: *Domitius ut valeat amicis*) despite his lacklustre games. On Roman friendship generally, and on the specialized use of the word 'friend' when canvassing for office, see ¶16 the definition of the word 'friend'.

For what new men. Quintus underscores Cicero's exceptionalism among the several new men canvassing for office in 64 (see §VII.5), a point he reprises at ¶14. Here, although the text is defective, the essential sense is recoverable. Watt 1958a prints Sedgwick's emendation (translated here), but most editors prefer the text printed in Schwarz and Hummel 1791: <*non multi homines*> *habuerunt* (the translation is then: 'for very few new men have had ...'), which reflects Cicero's phrasing at *Att.* 5.18.1. Schwarz 1720 had originally printed <*novi nulli*> *habuerunt* ('no new men have had ...'), an even stronger assertion; this emendation is accepted by Nardo 1970, 58 n. 12; Nardo 1972 (who prints <*nulli homines*> *novi*, which yields the same sense); Duplá, Fatás, and Pina Polo 1990; Lucrezi 2001.

a wide range of friends. Quintus' catalogue illustrates the comprehensive quality of Cicero's network of friends, which extends into the lower orders (see below **clubs**). Quintus' list, although it exhibits an overall tendency to move down the social scale, nevertheless eschews hierarchy (as do similar lists in Cicero's correspondence: e.g. *Fam.* 2.6.3; *Q. Fr.* 2.3.4). This list does not explicitly include the nobility, whose introduction is postponed until ¶4, nor does it specifically cite members of the senatorial order (the importance of senatorial friends is mentioned at ¶29; cf. ¶¶8, 53). Instead, in this list, these elites are included among the men whom Cicero has defended in court and the young men drawn to Cicero by his oratory, which focuses the reader's attention on Cicero's merits. The same focus obtains in Quintus' list of Cicero's supporters at ¶50.

publicans. Publicans (*publicani*) were rich men of the equestrian order (see next note), who formed companies (*societates publicanorum*) in order to provide many of Rome's public services (*publica*, hence their designation): e.g. the provisioning of Roman armies, the management of Rome's mines in Spain, and the collection of taxes, most notably in the province of Asia.

Out-sourcing on this grand a scale was necessitated by the Romans' insistence on maintaining a small government with only a rudimentary administrative staff. Owing to the enormous resources demanded for carrying out these essential functions, the companies formed by *publicani* were large and complex, and much about their operation remains murky (Badian 1972, 67ff.; Lintott 1993, 86ff.; Cottier, Crawford, Crowther, Ferrary, Levick, Salomies, and Wörrle 2008; Kay 2014, 192ff.).

Quintus begins his list of Cicero's friends with the *publicani* owing to their special status within the equestrian order (Brunt 1988, 151ff.), their collective clout (Badian 1972, 82ff.; Brunt 1988, 148ff.), and their close relationship with Cicero, a staunch supporter, whose rise was aided by his intimate relationship with the publicans (Mitchell 1979, 98ff.; Bleicken 1995, 14ff.; Berry 2003). As early as his aedileship, Cicero could claim to have devoted his career to the causes of the *publicani* (*Verr.* 2.2.181). At *Planc.* 23, Cicero lauds them as 'the flower of the Roman knights, the adornment of the state, the foundation of the republic', and he was a reliable supporter of their interests (e.g. *Leg. Man.* 17–18; *Agr.* 1.22–7; 2.102; *Att.* 6.1.16; 6.3.3). At the same time, the reputation of *publicani*, whose wealth derived from business investments and lending, instead of more honourable pursuits like agriculture and warfare (Cic. *Off.* 1.150), was susceptible of public criticism. It was held against P. Rupilius (cos. 132) that he began life as a publican (Val. Max. 6.9.8), and about T. Aufidius (pr. 67), another publican who advanced into the senate, it was said that his excellent service as governor in Asia (*MRR* 2.154) 'proved that his original condition [viz. his career as a publican] was owed to fortune' and not to his character (Val. Max. 6.9.7). Gaius Marius experienced the slur that he was a publican (Plut. *Mar.* 3), and the prosecutors of Gnaeus Plancius, whose father was a publican, could attack him on that very ground before a jury dominated by the equestrian order (*Planc.* 23–4). Even Cicero could view the profiteering of the publicans as disreputable (Cic. *Att.* 2.1.8), and in his public letter to Quintus on provincial administration he acknowledges, at length, the difficulty of working with the publicans in a totally honourable way (Cic. *Q. Fr.* 1.1.6–7, 32–6). Put differently, Cicero always ran a calculated social risk in championing the *publicani*. Here Quintus does nothing to palliate Cicero's connection with the publicans: quite the contrary, they come first on his list of the orator's valuable friendships, thereby signalling a relationship that constitutes a key aspect of Cicero's political identity.

the equestrian order. By any definition, equestrians were, like senators, very wealthy Romans. A knight (*eques*), although he might undertake public service (knights served as officers in the military and sat on juries in the city), did not follow a political career by holding magistracies or entering the senate. Consequently, knights enjoyed less prestige than senators. Still, owing to their wealth, their votes in the centuriate assembly were crucial for the success of any candidate (see §II.3). Cicero, who originated in an equestrian family, regularly advertised his connections with the order and throughout his career benefited from its support (Bleicken 1995; Berry 2003; ¶13).

Unlike senators, knights were unimpeded by law or custom from engaging in business, trade, or moneylending; on the factors inhibiting, though not eliminating, senatorial business affairs, including the *lex Claudia* of 218, see D'Arms 1981, 20ff. This is not to say that the equestrian order constituted a business or financial class, since many knights remained agriculturalists whose lifestyle and values corresponded closely with the senatorial order (Brunt 1988, 144ff.). But Rome's rich investors, including the *publicani*, were equestrians, and their financial resources were indispensable to senators, especially senators seeking higher offices, whose assets often consisted in estates and other properties (Welch 1996; Andreau 1999, 139ff.; Ioannatou 2006, 313ff.; Jehne 2016). Consequently, when Quintus draws attention to Cicero's close friendship with the equestrian order, he also brings to the fore the orator's traditional but distinctly ample resources for sustaining and advancing his career.

Exactly whom Quintus refers to with the expression *equestrian order* is unclear. Strictly speaking, knights were men possessing a public horse (*equites equo publico*) and assigned by the censors to one of the eighteen equestrian centuries, a group that included the sons of senators who had not yet entered upon a political career. But it seems clear that, in ordinary parlance, Romans used the word 'knight' to refer to anyone whose wealth met the obligatory minimum for equestrian order (which, under Augustus, was 400,000 sesterces: Plin. *NH* 33.32). At ¶33, Quintus distinguishes the equestrian order from the equestrian centuries, so perhaps his sense here is inexact, but ¶33 is bedevilled by textual difficulties that leave Quintus' usage there less than entirely certain (see commentary on ¶33). On the late republican sense of 'knight', see Nicolet 1966; Badian 1972, 82ff.; Wiseman 1987, 57ff.; Brunt 1988, 144ff.; Bleicken 1995, 54ff.; Linderski, 1995, 138ff.

municipalities that are devoted exclusively to you. An important constituency for any candidate. After the enfranchisement of Italy at the conclusion of the Social War (see **¶1 within a single, systematic form and in a logical order**), communities that were not Roman colonies (see **¶30 municipality, colony, prefecture**) became municipalities (*municipia*), the citizens of which had full citizen rights (the Romans also designated certain provincial communities *municipia*, whose inhabitants had only limited Roman citizen rights but whose magistrates regularly gained full Roman citizenship; Quintus does not here refer to these communities) (Sherwin White 1973, 159ff.; Bispham 2007, 161ff.; Laffi 2007). During the imperial period, municipalities maintained offices in Rome (Plin. *NH* 16.236; Suet. *Nero* 37.1; see Richardson 1992, 368; *LTUR* 4.350ff.). If this was also the case during the republic, these offices (like tribal offices: see ¶17 **fellow tribesmen**) will have received visits from glad-handing candidates. Prosperous citizens in the municipalities, knights, surely, but especially men who were enrolled in the first class, because they could afford to journey to Rome for the elections and because they were members of rural tribes, possessed valuable votes in the centuriate assemble (see §III.3). Consequently, the cultivation of the municipal elite was, by Cicero's day, absolutely essential (e.g. Cic. *Att.* 1.1.2; *Planc.* 21–2; *Sull.* 24; *Phil.* 2.76; Caes. *B.Gall.* 8.50; see Brunt 1988, 427ff.). The canvassing of municipalities, and other types of citizen communities, is discussed more fully at ¶¶30–2. Quintus' discussion of the importance of fellow tribesmen and of neighbours is also pertinent, inasmuch as Cicero's fellow tribesmen and neighbours extended themselves throughout Italy: see ¶17 **fellow tribesman**; ¶17 **neighbours**.

The devotion of the municipalities was a potential advantage for Cicero. It was not always the case that senators enjoyed good relations with municipal elites (Garnsey 1970, 189ff.; D'Arms 1984; Frier 1985, 261ff.). By contrast, Cicero's hometown of Arpinum was located near municipalities belonging to several tribes, and Cicero possessed villas in various regions of Italy, properties that expanded his personal and proximate ties to members of various municipalities (Shatzman 1975, 404ff.; Mitchell 1979, 102ff. Lomas 2004; ¶17 **neighbours**; §§VII.2 and VII.3). In addition, Cicero had, by 64, argued several important cases on behalf of municipal elites (e.g. *In Defence of Sex. Roscius* (Umbria); *In Defence of Aulus Caecina* (Volaterrae); *In Defence of Aulus Cluentius* (Apulia); see Mitchell 1979, 102ff.; see §VII), and he was conscientious in sustaining his relationship with municipalities (e.g. *Fam.* 13.4.1; 13.7.1). Municipal connections were valuable not only in their own right but also because they offered opportunities for conferring a favour on any senatorial and noble friends of a municipal defendant: this was plainly the case in Cicero's defence of Roscius, who enjoyed ties with distinguished noble families (see Cic. *Rosc. Am.* 15). Cicero also served as patron to various Italian municipalities (e.g. he was patron of Reate (*Scaur.* 27), Cales (*Fam.* 9.13.3), Capua (*Sest.* 9), and Locri (*Leg.* 2.15), though these relationships may well have arisen after his consulship). In general, see Deniaux 1993, 373ff. Mouritsen 2001, 121ff. has suggested that Cicero was exceptional in his cultivation of the municipalities, though of course that cannot be certain. Perhaps surprising in view of Cicero's exertions in establishing personal ties to Italy's municipalities, his letters, speeches, and essays reveal little sense of their local distinctiveness (Dench 2013, 127f.).

many men of every rank. Not to be taken literally, although from an elite perspective one need not go down the social scale too terribly far in order to satisfy the spirit of this claim (Mouritsen 2001, 107ff., goes so far as to maintain that candidates did not actively seek support at all social levels but did so only from prosperous ones). And at the very least Cicero had defended a freedman (*Clu.* 49), a woman of Arretium whose free status was challenged (*Caec.* 97), a comic actor (*Q. Rosc.*), and a scribe (*Clu.* 126; on the status of scribes, see Badian 1989). Cicero's sincere attitude towards the lower classes was hardly generous: for him, the urban masses were 'disgusting filth' and remained 'wretched, half-starved, ready to drain the treasury dry' (Cic. *Att.* 1.16.11; see Cic. *Att.* 1.19.4). In principle and in public, however, he believed one ought to offer one's assistance to every sort of person, including the poor (Cic. *Off.* 2.70–1).

clubs. Clubs (*collegia*) were religious and social organizations based largely on occupation and neighbourhood. Most of what we know about them derives from imperial, not republican, evidence. Still, certain features are clear enough. Membership was open to free, freed, and slave. Membership was voluntary, and contributions were expected. Members were organized into smaller units, called centuries (*centuriae*) or decuries (*decuriae*); assemblies were held and officers were elected, with various titles; the chief officer of a *collegium* was its *magister*. *Collegia* held meetings, suppers, celebrated sacred festivals, and formed corporations to provide for members' funerals. For the bulk of the urban population, *collegia* offered an opportunity for local prestige in a society that offered little in the way of dignity to the working poor. Consequently these organizations held a precious place in the mentality of the masses. The elite were aware of this and often acted as patrons to *collegia* (Clemente 1972; there is no evidence to suggest that Cicero acted as a patron to any *collegium*), and a very few *collegia* included some wealthy members (Treggiari 1969, 168f.). Quintus advises Cicero on how best to solicit the support of *collegia* at ¶¶30–2. On *collegia*, see Waltzing 1895–1900; Robertis 1938; Ausbüttel 1982; Linderski 1995, 165ff., 645ff.; Bollmann 1998; Tatum 1999, 25ff., 117ff.; Verboven 2007; Mayer 2012, 85ff.; ¶17 **neighbours**; ¶30 **all the clubs, the boroughs, and the neighbourhoods**

The potential political exploitation of *collegia* remained a senatorial worry. In 67 the tribune C. Manilius relied on the support of *collegia* to push through legislation, later abrogated, that benefited the voting rights of freedmen (Asc. 45C; Dio 36.42), and in 66 there was political violence that was blamed on the activities of some *collegia* (Cic. *Cat.* 1.15; Dio 36.44.3). Consequently, in 64, the senate passed a decree suppressing *collegia* deemed hostile to the republic and forbidding the celebration of the *ludi compitalicii*, unofficial games observed in Roman neighbourhoods by *collegia* in honour of the Lares Compitales, deities of the crossroads who watched over Roman neighbourhoods (Asc. 7C: these deities were officially honoured with an annual sacrifice, the Compitalia, which was unaffected by this decree) (see Linderski 1995, 165ff.; Lintott 1999b, 77ff.; De Ligt 2000; Lott 2004, 51ff.). How many *collegia* were suppressed by the senate's decree is unclear, and this passage is a reminder that respectable *collegia* and their activities subsisted as important elements in Roman social and political life (see Asc. 59C). Still, it is at least somewhat surprising that Quintus does not include here some positive qualification that would underscore the respectable quality of Cicero's relationship with these organizations and thereby avoid any potential confusion regarding his attitude towards the senate's decree. It is of course possible the senate's decree was passed later in the year (closer to the time of the neighbourhood games, which were celebrated after the Saturnalia).

young men. These will be young men of equestrian or senatorial status inasmuch as they are drawn to Cicero by their study of oratory; consequently, their inclusion here disrupts this passage's progression down the social order. A young man could be designated an *adulescens* (in this instance the word is *adulescentulus*, its diminutive) from the time he was a teenager until his late 30s. Young aristocrats, even when teenagers, took part in military service and sometimes appeared in public as orators (see §III.2). Some were politically active: e.g. young men were involved in both the Catilinarian conspiracy and its suppression (Cic. *Cat.* 14.5; *Cael.* 10; *Phil.* 2.16) and in the perturbations associated with the trial of P. Clodius Pulcher in 62 (sources assembled at Tatum 1999, 70f.). Some young men also were influential in determining the outcome of elections: e.g. C. Scribonius Curio (tr. pl. 50) (Cic. *Fam.* 2.6; *Phil.* 2.8); D. Brutus (cos. desig. 42) (Cic. *Fam.* 11.16); M. Brutus (pr. 44) (Cic. *Fam.* 11.17). At *Fam.* 2.6.3. Cicero claims that T. Annius Milo, a candidate for the consulship of 52, enjoys the support of elite and influential young men (denominated *iuventus*, 'the youth', instead of *adulescentes*). In 64 Cicero depended on the support of L. Domitius Ahenobarbus (cos. 54), with whom he and Quintus had enjoyed a long political relationship (Cic. *Att.* 1.1.3–4; *Verr.* 2.1.139); Cicero goes so far as to describe him as 'the man on whom my hopes for election rely most of all' (*Att.* 1.1.4). On young men in republican politics, see Allen, Jr. 1938; Eyben 1972, 1993; Isayev 2007.

their study of oratory. It was customary for young Romans of the elite class to associate themselves with distinguished senior men in order to acquaint themselves with the business of the forum, especially the courts, and to extend their personal connections (e.g. Cic. *Off.* 1.122; 2.46-7; *Amic.* 1; *Phil.* 2.3; *Sen.* 10; Plut. *Cat. mai.* 3.4; see §III.2). This relationship was deemed a form of friendship (Cic. *Fam.* 13.10.2) and is often described by scholars as *tirocinium fori* ('apprenticeship in the forum', a modern formulation: Powell 1988, 122) (see Bonner 1977, 84ff.; Scholz 2011, esp. 286ff.). By 64 Cicero was Rome's leading orator and a natural object of such associations (Quint. 12.11.6). The mature Cicero recognized in himself a model for younger orators (Cic. *Phil.* 2.20; *Att.* 2.1.3; 4.2.2.; *Q. Fr.* 3.1.11).

constant crowd of friends. By recurring to friends comprehensively Quintus completes his catalogue. At ¶¶34-8. Quintus discusses the particulars of marshalling daily attendance by supporters and the electoral significance of keeping large crowds in daily attendance.

¶4 See to it that...express their gratitude. Reciprocity constituted the basic stuff of Roman society. The exchange of favours was essential to friendship, patronage, commerce, and any form of political activity—not least because politics in Rome centred round the actions and ambitions of individuals instead of parties or factions (Meier 1980, 163ff.; Paterson 1985; Brunt 1988, 85f.; Hölkeskamp 2010, 8ff.; Steel 2013b, 42ff.; see §III.3). Romans did not seek an exact balance of favours: the performance of a favour (a *beneficium* or *officium*; see below **put you under an obligation**) imposed an obligation (*officium*) and garnered gratitude (*gratia*); the return of that favour dissolved neither obligation nor gratitude but instead tended to shift them back to the original benefactor; a constant exchange of favours established mutual obligation and gratitude (Saller 1982, 17ff.; Leunissen 1993; Verboven 2002, 35ff.; Griffin 2013, 30ff.; Rollinger 2014, 92ff.). Providing gifts and favours (*beneficia*) exhibited one's merit (e.g. Cic. *Off.* 2.53-4; on *virtus*, see ¶7; on industry, see ¶1 **assiduousness**) and generated fame (e.g. Cic. *Off.* 2.20-70, esp. 2.32; Sen. *Ben.* 2.33.3; Plin. *Ep.* 1.18.14; 5.1.13; on *gloria*, see ¶2 **your fame as an orator**). But benefactions were not exclusively for the purpose of achieving social splendour: by doing good to others, the aristocracy believed, they shackled them with inevasible debts of gratitude—or *gratia*—obligations so grave that, in many respects, *gratia* became an instrument of clout (MacMullen 1986; Jacotot 2013, 376ff.; Tatum 2015; see below **express their gratitude**). At the same time, an exchange of favours, it was widely assumed, had the potential for stimulating genuine personal affection (Cic. *Nat. D.* 1.121; *Off.* 2.23-6; Sen. *Ben.* 2.18.5; 2.21.1; cf. Arist. *Eth. Nic.* 1163a3-9). Reciprocity, in its various social manifestations, recurs throughout Quintus' detailed analysis of canvassing (¶¶16–53).

forceful reminders and solicitations. At *Fam.* 2.6.1–2, Cicero observes that a man of sensibility feels awkward when asking a favour from someone already indebted to himself but that, in any case, he should ask (*rogare*) and not insist on reciprocity. In urging Cicero to make solicitations (*rogando*), Quintus employs the correct diction, but his tone is far more insistent than what Cicero's letter describes as appropriate. At *Fam.* 2.6, Cicero is appealing to a long-standing and largely philosophical view on reciprocity, according to which a benefactor should neither remind the recipient of his favour of past kindnesses nor demand their repayment (e.g. Arist. *Eth. Nic.* 1162b22–34; *Eth. Eud.* 1243b; Ter. *An.* 43–4; Cic. *Amic.* 71; Sen. *Ben.* 2.10.5–11.3; see Konstan 1997, 79ff.; Griffin 2013, 39f.). From this perspective, approaching benefactions along the lines of an investment could be regarded as sordid. It is obvious that Quintus has no time for this elevated view—throughout the *Brief Handbook* he insists that Cicero insist on repayment for past favours (often, but not invariably, by way of the verb *rogare*: ¶¶5, 19, 21, 44, 47, 48). Quintus' direct attitude towards claims on reciprocity corresponds to normal Roman expectations and practice (see Verboven 2002; Hall 2009, 56ff.).

never be another opportunity. Not literally true, of course, but underscoring how essential for Cicero's campaign the backing of his supporters is (and indicating obliquely how grateful Cicero must be in response). This idea recurs at ¶¶19, 38. Quintus' emphasis on the importance of this opportunity (*tempus*) links the urgency of Cicero's campaign with the exceptional circumstances of any canvass (see ¶12 **required by your present situation**).

express their gratitude. Gratitude (*gratia*) is the crucial concept in the Romans' ideology of reciprocity. *Gratia* is the goodwill felt by the recipient of a favour. It is also the influence possessed by the dispenser of a favour: a man to whom favours are owed is *gratiosus*, that is, influential and popular. The obligation to repay debts of gratitude was strongly felt (e.g. Cic. *Off.* 1.47: 'for no duty is more necessary than that of expressing gratitude'; Cic. *Off.* 2.63: 'everyone hates a man who ignores a favour'; Sen. *Ben.* 3.1.1). Inasmuch as it was understood that one's debt in gratitude was proportional to one's capacity for repaying it (see Saller 1982, 16, collecting *testimonia*), the lower orders could and did benefit from elite liberality and as a consequence they, like their betters, resented any threat to this system of exchange (Cic. *Off.* 2.63: 'men of modest means deem this outrage [viz. ingratitude] their common enemy'). See Hellegouarc'h

1963, 202ff.; Moussy 1966; Weische 1966, 74ff.; Saller 1982, 21ff.; Verboven, 2002, 37ff. (and *passim*); Griffin 2013, 103ff.; Jacotot 2013, 376ff.; Rollinger 2014, 101ff.

Ideally, elections were decided by *gratia* (see Cic. *Att.* 4.15.8; *Q. Fr.* 2.15.4 on *gratuita comitia*, or 'elections decided by *gratia*', by which Cicero means elections that were not corrupted by *ambitus*, on which see ¶55 **bribery**). When campaigning for the consulship, Cicero remained aware of the importance of *gratia* to his success (*Att.* 1.1.4: 'indeed, you see...how important I reckon it to be that I not only preserve my existing *gratia* but that I actually expand it'). Cic. *Mur.* 70–1 emphasizes the importance of expressions of electoral support as a means by which humble citizens can repay debts of gratitude to public figures, and at *Planc.* 7–9 Cicero emphasizes that, in elections, *gratia* can count for more than personal merit. Indeed, the role of gratitude is a recurring one in discussions of elections (e.g. Cic. *Att.* 4.16.6; *Fam.* 2.6.3; 11.16.3; Dio 37.44.3). Unsurprisingly, then, the *Brief Handbook* repeatedly stresses the importance of *gratia* (see ¶¶8, 18–19, 23–4, 29, 32, 35–6, 38, 42, 44, 46, 56, 57), and Cicero is routinely, as here, depicted as *gratiosus*. How a candidate can garner *gratia* is the subject of the *Brief Handbook*'s extended analysis at ¶¶16–53. See also §III.3.

put you under an obligation. Cicero the candidate represented an opportunity for anyone seeking to invest social capital, and now, Quintus emphasizes (by way of hyperbole: 'there will never be another opportunity'), is the time to seize that opportunity. It was natural for Romans to seek to oblige those who could be useful to them in the future (e.g. Cic. *Off.* 1.48; 'we do not hesitate to confer obligations on those whom we expect to help us in the future'; see *Off.* 2.21–2). More than once Quintus makes it clear to his readers that there are men drawn to Cicero by the prospect of his subsequent gratitude (¶¶18, 21–2; see above **See to it that . . . express their gratitude**; and **express their gratitude**).

the goodwill of the nobles. The nobility (see below **nobles**) receive a separate, distinctive, and flattering treatment here (see ¶2 **new man**; §IV.5). When, however, Quintus recurs to his catalogue of Cicero's supporters at ¶50, the nobility are integrated into his list and come *after* publicans and the equestrian order. The nobility are not represented as being, in any sense, in Cicero's debt—a prudent move, inasmuch as it was widely believed that the very powerful disliked exhibiting gratitude (Cic. *Off.* 2.69; cf. Sen. *Ben.* 2.23.3). Although members of the nobility were inclined to abhor the idea of a new man occupying a coveted consulship (Sall. *Cat.* 23.6; *Iug.* 63.7), there was venerable precedent for noble support of a *novus homo*: the relationship between the noble L. Valerius Flaccus (cos. 195) and his protégé M. Porcius Cato (cos. 195); see Astin 1978, 9ff. And in fact most new men who rose in politics did so by attaching themselves to a great man, ordinarily a great general (Wiseman 1971, 176ff.). Cicero, too, cultivated the nobility, and exhibited himself as a loyal supporter of Pompeius. Still, he remained concerned about the nobility's attitude towards his candidature (Cic. *Att.* 1.1.2: 'when I have figured out where the goodwill of the nobility is directed, I will write to you'; *Att.* 1.2.2: 'it is public opinion that your friends, the nobility, are going to be hostile to my winning election'). In the end, however, the nobility supported his candidature (Sall. *Cat.* 23.6).

Quintus' Latin here (*novum hominem, hominum nobilium*) perhaps recalls Cicero's at *Verr.* 2.5.181 (*nobiles homines novorum hominum*), though expressions like these may have been common. If there is a reference to Cicero's earlier speech, however, it takes the form of a correction. Whereas Quintus compliments the clout of the nobility, in the *Verrines* Cicero complains about it ('I am aware how great the envy and how great the hatred that nobles feel for the excellence and industry of new men').

nobles. By the third century, by which time the political opportunities of patricians and wealthy, ambitious plebeians had become more or less comparable, a new elite, defined by office-holding, emerged (Hölkeskamp 2011a). Men from these families were 'known' (*nobiles*) owing to the political success of their ancestors, and men designated *nobilis* ('noble') come to dominate the consulship thereafter, especially in the late republic (Badian 1990). No ancient definition of nobility (*nobilitas*) survives, and perhaps the word never had a genuinely technical definition, but the preponderance of the evidence supports the view of Gelzer that nobles were men descending from a consul, a consular tribune, or a dictator (Gelzer 1969b). That such men were noble is, in any case, certain. An alternative theory grants nobility both to these men but also to patricians and to descendants of anyone who held any curule magistracy (Brunt 1982). The evidence will not permit the complete exclusion of this possibility. An excellent review of these matters is supplied by Burckhardt 1990. The nobility was not a closed caste. A non-noble who reached the consulship, although he did not thereby become a noble, ennobled his family: Cicero's son was a noble.

ex-consuls. Ex-consuls were highly influential (Jehne 2011b). But not every ex-consul in 64 was noble: e.g. C. Scribonius Curio (cos. 76), L. Gellius (cos. 72), and L. Volcacius Tullus (cos. 66) (see the evidence assembled by Badian 1990). Perhaps Quintus has only noble ex-consuls in mind here. Or perhaps he is intentionally blending two eminent categories, one of which, the ex-consuls, represents a station Cicero can aspire to reach (Cicero cannot become a noble; see previous note). In either case, the reference here is highly complimentary.

¶5 solicited assiduously. Nobles and ex-consuls are not here represented as owing Cicero any debt of gratitude, by way of contrast with the catalogue of friends rehearsed in ¶3 above—another strategic compliment. On Quintus' treatment of the nobility in the *Brief Handbook*, see ¶2 **new man.**

send your connections. Quintus' verb (*allegare*) refers to the Roman practice of sending personal representatives, usually mutual friends, to make a request (*adlegatio*). This practice, which obviously required more work by the petitioner, who had to persuade intermediaries to take part on his behalf, always signalled high esteem for the Roman approached in this way and was an important element in sustaining aristocratic cooperation and consensus. The purpose of *adlegatio* was not to intimidate anyone but instead to exhibit honour (see Cic. *Rosc. Am.* 25; *Verr.* 2.1.44; 2.1.136; 2.1.139; 2.1.149; *Fam.* 15.10.2; see Shackleton Bailey 1965, 286; Tatum 2017, a detailed discussion of *adlegatio* and its purposes). On the role of intermediaries in the imperial period, see Griffin 2013, 73ff.

our political opinions. Quintus identifies himself with Cicero's career and candidature (see ¶1 **our mutual affection**) and this identification is emphasized here by way of a shift to the first person plural (*LHS* 19ff.), a recurring feature of the *Brief Handbook* (¶¶5, 8, 57; see Nardo 1970, 119f.). The mature Quintus was in fact very hostile to popular rights, going so far, according to Cicero's *De legibus*, as to advocate abolishing the tribunate (Cic. *Leg.* 3.19–22).

the best men. Romans often referred to the wealthy in moral terms like *boni* ('good men') and *optimates* ('the best men')—or simply *optimi* ('the best men', a designation for men qualified to be senators: Festus 290L). The word *optimates* was often, as here, used in contrast with *popularis* ('champions of popular rights'; see next note), in which case the word takes on a political charge: it indicates advocates of the prestige of the senate (*senatus auctoritas*) in resistance to fellow aristocrats taking a stand on behalf of the sovereignty of the people (*maiestas populi Romani*). Although senatorial authority and popular sovereignty were each of them legitimate and fundamental principles in Roman government (see §§II.1; III.1), controversies over their application were not infrequent. *Optimates* and *populares* were not political parties, nor anything like coherent or stable political factions (for a different view, however, see Wiseman 2009, 13ff.). So potentially flexible were these designations that, in his famous description of the *optimates* at *Sest.* 96–9, Cicero includes under this rubric nearly every citizen of any class whose sense was good and whose finances were sound (see Kaster 2006, 317ff.). In general on *optimates*, see Strasburger 1939; Burckhardt 1990, 8ff.; Robb 2010; Mouritsen 2017b, 112.

champions of popular rights. A Roman politician could be labelled *popularis* ('a champion of popular rights') if he attempted to expand the entitlements of any segment of the Roman people, including the equestrian order, or somehow emphasized popular sovereignty at the expense of the senate's prestige. Some political figures, it is clear, held a principled view of popular rights. Others championed popular rights in order to gain political influence. Over the course of his career, a Roman politician might take actions that were both optimate and *popularis* in quality: e.g. Domitius Ahenobarbus (cos. 96) (Cic. *Leg. agr.* 2.19; Asc. 79–80) or the staunchly optimate M. Porcius Cato (pr. 54), who, during his tribunate, significantly expanded the grain subsidy (*MRR* 2.174f.). This was true of Cicero as well (see below). Popularity with the masses was an important aspect of a candidate's appeal to Romans of all classes (see §III.5). At the same time, there were extreme *popularis* politicians, like the Gracchi or L. Appuleius Saturninus (tr. pl. 103), who became public enemies (Steel 2013b, 15ff.). Consequently, it was important when competing for a consulship to avoid any imputation of demagoguery or political extremism. On the *popularis* in Roman politics, see Meier 1965; Seager 1972a; Meier 1980, 116ff.; Tatum 1999, 3ff.; Robb 2010; Mouritsen 2017b, 112ff.

Cicero, who would later describe himself as a *popularis* consul (Cic. *Leg. agr.* 1.35), had by 64 acted as an advocate of equestrian interests (see ¶3 **publicans;** ¶3 **the equestrian order,** and an important beneficiary of *popularis* reforms; cf. Meier 1965, 599ff.), criticized corruption in the nobility (Cic. *Verr.* 2.3.7); defended a *popularis* tribune (C. Cornelius (tr. pl. 67); see ¶19 **Gaius Cornelius**), delivered a speech on behalf of Pompeius (see below **Gnaeus Pompeius**), and at the very least publicly offered to defend C. Manilius (tr. pl. 66; see ¶51 **taken up the case of Manilius**), another *popularis* (on all these matters, see the detailed discussion at §VII.3–4). There was nothing subversive here, but an important part of Cicero's appeal to the prosperous classes whose votes mattered most in the centuriate assembly resided in his soundness and his reliability as a defender of the status quo, especially at a time of economic anxiety.

Did Cicero's rivals try to portray him as an extreme *popularis*? It was certainly a potential extension of electoral attacks on his condition as a new man (see ¶2 **new man**): new men were often associated with the tactics of *popularis* politicians (see Wiseman 1971, 173ff.). In any case, because an important tactic in Cicero's campaign was his depiction of Antonius and Catilina as corrupt intriguers working against the authority of the senate (see §VII.5), it was vital that Quintus underline Cicero's optimate perspective by disavowing any *popularis* inclinations here. Elsewhere in the *Brief Handbook* he even refers to the urban populace with the expression *multitudo* ('masses'; see ¶¶30, 44, 49, 51, 53), a somewhat disparaging term (Hellegouarc'h 1963, 514; see Bruggisser 1984). Quintus himself held strongly optimate views and remained an advocate of aristocratic prestige, at least according to Cicero (Cic. *Leg.* 3.17–22, 26, 34–7).

any speech that appeared to support popular rights. Quintus refers to Cicero's speech *On Behalf of the Law of Manilius (Pro lege Manilia)*, his public declaration of his willingness to defend Manilius (and his defence of Manilius in 65, if Cicero actually defended the man), and his defence of C. Cornelius (tr. pl. 67) in 65 (*Pro Cornelio*, extant only in fragments: Asc. 57–81C); on each of these matters, see §VII.3–4. Each of these undertakings was in the interest of Pompeius (see next note). At *Leg. Man.* 71, Cicero acknowledges the reality that his speech may have provoked enmity on the part of some, and P. Vatinius (cos. 47), when he was Cicero's enemy, claimed that *Pro Cornelio* offended the *boni* (*Vat.* 6, where Cicero points out that Vatinius' claim is contradicted by his election to the consulship in the next year).

Gnaeus Pompeius. Cn. Pompeius Magnus, Pompey the Great, was Rome's most illustrious figure during the 60s. Already commanding troops in his 20s, Pompeius helped to secure Sulla's victory in Italy and crush opposition to Sulla in Sicily and Africa; in 77 he helped to suppress the insurrection of M. Aemilius Lepidus (cos. 78), after which he campaigned against Sertorius in Spain. As an equestrian, he celebrated two triumphs and in 70, although under age, became consul despite having held no previous magistracy. In 67 he was awarded an extraordinary command against piracy, a military campaign he concluded with rapid and stunning success. He far surpassed his peers in military glory, and by 64 he was winning victories in the east as commander in the war against Mithridates. In doing so, Pompeius extended his connections and influence among senators and equestrians alike—all the while remaining fabulously popular with the masses. He also became extremely rich. On Pompeius' career, see Seager 2002. Although they were acquainted, and Cicero had served as a junior officer under the command of Pompeius' father (Cic. *Phil.* 12.27), the two men were not close in 64. The advantage of Pompeius' political support, however, was obvious to Cicero, who worked anxiously to secure it (Cic. *Att.* 1.1.2). The *Brief Handbook* returns to Pompeius' importance to Cicero's campaign at ¶¶14 and 51. After his election, Cicero insisted that his past support for Pompeius had been motivated by friendship (*familiaritas*) and by his political ambitions ('by my hope for office and grand prestige', Cic. *Leg. agr.* 2.49). In later years, however, Cicero began to view his early exertions on Pompeius' behalf as insufficiently requited by the great man (Cic. *Att.* 2.9.1, a bitter reference to his adulatory speeches for Pompeius; *Q. Fr.* 3.4.2).

The suggestion that Cicero's *Pro lege Manilia* and *Pro Cornelio* were delivered with Pompeius' interests in mind would not assuage hostility on the part of Pompeius' enemies. But currying favour with Pompeius was an activity Cicero shared with many nobles who were keen to accept appointments from Pompeius and share in the glory of his conquests (Seager 2002, 46ff.). For this reason, Quintus' confession of Cicero's opportunism here, in addition to flattering Pompeius, depicts Cicero as following a political course shared by many men who doubtless deemed themselves *optimates*.

¶6 young nobles. Quintus has already singled out the value of youthful support (on which see **¶3 young men**). The sons of nobles constituted the most distinguished, glamorous, and influential young men—and they possessed valuable votes in the equestrian centuries. Here Quintus adds nothing new to his previous advice, but he further extends his complimentary treatment of the nobility, all of which cushions the blow when he shifts to his attack on Cicero's principal noble rivals (see **¶8 But, you will say... Quite the contrary**).

have already won over. On the support Cicero enjoyed from the young noble L. Domitius Ahenobarbus, see **¶3 young men**.

¶7 nobles contending against you. For the next several sections (**¶¶7–12**), Quintus concentrates on the inadequacies of Cicero's noble competitors. Other rivals are ignored, but that is no proof they had dropped out. Quintus has already established Cicero's superiority to any candidates who are new men (**¶3 For what new men**), and men from old but non-noble senatorial families fall outside his analysis here (on Cicero's rivals for the consulship, see §VII.5).

In his treatment of Cicero's noble competitors, Quintus reprises themes characteristic of the rhetoric of new men: e.g. new men can be superior in industry and talent; nobles rely too much on their nobility. But, unlike other texts that contrast new men with nobility, the *Brief Handbook* does nothing to challenge the nobility's traditional claims to superiority (see **¶2 new man**). P. Sulpicius Galba and L. Cassius Longinus are dismissed lightly, and Antonius and Catilina are treated as deviant specimens of nobility, an attitude made clear by Quintus in his concluding remarks: there Quintus compares Cicero's candidature with that of the new man C. Coelius Caldus (cos. 94) and stresses the point that, although Coelius was an excellent man and was elected consul, it was *not* because he excelled his noble rivals in ability or in his worthiness to hold office (**¶11**). Cicero, by contrast with Coelius, is the beneficiary of good luck (*fortuna*) in that his competitors, unlike Coelius', are inadequate.

no one would dare. Wishful thinking. In fact, Cicero's *novitas* was the most serious obstacle to his election (see ¶2 **new man**; §VII.5).

their nobility...your merit. Merit (*virtus*), a quality associated with noble birth, was also claimed by ambitious new men and was important in the assertive rhetoric of new men (see ¶2 **new man**).

Publius Galba. P. Sulpicius Galba (pr. by 66) was both noble and patrician. The first to commence canvassing, he immediately met with rebuffs, a disadvantage that made him an easy target for Quintus' criticism (hence its brevity); see Cic. *Att.* 1.1.1; §VII.5. Elsewhere Galba is described in attractive terms (Cic. *Mur.* 17; Asc. 82C). Although here Galba is said to lack energy (see below), at *Mur.* 17 Cicero says that it was *gratia* that Galba wanted. The particulars of his career are not well known (*MRR* 3.201).

Lucius Cassius. L. Cassius Longinus (pr. by 66) derived from an ancient and noble family distinguished by numerous consulships. Many details of his early career are unclear (*MRR* 3.50f.), but, like Galba, he was so weak a candidate that Quintus did not need to waste many words in dismissing him. Our sources are not kind to him: elsewhere he is described as fat (Cic. *Cat.* 3.16) and stupid (Asc. 82C). He later joined the Catilinarian conspiracy (Cic. *Cat.* 3.9, 14, 25; 4.13; *Sull.* 36–39, 53; Sall. *Cat.* 17.3; 50.4). See Münzer 1897, 1738.

because they lack vigour. Literally 'sinews' (*nervi*), the seat of a man's strength, used figuratively not merely of physical vigour but also of political resources (Cic. *Att.* 15.4.1; *Fam.* 6.1.3; *Flacc.* 13; *Sull.* 24; *Phil.* 5.32). At *Off.* 2.36, Cicero makes the relevant claim that 'the multitude despise those whom they believe have no virtue [*nihil virtutis*], no spirit, no vigour [*nihil nervorum*]'. Although accusations of sloth were sometimes hurled at the nobility by new men (see ¶1 **assiduousness**; ¶2 **new man**), here Quintus narrows his focus: it is these two men, not the nobility as a class, who lack energy—and that is the reason they are doing so poorly at canvassing for the consulship.

¶8. But, you will say...Quite the contrary. Latin *at* ('but'), especially in conjunction with *immo* ('quite the contrary'), conjures up an imaginary speaker (hence the addition of 'you will say' in the translation; see *TLL* 1.996–7; *OLD* 194; *LHS* 492). Didactic epistles often include exchanges characteristic of dialogue (Hirzl 1895, 353ff.), as does epistolary prose generally (Hutchinson 1998, 113ff.; e.g. Cic. *Att.* 9.10.3; 10.12A.1; *Ad Brut.* 1.34.2). In this way, Quintus attributes to Cicero the (correct) observation that Antonius and Catilina are his most formidable competitors. He will go on, however, by way of a long passage of invective, to refute

Cicero's claim—not in order to persuade his brother, of course, but to parade before his readers a robust account of the vices of Antonius and Catilina.

Now, vituperation was not entirely foreign to didactic epistles (see, e.g., Inwood 2007), and the employment of negative examples for the purpose of delivering lessons about positive behaviour was traditional in Roman society (e.g. Hor. *Sat.* 1.4.105–6). Still, Quintus' deployment of invective here has more to do with electoral propaganda than with the moral instruction of candidates.

Canvassing entailed aggression. Consequently, invective was at once a natural and routine feature of any political campaign (Cic. *Fam.* 8.2.2; *Planc.* 85; *Off.* 1.38; Liv. 4.25.12; 22.34.2; see Steel 2011), a reality recognized by Quintus at ¶52, where he urges Cicero, as part of the pageantry appropriate to a political campaign, to smear his rivals' reputations. Vituperation was a regular feature of Roman oratory and so was common to political and forensic discourse alike (indeed, it was deemed essential to forensic oratory: Cic. *Font.* 37; *Mur.* 11; *Cael.* 6–8). Romans tended to attack their opponents by way of a broad array of aspersions, on the view that *any* moral lapse in an individual implied *every* moral lapse (Cic. *Inv. rhet.* 2.33; *Rhet. Her.* 2.5), and that is also the pattern one finds in the *Brief Handbook*. These invective tropes were largely conventional and were staples of a rhetorical education (e.g. Cic. *Inv. rhet.* 1.34–6; 2.28–31; 2.177–8; *Rhet. Her.* 3.10–15). At ¶54, Quintus suggests that invective is ineffectual against a good candidate (see ¶54 **escape animosity, gossip**).

Romans resorted to calumniation in order to discredit and shame their opponents and to set themselves up as foils to their opponents' vices. In this way, invective as moralizing could be regarded as a service to the larger community, which was expected to share the calumniator's moral outrage. In addition, if invective was done with style, it could be highly entertaining and reflect well on the intelligence and education of the reprover (Cic. *De or.* 2.236). How seriously invective was taken by audiences, or even by its recipients, is unclear to us and in any case must have varied a good deal. At ¶41, Cicero is encouraged to suggest to voters that, in reality, he could be well disposed toward his competitors. This was certainly possible in practice: although Antonius was harshly abused by Cicero during the political contest between them (see below **cut-throats since their childhood**), the two men cooperated during their joint consulship and thereafter sustained a dutiful if not close relationship (e.g. Cic. *Fam.* 5.5; *Att.* 1.12.1; *Flacc.* 95; *Pis.* 5), including Cicero's unsuccessful defence of Antonius at his trial in 59 (Alexander 1990, 119f.). On Roman invective, see Syme 1939, 149ff.; Corbeill 2002; Craig 2004; Arena 2007; the essays in Smith and Covino 2011; Hammar 2013; Beard 2015, 99ff.

In what follows, Antonius and Catilina are each of them alleged to be violent, lubricious, wilful plunderers, and in financial difficulty. It is nonetheless apparent that, in the *Brief Handbook*, Catilina is by far the worse of the two. Quintus' attacks on Antonius and Catilina reveal numerous close similarities with Cicero's *Tog. cand.*, a speech delivered late in his campaign (see §VII.5). So close in concept and phrasing are these parallels (they are discussed below in the appropriate entries) that their resemblance has long been an important part of the argument against the *Brief Handbook*'s authenticity, the assumption being that it is unlikely that Cicero should have borrowed his ideas or their phrasing from Quintus (Eussner 1872; Hendrickson 1904; Waibel 1969). But there is no obvious reason to believe that the invective elements in either work are original to them (Laser 2001, 118): by 64, Antonius and Catilina had had quite enough experience of public life to have attracted an ample share of abuse. It was more effective for Quintus and Cicero to elaborate, however unfairly, elements in the existing notoriety of each man than to concoct original sins. It is in any case probably a mistake to view the resemblances between the *Brief Handbook* and *Tog. cand.* in terms of literary intertextualities. It is more likely that we have to do with what, in modern terms, could be called 'talking points', recycled throughout this campaign as frequently as were complaints about Cicero's status as a new man (on the organization of opinion within a political campaign, see §III, esp. §III.7). The invective in the *Brief Handbook* is not identical with what one finds in *Tog. cand.*, a fact that is not attributable simply to the fragmentary nature of the latter: *Tog. cand.*, for instance, accuses Antonius of keeping a gang of shepherds as a private army (Asc. 87C) and blames him for acting as a chariot driver (Asc. 88C); neither item appears in the *Brief Handbook*.

Antonius. C. Antonius (cos. 63) was a son of the brilliant orator, M. Antonius (cos. 99; cens. 97), who was much admired by Cicero (see §VII.5), and the uncle of the triumvir Mark Antony (cos. 44). He was nicknamed by others 'Hybrida', an unflattering moniker meaning 'half-breed', which without subtlety implied bad things about his mother (Plin. *NH* 8.213; see Buongiorno 2006 for a review of the varying explanations of the social significance of Hybrida). Antonius served under Sulla, profiting both in provincial service and in the proscriptions; in 76 he was brought to court for his excesses as a Sullan officer in Greece, but escaped by appealing to the tribunes (see ¶9 **citizen slaughter**). In 70, he was expelled from the senate on account of his unsavoury past and his debts. By way of election as tribune, probably in 68, he returned to the senate. As tribune, he passed the epigraphically preserved *Lex Antonia de Termessibus* ('the Antonian Law regarding Termessus') rehabilitating the city of Termessus Maior in

Pisidia (see *RS* 331ff.). Praetor in 66, owing to Cicero's support (*MRR* 2.151f.), consul in 63, he led the campaign in the field against Catilina and was hailed *imperator* ('conquering general'). After governing Macedonia from 62 to 60, he was condemned for his abuses there in 59 despite a defence by Cicero. In 44, however, he was pardoned by Caesar, and in 42 he became censor. A man of little talent or integrity, his high birth brought him, even in the teeth of his failures, every benefit and office of senatorial society. See, further, Klebs 1894, 2577ff.; Drumann and Groebe 1899, 390ff.; *MRR* 2.531; 3.18; Ferriès 2007, 338f.; on Antonius' activities during the campaign of 64, see §VII.5.

Catilina. L. Sergius Catilina derived from patrician but not recently distinguished stock. He served with Cicero and Pompeius under Cn. Pompeius Strabo during the Social War (*ILS* 8888 = *ILLRP* 515), and he was later a Sullan lieutenant. During the proscriptions he was conspicuous for his violence and profiteering. Elected praetor for 68, he thereafter governed Africa for two years, where his corruption disturbed the senate and formed the basis for suspicion and prosecution that prevented his standing for the consulship of 65 or 64. In the end he was acquitted, and stood unsuccessfully for the consulship of 63 and 62, after which he organized his infamous conspiracy. His designs were uncovered by Cicero, and Catilina's forces were defeated in the field by Antonius. Owing to the hostile treatment of the ancient sources, not least the speeches of Cicero, Catilina is difficult to recover. Still, it is clear enough that he was a man of genuine capacity, capable of inspiring friendship and loyalty in many (see Cic. *Cael*. 12–14). His reversals after his obviously disreputable tenure in Africa, however, seem to have damaged his prospects beyond repair, though that will not have been obvious in 64 (see Cic. *Sull*. 81). See, further, Steel 2013b, 150ff.; Levick 2015; *MRR* 3.192; on Catilina's campaign in 64, see §VII.5.

industrious, hard-working. By enumerating the qualities that render any candidate formidable, Quintus actually rehearses Cicero's virtues and reminds his readers that neither Antonius nor Catilina possesses them.

blameless. *Innocens* ('blameless') regularly describes a Roman conspicuous for his unselfish and moderate administration of public affairs; in imperial inscriptions it is commonly associated (as here) with the vocabulary of hard work (e.g. *diligentia*; *industria*; see ¶1 **assiduousness**). More generally it refers to anyone who has exhibited no faults in public or private life. See Hellegouarc'h 1963, 283; Forbis 1996, 64ff. The idea recurs, along with bravery and eloquence, in Quintus' description of the ideal consul at ¶13.

classes that constitute the juries. By the terms of the *lex Aurelia iudiciaria* of 70 (*MRR* 2.127), juries for the standing courts in Rome (on which see Lintott 1999a, 157ff.) were composed of men drawn in equal numbers from three groups: senators, knights, and *tribuni aerarii*. Little is known of this third group, but in certain circumstances, especially in regard to jury service, they could be addressed and treated as if they were knights (e.g. Cic. *Tog. cand* (Asc. 86C); *Clu.* 121; *Font.* 36; *Flacc.* 4; *Rab. Post.* 14; see ¶3 **the equestrian order**). References to men who constitute juries are, consequently, often circumlocutions meant to indicate knights (see Bleicken 1995, 32ff.; Berry 2003, 222ff.). But here the formula gives palpable expression not merely to Cicero's eloquence but also to the practical reality of his eloquence: his clout in the courts. This was a very important source of influence (see ¶2 **your fame as an orator**). Quintus returns to this influence as a means of inhibiting criminal behaviour on the part of Antonius and Catilina at ¶56.

cut-throats since their childhood. Accusations of violence were conventional in Roman invective. Still, inasmuch as at the time of this campaign Catilina may have been under indictment before the *quaestio de sicariis* (the murder court) for his activities during the proscriptions (see ¶9 **citizen slaughter**), the charge possibly carried more than a routine degree of currency. The word *sicarius* ('cut-throat') means literally 'dagger-man'. It is frequently paired with low-life creatures (e.g. 'gladiator' or 'slave'; see Cic. *Rosc. Am.* 8; *Cat.* 2.7; 3.8; *Sest.* 77, 88), and at Cic. *Dom* 45 it is (as here) associated with indebtedness (see below **deeply in debt**). The insult was common (Cic. *Rosc. Am.* 39; *Verr.* 2.1.9; *Sest.* 39; *Pis.* 38; *Phil.* 13.23), and enemies denounced even Cicero as a *sicarius* (Cic. *Mil.* 47). Quintus' treatment of Antonius and Catilina opens and closes with knives: he commences by describing the two as cut-throats; he concludes by asserting that the Roman people would never, by electing them to consulships, unsheathe two daggers (*duas...sicas*) against the state (¶12).

wanton. Accusations of personal immorality, typically delivered in more lip-smacking detail than anything in the *Brief Handbook*, were conventional and pervade Roman political discourse. Instances are too numerous to cite in bulk (but see Liv. 39.42.5–12 (elder Cato); Cic. *Dom.* 36, 139; *Har. resp.* 42, 55; *Pis.* 70, 86; *Sest.* 18; *Mil.* 59, 72–85; see Opelt 1965, 154ff. for further examples). Cicero, too, was assailed for alleged immorality (Cic. *Dom.* 93; Plut. *Cic.* 7.7; [Sall.] *In Cic.* 2; Dio 46.18.4–6). Antonius was destined to hear worse than he receives here: M. Caelius Rufus (pr. 48), in his later prosecution of Antonius, depicted the man as drunk and lying amid a bevy of courtesans (Quint. 4.2.123–4). On moralizing in republican Rome, see Edwards 1993 and Langlands 2006.

deeply in debt. This was a common slur, but a topical one in 64 owing to widespread anxiety about indebtedness and the threat it posed to civic stability (see §VII.5). Romans took a harsh view of indebtedness, not least because the possession of wealth was essential to one's public standing, and bankruptcy was viewed as a moral failure: a profligate man was unsound and therefore dangerous to the social order. Consequently, accusations of financial embarrassment were frequent in Roman invective (e.g. Cic. *Verr.* 1.21; 3.65; *Cat.* 1.9; 1.13; 2.11; 3.14; 4.5; 4.10; *Dom.* 25; *Pis.* 12; *Sest.* 9, 98–9, 111; *Phil.* 2.42–5; 3.1; 5.6; 13.26; Schol. Bob. 87 (Stangl)). Cicero's indebtedness later in life also attracted hostile attention (Dio 46.18.3). On solvency and Roman morality, see Hellegouarc'h 1963, 532ff.; Opelt 1965, 162; Edwards 1993, 173ff.; Pina Polo 2016.

one of these men. Antonius.

sold at auction. Hyperbole, if not a complete falsehood. Quintus' language here (*bona proscripta*) refers to a civil procedure described as 'the sale of one's possessions' (*bonorum venditio* or, as here, *proscriptio*: Cic. *Quinct.* 56; *Leg. agr.* 1.4; *Flacc.* 74, 247; see Greenidge 1901, 284ff.; Schulz 1951, 526ff.; Crook 1967, 173ff.; Johnston 1999, 108ff. This procedure should not be confused with state confiscation, *publicatio bonorum*, or the consecration of one's property to the gods, *consecratio bonorum*: see Salerno 1990; Allély 2003; Couhade-Beyneix 2003; Hinard 2011, 131ff.; Ferriès 2016.) Its purpose was twofold: to bring relief to creditors and to punish the debtor, who was officially disgraced (viz. declared *infamis*, a condition that entailed important legal liabilities; see Lintott 1999a, 71f.): Cic. *Quinct.* 48–51 describes this procedure and the dishonour it brought on anyone subjected to it. In his *Tog. cand.*, Cicero alleges that debt forced Antonius to sell his properties in the country, a turn of events that rendered him a dangerous figure (Asc. 87C). Quintus alleges a far deeper disgrace, and his claim is almost certainly a false one. Still, Antonius' debts were extreme enough for him to be removed from the senate in 70 (see below **expelled from the senate**). On auctions in Rome, public events that carried social as well as financial significance, see Andreau 1999, 38ff.; García Morcillo 2008.

he could not compete, in an impartial trial, with a Greek. This episode was also mentioned by Cicero in *Tog. cand.* and is recounted in more detail at Asc. 84C (see Marshall 1985b, 293f.; Lewis 2006, 293). It is also rehearsed, in garbled form, at Plut. *Caes.* 4.2–3 (on which passage, see Pelling 2011, 145ff.). Antonius, it appears, while serving in some capacity under Sulla during his eastern command against Mithridates (Asc. 84C, perhaps in 84; see *MRR* 2.61f.), abused his position in order to cheat certain men in Achaea: Asconius claims they were 'plundered'; in Plutarch, Antonius is said to have taken bribes. Subsequently, in 76, by way of the advocacy of Julius Caesar, a complaint was brought before the peregrine praetor, M. Terentius Varro Lucullus (cos. 73), whose responsibilities included litigation between citizens and foreigners (Brennan 2000, 441ff.) The praetor ruled against Antonius, who appealed to the tribunes, at least one of whom intervened to quash the praetor's decree (on the tribunes' authority in such matters, see Greenidge 1901, 290ff.; Lintott 1999a, 125ff.). The incident was apparently a sensational one, and Antonius' action was adduced by the censors of 70 as one of the reasons for his expulsion from the senate (Asc. 84C).

The exact legal nature of the proceedings against Antonius remains unclear: Buckland 1937, 43, proposes an unspecified criminal action. Damon and Mackay 1995, make a good case for a civil claim of property under the formulary system (*condictio*; see Schulz 1951, 611ff.) but one innovative enough to be impeachable (hence the successful appeal to the tribunes). The evidence, such as it is, will also support the view that Caesar's clients asked the praetor to rescind prior transactions conducted with Antonius on the grounds that they were made under duress (*in integrum restitutio*; see Schulz 1951, 68f.), an idea originally suggested but subsequently abandoned by Buckland (who was too affected by the overblown language in Asconius' narrative—e.g. 'plundered'—which will owe itself to its rhetorical origins). Antonius' oath reflects a remedy in civil law open to any defendant who believes the judge (*iudex*) appointed to his case will be unfair (*eiurare*: Greenidge 1901, 266; Brunt 1988, 230), and that may have been the basis of Antonius' objection in his case. But that will not explain his summoning of the tribunes. Damon and Mackay propose that Antonius objected to the praetor's formula for deciding his case, a complaint that could invite tribunician intervention. Our sources indicate that Antonius summoned the tribunes and swore his oath *after* his case had been decided, and it was perhaps this exceptional escape from justice that generated opprobrium.

Antonius' oath clearly attracted ridicule. According to Asconius, he simply swore that 'he could not get justice' (*aequo iure uti non posset*), but Cicero in *Tog. cand.* (Asc. 84C) and the *Brief Handbook* here represent Antonius' complaint in more embarrassing terms: he admits that he cannot compete in litigation with a Greek—notwithstanding Roman distrust of Greeks giving evidence (Cic. *Flacc.* 9–12), or the advantage of being a Roman noble in a Roman court (Plutarch, who knew the formulation of Antonius' oath, mistakenly believed the case was heard in Greece). Doubtless Antonius meant his oath to indicate in strong terms the unfairness of his predicament, but it could also be taken as an astonishing confession of oratorical and legal and social ineptitude—and that is clearly how Cicero and Quintus chose to regard it (charges of forensic ineptitude were common in Roman invective: e.g. Cic. *Clu.* 58–9; *Leg. agr.* 2.13; *Pis.* 1; *Har. resp.* 13–14; *Dom.* 3; *Planc.* 47, 83; *Cael.* 8, 27; *Phil.* 2.42–3; 5.19–20). Antonius' oath remained a source of embarrassment: when prosecuting Antonius in 59, M. Caelius Rufus (pr. 48) put it to work in ridiculing the defendant (Quint. 9.3.58: 'the Greek began to be astonished with joy'). A less plausible view of Antonius' oath is offered by Buller 1987.

expelled from the senate. The *lex Ovinia*, passed at some time before 312 (*MRR* 1.158f.), assigned to the censors the responsibility of revising the membership of the senate (*lectio senatus*; see Lintott 1999a, 68ff.), an undertaking that preceded the census proper and the ritual purification of the city (*lustrum*), events which took place approximately every five years (Lintott 1999a, 115ff.). Romans believed that one's status in society should be determined by wealth and by character; consequently, the *lectio senatus* entailed scrutiny of each senator's personal morality (Astin 1988, 14ff.): a Roman deemed deficient by both censors was expelled from the senate (grounds for exclusion: Lintott 1999, 71f.). There was no appeal. Antonius was ejected in the revision conducted by the censors of 70 (see next note), a purge of sixty-four senators, including a former consul (see *MRR* 2.126f.). The censors' objections to Antonius included the claims that he had cheated Roman allies, rejected a judgment against him (see above **he could not compete…with a Greek**), and was heavily in debt (see above **sold at auction**) (see Asc. 84C). Antonius regained his place in the senate when he was elected tribune, probably in 68 (*MRR* 2.138); a *lex Atinia*, of uncertain date, secured the automatic adlection into the senate of ex-tribunes (Gell. *NA* 14.8.2; App. *B.Civ.* 1.28.126; see Tatum 2009a). Antonius' expulsion remained a natural target for his enemies. At the same time, when it suited his forensic purposes, Cicero could minimize the significance of senatorial expulsions by censors (Cic. *Clu.* 119–22) and it was widely appreciated in Rome that the revision of the senate could entail political sharp practice (see, e.g., Astin 1985; Tatum 1990).

estimable censors. The censors of 70 were Cn. Cornelius Lentulus Clodianus (cos. 72) and L. Gellius Publicola (cos. 72).

one of our competitors. Quintus' use of the plural again identifies the political careers of the two brothers and emphasizes their family solidarity. Cicero and Antonius were elected in 67 each to a praetorship for 66. Cicero was elected at the top of the poll; Antonius was elected to the third place but, according to Cicero, only with his assistance (Asc. 85C). In Cicero's *Tog. cand.*, Antonius is reproached for his ingratitude for this earlier favour. In the *Brief Handbook*, however, there is no hint of this episode: instead Antonius' campaign for the praetorship is criticized for its unsavoury nature.

Sabidius and Panthera. Their identities are unknown, but there is no reason to conclude that they are fictions. The *nomen* Sabidius (on Roman nomenclature, see Appendix A) is attested during the republic at Minturnae (*ILLRP* 724 = *CIL* 1².2682; *ILLRP* 729 = *CIL* 1².2699) and an inscription from Terracina reveals a senatorial Sabidius (*ILLRP* 387 = *ILS* 8962 = *CIL* 1².836), M'. Sabidius M'. f. ('Manius Sabidius, son of Manius'), whom Münzer 1920, 1570, identifies with this Sabidius, though without good reason. Still, M'. Sabidius suffices to demonstrate that the name *can* refer to a member of the senate or equestrian order (David et al. 1973, 262). Panthera is a *cognomen*, attested in Italy in the republic (*CIL* 9.483; *CIL* 10.8058) and attached to a decurion of Pisa, L. Otacilius Q. f. Panthera (*ILS* 140 = *CIL* 11.1421); the *cognomen* is most famously applied to Cn. Aufidius (tr. pl. 170) (but see *MRR* 1.423 n. 6) for his success in passing legislation permitting the importation from Africa of panthers for games in the circus (Plin. *NH* 8.64). This Panthera, then, *could* be either an Aufidius or an Otacilius, each a family name represented in the senate (see, e.g., *MRR* 2.535, 597) and among the knights (see Nicolet 1974, 794ff., 967; cf. David et al. 1973, 262ff.). If it is correct that Quintus designates these men as Antonius' electoral representatives during the praetorian elections of 67 (see next note), then they are here represented as members of the equestrian or senatorial orders notwithstanding the contempt with which Quintus mentions them.

when he owned no slaves which he could offer at auction. The meaning of the text here is uncertain owing to the ambiguity of the Latin expression *ad tabulam* (here translated 'at auction'): Antonius lacked 'those whom he might put *ad tabulam*.'

Because *ad tabulam* can mean 'on an auction notice', this sentence can be understood as alleging that an impecunious Antonius could not even find slaves in his household whom he might sell in order to obtain the cash needed for his campaign for office. This slur then helps to explain the subsequent 'although' (*tamen*) introducing the scandal of Antonius' actually purchasing a slave girl (and so presumably going even further beyond his means) whom he kept as a concubine. This is the suggestion of Constans 1940, 275, and it is widely accepted by editors and translators (e.g. Watt 1958a; Henderson 1972; Fedeli 1987; Shackleton Bailey 1988; Duplá et al. 1990; Boriaud 1992; Shackleton Bailey 2002; Prost 2017, 6).

But there is an older explanation. At elections, ballots were counted and recorded on a tablet (*tabula*), a process overseen by officials called guardians (*custodes*), some of whom were appointed by the candidates themselves; this stage in the election process was described by the expression *ad tabulam* (Varro, *RR* 3.5.18; see Taylor 1966, 54ff.; Staveley 1972, 175ff.), and it is possible to see in this passage a reference to that procedure (e.g. Buecheler 1869, 29; Tyrrell and Purser 1904, 158; Romano 1961–2, 157; Nardo 1970, 86; Laser 2001, 121; Cooley, Murrell, Taylor, and Thorpe 2009, 15). In order to take *ad tabulam* in this sense, however, one must postulate a lacuna in the text. Wesenberg 1872 proposed reading <*alios*> *ad tabulam*, which permits the sentence to be translated as, 'He was one of our competitors when we stood for the praetorship, when Sabidius and Panthera were his friends and he had no others to appoint as his representatives at the tabulation of the votes.' Taken this way, the passage underscores Antonius' deficit in distinguished connections.

It was the apparent obscurity of Sabidius and Panthera that led Constans to reject this approach to this passage, but that is to miss the point. Still, taking *ad tabulam* in this sense makes nonsense out of *tamen* ('although'), a problem that has been emended away by Shackleton Bailey, who reads *quo iam in magistratu* for *quo tamen in magistratu* (Shackleton Bailey 1988; Shackleton Bailey 2002), which, if accepted, gives us: 'He was one of our competitors when we stood for the praetorship, when Sabidius and Panthera were his friends and he had no others to appoint as his representatives at the tabulation of the votes. Then, during his actual praetorship, he bought a girl from the stands at the slave market, whom he indiscreetly kept at home as his lover.'

Which construction of *ad tabulam* is to be preferred? Constans's reading requires less in the way of emendation, but the older approach makes (slightly) better sense of the passage's introduction of Sabidius and Panthera. Throughout his treatment here, Antonius is ridiculed for his inappropriate associations: he is too poorly connected to beat a foreigner in court, he had unfit friends in his previous campaign, he prefers a slave girl to his wife, and during his current campaign (see below **sleazy foreign mission**) he shuns the Roman people.

bought a slave girl from the stands. The expression *de machina* ('from the stands') marks the circumstances as unelevated. In this sense, the expression is elsewhere found only at Petr. *Satyr.* 74.13, where Trimalchio reminds his wife, Fortunata, that he acquired her from this same source.

as his lover. Slaves were sexually available for exploitation by their owners (Bradley 1984, 118ff.; Bradley 1994, 28f.). Nevertheless, it was disgraceful to keep and to display a slave (or even a freedwoman) as one's concubine if one possessed a wife (Evans-Grubbs 1993). Antonius' conduct while holding a praetorship besmirches his office.

remaining in Rome. On the importance of remaining in the city in order to canvass voters, see ¶43.

imploring the Roman people. On the servile posture required of candidates for office, see §III.4.

plunder all the innkeepers. Inasmuch as innkeepers were proverbial for their dishonesty (see Hor. *Sat.* 1.5.4; Iuv. 9.108), this expression is meant to be a witty exaggeration. Still, a senator on a *legatio libera* (see next note) was in a position to exploit the hospitality of others. Accusations of plundering recur in Roman invective (e.g. Cic. *Rosc. Am.* 23–4, 146–7; *Verr.* 2.46–7; 5.131; *Pis.* 9; *Sest.* 15; *Phil.* 2.92). On important aspects of the reality of Roman plundering, see the essays in Ferriès and Delrieux 2014.

sleazy foreign mission. A *legatio libera* ('foreign mission') was an embassy undertaken by a senator on behalf of the state. In practice, however, such missions had become junkets that cost a senator nothing—and imposed expensive demands on local communities that he visited—yet enabled him to deploy the full majesty of the Roman senate to his personal advantage; for instance, senators exploited missions in order to secure foreign investments (e.g. Cic. *Flacc.* 86; *Leg. agr.* 1.8; 2.45; see Linderski 2007, 307ff.). By the late republic this practice was increasingly viewed as sordid. Cicero strongly disapproved of it (but see *Flacc.* 86, where he defends it on behalf of his client), and during his consulship attempted to curb the practice (Cic. *Leg.* 3.18, where Cicero denounces such missions by insisting that 'nothing is more sleazy').

What, precisely, Quintus has in mind here is unknown. Buecheler 1869, 29f., introduced, by way of emendation, the idea that Antonius had taken a mission to Cappadocia, but his suggestion has not found favour and was adequately refuted by Sjögren 1913, 119f. Antonius was certainly present in Rome during the final phase of canvassing, but he may have absented himself previously, perhaps by way of a 'foreign mission', to seek important votes in the Gallic provinces, an action that Cicero also considered undertaking by way of accepting a legateship (Cic. *Att.* 1.1.2; see §VII.5).

¶9 good gods! The transition is highly rhetorical; in this way, Quintus signals to his readers that Catilina is even worse than Antonius. See Cic. *Sest.* 19 (where Cicero is shifting from his denunciation of A. Gabinius (cos. 58) to C. Calpurnius Piso (cos. 58)): 'As for the other one—oh good gods! [*alter—o di boni*].'

What...apart? A fictional dialogue ensues (see ¶8 **But, you will say...** **Quite the contrary**).

distinction. Quintus immediately begins to challenge any Catilinarian claim to superiority or even excellence. Although *splendor* ('distinction') is regularly linked to the prestige of the equestrian order and to municipal elites, it can also be applied to the reputations of leading senators (see Hellegouarc'h 1963, 488ff.). At ¶52, Quintus insists that Cicero's campaign be distinguished (*splendida*).

he possesses... †Catilina†. The text is obviously corrupt here (the assertion that Catilina enjoys the same nobility as Catilina is patent nonsense): either *Catilina* should be emended to *Antonius* (so Manutius) or simply excised (so Muretus). The translation then becomes either 'he possesses the same nobility as Antonius', or 'he possesses the same nobility.'

same nobility. On nobility (*nobilitas*), see ¶4 **nobles.** Catilina and Antonius were each of them noble. Antonius' family was more recently ennobled (it seems likely that his father, the consul of 99, was the first of his line to reach the consulship; see Badian 1990, 388), but this gave him the advantage of his father's recent and still remembered fame (on the significance of this advantage in Roman elections, see Hopkins and Burton 1983). Catilina's successful ancestors, on the other hand, lay in the remote past.

greater courage. Catilina's *virtus* ('courage', but see ¶1 **assiduousness**) is conceded by Cicero at *Cael.* 12 and is reflected in Sallust's characterization of the man (e.g. Sall. *Cat.* 5, 60–1). Doubtless he advanced his reputation for bravery during his campaign (see §VII.5). Here Quintus draws an apparent distinction between nobility (*nobilitas*) and *virtus*, which attributes to Catilina's fictitious supporter a recurring claim in the rhetoric of the new man (see ¶2 **new man**). This distinction also adds point to the subsequent claim that Antonius is a coward (see next note).

afraid of his own shadow. At Cic. *Att.* 15.20.4, Cicero calumniates Mark Antony with a similar expression (see Prop. 2.34.19–20). In Roman vituperation, the aspersion of fear or cowardice appears less frequently than other common allegations, such as low birth, cruelty, decadence, or indebtedness. Still, it recurs often enough to be deemed a stock insult (e.g. Cic. *Verr.* 2.5.74; *Mil.* 41; *Phil.* 2.71–4; Caes. *B.Civ.* 1.4; Dio 46.28.1; see Opelt 1965, 190ff.).

does not even fear the law. It is possible that Catilina was tried for violating a Vestal Virgin in 73 (see Alexander 1990, 83) and he was certainly tried and acquitted in 65 for extorting money from Africa when he governed that province in 67–66 (see Alexander 1990, 106; see next note). At some point in 64, he was under indictment for violence perpetrated during the Sullan proscriptions (see next note). It was a record that left him vulnerable to derogation by his enemies. In his *Tog. cand.*, Cicero denounced Catilina for his lawlessness (Asc. 86C: 'he violated laws, tribunals, courts'), an accusation he repeated at *Cat.* 1.18 ('not only have you ignored the law and the courts but you have succeeded in overturning and shattering them').

Born…murdering Roman knights. In a single sentence the *Brief Handbook* rehearses the whole of Catilina's disreputable life, from the moment of his birth through his early adulthood (for a close analysis, see Kierdorf 1966). This technique can be paralleled in Ciceronian invective; e.g. *Dom.* 126, abusing A. Gabinius (cos. 58): 'we have witnessed the immorality of his boyhood, his youthful lasciviousness, the disgraceful poverty of the residue of his life, the criminality of his consulship'.

his father's poverty. The same charge is repeated at Sall. *Cat.* 5.7. Catilina's family, though noble, had not attained consular office since the fourth century. The imputation of poverty draws attention to the (relatively) fallen condition of the Sergii. Furthermore, because this campaign took place at a time of genuine anxiety about indebtedness (see §VII.5; **¶8 deeply in debt**), this slur reminded readers of Catilina's unreliability and likely rapacity. On the rhetoric of financial embarrassment, see **¶8 deeply in debt**.

reared in debauchery…sister. The text and its specific meaning are uncertain. But the gist is obvious enough. The MSS supply *sororum stupris* ('debauchery with his sisters') or *sororis stupris* ('debauchery with his sister'), and each is printed in various editions. Watt's elegant suggestion, *sororiis stupris* (either 'debauchery with his sisters' or 'sister'), is inspired by Cic. *Sest.* 16, where it is an aspersion aimed at P. Clodius Pulcher (tr. pl. 58); the adjective *sororiis* is easily corrupted to *sororis*. We know nothing of Catilina's sister or sisters. The man's depraved lifestyle, however, is also adduced by Cicero in *Tog. cand.* (Asc. 86C; 91C) and *Sull.* 70, and is described in imaginative detail by Sall. *Cat.* 14–16. Still, none of these sources suggests Catilinarian incest, although incest is a reasonably common reproach in republican invective (e.g. *Pis.* 28; *Har. resp.* 9; [Sall.] *In Cic.* 2; Plut. *Cat. min.* 54.1–2; Dio 46.18.6; but see Kaster 2006, 409ff.). For this reason, Buecheler 1869, 30, saw in this passage a criticism only of Catilina's sister's immorality and therefore commentary on the moral environment of Catilina's upbringing. But here the *Brief Handbook* seeks to blacken Catilina's reputation; consequently there is no reason to ignore its allegation of incest. That youthful depravity naturally led to every other vice was a staple of Roman invective (see Langlands 2006, 281ff.).

grown to manhood…slaughter. This phrase, like its predecessor, is alliterative in Latin (*corroboratus in caede civium*); after *in caede* ('in the

slaughter of…') the word 'citizens' (*civium*) comes as a shock, though in
the rhetoric of Roman invective this phrase may not have been uncommon (see Cic. *Sest.* 79). In *Tog. cand.*, Cicero describes Catilina as a man
'who has butchered so many citizens' (Asc. 84C: *is qui tot cives trucidavit*)
and claims that 'he bloodied himself in wicked slaugher' (Asc. 86C: *caede
nefaria cruentavit*). These references are to the proscriptions (see next note).

citizen slaughter. This expression can refer either to the civil war of 83–82
or the proscriptions that followed it. The civil war of 83–82 was fought by
L. Cornelius Sulla (see below **Sulla**) against a Roman government dominated at the time by his political enemies, who had outlawed him. In 82,
after achieving victory and making himself master of the city, Sulla instituted the proscriptions: lists were posted that named public enemies who
could be killed with impunity by anyone; their possessions were confiscated by the state; their children and grandchildren suffered loss of civil
rights. It was a grisly incentive that by bringing the heads of the proscribed
to Sulla one could earn a financial reward from the treasury. This persecution of Sulla's enemies was not limited to Rome but extended to Italian
municipalities. The period of the proscriptions was brief, but bloody and
was exacerbated by unsanctioned killings and thefts of property (see
Hinard 1985; Seager 1994, 187ff.; Keaveney 2005, 124ff.; Hinard 2011, 75ff.;
Steel 2013b, 97ff.; Ferriès 2016). Catilina commanded troops as a Sullan
legate during the civil war (see Sall. *Hist.* 1.46 (McGushin); *MRR* 3.192)
and he played a part in the proscriptions. The proscriptions horrified the
Romans: in the municipalities, past involvement in the proscriptions
became a disqualification for public office (*Tab. Heb.* 122). In 64, the year
of Cicero's candidature, there was a strong backlash against those who had
excelled in cruelty and avarice during the proscriptions: M. Porcius Cato
(pr. 54), quaestor in that year, in his reform of the treasury, targeted men
who had illicitly profited during the proscriptions, and Julius Caesar, who
sat as presiding judge of the *quaestio de sicariis* (the murder court; see
Cloud 1994, 505ff.; Lintott 1999a, 157ff.), accepted cases against individuals who had killed citizens during the proscriptions, two of whom,
L. Luscius and L. Bellienus (who was an uncle of Catilina according to
Cicero; see Asc. 91C), were convicted (see Cic. *Leg. agr.* 1.12; Sall. *Hist.* 4.1
(McGushin); Plut. *Cat. min.* 17.4; Suet. *Iul.* 11; Dio 37.10.2). At some point
in 64, possibly after the elections, L. Lucceius charged Catilina before
this court, but Catilina enjoyed elite support and was acquitted (his trial
certainly took place after the elections; see Hinard 1985, 204ff.; Alexander
1990, 108f.). In his *Tog. cand.*, Cicero suggests that Catilina had already
been accused at the time of that speech's delivery (Asc. 90C); however,
Asc. 91C states that Lucceius indicted Catilina *after* the consular elections.

At the very least, Lucceius' intentions must have been made clear by the time Cicero and Catilina were competitors for the consulship (see Marshall 1985b, 292; Lewis 2006, 299). This looming prosecution, in conjunction with an atmosphere of renewed hostility against the events of the pro-scriptions, animated Cicero's and the *Brief Handbook*'s invective against Catilina, which was doubtless circulated constantly during this campaign.

by murdering Roman knights. Sulla's proscriptions took the lives of more knights than senators (see Cic. *Clu.* 151; App. *B.Civ.* 1.95; see Hinard 1985, 116ff.). Casting Catilina as a slayer of knights unmistakably contrasts him with Cicero, their champion (see ¶3 **the equestrian order**). Quintus emphasizes the suffering of the equestrian order: only one senatorial vic-tim is singled out, though his death is described at great length (M. Marius Gratidianus at ¶10). By contrast, Cicero, in his *Tog. cand.*, depicts Catilina as a menace to every level of society (Asc. 89C).

Sulla. A major figure in late republican history, L. Cornelius Sulla Felix (cos. I 88), served creditably under C. Marius (cos. I 107) in the Jugurthine and Cimbrian wars and won distinction during the Social War, after which he became consul and was assigned the command of the war against Mithridates Eupator. His command was transferred to Marius, however, and in response Sulla led his troops against Rome, an unprecedented and shocking event. Afterwards, while Sulla was in the east campaigning against Mithridates, control of Rome was regained by Marius and L. Cornelius Cinna (cos. I 87), who with their supporters dominated politics in the city: Sulla's command was rescinded and he was outlawed. In 83 Sulla, however, returned to Italy. Civil war supervened, Sulla emerged as victor, and he was named dictator. The proscriptions (see above **citizen slaughter**) followed. But Sulla also reorganized the state, mostly along traditional lines. Sulla abdicated his dictatorship sometime in 81 and was consul for the second time in 80. Thereafter he retired from public life, dying in 79. (See *MRR* 3.73ff.; Seager 1994; Keaveney 2005; Santangelo 2007; Steel 2013b, 97ff.; Eckert 2016.)

Gauls. Catilina's command of a contingent of Gauls is not mentioned else-where. It may be only a fictional embellishment for rhetorical effect. If not, one is left with conjecture. We are probably not to imagine an informal bodyguard of Gauls, like the one recruited by Julius Caesar (Caes. *B.Civ.* 1.41). But it is possible that Catilina, when serving as legate to Sulla, was placed in charge of auxiliary forces recruited from Cisalpine Gaul (see Brunt 1971, 435ff., who discusses military recruitment during the Social War and the Sullan civil war), who are for rhetorical effect described here in misleading terms (Cic. *Pis.* fr. ix; see Nisbet 1961a, 53). In what follows,

Quintus indicates that these Gallic forces executed numerous equestrians, some of whom are also named as Catilinarian victims at Asc. 84C (in which text no context for their deaths is supplied). Which means that, even if Catilina's command of so-called Gauls was real and legitimate, it is here deformed into something horrible. Quintus again extracts force from contemporary hostility against Sulla's proscriptions (see above **citizen slaughter**) and he amplifies these strong feelings by invoking traditional Roman fears of marauding and barbaric Gauls (on which aspect of Roman society, see Williams 2001).

we still remember. An appeal to universal knowledge, typically formulated along the lines of 'who does not know' or 'we are all aware', was so common in Greek oratory that the device was deemed a hackneyed one ([Dem.] 40.53; Arist. *Rhet.* 1408a32–36; see Ober 1989, 149f.; Pelling 2000, 28). This practice persisted in Roman rhetoric (e.g. Cic. *Verr.* 2.4.14: 'who of us doesn't know?' (*quis vestrum … nescit?*); *Caec.* 28: 'indeed, we had all remembered…' (*miminerant enim omnes*); *Flacc.* 83; *Har. resp.* 32; *Sest.* 133; *Planc.* 33). Although this technique was an aggressive one, designed to impose agreement in the absence of facts (see [Dem.] and Aristotle above), here it also helps to create a sense of community on the part of Cicero, Quintus, and his readers—who are all of them depicted as appalled by Catilina's lethal Gauls.

mowing off the heads. 'mowing off' (*demetebant*) is the generally accepted correction of the MSS' *demebant* ('they were cutting off'), which usually refers to the trimming of hair or nails.

men like Titinius … Tanusius. These names are given in plural forms, a common means in Latin of indicating types (*LHS* 19). The impression, then, is that many equestrians (like these men) were slain, and not just those whose names are supplied here. A list of Catilinarian victims similar to the names mentioned in ¶¶9–10 is provided by Asconius (84C), who takes them from Cic. *Tog. cand.* Both texts name L. Tanusius, Q. Caecilius (but see below **Quintus Caecilius**), and M. Marius Gratidianus (see ¶10). Asconius omits Cn. Titinius and Nanneius, but includes M. Volumnius (not mentioned by Quintus, perhaps because he was not a knight; see Nicolet 1974, 1081f.; Hinard 1985, 410f.). Neither text includes Catilina's brother (Plut. *Sull.* 80.2; *Cic.* 10.3) or the senator M. Plaetorius (Val. Max. 9.2.1). (See, further, Nicolet 1964; David et al. 1973, 257ff.)

Titinius. Otherwise unknown (Nicolet 1974, 1037f.), but sometimes identified with the Cn. Titinius who was among the knights who opposed M. Livius Drusus in 91 (Cic. *Clu.* 153; see Hinard 1985, 401f.). If so, he was a reasonably prominent figure. The name is too common to establish a connection between this man and the equestrian and senatorial Titinii of Minturnae, who were known to be hostile to Marius (Plut. *Mar.* 38.4).

Nanneius. An unknown figure. The near consensus of the MSS reads *Nannius*, which is regularly corrected to *Nanneius*. Each name is attested, but in no case does it explicitly denominate a senator or an equestrian (see the references assembled by Solin and Salomies 1988, 125). *Nanneius*, however, appears in literary as well as epigraphical contexts, including a letter by Cicero (Cic. *Att.* 1.16.5 (but perhaps misleadingly: see Wiseman 1974, 147ff.); see also Martial 5.14.2; 11.61.1). Hence the preference of critics. But there can be no certainty.

Tanusius. L. Tanusius (the praenomen is provided by Asc. 84C). Nothing more is known of him. It is not impossible that he was related to Tanusius Geminus, a late republican annalist and (possibly) a senator (see *FRHist* 1.391ff.). The wife of T. Vinius, proscribed in 43 but spared owing to his wife's efforts, was a Tanusia (App. *B.Civ.* 4.187; Dio 47.7.4; Suet. *Aug.* 27.2).

Quintus Caecilius. The reading of the MSS is *Q. Caucilius*, but most editions correct this to *Q. Caecilius*, who is named among Catilina's victims at Asc. 84C. The late republic was awash with equestrian Caecilii (see Nicolet 1974, 806ff.), and so the name is unsurprising. But only the *Brief Handbook* includes the information that Q. Caecilius was Catilina's brother-in-law (though this may be illusory, inasmuch as the relevant bits of Cic. *Tog. cand.* are lost). With this discrepancy in mind, and because the name *Caucilius* is epigraphically attested (even if not explicitly of an equestrian; see Schulze 1904, 213, 441), Shackleton Bailey (1988 and 2002) prints *Q. Caucilius*. His conservatism is probably unnecessary here but must remain a real possibility. This man's wife is likely to have been an allegedly debauched sister of Catiline (see above **reared in debauchery . . . sister**).

¶10 Why should I go on. Twice in this paragraph (see 'Why should I now write . . .') Quintus deploys rhetorical questions in *praeteritio* (the rhetorical ploy of pretending to pass over certain details while actually relating them), all of which adds to the self-consciously rhetorical register of this portion of the *Brief Handbook*. The immediate impression given by the text is that, in view of the matters related above, nothing could damage Catilina's reputation further—after which even greater iniquities are described.

Marcus Marius. M. Marius Gratidianus, like Cicero a native of Arpinum, was a relation of the orator: Gratidianus' father, M. Gratidius, was brother-in-law (by way of the marriage of his sister, Gratidia) to Cicero's grandfather (see fig. 1). Consequently, Cicero was Gratidianus' first cousin once removed. Gratidius was himself married to a sister of Gaius Marius. At some point, Gratidianus was adopted by M. Marius (a brother of Gaius Marius and originally Gratidianus' uncle). A late source (the Berne Scholiast on Lucan 2.173) claims that Catilina was married to a sister of Gratidianus, but this seems unlikely (Marshall 1985b, 292). In politics, Gratidianus supported Gaius Marius and L. Cornelius Cinna (cos. I 87). Tribune in 87 (or 86), he fled Rome along with Cinna, returned with the Marians, and, in the midst of the Marian terror, was prepared to prosecute Q. Lutatius Catulus (cos. 102), who anticipated his fate by suicide (*MRR* 2.47; 3.140). As praetor in 85, when all the praetors and tribunes endorsed a measure regulating the exchange rate between bronze and silver coinage (which had become unstable and unpredictable owing to the political turbulence of 88 and 86), Gratidianus, by issuing an independent edict, usurped the credit for this measure (on the nature of this measure, regularly misunderstood, see Crawford 1968; see also Verboven 1994). As a result, he became extremely popular, to the degree that statues in his honour were erected throughout the city (Cic. *Off.* 3.80; Plin. *NH* 33.132; 34.27; see *MRR* 2.57). He was praetor for a second time, in 84, 83, or (very likely) 82. He was slain during the proscriptions (*MRR* 3.140f.). Although a relation, Cicero is critical of Gratidianus for his unethical opportunism during his first praetorship (Cic. *Off.* 3.80–1); he also criticizes Gratidianus at *Leg.* 2.36, although the point of that passage remains unclear. (See Münzer 1930, 1825; Rawson 1991, 562ff.; Dyck 1996, 598ff.)

Quintus goes on to supply a gruesome account of the death of Gratidianus. He is driven through the city of Rome by Catilina, tortured at the tomb of Lutatius Catulus (his judicial victim during the Marian terror), and beheaded. His head is then carried off (to Sulla, although Quintus does not say so). The death of Gratidianus was a celebrated instance of cruelty, related by numerous sources in more than one version (Cic.

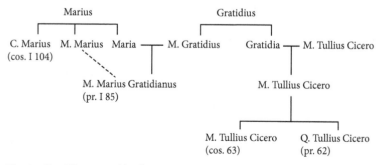

Fig. 1. Gratidianus and his kinsmen.

Tog. cand. frr. 5, 14 15; Asc. 84, 87, 90C; Sall. *Hist.* 1.36; 48.14 (McGushin); Liv. *Per.* 88; Val. Max. 9.2.1; Luc. 2.160–73; Sen. *Dial.* 5.18.1–2; Plut. *Sull.* 32.2; Flor. 2.9.26; Firm. Mat. *Math.* 1.3.35–45; Oros. 5.21.7–9; Schol. Bern. 61f. Usener). Catilina is the perpetrator in most versions, but Livy, Valerius Maximus, and Seneca make Sulla the culprit; the Berne Scholiast blames Q. Lutatius Catulus (cos. 78), the son of the man prosecuted by Gratidianus. On the nature of this tradition and the persistent controversy over who was responsible for Gratidianus' death, see Marshall 1985a; Damon 1993, 282; Spina 1996; Dyck 1996, 599; Hinard 2011, 143ff.

Although it is by no means certain that Catilina was responsible for Gratidianus' death, this calumny was very much ventilated in 64. Cicero relates the event in *Tog. cand.* (Asc. 84, 87, 90C). There he emphasizes the decapitation and its aftermath, evidently stressing the disgusting spectacle of Gratidianus' head being carried through the city to be delivered to Sulla, who was in the Temple of Apollo (this is confirmed by the nature of Asconius' comments on the speech). Quintus' version, by contrast, concentrates on Gratidianus' humiliating treatment before his execution (the fragmentary nature of Cicero's speech keeps us from knowing whether or not Cicero dealt with this). Quintus does not mention his or Cicero's kinship with Gratidianus; Cicero, however, may have done (Asconius includes that information in his commentary by remarking on the closeness of their relationship, an exaggeration that suggests that Cicero made some mention of their connection).

beloved of the Roman people. Owing to the edict he promulgated during his first praetorship, his statues were erected throughout the city (see above **Marcus Marius**). If we can believe the younger Seneca, the people went so far as to make offerings of frankincense and wine at Gratidianus' statues (Sen. *De ira* 3.18.1; see Marco Simón and Pina Polo 2000). The point here, however, is not so much to render Gratidianus more attractive to the reader but instead to accentuate the horrific quality of his humiliation and suffering in the presence of the Roman people. Still, *populus* is the word chosen by Quintus instead of *multitudo*, perhaps in order to avoid the suggestion that Gratidianus was a demagogue (see ¶5 **champions of popular rights**).

flogged. Quintus refers to a form of military corporal punishment: Gratidianus is repeatedly struck by the blows of a *vitis*, a staff that each centurion carried as a symbol of his office and employed in administering disciplinary beatings on soldiers (Watson 1969, 125). Gratidianus' treatment is thus a perversion: a civilian is said to be subjected to a punishment that is possible only outside the city and in a military context. On the disgrace associated with such punishment, see Walters 1997, 37ff.

through the entire city. Degrading treatment along these lines was apparently common during the proscriptions (App. *B.Civ.* 1.95). Quintus' treatment of this episode contrasts with Cicero's in *Tog. cand.* There the orator stresses the journey of Gratidianus' severed head through the whole of the city, whereas Quintus dwells on Gratidianus' painful and humiliating delivery to the site of his execution. The version related by Val. Max. 9.2.1 shares this feature.

in full view of the Roman people. Cicero, in his *Tog. cand.* (Asc. 87), employs the same expression (*inspectante populo*) in describing the circumstances of Gratidianus' decapitation. But the expression is a commonplace (Cic. *Dom.* 62; *Vat.* 34; *Cael.* 47; *Phil.* 2.21; 3.12; cf. *Div.* 1.32).

the tomb. A *bustum* ('tomb') was an enclosure, used repeatedly for members of the same family, in which funeral pyres were constructed and where cremated remains were interred (Richardson 1992, 351). Several sources make it clear that the site of Gratidianus' death was the *bustum* of the Lutatii Catuli (Luc. 2.173–6; Sen. *Dial.* 5.18.1–2; Flor. 2.9.26; Oros. 5.21.7–9), the location of which is unknown (the proposal by Tyrrell and Purser 1904, 159, that the *bustum Basili* is meant, on the grounds that it was often the scene of violence, is unnecessary). However, Quintus' *bustum* is not specified here. Nisbet 1961b, 86f., adduces this point as an argument that the work is spurious: a later writer, he urges, misunderstood something obscure (and unpreserved) in *Tog. cand.* and as a consequence believed Gratidianus was executed at his own *bustum*. The version of Gratidianus' death in the *Brief Handbook*, however, is different from Cicero's (see above **Marcus Marius**), and a later writer, in view of the evidence cited above, could hardly have misunderstood the significance of the *bustum* in Gratidianus' story. It is of course possible (as Nisbet observes) that something has dropped out of the text here. Still, if the tale of Gratidianus' death was current in anti-Catilinarian invective in 64 (see above **Marcus Marius**), it may have been felt by the author that specificity was unneeded here. Quintus is similarly elliptical in referring to Gratidianus' head being carried to Sulla (see below **carried the head**). Buecheler 1869, 31, suggested that by omitting Catulus' name the *Brief Handbook* evaded the element of revenge in the episode, but then why introduce the *bustum* at all? A similar (and unlikely) story is told by Valerius Maximus (9.2.2) about the death of either L. Julius Caesar (cos. 90) or C. Julius Caesar Strabo (aed. 90)—the account is garbled—whom Marius slew at the tomb (*bustum*) of Q. Varius Severus (tr. pl. 90) during the Marian terror.

stood there, still alive. Watt and other editors follow the MSS and read *vivo stanti* here, but *stanti* ('standing') cannot be right (Damon 1993,

281ff.). Shackleton Bailey (1988 and 2002) prefers Puteanus' conjecture *spiranti* ('breathing'). When *vivo* and *spiranti* are used in conjunction they regularly require a connective (evidence at Damon 1993, 285). Shackleton Bailey, then, reads <*vix*> *vivo et spiranti*, yielding the translation: 'Catilina took a sword in his right hand, grabbed the hair of Marius' head with his left, and cut through the man's neck when he was barely living and breathing'. Shackleton Bailey introduces *vix* ('barely') on the grounds that it is necessary in order to emphasize the extent of Gratidianus' torture; that is, only when the man was no longer sentient and could no longer feel the pain of his torture did Catilina end his life (Shackleton Bailey 1994). Damon 1993, 286ff. prefers simply *spiranti* (in her view *vivo* was introduced as a gloss on *spiranti*), which also renders acceptable sense. If the author chiefly wanted to make the point that Gratidianus was still alive at the moment of his decapitation, he might well have written *vivo etiam et spiranti* ('still alive and breathing'), which must have been a cliché in Latin (see Cic. *Dom.* 134).

carried the head. Catilina, it is clear from other versions (see above **Marcus Marius**), carried the head to Sulla. Quintus apparently expected his readers to be sufficiently familiar with the episode to know that.

streams of blood. According to Plutarch (*Sull.* 32.2), Catilina washed his hands in the sacred water of the Temple of Apollo after he delivered Gratidianus' head to Sulla.

actors and gladiators. Notwithstanding the popularity of actors and gladiators, or the celebrity and success of certain individuals (e.g. the actor Q. Roscius Gallus, whom Sulla enrolled in the equestrian order; Macr. *Sat.* 3.14.3), these professions were regarded as dishonourable by the Romans, and their practitioners suffered legal disgrace (*infamia*; see ¶8 **sold at auction**): see Edwards 1993, 123ff.; Wiedemann 1992, 28ff.. Gladiators were also dangerous because they could be put to use as personal retainers (Wiedemann 1992, 122f.; Nippel 1995, 49), and the word *gladiator* was a common term of abuse in Latin (see Opelt 1965, 136): Catilina is called a gladiator at Cic. *Cat.* 1.29; 2.24; *Mur.* 50, 83. These prejudices are operative here. Although Sulla (to his discredit) cavorted with actors (Plut. *Sull.* 2.4; 33.3; 36.1–2; Macr. *Sat.* 3.14.3), this allegation is not elsewhere levelled against Catilina: neither actors nor gladiators are included among his disreputable associations by Sallust (*Cat.* 14–16). Still, it is possible that in his *Tog. cand.* Cicero introduced an exceptionable connection between Catilina and gladiators (Asc. 88C)—especially if this fragment is to be read in conjunction with Cicero's accusation that Antonius maintained a menacing army of unemployed shepherds for unspecified violent purposes (Asc. 87C). By implicating Catilina in the immorality of actors and the violence of gladiators, Quintus supplies a thoroughly Roman slur (actors were not held in contempt in Greek culture). But the aspersion is not an especially frequent one. At Sall. *Iug.* 85.39, Marius insists that he does not possess an expensive actor (by implication, this is in contrast with his enemies); Mark Antony's relationship with actors is deprecated by Cicero (*Phil.* 2.62–7, 101; 8.26); Tacitus criticizes Nero for his association with actors (*Hist.* 2.71) and gladiators (*Ann.* 13.25); it was held against the young Titus that he caroused with performers (Suet. *Titus* 7.2); SHA, *Heliogab.* 15.1 mentions, among Elagabalus' disgraceful companions, charioteers and actors. The possibility of an attraction to actors or gladiators aroused genuine aristocratic anxiety: in AD 19 a senatorial decree censured young aristocrats who went so far as to fight as gladiators or perform as actors (see Lebek 1991).

opprobrium and...scandal. In 73 the Vestal Virgin Fabia was tried for violating her vows (sources assembled at Alexander 1990, 83)—allegedly with Catilina, who may also have been prosecuted (see Sall. *Cat.* 15.1; Oros. 6.3.1). Fabia was acquitted (Catilina, too, if he was also indicted). But the calumny persisted in anti-Catilinarian invective, thereby setting the brothers Cicero a problem: they could hardly ignore the smear but at the same time they could not repeat it as if it were a fact because Fabia was half-sister to Terentia, Cicero's wife (Plut. *Cat. min.* 19.3; see Treggiari 2007, 31), and because the status of any innocent Vestal Virgin demanded public respect, which their influential families were certain to defend (Gallia 2015, 80ff.). Consequently, any suggestion that Fabia was guilty had to be deflected—without rehabilitating Catilina's reputation. Hence the careful formulation here, which is more or less the same as Cicero's in his *Tog. cand.* (Asc. 91C: 'you have lived in such a way that there is no place, however sacred, where your approach does not drag along an accusation, even when there is no fault in that place'). Each passage delicately reproaches Catilina's character but also insists on the unnamed Fabia's innocence. Further on Fabia, see Wildfang 2006, 96f.; DiLuzio 2016, 233f.

procured himself intimate friends. The verb used here, *comparare*, can (but need not) mean to acquire by disreputable means or for improper purposes (*OLD* 373, definition 5). Quintus now reviews six unsavoury friends of Catilina. Catilina's friendships are entirely utilitarian and, more importantly, entirely disreputable. As such they contrast sharply with Cicero's wide and distinguished network of friends (¶3 **the number and variety of your friends**) and exhibit electioneering tactics of the worst order (see ¶16 **the definition of the word 'friend'**).

In his review, Quintus begins in the senate house (*curia*), shifts to the auction halls (*atria*), and concludes in a reference to the equestrian order. It has been objected that this list of Catilina's friends diverges from Cicero's regular habit in his speeches, whereby he catalogues individuals and groups along hierarchical lines (Nisbet 1961b, 87; see §V.1). But that was not Cicero's invariable habit when writing letters (e.g. Cic. *Q. Fr.* 2.3.4; *Fam.* 2.6.3), and the *Brief Handbook* has already demonstrated that its lists will not be determined by that principle (see ¶3).

like Curius... Vettius. Plurals are employed to indicate that these men represent types—that is, they are typical of the sort of men attracted to Catilina's friendship (see ¶9 **men like Titinius... Tanusius**). On the identities of the men in the *Brief Handbook*'s list, see the detailed, if sometimes speculative studies by Nicolet 1972 and David et al. 1973, 264ff. Laser 2001, 129, observes that this list of names does not include the most notorious members of the Catilinarian conspiracy, an odd omission if the *Brief Handbook* is a later forgery.

Curius. Q. Curius was expelled from the senate in 70 (Sall. *Cat.* 23.1; App. *B.Civ.* 2.3) but subsequently regained his rank. He joined but later betrayed the Catilinarian conspiracy (Sall. *Cat.* 23.2; 26.3) and attempted, unsuccessfully, to implicate Caesar (Suet. *Iul.* 17). Asc. 93C reports that, at an unknown point in his career, he was condemned on an unknown charge. The man was ridiculed for his pedantry by C. Licinius Calvus (Asc. 93C = fr. 1 Courtney, but see Courtney 1993, 202), and he was deployed against Catilina by Cicero in his *Tog. cand.* (Asc. 93C). (See *MRR* 3.78.)

Annius. Q. Annius (Chilo?) was a senator who remains little known apart from his participation in the Catilinarian conspiracy (Sall. *Cat.* 17.3; 50.4; *MRR* 3.15).

Sapala. Perhaps a name of Gallic extraction: *Sapalus, Sapalo, Sapula,* and similar names are commonly attested in Celtic regions, including Cisalpine Gaul (Harvey 1980, 116). Because a Roman Sapala is otherwise unknown, it is sometimes emended to *Scapula,* a familiar *cognomen*. Nicolet 1974, 998f., and David et al. 1973, 269f., who accept this emendation, draw attention to the existence in the late republic of the Quinctii Scapulae, an equestrian family linked to business in the auction halls (see below **auction halls**). It would not be implausible for one of Catilina's friends to be an equestrian Quinctius Scapula, but inasmuch as the point of this passage is to adduce discreditable friends, it is perhaps safer to assume that Sapala (or even Scapula) refers to a freedman (or a free man of modest origins) in the ranks of the personnel of the auction halls.

Carvilius. This name is familiar and distinguished: it is borne by senators, including consuls. Nicolet 1974, 827, and David et al. 1973, 270f., attempt to connect this man with the Carvilii Polliones, an equestrian family attested in the late republic. But distinguished names were also borne by the freedmen of distinguished families (and their descendants), and again it is unnecessary to identify Catilina's friend with anyone of equestrian rank.

auction halls. *Atria* ('auction halls') most naturally refers to the *atria Licinia*, the auction halls which were perhaps located north-east of the Roman forum (Richardson 1992, 41; *LTUR* 1.132; Carandini 2017, 289f.). These auction halls were centres of vital and profitable economic activity, the agents of which were often (but not invariably) wealthy freedmen (see Andreau 1999, 38f. and 48f.; see also *RS* 384f.; Hinard 2011, 431ff.).

Pompilius. This is a common name, although nothing further is known of this man. Nicolet 1974, 988f., proposes reading *Popilius* here, identifying Catilina's friend with P. Popilius, who, although the son of a freedman, rose to become a senator. He was excluded from the senate, however, in the census of 70 (Cic. *Clu.* 131–2), on the grounds that he had been corrupted while serving as a juror. The suggestion is an intriguing one, and this Popilius would be a figure discreditable enough to suit Quintus' purposes here.

Vettius. L. Vettius, an equestrian from Picenum. Like Cicero and Catilina, he served under Pompeius' father during the Social War (*ILS* 8888 = *ILLRP* 515). He later enriched himself during the Sullan proscriptions (Sall. *Hist.* 1.48 (McGushin); cf. Cic. *Att.* 2.24.2–4; Suet. *Iul.* 17), and it is doubtless for this behaviour that he is adduced here (see ¶9 **citizen slaughter**). In 63 he provided information on the Catilinarian conspiracy (in which he had earlier been a participant) and attempted (unsuccessfully) to implicate Caesar. In 59, stimulated by motives that remain obscure, he claimed to uncover a plot against Pompeius involving several distinguished men: when his allegations failed to persuade, he was confined and subsequently murdered during his confinement (see further Gelzer 1969a, 90f.; Mitchell 1991, 111f.; Seager 2002, 98f., 180).

brazenness. This is the only occurrence in the *Brief Handbook* of *audacia*. In political polemic, *audacia* was often deployed to indicate an opponent's passion for subverting the established political order (Wirszubski 1961; Weische 1966, 28ff.): in 63, at the time of the Catilinarian conspiracy, Cicero referred to Catilina's *audacia* with that sense (Cic. *Cat.* 1.1; 1.4; 2.1; 3.17; *Mur.* 17) and Catilina subsequently becomes a paradigm of political subversion (e.g. Plut. *Cic.* 10.4; Dio 36.44.4; cf. Quint. *Inst.* 2.16.7). In view of the efforts in 64 of Cicero's campaign to portray both Antonius and Catilina as dangerous figures during a time of economic anxiety (see ¶8 **But, you will say…Quite the contrary; ¶8 deeply in debt;** §VII.5), Quintus has doubtless chosen this word carefully. But its political implications immediately give way to something even ghastlier when Quintus goes on to accuse Catilina of child abuse (see next note, and below **children**).

facility and skill. Skill (*ars*) is conjoined with facility (*efficacitas*, an uncommon word but used once by Cicero at *Tusc.* 4.31) in a perverse deformation of ¶1 **talent**, where Quintus expresses his desire to combine his *ars* (viz. the *Brief Handbook*) with Cicero's talent (*ingenium*). At ¶1, Cicero's aspiration is the consulship; Catilina, by shocking contrast, puts his talents to work in order to rape children.

children. Literally 'children wearing the *toga praetexta*', that is, freeborn children of Roman citizens. Boys wore the *toga praetexta* until they donned the *toga virilis*, usually around the age of 15 (Dixon, 1992, 101; Edmondson 2008, 26ff.). During the republic, girls also wore the *toga praetexta* (e.g. Cic. *Verr.* 1.113), traditionally until the time of their first marriage (George 2001, 183ff.; Olson 2008). The *toga praetexta* signified the respect that was owed to children (e.g. Hor. *Ep.* 5.7; Pers. *Sat.* 5.30). *Liberos* ('children') is masculine here, but the masculine plural is regularly used to indicate boys and girls (and can in fact be used in referring to a single girl) (*KS* 87). Catilina's depravity, then, is comprehensive. Sexual relations with freeborn children were deemed abominable by the Romans and were denominated by the term *stuprum* ('illicit or immoral sex'); a *lex Scantinia*, of uncertain date but possibly as early as 149 (*MRR* 1.460 n.3), outlawed some activities associated with *stuprum* and these very likely included sex with freeborn boys (see, further, Fantham 1991; Skinner 2005, 199f.; Wiliams 2010, 103ff., 120ff.).

Africa. Catilina was propraetor in Africa in 67–66 (*MRR* 2.147). His tenure as governor was so objectionable that, even before it was concluded, an African delegation had travelled to Rome in order to lodge its complaints with the senate (Asc. 85C). In 65 he was tried for provincial extortion (*de repetundis*), a charge on which Cicero briefly considered defending Catilina in the hope of making him an ally in the consular elections (*Att.*1.2.1). Although Catilina was apparently regarded as guilty (Cic. *Att.* 1.1.1), he enjoyed eminent support at his trial and was acquitted. Cicero insisted that the senators on the jury tended to vote for condemnation (Asc. 89C), and he later claimed that Catilina's prosecutor, P. Clodius Pulcher (tr. pl. 58), had been bribed to fumble the case (Cic. *Har. resp.* 42;

Pis. 23; but see Tatum 1999, 53ff.). On this trial, see Alexander 1990, 106f. An acquittal could, of course, be viewed as a triumph, and doubtless Catilina cast his trial in that light. But trials were ordeals, in which defendants were subjected to withering abuse (see ¶8 **But, you will say… Quite the contrary**), and a man's enemies could, and in Catilina's case certainly did, recur to past accusations as proof of bad character. Quintus concludes his list of Catilinarian vices and crimes by adducing this trial: it was the most recent and therefore most familiar of Catilina's disgraces, and it allowed Catilina to be represented as simultaneously greedy and cruel (the crime of extortion was often associated with cruelty: see Seager 1997), which reprised Quintus' animadversions on Catilina's conduct during the proscriptions (see ¶9 **citizen slaughter**). Cicero also made much of Catilina's trial in his *Tog. cand.* (Asc. 86–7, 89, 92C).

Read them. Witnesses did not invariably appear in court. Instead, they could provide written depositions (*testimonium per tabulas*; see, e.g., Cic. *Q. Rosc.* 43; *Cael.* 55; Quint. 5.7.32; Greenidge 1901, 488ff.; Steck 2009, 83ff.). And although Romans did not produce transcripts at trials, memorable remarks and speeches were sometimes preserved (not always by their authors). The commentary of witnesses, and their interrogation, could be extensive, colourful, and wide-ranging: Cicero's speech *In Vatinium* reflects his interrogation of P. Vatinius (cos. 47), a witness for the prosecution, during his defence of P. Sestius (pr. 54) in 56 (Alexander 1990, 130f.). The evidence of African witnesses against Catilina is also cited by Cicero in his *Tog. cand.* (Asc. 87C). Undoubtedly this material, or perhaps forgeries masquerading as depositions (see §III.9), was circulated by Cicero's campaign in an attempt to undermine confidence in Catilina's integrity.

left that trial as impoverished. Catilina, it is here alleged, secured his acquittal through bribery, a conventional complaint on the part of anyone who believed there had been a perceived miscarriage of justice. At the same time, jury tampering was a Roman reality (see Cic. *Verr.* 1.36–42, a tendentious denunciation of jury corruption, with emphasis on the schemes of Verres). Notorious instances of suborned, or at least allegedly suborned, juries include: Terentius Varro (Cic. *Verr.* 1.40; *Clu.* 130); Oppianicus (Cic. *Clu.* 62ff.; *Verr.* 1.29; 1.39; 2.79; *Caec.* 28; *Brut.* 241); P. Clodius Pulcher (Cic. *Att.* 1.16.5; *Har. resp.* 36ff.; Val. Max. 9.1.7; Plut. *Cic.* 29.5; Dio 37.46.3; Schol. Bob. 86, 90, 91, 173 (Stangl)). In his *Tog. cand.* Cicero rather desperately insists that, by voting to acquit, the jurors in Catilina's case were preserving him for a future and more severe punishment (Asc. 87C). There is no hint in that speech of Catilinarian jury tampering. Cicero may, however, have raised the question of the prosecution's collusion (see above **Africa**); Asconius, in his commentary, addresses the matter (Asc. 87C).

impoverished. Quintus insists (falsely) that Catilina's bribes left him penniless (reprising criticism lodged at ¶8 **deeply in debt**). This aspersion may have been conventional (see, esp., Cic. *Har. resp.* 6; Quint. 8.3.1, quoting Cicero's fragmentary speech *In P. Clodium et Curionem*). Although juries were composed of elites (see ¶8 **classes that constitute the juries**), the alleged impecuniousness of some of them is adduced here in order to explain their susceptibility to Catilina's bribes (see Cic. *Clu.* 66).

another trial. It appears that, in trials for extortion (see above **Africa**), an acquitted man could not be tried a second time for offences alleged to have taken place up to that time, but this remains unsettled (see Lintott 1992, 137ff.; *RS* 106). Perhaps Quintus is merely slinging mud. Or perhaps he has in mind Lucceius' plans for prosecuting Catilina in the murder court (see ¶9 **citizen slaughter**). Cicero, in his *Tog. cand.*, also insists that Catilina will soon face another trial (Asc. 87C).

¶11 better luck. Quintus concludes his discussion of Cicero's standing as a new man by way of an extended comparison with the election of the new man C. Coelius Caldus (see next note). Once again, Quintus is careful, in advancing Cicero's merits, not to offend the nobility. This is made clear at the beginning when he attributes Cicero's likely elevation to office at least in part to his good luck (*fortuna*): that new men owed their success to *fortuna* was a view held by the nobility (see Wiseman 1971, 109, who assembles testimonia). Although Quintus does not fully embrace that perspective here, he insinuates it into his final appraisal of Cicero's prospects in this section of the *Brief Handbook*: it is Cicero's good luck that he is not competing with the likes of Coelius' noble rivals but instead with the likes of Antonius and Catilina. At ¶27, Quintus again draws attention to Cicero's good luck (*casus*) in having such atrocious and ill-equipped rivals.

Gaius Coelius. Gaius Coelius Caldus, as tr. pl. in 107, carried a law extending the secret ballot to treason cases tried before the people, then the sole remaining public assembly excluded from the requirement of the secret ballot (*MRR* 1.551); in the same year he successfully prosecuted C. Popillius Laenas on a charge of treason on the grounds that he had negotiated a disgraceful surrender while serving as a legate in Gaul (*MRR* 1.552). The date of his praetorship remains uncertain: the usual view is that he was praetor in 100 or 99 and that he was allocated Nearer Spain as his province (*RRC* 457ff.; *MRR* 3.59–60; but see Brennan 2000, 673, for another possibility). Elected consul for 94, he became governor of Gaul, where he was acclaimed *imperator* ('victorious general') and where he apparently remained until his death in 85. Important facets of his career can be recovered only from the coins minted by his grandson in 51 (*RRC* 457ff., on which see Badian 1998), who in 50 served as Cicero's quaestor in Cilicia (*MRR* 2.250). Coelius was much admired by Cicero, who often claimed him as a model for his own career (Cic. *Verr.* 2.5.181; *Mur.* 17; see Blom 2010, 158ff.). But here Coelius is less an exemplar than a *comparandum*. Cicero is not instructed to shape his canvass along the lines of Coelius'. In the *Brief Handbook*, it is a noble, C. Aurelius Cotta (cos. 75), who is singled out as the man whose canvassing technique Cicero should imitate (see ¶47).

It is not at all certain that Coelius was the last new man to attain the consulship before Cicero's election in 64. It is routinely observed that Cicero tends to ignore the new men M. Herennius (cos. 93), C. Norbanus (cos. 83), and M. Tullius Decula (cos. 81) (Wiseman 1971, 108f.; Blom 2010, 162). Herennius, however, was probably not a *novus* (see Badian 1990, 389). As for the remaining two, there are insufficient testimonia to draw certain conclusions. Decula's status must remain uncertain (Badian 1990, 391), and Evans 1987, 121ff., has argued that Norbanus was not a new man. In the case of Norbanus, even if he was in fact a new man, his disreputable career rendered him anathema to Cicero (see Wiseman 1971, 108f.; Hinard, 2011, 147ff.).

not so long ago. The word *nuper* (regularly translated 'recently') was very flexible: it commonly refers to events decades old (and can in fact extend to events centuries earlier); see Linderski 1995, 104f. In this instance it looks back more than thirty years, from 64 to 95. The word, then, strikes a balance between the novelty of a new man's election and its propriety (Coelius operates here as an admirable example of the value to Rome of recognizing the merit of new men).

two men. One of these men was L. Domitius Ahenobarbus (*MRR* 2.12), who was elected with Coelius. Little is known about this Domitius: his praetorship in Sicily was remembered for its cruelty (Cic. *Verr.* 4.2.17; Val. Max. 6.3.5) and his death for its violence (he was murdered at the door to the curia in 82; see Vell. 2.26.2; App. *B.Civ.* 1.88). See, further, Carlsen 2006, 50ff. His nephew, L. Domitius Ahenobarbus (cos. 54), was one of Cicero's principal noble supporters in 64 (Cic. *Att.* 1.1.3), a circumstance that will have helped to stimulate the lavish compliments employed in this paragraph—and underscores the reality that Cicero very much needed noble backing if he hoped to win the consulship. The identity of the other noble, who was defeated in the elections of 95, remains unknown. Badian 1964, 93f., makes a plausible case for C. Valerius Flaccus (cos. 93; see *MRR* 3.211), but this argument falls apart if Coarelli is correct in concluding that this man served in Asia as governor during 98–95 (see Coarelli 1982). See, further, Brennan 2000, 552.

talent. Cicero also possesses talent (*ingenium*; see ¶1 **talent**), the common property of capable new men and capable nobles.

honour. The word *pudor*, in political discourse, registers a sense of propriety and restraint in positions of responsibility (see ¶8 **blameless**). The word also signals the personal morality of Coelius' noble rivals, in contrast to the vices of Antonius and Catilina (see above ¶¶8–10). Although it is used only here in the *Brief Handbook*, it is a regular item in catalogues of aristocratic virtues (e.g. Cic. *Mur.* 30; see Hellegouarc'h 1963, 283, and, more generally, Kaster 2005, 28ff.).

favours. This is the first occurrence of *beneficium* ('favour'; see ¶4 **put you under an obligation**) in the *Brief Handbook*, but the word, like the idea of reciprocity it conveys, will suffuse the second section of the work (¶¶13–53), which it anticipates here: ¶¶13, 16 (where *beneficia* are vital to friendship), 18, 19, 21 (where *beneficia* are vital to gaining electoral supporters), 26, 30, 37, 40, 46. Here the word indicates the high degree of *gratia* ('influence') both nobles possessed; Cicero shares the same resource (see ¶4 **express their gratitude**).

matchless technique and assiduousness. Technique (*ratio*) and assiduousness (*diligentia*) reprise Quintus' opening assertion that Cicero possesses these vital assets, especially when he is equipped with the *Brief Handbook* (see ¶1 **assiduousness**; ¶1 **within a single, systematic form and in a logical order**). Coelius' noble rivals succeeded not simply because they were noble or even virtuous, but because they were adept at canvassing (see Morstein-Marx 1998, 278f.; ¶47 **master in the art of canvassing**).

¶12 nature…studies…methodology. This combination (*natura… studia…ratio*), features of Cicero's profile that he shares with the nobles adduced in the previous section, was emphasized from the beginning of the *Brief Handbook* (see ¶1); the reprise is made clear by the recurrence of *usus* ('practice'), used only here and at ¶1. As the work insists from its commencement, Cicero already possesses all that is required for electoral success. Still, campaigning for office does not come naturally to the aristocratic temper, hence the need for Quintus' urging here.

methodology. By 'methodology' (*ratio*), Quintus refers to the advice included in the *Brief Handbook* (see ¶1 **within a single, systematic form and in a logical order**). The application of traditional canvassing practices, which receive rational exposition in the *Brief Handbook*, constitutes one of Cicero's advantages despite his condition as a new man—just as a mastery of these practices was an asset belonging to Coelius, noble rivals (see ¶11 **matchless technique and assiduousness**).

required by your present situation. By 'present situation' (*tempus*) Quintus plainly refers to Cicero's canvass. Quintus, naturally enough, often resorts to *tempus* in order to underline the urgency of canvassing (e.g. ¶¶4, 19, 21, 24, 38). At the same time, the traditional requirements of canvassing were not entirely suited to aristocratic tastes (see §III.4), and Quintus also deploys *tempus* in order to emphasize the very special circumstances of canvassing and the peculiar moral conditions canvassing entails (see especially ¶¶25, 45–6; cf. ¶16). Cicero uses *tempus* in this same sense, and by way of making it clear that canvassing presents a candidate with extraordinary demands, at *Att.* 1.1.4. He makes a similar distinction, when political and philosophical inclinations pull in different directions (*Off.* 2.57–8, a political exception to *Off.* 2.55; *Off.* 2.60). A concern over this tension also animates Cicero's *De republica* and *De legibus* (Atkins 2013, 62ff., 188ff.). As a practical matter, the Romans believed, unsurprisingly, that the exigencies of any situation might dictate one's behaviour (e.g. Cic. *Clu.* 139, on Cicero's reaction to his *tempus*; see Cic. *Fam.* 1.19.18; 1.9.21; *Inv. rhet.* 2.156–78; Quint. 3.5.18; 5.103–5). But Quintus' usage here is also influenced by contemporary philosophical interests. Cicero, in his philosophical writing, was preoccupied by the relevance of circumstances to right action (Woolf 2007; cf. McConnell 2014, 39ff.). At *Off.* 1.31–2, he employs the word *tempus* in translating the Greek word *peristasis* (see *Att.* 16.11.4), which, by the Hellenistic period, had become a technical term for a situation that was, in moral terms, somehow special or even difficult (White 1978, 111ff.; cf. Fortenbaugh 1993; Langlands 2011; Brown 2014). That sense of *tempus* obtains at ¶¶25 and 45–6, where it forms part of Quintus' design, whenever he must address the compromises to aristocratic decorum required by canvassing, to foreground Cicero's aristocratic probity and to give at least some moral cover to these traditional and necessary if potentially unattractive features of canvassing (Tatum 2007, 129ff.). See also ¶16 **the definition of the word 'friend'**; ¶25 **you can honourably do**; ¶42 **when canvassing**; ¶45 **to your situation**.

you can and should do. The practices encoded in the *Brief Handbook* represent *normative* practices (see ¶1 **anything new**; §IV.4).

notable for their vices. This expression (*vitiis nobiles*) relies on the literal sense of *nobilis*, or noble, for its effect: that is, *nobilis* means 'known' (see ¶4 **nobles**): Antonius and Catilina are more notorious for their immorality than distinguished for the excellence of their birth.

with a single vote, to draw two daggers. The two daggers are plainly Antonius and Catilina, and this striking line reprises their description at ¶8 as 'cut-throats since their childhood'. A wicked citizen could draw 'two daggers' with a single ballot because, in consular elections, each voter cast two votes (for the two available consulships; see §II.3). A similar conceit, in very similar language, is employed by Cicero in his *Tog. cand.* (Asc. 93C), and this line was very probably put to use during Cicero's campaign along the lines of a modern political slogan (see §§III.11; VII.5). Still, some have seen in this resemblance evidence that the *Brief Handbook* is a later forgery (see §V.5).

¶13 I have explained. This transitional passage concludes Quintus' examination of Cicero's condition as a new man. It concedes that Cicero must be the object of envy on the part of others, notwithstanding his merits, indeed, to some extent on account of his merits. Quintus then finishes by associating Cicero's opposition with members of the political class who are hostile to Pompeius, reprising his notice from ¶5 **Gnaeus Pompeius**.

sheer enormity. A new man's undertaking to stand for the consulship, Quintus admits, is a bold undertaking, a concession that both compliments Cicero and acknowledges the dominance of the nobility in Roman elections.

worthy of that office. Cicero is universally deemed worthy (*dignus*) of election. On the importance of *dignitas* ('prestige') to winning office, see §III.2. On the use of *dignus* as a recommendation to office in Pompeian election posters, see §III.7.

resentful. For the Romans, accomplishment inevitably inspired *invidia* ('envy'). *Invidia* could be felt in response to another's success, whether it was merited or not and whether it blighted one's own prospects or not (Hellegouarc'h 1963, 195ff.; Kaster 2005, 84ff.). *Virtus* was especially believed to stimulate envy in others (*Rhet. Her.* 4.36; Cic. *Cat.* 1.28–9; *Balb.* 15–18; *Rab. Post.* 48; *Phil.* 8.29–31; Sall. *Cat.* 3.2; 37.3; *Iug.* 10.2; see Kaster 2005, 182 n. 15), an assertion the *Brief Handbook* also makes at ¶39. The impediment of *invidia* is natural, and so Quintus does not here deprecate the feeling. And in Quintus' view it is not only the nobility who envy Cicero, it is other new men and the public at large (see below **closely attached to you in friendship**).

the man who is brave. Quintus has already credited Cicero with eloquence (¶¶2, 8) and blamelessness (see ¶8 **blameless**). Here, and only here in the *Brief Handbook*, Cicero is described as brave (*fortis*), an obvious compliment, which contrasts with the cowardice attributed to Antonius (see ¶9 **afraid of his own shadow**).

how great your prestige will be. Once elected consul, Cicero will potentially excel at least some ex-consuls—and they know it. That Cicero's election should be resisted on this ground was to be expected; at the same time, the competitiveness of the Roman aristocracy renders such an attitude unexceptionable. And, in any case, Quintus simply raises the possibility: he does not go so far as to attribute envy or obstruction to the ex-consuls, whom he does not wish to offend. On the importance of ex-consuls, see ¶4 **ex-consuls.**

men from consular families…the station of their ancestors. It was expected of young nobles that they would replicate the success of their ancestors: anything short of that was potentially disgraceful (e.g. *ILS* 4, 6; Cic. *Off.* 1.116; Caes. *B.Gall.* 7.80; Liv. 1.22.2; see Earl 1967, 11ff.; Hölkeskamp 2010, 122ff.). This reality was a strong motive in noble hostility against new men in the consulship (Wiseman 1971, 101ff.) and exacerbated any noble's fear of defeat in elections for office (*dolor repulsae*).

closely attached to you in friendship. Envy was incompatible with genuine friendship (e.g. Cic. *Amic.* 59–60; cf. *Amic.* 14; *Att.* 1.13.4; *Fam.* 14.1.1), and although competition for office could ruin a friendship (Cic. *Amic.* 34) it ought not to do so (Cic. *Amic.* 63); see Brunt 1988, 369. The importance of friendship to electoral success has already been observed (see ¶3 **the number and variety of your friends**), and friendship constitutes a major theme of the *Brief Handbook* (¶¶16–40; see ¶16 **the definition of the word 'friend'**).

¶14 the public. The word here is *populus*—the men who voted in assemblies—and not the less respectable *multitudo* (see ¶5 **champions of popular rights**). The success of the nobility in consular elections was a reflex of the conservatism of voters of every class, including men of the first class as well as the knights out of whose ranks new men emerged.

in the fashion of recent years. Since the final enfranchisement of the Italians in the census of 70 (see ¶1 **within a single, systematic form and in a logical order**) there had not been a new man in the consulship. It had, in fact, been at least twenty years, and possibly longer, since a new man had been elected (see ¶11 **Gaius Coelius**). At the same time, this expression suggests to readers that there is nothing traditional or venerable about the modern aversion to electing new men.

angry with you…cases you have pleaded. Quintus turns now to a different source of opposition to Cicero's candidature—namely, political figures he may have offended by defending C. Cornelius (tr. pl. 67) (see ¶5 **any speech that appeared to support popular rights**). As he did previously, Quintus here connects Cicero's forensic performances with his support for Pompeius (see ¶5 **Gnaeus Pompeius**). Quintus here emphasizes Cicero's enthusiasm for the great man and makes it clear, both to him and to other readers, that Cicero is willing to incur hostility from some quarters on Pompeius' behalf. Similarly, in his public letter to Quintus on provincial administration, Cicero expresses approval if Quintus has incurred enmity for the right reasons (Cic. *Q. Fr.* 1.1.19; 1.26).

increasing the glory of Gnaeus Pompeius. Only Pompeius' personal enemies—men like M. Licinius Crassus (cos. I 70) or L. Licinius Lucullus (cos. 74) or M. Porcius Cato (pr. 54)—could be hostile to Cicero on account of his past enthusiasm for Pompeius, or so Quintus indicates here. Nor could readers overlook the fact that one of Pompeius' bitterest enemies was also an ardent supporter of Cicero's candidature—namely, L. Domitius Ahenobarbus (cos. 54)—whose brother Pompeius had executed during the civil war between Sulla and the residue of the Marians (Plut. *Pomp.* 11–12; [Sall.] *Ep.* 1.4.1; Val. Max. 6.2.8; see Carlsen 2006, 53ff.).

¶16 a campaign for high office. Here the *Brief Handbook* commences its systematic analysis of canvassing, which constitutes the bulk of the work (¶¶16–53). The style becomes austerely didactic and throughout this section the work presents itself as the art of canvassing that was promised in ¶1. Canvassing is classified into two main components: gaining the support of friends (¶¶16–40) and gaining the goodwill of the people (¶¶41–53). This division was apparently conventional: in assessing the prospects of two candidates for the consulship of 64 Cicero appraises them in terms of their resources 'in friends and public reputation' (*Att.* 1.1.2: *et ab amicis et existimatio*), a classification strikingly similar to Quintus' (Morstein-Marx 1998, 262). Quintus' division between the support of friends and the goodwill of the people is made untidy by the very broad and strictly utilitarian definition of friendship that he adopts (see below **the definition of the word 'friend'**), a move that admits the candidate's relationships with crowds composed of men at every social level, even the lowest levels of society (see especially ¶¶34–5), into his category of securing friendly supporters (see Fezzi 2007, 21). Quintus' division is further eroded when friendship makes an important appearance in his discussion of acquiring popular goodwill (¶42). The author is aware of his imperfect distribution and he defends his organizational scheme at ¶49.

The appropriate means for acquiring and exploiting the energies and affections of others was a topic of Greek philosophical thought and of obvious interest to elite Romans. An obvious parallel for Quintus' account here is Cicero's discussion, at *Off.* 20–71, of the topic 'how we can excite and arouse the enthusiasm of others in support of what is useful to us' (*Off.* 2.20). Cicero's *De officiis* relies heavily on the Stoic Panaetius' *Peri kathekontos* (*On Duty*) and on the philosophical tradition behind it (Dyck 1996, 353ff.; Gill 2003, 40ff.). Like Quintus, Cicero breaks down the methods for winning the support of others into several strategies. Presumably Quintus' organization of material owes something, at least in inspiration, to philosophical sources whose exposition was analytic along the lines of Panaetius. But there any observable similarity ends, and it is worth observing that, whereas Cicero's (and Panaetius') organization of material is somewhat rambling and anything but neat (see Dyck 1996, 387ff.), the untidy features of Quintus' arrangement are not accidents but actually help him to fashion his version of the correct and moral approach to canvassing for office (see ¶42 **someone becomes friendlier to you**; ¶49 **departed from my own system of classification**).

divides itself. Any systematic analysis of a topic, it was generally assumed, should begin with a definition—often, as here, by way of division and classification (see, e.g. Cic. *Off.* 1.7; *Rep.* 1.38; *De or.* 1.209; 2.108; *Part.* 41; *Top.* 9; 26; ¶1 **within a single, systematic form and in a logical order**; §IV.4).

There is an important moral dimension to Quintus' organizational scheme. In the section on popular goodwill (¶¶41–53), the candidate's dealings with his public tend to be either impersonal or so extremely utilitarian, even self-serving, that only the unusual circumstances of a canvass can render them suitable specimens of behaviour (see especially ¶¶42, 44–9), an aspect of campaigning adumbrated earlier in the work (see ¶12 **required by your present situation**). Consequently, these actions are quarantined in Quintus' analysis from the more obviously satisfactory moral situation obtaining even in Quintus' greatly expanded conception of friendship that is the basis of ¶¶16–40 (see below **the definition of the word 'friend'**). This is not to say that the acquisition of popular goodwill is immoral in Quintus' exposition, but it does entail activities that are designated by Quintus as simultaneously problematic and necessary, and so require special, and separate, treatment.

support of friends. Quintus has already emphasized Cicero's extensive network of friends (see ¶3 **the number and variety of your friends**). There Quintus adduced them as compensation for Cicero's narrow resources as a new man. Here, reprising the point, Quintus explains how Cicero should go about acquiring new friends, confirming the support of existing friends, and—most importantly—deploying his friends in advancing his candidature. A man with political ambitions needed many friends (e.g. Cic. *Off.* 29–30; see Tatum 2015, with further bibliography), and activating their energies on one's behalf, although crucial at elections, was never a simple matter (Meier 1980, 180; Brunt 1988, 428f.; Yakobson 1999, 85f.).

goodwill of the people. Quintus' treatment of gaining the goodwill of the people (*popularis voluntas*), the second element in his definition of canvassing, is postponed until ¶41, where he describes his advice as 'the correct method for dealing with the people' (*popularis ratio*). At ¶49, he makes it clear that by gaining the goodwill of the people he means 'enhancing one's reputation with the public at large' and 'the means by which you may win over the masses'. Winning popularity with the public, including the lowest classes, is thus signalled as a requirement for success in any canvass for the consulship (see §§II.4, III.3–5). After his election, Cicero attributed his success to the goodwill of the people (e.g. *Leg. agr.* 2.4; *Vat.* 6; *Brut.* 321). And *popularis voluntas* appears to have been a natural factor in the analysis of any election (e.g. *Mur.* 2; *Planc.* 54; see Hellegouarc'h 1963, 183ff.).

assiduousness directed at gaining the support of friends. This is the subject of ¶¶16–40. Quintus' discussion is detailed and involves multiple sub-classifications. Below is an outline of the basic organization of this section of the work:

(A) retaining the support of existing friends (16–24)
    (a) retaining friends (16–17)
    (b) deploying friends according to their uses (18–20)
    (c) three methods for stimulating the support of friends (21–4)
        (i) favours (21)
        (ii) the expectation of favours (22)
        (iii) voluntary supporters (23–4)

(B) acquiring a broad range of friends (25–33)
    (a) the easy availability of new friends (25–8)
    (b) taxonomy of friends one must acquire (29–33)
        (i) men who are influential in the forum (29)
        (ii) men who are influential within various organizations (30–2)
        (iii) knights (33)

(C) attendance (34–8)
    (a) definition of attendance (34)
    (b) morning greeting (35)
    (c) escort to the forum (36)
    (d) attendance in the forum (37–8)

(D) false friends (39)

(E) taxonomy of enemies (40)
    (a) men offended by Cicero
    (b) men who dislike Cicero for no reason
    (c) men who are friends of Cicero's rivals

favours and the reciprocation of favours. In his discussion both of gaining the support of friends and exciting the goodwill of the people (¶¶41–53), Quintus remains concerned with reciprocity between the candidate and various segments of his public (see ¶4 **See to it that... express their gratitude; ¶4 express their gratitude**). Although Quintus demonstrates his awareness of the most elevated, selfless, and philosophical notions of friendship, his working definition in the *Brief Handbook* is more utilitarian in nature (see ¶16 **the definition of the word 'friend'**). Nevertheless, it must be recalled that, for the Romans, whether or not they were thinking like philosophers, a reliable exchange of favours constituted a genuine basis for *amicitia*, or friendship (e.g. Cic. *Mur.* 24; *Off.* 1.56, describing the relationship not as *amicitia* but *communitas* or *societas*; 2.21, 23–6, 29–32, 52–64, favours generate affection; *Nat. D.* 1.12; Sen. *Ben.* 2.18.5; 2.21.2; cf. Thuc. 2.40.4; Xen. *Mem.* 1.2.7; 2.9.8; 3.11.11; Arist. *Eth. Nic.* 1381b35; Epicurus, ap. Diog. Laert. 10.120; *Sent. Vat.* 23; Griffin 2013, 36ff.). Consequently, Quintus' ample extension of friendship in this section (¶¶16–40), based largely on reciprocity alone, is able to sustain something of the moral halo associated with elevated connotations of friendship. (See below **the definition of the word 'friend'**).

long-standing familiarity. Although this section of the *Brief Handbook* is devoted mostly to friendships that are primarily utilitarian in nature, Quintus is careful, here and elsewhere, to evoke loftier conceptions of friendship—gestures that underline how, for Cicero, an elevated conception of friendship is the natural one, even if it must be adapted to the unique moral requirements of canvassing.

an accommodating and agreeable nature. When Quintus encourages Cicero to be ingratiating with the masses (see ¶42 **Then**), although he will recur to Cicero's natural aristocratic charm and bonhomie (*comitas*), it is there described as inadequate to the task of winning over the masses. It seems, however, that Cicero did in fact possess an accommodating nature (*facilitas*), or so Caesar believed: he is reported as remarking of Cicero that 'if any man is accommodating [*facilis*], it is he' (Cic. *Att.* 14.1.2). By contrast, Quintus was not regarded as adept in winning friends (Cic. *Q. Fr.* 1.2.7).

the definition of the word 'friend'. The circumstances of canvassing for office were deemed extraordinary (e.g. Cic. *De or.* 1.112; see, further, §III.4; Tatum 2007) and this point is emphasized more than once in the *Brief Handbook* (see ¶12 **required by your present situation**; ¶25 **you can honourably do**; ¶42 **when canvassing**; ¶45 **to your situation**). Here Quintus reminds Cicero and his readers of something they already know, which is that the word 'friend' (*amicus*) is socially very adaptable, not least in the context of canvassing for office.

Romans used the word *amicus* in two distinct but not entirely unrelated registers: (i) as an ideal, friendship (*amicitia*) was based on goodwill and mutual affection (*amicus* and *amicitia*, derive from *amor* ('love'); see Cic. *Amic.* 26, on which see Powell 1990, 93f. Trustworthiness (*fides*) and virtue were essential; see ¶39 **deceit, treachery, and faithlessness**. So, too, common interests and pursuits. A man was unlikely to have an abundance of genuine friendships (Cic. *Amic.* 20), nor was it likely that a genuine friendship could exist when individuals were separated by too great a social divide (see Cic. *Amic.* 69 on the problem of unequal friendships). Although friendship entailed reciprocal good services, it did not arise from neediness or mere utility. (ii) *amicus* could also be applied, by way of courtesy, to acquaintances, even inferior acquaintances such as clients and supporters, with whom one shared a relationship of more or less strict utility; Cicero describes such friendships as *mediocres amicitiae*, or 'ordinary friendships' (Cic. *Fin.* 2.84). And this is the form of friendship recommend to Quintus when, as governor of Asia, he forms local acquaintances (Q. *Fr.* 1.1.11). Even when used in this sense, the positive connotations of ideal friendship were nonetheless evoked (otherwise this use of *amicus* could hardly be a compliment), nor was this usage deemed crafty or dissimulating; the well-known dictum of Syme, '*amicitia* was a weapon of politics, not a sentiment based on congeniality' (Syme 1939, 12), is excessive, reductive, and in any case goes beyond the pale of Roman sensibilities. The sheer abundance of friends required for political success in Rome, especially electoral success (see, e.g. Cic. *Planc.* 25: 'the solicitation of votes itself is always most influential when it is actuated by the claims of friendship [*officio necessitudinis*]'; see *Mur.* 7) was accessible only by way of a more or less utilitarian concept of friendship. Consequently, Quintus' extension of the definition of *amicus* here is neither surprising nor exceptionable. It is instead notable that Quintus represents Cicero, and his readers, as men for whom the ideal conception of friendship is the most natural one. Only the extraordinary circumstances of canvassing permit them to strain their elevated views on friendship. On friendship in Roman society, see Saller 1982, 11ff.; Brunt 1988, 351ff.; Powell 1990, 21ff.; Spielvogel 1993; Powell 1995b; Konstan 1997, 122ff.; Citroni Marchetti 2000, 3ff.; Verboven 2002, 35ff.; Tatum 2007, 119ff.; Konstan 2010; Griffin 2013, 31ff.; Rollinger 2014, 52ff.

makes a habit of visiting your home. Here Quintus adumbrates his discussion of a candidate's morning greeting (*salutatio*; see ¶35 **morning greeters**), where he explicitly observes that 'most morning greeters are common folk' (¶35). He nevertheless includes these visitors within his discussion of gaining friends.

Nevertheless. In this way Quintus again underlines his awareness of the superior quality of friendships that transcend the circumstances of canvassing (see above ¶13 **closely attached to you in friendship**), though, here too, their utilitarian advantages are recognized ('it is also very helpful'; see Laser 2001, 135). A list of the kinds of men 'more legitimately' regarded as friends' follows, the range of which is summarized under the rubric of 'any other close tie', or *necessitudo*, an important relationship in Rome combining reciprocity and responsibility (e.g. Cic. *Inv. rhet.* 2.35; *Fam.* 11.22.1; 13.55.2) with (at least in principle) affection (Cic. *Sest.* 6; *Phil.* 2.40; see below **any other close tie**). Quintus' list here is roughly parallel with lists at Cic. *Inv. rhet.* 2.35 and *Clu.* 94 (cf. *Brut.* 166) and was doubtless a standard one. Quintus revisits the importance of 'long-standing familiarity' at ¶25.

by blood or by marriage. That is, connections of natural kinship (*cognatio*) or arising from a relationship established through marriage (*adfinitas*). Friendship predicated on *adfinitas* is routinely asserted and commonly attested (see Hellegouarc'h 1963, 65ff.; Moreau 1990; Treggiari 1991, 107ff.; Zmeskal 2009). The friendship exhibited by the relationship between a father-in-law and a son-in-law was deemed especially close, but other marriage ties helped to consolidate friendships; for instance, Cicero's friendship with Atticus was reinforced when Quintus married Atticus' sister Pomponia. By contrast, a distinction is sometimes drawn between *cognatio* and friendship (e.g. Cic. *Fin.* 5.65; Quint. 4.1.7), nor, in Greek thinking about the matter, are kin routinely identified as friends (Konstan 1997, 53ff.). Nevertheless, even if their conjunction is infrequent in our sources, it is obvious that *cognatio* and friendship were compatible categories in the Roman republic: (e.g. Cic. *Verr.* 2.2.64 (Verres asserts his *cognatio* as well as his friendship with L. Metellus (cos. 68)); *Verr.* 2.4.72; *Phil.* 5.6; *Rhet. Her.* 4.69 (friendship emerges from kinship). In any case, the guiding principle in this sentence is *necessitudo* ('close tie'), a category that includes both connections by marriage and blood relations (e.g. Cic. *Verr.* 1.19; *Clu.* 199; *Sest.* 6; Val. Max. 6.2.3; Sen. *Ben.* 3.18.1; Plin. *Ep.* 10.87.3; Gell. *NA* 13.3.4; see Cosi 2002, 15f.; 29f.).

The possession of a powerful family and its network of supporters and dependants was regarded as a major source of influence at Rome, to the degree that Sallust's Marius, speaking as a new man, could complain, in the case of the nobles, about 'the might of their kindred and relations' (Sall. *Iug.* 85.4, *cognatorum et adfinium opes*; cf. *Rhet. Her.* 1.8; Cic. *Brut.* 166; *Att.* 4.16.6; *Fam.* 8.2.2), and the exertions of kin are often in evidence in our accounts of elections (e.g. Liv. 22.34.1–35.4; 35.10.1–10; 39.32.5–13; 40.28.8; Cic. *Scaur.* 32; Asc. 25C); see, further, Scullard 1973; Hölkeskamp 2010, 30ff.; Scholz 2011, 89ff.; Harders 2017.) At the same time, it is vital not to exaggerate the importance of family connections in the exercise of Roman politics or even in winning elections (Meier 1980, 175ff.; Brunt 1988, 443ff.; Tatum 2015, 259ff.); or, put differently, even kith and kin had to be cultivated by an aspiring candidate (Meier 1980, 177). And sometimes kin found themselves in competition for an office (e.g. Liv. 35.24.4–6, with Tatum 2001; Liv. 40.37.6–9). Here Quintus dutifully mentions Cicero's traditional connections, and the *Brief Handbook* itself constitutes proof of family solidarity behind Cicero's candidature. Still, Quintus cannot, and does not, expand on familial clout for the obvious reason that Cicero, a new man, lacks it on the probable scale of his rivals (hence the attack, at ¶28, on Antonius' capacity for winning and keeping friends).

religious fraternity. A *sodalitas* ('religious fraternity') was an association of elite men linked to the cult of a specific divinity. The institution went back to archaic times, one reminder of which is the *lapis Satriacanus*, a late sixth- or early fifth-century inscription commemorating a dedication to Mars by the *sodales* ('companions') of Poplios Valesios (that is, Publius Valerius) (see Cornell 1995, 144f.). These fraternities fostered close ties and were enhanced through mutual support (Cic. *Verr.* 1.93; *Cael.* 26; *Sull.* 7; *Brut.* 166; cf. *Mur.* 56; *Amic.* 45), friendly social intercourse (such as banqueting: *Rhet. Her.* 4.64), and personal affection (Cic. *Planc.* 29; *De or.* 2.200; *Fam.* 12.14.7); they entailed a relationship so profound that *sodales*, like individuals connected by ties of blood or marriage or bound together by *clientela* (see below ¶17 **clients**), were legally disqualified from judging one another (*Lex Rep.* 20 (*RS* no. 1, see *RS* 67); Cic. *Verr.* 2.1.44; *Mur.* 56; *Cael.* 26; see Brunt 1988, 416f.; *RS* 100f.). It was natural that aristocratic unions of this nature should prove influential, and their entirely legitimate, indeed morally elevated, utility in political campaigns is adduced here and again at ¶19.

This same term, *sodalitas*, was also used to refer to highly organized companies engaged in inappropriate and, eventually, illegal electioneering activities, though such a society was perhaps more correctly denominated a *sodalicium* (see Cic. *Planc.* 36–7; *Cael.* 16). The distinction was in any case often blurred, though it is obvious that here Quintus' reference to fraternities is not meant to evoke sordid electioneering practices. The influence of fraternities, legitimate or otherwise, was undeniable. When canvassing for the consulship, Caesar was careful to cultivate not just Pompeius and Crassus but also the many fraternities they had in their pockets (Dio 37.54.3). On fraternities and illegal electioneering, see ¶57 **dishonest electioneers . . . bribery agents**; §§III.6, III.10. On *sodalitates* of both the elevated and the sordid varieties, see Hellegouarc'h 1963, 109f.; David et al. 1973, 275ff.; Linderski 1995, 205–27ff.; Mouritsen 2001, 149ff.; Cosi 2002, 33ff.; Linderski 2007, 619f.; Feig Vishnia 2012, 140ff.

any other close tie. On *necessitudo*, the elevated relationship existing between *necessarii* ('personal connections'), see above **Nevertheless**. Quintus postpones mentioning fellow tribesmen and neighbours until the next section, but these men were also Cicero's *necessarii* (Cosi 2002, 59ff., 79ff., assembles the relevant testimonia). The integrity of *necessitudo* is introduced again at ¶56, where *necessarii*, according to Quintus, cannot be corrupted by electoral bribery (see ¶56 **to whom they have strong ties**). On Cicero's concept of this relationship, see Rowland 1970; the standard treatment of *necessitudo* remains Cosi 2002; further on *necessitudo* and its importance in the *Brief Handbook*, see Pani 2007.

¶17 the most intimate members of your household. Romans employed the term *domus* (their word for the mansions occupied by the rich) to refer broadly to all members of a household, including clients, freedmen, and slaves. The Romans' notion of *domus* could extend further to indicate non-resident relations on both sides of a family (Saller 1994, 80ff.; Hölkeskamp 2014). Quintus' *domesticus* here activates this sense of *domus* but operates even more broadly than *domus*: Quintus immediately turns to fellow tribesmen and neighbours as well as clients, freedmen, and slaves. Fellow tribesmen and neighbours are routinely mentioned in tandem (Cic. *Rosc. Am.* 47; *Har. resp.* 56; *Vat.* 59; *Planc.* 43), and both are mentioned along with clients at Cic. *Mur.* 69, but neither fellow tribesmen nor neighbours were, as such, a part of one's *domus*. In his public letter to Quintus on provincial administration, Cicero insists that strict household discipline is important for sustaining one's prestige (*dignitas*: *Q. Fr.* 1.1.18). On Cicero's household in Rome, see Mouritsen 2017a.

fellow tribesmen. A Roman tribe (*tribus*) was a voting district, not a kinship group, hence the natural association of tribesmen with neighbours (see previous note). At the same time, men from rural tribes routinely migrated to the city (Cic. *Sest.* 109; Purcell 1994, 644ff.) and, though resident in the city, preserved their original tribal affiliation (Forni 1966, 148f.). Furthermore, tribal districts were not contiguous and in fact could be widely dispersed throughout Italy. Consequently, although the relationship between fellow tribesmen was sometimes territorial, that was not invariably the case: the tribal relationship overlapped with neighbourliness (see next note) but was not identical with it.

One's tribe was an important affiliation, essential to one's identity as a citizen and therefore included in one's formal nomenclature. Cicero's tribe was Cornelia. Mark Antony, the triumvir, also belonged to the Cornelian tribe (*MAMA* 6.104), which makes it highly likely, though not a certainty, that Cicero's rival, Antonius, was his fellow tribesman. It may not have been uncommon for two candidates in a single election to derive from the same tribe, a circumstance that plainly raised the stakes in the competition for fellow tribesmen (see Brunt 1988, 430).

Voters were solicited by way of tribes, even for elections decided by the centuriate assembly (the first class of which was organized along tribal lines: §III.3). The thirty-five tribes maintained offices in the city (Cic. *Mur.* 72; Suet. *Iul.* 41) as well as communal burial sites (*ILS* 6054–5). Each tribe had officials, curators (*curatores*) and treasurers (*divisores*), and kept a register of its membership—all elements that emphasized tribal solidarity (despite the reality that tribal districts could be widely dispersed throughout Italy). This degree of organization rendered tribes convenient as well as essential sites for soliciting electoral support. Familiarity with one's fellow tribesmen (*tribules*) was common (Cic. *Sex. Rosc.* 47; *Att.* 1.18.4; *Fam.* 13.23.1; Varro, *Rust.* 3.2.1), as were benefactions toward one's fellow tribesmen (Cic. *Mur.* 69, 72–3; *Q. Fr.* 3.1.1). This was especially the case for candidates (e.g. Cic. *Planc.* 42–5; *Att.* 4.16.6; *Fam.* 2.16; App. *B.Civ.* 1.65), who routinely offered gifts to their fellow tribesmen (distributed by tribal treasurers) along with banquets and seats at the games (e.g. Cic. *Mur.* 72–3; see ¶55 **bribery**). So strong was the assumption of tribal solidarity that it was regarded as a disgrace should a candidate not carry the votes of his tribe (Cic. *Vat.* 36; *Planc.* 20; cf. *Att.* 2.1.9). Candidates solicited their own tribes vigorously and urged friends from other tribes to canvass them on their behalf: Cicero makes the point that this was his practice whenever he canvassed for office (*Planc.* 45–6), and, when he became a distinguished ex-consul, he campaigned among the tribes on behalf of his friends (*Planc.* 24–5). The fundamental discussion of tribes is Taylor 1960, but see also Smith 2006, 236ff. On the importance of tribes in Roman society and especially in political campaigns, see *StR* 3.196ff.; Taylor 1949, 50ff.; Wiseman 1971, 130ff.; Lintott 1999a, 50ff.; Yakobson 1999, 97ff.; Cosi 2002, 79ff.

neighbours. Physical neighbours (*vicini*) shared a natural connection. Neighbourhoods were the basic and essential environment of daily life. Consequently, neighbourliness (*vicinitas*) was central to Roman sensibilities and an important motive for mutual support and cooperation (Dutoit 1969; Palma 1988; Lomas 2012, 198ff.). By *vicus* (or, less precisely, *vicinitas* in the sense of 'neighbourhood'; see *OLD* 2055) a Roman could refer to an urban neighbourhood that possessed its own internal organization (with its own officials) and shared cult (by way of participation in the Compitalia; see ¶3 **clubs**), in each of which aspects the city's clubs also played an important role (Flambard 1981; Vanderbroeck 1987, 112ff.; see ¶3 **clubs**). Or he could refer to a rural district or a village, regions also characterized by a corporate identity (Witcher 2005, 123). The bulk of our knowledge of *vici* derives from the imperial period, by which time significant innovations had been introduced.

Vici were not shy about expressing political sentiments: one *vicus* erected a statue in honour of Sulla (*CIL* 6.1297 = *ILS* 872 = *ILLRP* 352), and *vici* could be politically active at any time (e.g. Cic. *Rab. perd.* 8; *Sest.* 34; *Dom.* 54; see Nippel 1988, 112). Neighbourliness (*vicinitas*) was deemed a vital factor in the outcome of elections (e.g. Cic. *Mur.* 47; 69; *Vat.* 39; *Planc.* 19–23; 43; *Har. resp.* 56; see Wiseman 1971, 47ff.).

For aspiring politicians, the realities of *vicinitas* were altered drastically in the aftermath of the Social War when Roman citizenship was extended throughout Italy (see ¶1 **within a single, systematic form and in a logical order**). Hence the practice of securing strategically situated villas up and down the peninsula in an effort to expand significantly the range of one's *vicini* (on Cicero's properties, see Shatzman 1975, 404ff.; Mitchell 1979, 102ff.; Lomas 2012, 198ff.; see ¶3 **municipalities that are devoted exclusively to you**; §VII.2). Quintus refers to Italian neighbourliness frequently, often by way of related associations like municipalities or prefectures (see ¶¶3, 24, 30–2, 50), recurrence that renders *vicinitas* one of the associations most strongly emphasized in the *Brief Handbook*: see Cosi 2002, 72ff.; Pani 2007, 308. On *vici*, see Fraschetti 1990, 192ff.; Purcell 1994, 9, 673ff.; Tarpin 2002; Capogrossi Colognesi 2002, 104ff.; Cosi 2002, 70ff.; Lott 2004; Bispham 2007, 81ff.; Feig Vishnia 2012, 35ff.; Mignone 2016, 170ff.

clients. This is the only reference to clients in the *Brief Handbook*. On the patron–client relationship in Rome (*clientela*), see ¶2 **deemed worthy of being patron**; §III.3. The view that *clientela* was central to the outcome of Roman elections—it was once simply assumed that men were elevated to office by the votes of their own clients and the clients of their aristocratic supporters—has rightly been rejected, and the analysis of political support found in the *Brief Handbook*, which has little to say about *clientela*, plays an important part in this modern argument (Brunt 1988, 382ff.; Morstein-Marx 1998; Yakobson 1999, 66ff.; Mouritsen 2001, 67ff.; Fezzi 2007, 16f., but see Briscoe 1992; see, further, §III.3). This is not to say, however, that *clientela* played no role in political campaigns. Clients could, if they chose, serve as useful surrogates (see ¶31 **candidates on your behalf**): men who identify themselves as clients appear in Pompeian posters beseeching readers to elect their patrons (e.g. *CIL* 4.822, 933, 1016, 7605; see §III.7). It was a common Roman complaint that among the nobility's daunting resources at elections was its advantage in *clientela*, a superiority that stimulated envy (*invidia*) on the part of those who were without it (see especially Sall. *Iug.* 85.4; cf. *Rhet. Her.* 8; Cic. *Clu.* 94; *Part. or.* 87). This advantage derived from the significance of the social superiority exhibited by playing the part of an energetic patron, whose exertions were repaid by the public attendance which was vital to electoral success (see, further, §§III.3, III.5; ¶34 **attendance**). It will often have been the case that a noble's inherited *clientela* gave him an advantage in the matter of attendance that was unavailable to others. When Quintus turns to attendance, however, he does not explicitly invoke *clientela*—not because the institution was irrelevant but because Cicero's clients were too few to matter: his supply of supporters, the bulk of whom were probably not clients in any strict sense, derived from his exertions as an orator. And inasmuch as the *Brief Handbook* avoids rhetoric that is hostile to the nobility as a whole (see ¶2 **new man**), it is unsurprising that Quintus does not address Cicero's disadvantage by way of a complaint about the nobility's dominance in *clientela*. Instead, clients are here included in a catalogue of important personal connections, along with fellow tribesmen and neighbours, but without further or extended commentary. In this way Quintus supplies Cicero with the proper and conventional image of a sound candidate. In his *Tog. cand.*, Cicero, instead of complaining about the nobility and its advantages in *clientela*, claims that Antonius' unsavoury behaviour ill equips him to have clients at all (Asc. 86C). On *clientela* in Roman society, see Eilers 2002, 1ff.; Deniaux 2006. On *clientela* in the *Brief Handbook*, see, further, Morstein-Marx 1998.

freedmen. A freedman's former master became his patron, to whom he owed not *fides* but instead legally defined deference (*obsequium*); consequently, freedmen are not routinely described as clients, and the collocation of client and freedman is a familiar one: e.g. Cic. *Inv. rhet.* 1.109; *Caec.* 57; cf. *Dig.* 47.2.90. Freedmen were regarded as part of the *domus* (Cic. *Fam.* 13.23.1; 13.46) and are adduced here for that reason. On freedmen who are influential in canvassing, see ¶29 **many freedmen**. On freedmen, see Treggiari 1969; Bradley 1994, 154ff.; Mouritsen 2011 and, with special attention to Cicero, Mouritsen 2017b.

gossip. Quintus offers a practical purpose for seeking popularity in one's own household: to avoid malicious slander. Quintus is not here offering advice on how to cover up one's personal scandals, but instead is underscoring how vulnerable each Roman's reputation was to the indiscretion of his household, whose very intimacy gave them credibility. Perhaps with this reality in mind, the elder Cato forbade his slaves to answer anyone's questions about their master's activities (Plut. *Cat. mai.* 21.1). Cicero, both in his public letter to Quintus on provincial administration and in their private correspondence, stressed the importance for public figures of carefully managing their slaves and freedmen (Cic. *Q. Fr.* 1.17; 1.2.1–3). During the final phase of any political campaign, even a whiff of the wrong sort of rumour (*aura rumoris*) could ruin a candidate's chances (Cic. *Mur.* 35; *Mil.* 42) and everyone was apparently keen to keep up with any speculation about the prospects of candidates for the consulship (e.g. Cic. *Att.* 2.4.4). By contrast, the support of one's family and a reputation for strong family loyalty (*pietas*) did much to advance a candidate's prospects (Cic. *Planc.* 29; *Off.* 2.46). On the influence of rumour in Roman society generally, see Laurence 1994; Dufallo 2001; O'Neill 2003; for an important treatment of rumour in literature, see Hardie 2012. On the agents of gossip in Rome, see Rosillo López 2017, 175ff. Cicero's public reputation is again taken up at ¶50, a discussion that does not include his household's views.

¶18 friends, whatever their category. Quintus reprises the theme of Cicero's extensive connections (see ¶3 **the number and variety of your friends**), but here he appears to focus on members of the upper classes.

pageantry. Pageantry (*species*), in Quintus' organizational scheme, is one of the means of winning the goodwill of the people: see ¶41; ¶52 **full of pageantry**. Quintus has already urged Cicero to show off his friends (see ¶3 **exhibit to the public**).

distinguished by office and by lineage. Nobles and ex-consuls, on whom see ¶4 **nobles**; ¶4 **ex-consuls**. Morstein-Marx 1998, 276, rightly observes that Quintus does not explicitly indicate that nobles are valuable to Cicero on account of the clients whose votes they can deliver; their impression on the electorate derives from their prestige.

even if they do not devote themselves. Highly, perhaps excessively, complimentary, but further evidence of the *Brief Handbook*'s determination to win over (and not to challenge) the powerful (see ¶2 **new man**). The value of conspicuous attendance by distinguished men is again mentioned at ¶50. Even young men at the start of their careers were urged to burnish their reputations through an association with distinguished public figures (Cic. *Off.* 2.46).

guaranteeing your legal rights. Although the consul presiding over an election had at least a theoretical right to refuse to announce a candidate's victory, in practice this will have been settled at the time of the *professio* (see §III.3). Nevertheless, the goodwill of the presiding magistrate was obviously to be desired, not least because consuls could and occasionally did insert themselves into electoral contests (Rilinger 1976; Pina Polo 2011, 289f.). So, too, and often sensationally, did tribunes (e.g. Liv. 25.2.6–7; Liv. 32.7.8–12; Cic. *Brut.* 226; Asc. 25C; Quint. 6.3.75; Plut. *C. Gracch.* 8.1). Both consuls and tribunes were in a position to offer protection from inappropriate legal or political attacks, and both offices had the authority to allow a candidate to address the people if he should wish to do so (Lintott 1999a, 94ff. (consuls), 121ff. (tribunes); on the consul's role at elections, see Pina Polo 2011, 192ff., 284ff.). In the event, during the campaign of 64, the candidates Antonius and Catilina were actively supported by the tribune Q. Mucius Orestinus (see §VII.5).

delivering the votes of the centuries. This expression (*centurias conficere*) occurs only here and at Cic. *Fam.* 11.16.3, a coincidence adduced by Waibel 1969, 38f., as evidence that the *Brief Handbook* is inauthentic. But the expression was probably commonplace (*conficere* is used in this sense, with tribes instead of centuries, at Cic. *Planc.* 45), even if the construction is poorly attested. Likewise *centurias tenere*, used in a similar sense ('to secure centuries'), appears at Cic. *Fam.* 11.16.3; and ¶33.

centuries. The crucial centuries belonged to the equestrian order and the first class (see §II.3). Within any century, authority was doubtless unstable and a focus of incessant contest on the part of 'men of exceptional influence'. Still, a candidate had to stake his chances on the men he deemed most likely to bring voters his way, and the chain of relationships could be complex: in 43, for instance, L. Lamia, a candidate for the praetorship, was able to turn to the ex-consul Cicero (who, in addition to being Lamia's friend, was indebted to him for past political favours); consequently, Cicero wrote to the consul-designate, D. Brutus, whose influence in the equestrian centuries Cicero believed to be decisive (*Fam.* 11.16.3). This kind of pattern was very probably a common one. Other men are described by Cicero as comparably compelling in important centuries: Domitius Ahenobarbus (*Att.* 1.1.3; *Verr.* 1.139); Cornelius (see ¶19 **Gaius Cornelius**); L. Pinarius Natta (noble but not yet a senator at *Mur.* 73); C. Scribonius Curio (noble but merely an ex-quaestor at *Fam.* 2.6; cf. *Phil.* 2.4). Festus, *Gloss. Lat.* 184.15, suggests that each century was presided over by an officer, called a centurion (*centurio*), possibly appointed during the census (Nicolet 1980, 264). Such an appointment was a conspicuous distinction, and it may have been by way of these men that the votes of individual centuries were solicited.

have, or expect to have, control. By the time of his candidature, Cicero had already acquired considerable influence among the electorate as evidenced by his election to the praetorship at the top of the polls (see

§VII.2). Which meant that, for aspiring politicians, he was in a position to reciprocate their exertions on his behalf—and all the more so should he become a consular. Owing to this dynamic, whereby a candidate's election raised the status and prospects of his supporters (e.g. Cic. *Brut.* 242–3), political figures routinely reached deals with one another for dispensing their electoral influence to their common advantage (Cic. *Att.* 2.1.9; *Plan.* 45–48, 54).

a tribe or a century. Owing to the tribalized organization of the centuriate assembly (see §II.3), 'tribe' and 'century' can be used almost interchangeably in discussing the collective units that must be won over.

or some other advantage. A clumsy addition that tends to universalize the reciprocity Quintus is invoking here, perhaps in anticipation of Quintus' extended remarks on reciprocity at ¶21. Or perhaps in recognition of the reality that not everyone capable of delivering votes had political aspirations: the *publicani* (see ¶3 **publicans**), for instance, were very influential in their tribes (Cic. *Planc.* 23–4).

in recent years, men eager for advancement. The natural sense of *ambitiosi* here suggests Quintus has in mind men active in canvassing and keen to benefit from it—that is, aspiring political figures and their aspiring operatives. Quintus suggests that 'in recent years' there has been an intensification of such activity, a reference to the political effects resulting from the enfranchisement of the Italian allies (see ¶1 **within a single, systematic form and in a logical order**): there were now more men who possessed the resources to pursue a senatorial career and, inevitably, more men looking to benefit from acting on their behalf in soliciting tribal support. Quintus will return to the solicitation of these men at ¶24.

¶19 if men were sufficiently grateful. Quintus underlines how Cicero has acted, throughout his career, in such a way as to merit gratitude (see §VII). The question to be determined in this election, then, is whether those whom he has benefited will act appropriately, itself a recurring theme of the work (see ¶4 **See to it that…express their gratitude**). In this way, Quintus places the moral responsibility for electing Cicero on the men he has aided in the past (see ¶21 **goodwill and keen electoral support**). At the same time, it is clear in the *Brief Handbook* that the possession of gratitude did not render canvassing unnecessary (Yakobson 1999, 86). In what follows, Quintus names specific individuals and groups, drawing his readers' attention to their conduct in this election.

during the past two years. Here Quintus emphasizes the two-year gap (*biennium*) that was obligatory between the praetorship (which Cicero held in 66) and the consulship (which he hoped to hold in 63), even if, at the time of writing (see **¶1 lasting but a few months**), the past two years extended into 66. Quintus has already defended certain aspects of Cicero's forensic activities during this period (see **¶5 any speech that appeared to support popular rights**). Here the effect is to emphasize Cicero's energetic exertions in the courts since his last election, at which time old debts could perhaps be regarded by some as repaid, and the fresh moral obligations they entail.

four religious fraternities. On *sodalitates*, see **¶16 religious fraternity**. It is not obvious what determined the order of Quintus' list of Cicero's defendants: the order of their trials offers a natural possibility, which avoids invidious comparison. By citing specific recent cases, Quintus diverges from the generalities of his earlier discussion of Cicero's advocacy and the gratitude it has earned (**¶¶2–4**).

men of immense influence. Quintus describes the whole of the membership of these four *sodalitates* as important men, which may have been so, but by generalizing here he compliments both Cicero's defendants and their fellow *sodales*, whatever their relative clout.

Gaius Fundanius. We cannot identify this man with certainty. There exists evidence for at least two senators of this name in the first century. (i) One was quaestor in 101 and a senator in 81 (see *RRC*, 328; *OGIS* 441.20–21). This man may also be the Fundanius who was Varro's father-in-law (Varro. *Rust.* 1.2.1). (ii) The other possibility, probably the son of the first Fundanius, was tribune between 72 and 68—perhaps most likely in 68 (*ILS* 38 = *RS* 333ff.; see Syme 1979, 557ff.)—and was, at some point, a curator of roads (*ILS* 5800); *curator viarum* was a useful post for acquiring influence in elections (see Cic. *Att.* 1.1.2; Wiseman 1971, 139; §III.2). He is very likely the same Fundanius who is attested as a friend of Quintus and Cicero in 59 (Cic. *Q. Fr.* 2.10). Whoever precisely this Fundanius was, Cicero deemed his speech in defence of the man important enough to publish it—perhaps in part to advertise his favour to Fundanius' *sodalitas*—but it survives only in fragments so meagre that it is impossible to recover the nature of Fundanius' trial (see Crawford 1994, 57ff.). (See, further, David et al. 1973, 271ff.; Crawford 1994, 57ff., with further bibliography.)

Quintus Gallius. Aedile in 67 and praetor in 65 (*MRR* 2.144, 158), in which office he presided over the trial of Gaius Cornelius (see next note). After his election to the praetorship of 65, Gallius was charged *de ambitu* for his illicit presentation of a gladiatorial show during his campaign and defended by Cicero, who published his speech (see Crawford 1994, 145ff.).

The date of his trial is controversial. Cicero alludes to this event, without naming Gallius, in his *Tog. cand.*, prompting the following information from Asconius: 'he appears to mean Q. Gallius, whom he later defended on a charge *de ambitu*' (Asc. 88C). This comment has often been interpreted to mean that Cicero's defence of Gallius took place after the delivery of *Tog. cand.*, which appears to contradict the evidence of the *Brief Handbook* (hence an argument against its authenticity: Henderson 1950, 11). Ramsey 1980b argues that there is no contradiction: Quintus' expression *in causis ad te deferendis* ('when they brought you their cases') need only indicate engaging Cicero's services, a relationship that entailed the gratitude of Gallius' fraternity whenever the actual trial took place, even if it had not taken place by 64 (see ¶¶44–8); trials in Rome could be delayed for various reasons and Ramsey suggests that that was the case with Gallius' trial—which could certainly not have taken place during 65, when his praetorship gave him immunity from prosecution. It is simpler, however, to assume that *postea* ('later') in Asconius' note means nothing more than 'after the episode just mentioned' (viz. Gallius' gladiatorial show) and not after the delivery of *Tog. cand.* (Zumpt 1871, 529 n. 4; cf. Lewis 2006, 296), in which case the trial will have taken place in late 66, after Gallius' election but before he took office (consistent with Quintus' 'past two years'), or, less likely, in 64, after his praetorship (which requires the assumption that he did not take up a province, which seems unlikely in the case of a man facing a prosecution). (See, further, David et al. 1973, 273ff.; Crawford 1994, 145ff.)

Gaius Cornelius. C. Cornelius was Pompeius' quaestor (Asc. 57C) and tribune of the plebs in 67, during which year he undertook an extensive, but only partially successful, legislative agenda, most of which were designed to curb magisterial and senatorial excesses (*MRR* 2.144). He was tried for treason (*maiestas*) in 65 and successfully defended by Cicero, who undertook the case in part in order to win favour from Pompeius, in part—at least according to Cicero in a later speech (*Vat.* 5)—because Cornelius was his friend (*amicus*). See the detailed discussion at §VII.4. See also ¶5 **any speech that appeared to support popular rights;** ¶51 **defended Cornelius.**

Gaius Orchivius. Praetor in 66 (*MRR* 2.152), his trial probably took place in 64, after he returned from a provincial command, but neither the date of his trial nor the charge against him are attested (see David et al. 1973, 275; Crawford 1984, 73ff.). In this case, Cicero apparently did not publish his defence speech.

for I was there. Thus Quintus here joins with Cicero in putting pressure on the religious fraternities to keep their promises by introducing himself as a witness to the fraternities' promises; see ¶5 **our political opinions.**

by frequent admonitions... their gratitude. Reprising earlier advice: see
¶4 forceful reminders and solicitations; ¶4 never be another opportunity.

people will be stirred. This is probably a generalizing conclusion, hence
the translation of *homines* as 'people'. Although *homines* could here operate as a demonstrative—on which view the word should be translated as
'they' or 'these men' and refer specifically to the members of the religious
fraternities just discussed by Quintus—that use of *homines* is strikingly
colloquial (*LHS* 198) and stylistically out of place here (so, rightly,
Buecheler 1869, 40). Having begun with a general observation on men's
gratitude, Quintus now concludes with a similarly comprehensive comment.
His reference to 'the expectation of reciprocity', somewhat awkwardly
introduced here, anticipates ¶21.

recent favours. Reprises the emphasis of 'during the past two years'
(see above).

¶20 clearly defined and specific duty. *Munus* (here translated 'duty'
and also found at ¶¶37, 57) is used interchangeably with *officium* for
variation—a Ciceronian practice (Dyck 1996, 109).

¶21 best incentives for... electoral support. Quintus employs the verb
ducere here in its specialized sense of offering support for someone's
candidature for office (see Warrior 1990).

goodwill and keen electoral support. The conjunction is significant and
underlines the specific brand of goodwill Quintus has in mind here. Every
facet of canvassing to be discussed in the subsequent paragraphs (¶¶21–39)
is subtended by this analysis of electoral goodwill: all entail reciprocity,
the expecting of future favours, and affection (matters change, but only a
little, when Quintus comes to dealing with the people at ¶40). At no point
in this discussion does Quintus adduce an alliance based on political
ideology. Cic. *Fam.* 2.6 illustrates Quintus' emphasis here on the importance of an exchange of favours in recruiting electoral support: Cicero,
writing to Scribonius Curio in 53, presses him to aid in T. Annius Milo's
canvass for the consulship; the letter concentrates almost entirely on
favours done (Milo's to Cicero; Curio's and Cicero's to one another) and
on favours to come (on the part of both Cicero and Milo) if Curio
cooperates.

    Benevolentia ('goodwill'), used only here in the *Brief Handbook*, was
essential to friendship (Cic. *Amic.* 19) and was a natural response to benefactions (Cic. *Off.* 2.32; cf. Arist. *Eth. Nic.* 1167a15; see Hellegouarc'h 1963,
149f.), all of which renders its presence in this section, which concentrates
on 'gaining the support of friends' (¶16), entirely suitable—and renders

Quintus' insistence on the obligations of gratitude a bit less brusque. Quintus' use of *benevolentia* here diverges from Cicero's at *Off.* 2.19–22: there Cicero observes the importance of *benevolentia* for exciting others' enthusiasm on one's behalf, but distinguishes it from gratitude or the expectation of favours. At *Off.* 2.32, however, when he attributes the acquisition of *benevolentia* to benefactions and a willingness to confer benefactions, Cicero's view closely approximates Quintus'.

genuine personal affection. Notwithstanding canvassing's capacious definition of the word 'friend' (¶¶16, 25), Quintus continues to remind readers that canvassing is also a circumstance animated by elevated notions of friendship.

no one will ever respect them. Again, the moral responsibility for Cicero's election resides with men whom he has assisted in the past (see ¶19 **if men were sufficiently grateful**). On the importance of reciprocity and the disgrace of ingratitude, see ¶4 **See to it that... express their gratitude.**

¶22 help and protection. Although *auxilium* ('help and protection') here refers primarily to Cicero's capacities as an advocate, it also suggests his future capacity as a consul. Providing *auxilium* to his fellow citizens, an activity naturally associated with the services of a tribune of the people, was also a consul's duty (Liv. 2.27.2; cf. e.g. Cic. *Verr.* 2.72; *Rab. perd.* 10; *Mur.* 82; *Red. sen.* 10; *Dom.* 12; *Sest.* 25; *Pis.* 34).

keeping an eye. Romans were by nature censorious and did in fact keep an eye on one another (Pöschl 1961; Veyne 1983; Kaster 2005, 84ff.). The importance of Cicero's careful assessment of his supporters—a reminder to readers that the candidate, too, has expectations and will remember who does and does not disappoint—recurs at ¶¶24, 35 (where he is urged to be conciliatory with unreliable supporters among the public), 36, 39. At ¶55, Cicero is advised to monitor his rivals' attempts at illegal electioneering.

¶23 by adapting your conversation. Cicero is urged to be accommodating in order to encourage men who are already well disposed to him—an action, it is here claimed, that will lead to a deeper friendship. This idea recurs, in a somewhat diluted form, at ¶42 **what you lack by nature**, where Cicero is advised to be ingratiating.

friendship... real intimacy. A utilitarian friendship gained during a canvass for office (*amicitia* in the sense prescribed at ¶16 **the definition of the word 'friend'**) becomes more attractive if Cicero indicates that there is a possibility for the relationship to become a close and stable one. In other words, supporters as well as candidates seek to acquire fresh, attractive personal connections during an election campaign; this idea recurs at ¶26.

¶24 men who are influential in their neighbourhoods and municipalities. Almost the same expression occurs at Cic. *Mur.* 47, indicating that it was something of a formula, though there Cicero also honours these men by describing them as 'good' (*viri boni*) (see **¶3 municipalities that are devoted exclusively to you; ¶17 neighbours**). Immediately below Quintus speaks instead of 'fellow tribesmen' (see **¶17 fellow tribesmen**). Because membership in these various and active organizations overlapped, it was efficient to adduce them in clusters.

prosperous men. The focus remains on elites, even if in reality these are men whose stature was less grand than that of senators and knights.

no previous inclination to exercise their influence. Quintus turns to a fresh category of supporter: men who are disinclined to involve themselves in canvassing on anyone's behalf. The actual number of voters each year was quite small, nor is it obvious that a majority of Romans living in the city itself participated in the rituals of canvassing (see §II.4). For any candidate, then, it was advantageous if he could inject new supplies of supporters into his campaign (Mouritsen 2001, 92ff., with bibliography in n. 4). Activating the exertions of influential men, including the apolitical, was, if successful, an obviously useful tactic. In the absence of previous favours or expressions of goodwill, these men require careful cultivation— *inservire* is Quintus' verb here—which is to say, Cicero must treat them with extreme deference and put his services at their disposal. On the use of servile expressions in describing canvassing, see §III.4.

other men, however. It cannot always have been clear to men of the senatorial order which figures in the lower levels even of prosperous society carried the most clout, not least because there was always competition for local prestige and so there were conflicting claims for local preeminence; on local prestige, see Tatum 1999, 146ff. Obviously, Cicero must choose the right men.

¶25 you can honourably do. Quintus here reprises and summarizes views expressed in **¶¶16–17**, but with a different orientation. Aristocrats found certain aspects of canvassing for office unpleasant and embarrassing (see §III.4). Here Quintus does not so much offer advice as extend moral cover to the varied and utilitarian connections Cicero must acquire and exploit during his campaign, all of which are justified only by the special circumstances of a political campaign (see **¶12 required by your present situation; ¶42 when canvassing; ¶45 to your situation**). He portrays Cicero, and his readers, as naturally unwilling to turn away from ideal (and philosophical) conceptions of friendship toward practical ones (see ¶16 **the definition of the word 'friend'**) and stresses that *only* during a campaign can one act this way honourably and in accordance with the decorum expected of a senator (*honeste*—here contrasted with *absurde*; see Jacotot 2013,124ff.; see, further, Tatum 2007). Notwithstanding this special provision, the techniques Quintus goes on to prescribe in ¶26 are unobjectionable from any perspective: there Cicero is encouraged to transform potentially utilitarian friendships into genuine ones.

make friends with whomever you like. This extension of friendship permits Quintus to include advice on morning audiences and attendance in the forum (¶¶34–8), activities that involved mass participation by the lower classes (¶¶34–5), under the rubric of 'gaining the support of friends' (¶16). In ordinary discourse such attendants were frequently denominated as friends (e.g. Cic. *Att.* 1.18.1 (cf. the complaints of Sen. *Ben.* 6.34); see Goldbeck 2010, 236ff.).

¶26 one of your rivals. Why one? Voters cast two ballots for the consulship (§II.3), so nothing prevented anyone from voting both for Cicero and one of his rivals. Perhaps Quintus wants to remind readers of the unsavoury alliance (*coitio*) between Antonius and Catilina against Cicero (see §VII.5). Or perhaps Quintus is reacting to the likely reality that most voters, even during the final phase of canvassing, were undecided about at least one of their votes for consulship (cf. Yakobson 1999, 85; §II.4).

provided he was made. Cicero's success, Quintus here insists, relies more on his forging real friendships than simply accumulating utilitarian ones. Despite the admonitions of the previous section, Cicero is urged to base the new associations of his political campaign on honest esteem and reciprocity rather than mere expediency: the resulting friendships should therefore be 'secure and lasting', not *suffragatoria*—that is, just for the purpose of winning a vote (*suffragium*). This reprises the sense of ¶23 and strongly mitigates the necessary compromise with normal behaviour prescribed at ¶25 (see ¶25 **you can honourably do**).

¶27 stroke of luck. At ¶11, Quintus comments on Cicero's good fortune (*fortuna*) in having unacceptable rivals; here it is a matter of chance (*casus*) that Cicero has the advantage of competing against nobles of an inferior quality. On the significance of these references, see ¶11 **better luck.**

your competitors. Presumably Quintus refers only to Antonius and Catilina. At ¶17, P. Sulpicius Galba and L. Cassius Longinus are criticized for lack of vigour but not their immorality.

whose friendship must be despised or shunned. Quintus reprises his previous invective against Antonius and Catilina (¶¶8–12) in order, once again, to lend an important moral quality even to the utilitarian friendships entailed by an electoral campaign (see ¶16 **the definition of the word 'friend'**). In his *Tog. cand.*, Cicero also insists that Catilina is incapable of attracting friends, whereas Antonius is unable to attract clients (Asc. 84C). But inasmuch as Antonius was elected consul, this allegation cannot, from any practical perspective, have been true of him. And at *Cael.* 12–13 Cicero makes the point that Catilina was very good at winning friends (see Sall. *Cat.* 14–16).

what I am recommending to you. The content of the *Brief Handbook* is again marked as normative (see ¶1 **anything new**; §IV.4), and again the point is made that success at consular elections demands skill in the art of canvassing (see ¶11 **Gaius Coelius**; ¶47 **master in the art of canvassing**; see Morstein-Marx 1998, 278f.).

¶28 address them by name. Was Antonius bad with names? At ¶¶41–2, in discussing 'dealing with the people', Quintus stresses the importance of recognizing people by name (see Plut. *Crass.* 3.5; Petron. *Sat.* 44). Naturally this capacity was even more central in exchanges between friends, and it was essential in canvassing (Cic. *Mur.* 77). At *Red. sen.* 13, Cicero attacks Piso because he lacks any interest in getting to know people (*cognoscendorum hominum studium*). For a humorous take on the importance of knowing names, see Hor. *Ep.* 1.6.49–55. Or is Quintus here alleging that Antonius is overly reliant on *nomenclatores*, assistants (most often slaves) employed by elites to remind or inform them of others' names? This practice was widespread at morning audiences but banned in political campaigns (by what specific measure we do not know). The younger Cato was exceptional in observing the electoral ban on *nomenclatores* (Plut. *Cat. min.* 8.2), for which he won the moral approval of others even if he failed in his bid for the consulship (Broughton 1991, 37). Quintus here, and again at ¶32, assumes that his readers will feel obliged to disapprove of the practice (see Cic. *Mur.* 77; Plin. *NH* 29.19; Vogt 1978; Kolendo 1989). In reality, Cicero employed a *nomenclator* (Cic. *Att.* 1.4.5). In any case, knowing names was just the beginning of a relationship: at ¶31 Quintus tells Cicero that, in order to win friends, he must be more than a mere *nomenclator*.

supreme glory, prestige, and a record of grand accomplishments. Only a superman can forgo the traditional obligations of canvassing if he wishes to win office. Quintus leaves it to his reader to recall men of such stature, any list of which could include, in recent years, Pompeius, whose extraordinary consulship in 70 was made possible and inevitable by a senatorial decree exempting him from the normal legal requirements of standing for the office (Cic. *Leg. Man.* 62; Plut. *Pomp.* 21; *Crass.* 12; Liv. *Per.* 97; see Seager 2002, 36f.). From the distant past he might have mentioned: Q. Fabius Maximus Rullianus, who won an unsought consulship in 299, but declined it (Liv. 10.9.10; whether or not he was elected aedile for 299 remains unclear; see Oakley 2005b, 139ff.); Fabius, was consul in 297, though he did not stand, along with P. Decius Mus, who also did not stand (Liv. 10.13.5–13, an action repeated in 295: Liv. 10.22.2); Scipio Africanus, elected in 211 to an extraordinary command in Spain without campaigning for the office (Liv. 26.18.7–10; see *MRR* 1.280); T. Manlius Torquatus (cos. I 235), nearly elected consul in 211 against his will (Liv. 26.22.2–6); L. Aemilius Paulus (cos. I 182), who was pressed by the public to make himself a candidate for the consulship of 168 (Plut. *Aem.* 10.2; see *MRR* 1.427); and Scipio Aemilianus, 'who never campaigned for the consulship, [but] was twice elected consul' (Cic. *Amic.* 11), for 147 and 134 (*MRR* 1.463, 490). Quintus does not represent Cicero, or any of his rivals, as a superman of this quality. And in fact Cicero went to some trouble to remind his contemporaries that he intended to canvass in the traditional manner (Cic. *Att.* 1.1.2: 'as for me, I shall be absolutely assiduous in meeting a candidate's every responsibility').

Although, throughout the *Brief Handbook*, Quintus accepts the precedence of the nobility (see ¶2 **new man**), here he omits the role of nobility and family reputation (*commendatio maiorum*) in advancing candidates to high office (see §III.2). There is nothing subversive here: Quintus has already addressed the issue of his rivals' nobility (¶¶7–11). Here he affirms the notion that Rome's political aristocracy was predicated on merit, an idea as appealing to the nobility as it was to anyone else (see Hölkeskamp 2004, 32ff.; Hölkeskamp 2010, 89ff.).

glory. *Gloria*, won chiefly but not exclusively in war, designated the highest of traditional aspirations on the part of the Roman aristocracy; it was intimately (and unsurprisingly) associated with prestige (*dignitas*) and the attainment of high office (Earl 1967, 30ff.; Hellegouarc'h 1963, 369ff. In his *De officiis*, Cicero supplies a lengthy discussion of the elements of *gloria* (*Off.* 2.31–51), including the role of eloquence (*Off.* 2.48–51; see Long 1995; Dyck 1996, 409ff.).

useless…without talent. This kind of abuse was characteristic of the new man's critique of the nobility. Here, however, it is applied specifically to Antonius and not to the nobility at large. (See, further, ¶2 **new man**.)

monumental negligence. Cicero's success over Antonius is assured by his virtues and by his previous exertions in winning widespread support, to the extent that only a failure to canvass correctly can cost Cicero this election. Quintus makes a similar point when he brings his advice to a close at ¶57

¶29 friendships. Friendship remains the central connection in this section; here its utility is indicated explicitly (see ¶3 **the number and variety of your friends**).

first and obvious thing. An obvious compliment to the most distinguished orders, whose immediate link to the remaining orders does them no dishonour; here the nobility are not distinguished from the residue of the senatorial order (see Quintus' exposition of Cicero's connections at ¶¶2–4).

industrious and influential. These qualities first appear at ¶8, where they describe Cicero. Here Cicero's smaller-fry supporters are assimilated to the candidate himself, a depiction that culminates in ¶31 when they become his surrogate candidates (*quasi candidati*; ¶31 **candidates on your behalf**).

men living in the city. Quintus here focuses on modestly prosperous men, or prosperous men lacking the status of senators or knights, not on the urban masses (Buecheler 1869, 45). This is a range of Roman society that remains elusive to modern scholarship (see, e.g., Treggiari 1969, 87ff.; Badian 1989; Purcell 1994, 644ff.; Tatum 1999, 17ff.; Yakobson 1999, 42ff.). The influence of men of this category was also susceptible of negative imputations (e.g. Plaut. *Trin.* 199–222; see Damon 1997, 109f.). At *Ep.* 1.6.49–50, Horace lampoons the man striving for influence (*gratia*) and pageantry (*species*; see ¶52 **full of pageantry**) by gaining the acquaintance of men capable of delivering (or denying) the support of tribes: he is urged to address them, not merely as friends, but as father or brother.

many freedmen. As Quintus makes clear, they owe their influence to their exertions: he does not speak of their usefulness as voters. Freed slaves became citizens, who enjoyed the right to vote, although the value of their votes was limited because nearly all freedmen were assigned to the four urban tribes. Exceptions were made in the case of some wealthy freedmen whose sons were more than five years old (Liv. 45.15.1–3). Even in the urban tribes, and here Quintus specifies freedmen who are active in the city, wealthy freedmen presumably could be assigned to the superior classes of the centuriate assembly—unless one accepts the view, proposed by Mouritsen 2001, 94 (see Mouritsen 2011, 75f.), that all freedmen were enrolled among the centuries of non-combatants, in which case their votes were all but valueless (see, however, Taylor 1960, 139f.). Nonetheless, here Quintus concentrates on the activities of freedmen. An illustration (perhaps but not certainly anachronistic) of the activities of freedmen supporters is supplied at Plut. *Aem.* 38.3, where the supporters of Scipio Aemilianus, in his bid for the censorship, are said to include 'low-born ex-slaves, men who busied themselves in the forum and had enough influence to gather a mob and to force any issue by way of vigorous canvassing or demonstrations'.

Freed slaves owed their former masters a degree of deference and the performance of stipulated duties (*obsequium*; see Treggiari 1969, 68ff.; Bradley 1994, 154ff.; Mouritsen 2011, 36ff.), and the freedmen of senators often acted as their political agents (see Treggiari 1969, 178ff.), but there is no suggestion here that this relationship with their former masters inhibited the political activities of freedmen in any way. Quite the reverse, since they are available for Cicero to cultivate (Yakobson 1999, 86). Cicero is urged to approach these freedmen in the same highly honorific manner as he was advised to court nobles and ex-consuls at ¶5 (see ¶5 **send your connections**). On freedmen in Roman politics, see further Treggiari 1969, 162ff.; Mouritsen 2011, 65ff.

¶30 all the clubs, the boroughs, and the neighbourhoods. The manuscripts read and Watt prints *conlegiorum omnium*, duly translated here. But Mommsen's emendation of *omnium* to *montium* is very probably correct, in which case the text should read: 'take stock of the whole of the city, of the clubs, of the *hills*, of the boroughs', etc. (*StR* 3.114 n. 5). Mommsen's proposal, based on the rough parallel provided by Cic. *Dom.* 74 (*nullum est in hac urbe collegium, nulli pagani aut montani*... 'there is no club in this city, no members of a borough or of a hill...'), introduces here the 'hill', a local urban administrative unit closely associated with the *pagus* ('borough'), itself an important administrative unit. Each was linked with *collegia* ('clubs'). *Montes* and *pagi*, like *collegia*, could deliberate and pass decrees (Cic. *Dom.* 74; see *ILLRP* 699–701) and were active in numerous aspects of urban life. The distribution of these districts, known chiefly from epigraphical traces, was untidy: the Aventine, for instance, was the location of a *pagus* (*CIL* 14.2105), and there was a *pagus montanus* on the Esquiline (*CIL* 6.3823 = 31557); at the same time, Varro (*Ling.* 6.24.5–7) defined *montani* as inhabitants of the *pagi* on the seven hills of Rome (members of a *mons*, however, were also called *montani*: e.g. *ILLRP* 698). All these organizations elected officers (*magistri; flamines*: see, e.g., *ILLRP* 696–704). See further Flambard 1981, 149ff.; Crook 1986; Fraschetti 1990, 123ff., 134ff., 173ff.; Purcell 1994, 673ff.; Capogrossi Colognesi 2002; Tarpin 2002, 177ff.; Feig Vishnia 2012, 35ff.; see ¶3 **clubs**; ¶17 **neighbours**.

leaders of these organizations. The chief figures in these urban organizations are not obviously identical with the men described in ¶24 as 'influential in their neighbourhoods'. Such men are hardly excluded here, but Quintus' focus is instead on men who are active leaders within clubs, hills, and boroughs, many of whom will have been shopkeepers and craftsmen (Vanderbroeck 1987, 54ff.; Tatum 1999, 142ff.). Their local prestige—that is, their everyday influence over their fellow members, who may care more about the approval of their organization's officers than they do about the career prospects of an ambitious senator—could prove helpful to a candidate seeking popularity among the masses. At the same time, the conspicuous solicitations of a candidate—with the clear indication to their fellow members that these leaders enjoyed superior connections— will have enhanced the leaders' local prestige. Members of the senatorial order were interested in granting modest honours to these leaders: such men, for instance, could enjoy the distinction of being present at public acts presided over by Roman magistrates (see, e.g., *ILLRP* 704, where *magistri* of *vici*, some of them freedmen, are present with the aediles at a dedication). The use of intermediaries recommended here by Quintus was no obstacle to Cicero's direct solicitation of the lower orders (*pace* Mouritsen 2001, 143), a topic reserved for ¶¶41–53.

Because some figures at this social level erupted into violent political activity during the 50s, especially in cooperation with P. Clodius Pulcher (aed. 56), our accounts of them are frequently hostile (otherwise men at this social level tend to sink into obscurity in our literary sources), but that bias in our sources should not be mistaken for the normal elite view of such persons (see Treggiari 1969, 168ff.; Vanderbroeck 1987, 52ff.; Nippel 1995, 71ff.; Lintott 1999a, 74ff.; Tatum 1999, 146ff.; Yakobson 1999, 86ff.).

the rest of the multitude. It is possible to take Quintus' formulation (*reliquam multitudinem*) to refer strictly to the many who constituted the remainder of each organization cited here (so Lintott 1990, 10; Morstein-Marx 1998, 277) and not to the whole of the urban masses. But inasmuch as Cicero is here urged to take stock of 'the whole of the city' by way of these very organizations, it is the comprehensive sense of this expression that is likeliest here.

divided into tribes. The extension of Rome's existing rural tribes over the whole of Italy after the Social War resulted in a highly complex and non-contiguous distribution, a state of affairs which, especially after the census of 70, drastically altered the Roman electorate (Taylor 1960, 101ff.; ¶1 **within a single, systematic form and in a logical order;** §II.3). Quintus now turns from the city to voters in the rest of Italy. Although it was only after the Social War that Roman citizenship extended up and down Italy, canvassing the rural tribes was important in campaigns for office as early as the fourth century (e.g. Liv. 7.15.13, with Oakley 1998, 177). Winning over voters in the rural tribes (especially voters from the higher classes) was crucial to any candidate's success in the centuriate assembly (§II.4).

municipality, colony, prefecture. The sequence is highly conventional: e.g. Cic. *Sest.* 32; *Phil.* 4.7 (varied by Cicero at *Pis.* 51 and *Phil.* 2.58); *Este Fragment*, lines 5, 10 (*RS* 319); *Tabula Heracleensis, passim* (*RS* 363ff.). On municipalities, see **¶3 municipalities that are devoted exclusively to you.** As early as the fourth century, Rome began to establish citizen colonies; by the time of the late republic, the political organization of colonies, although varying somewhat from place to place, largely resembled that of Rome (Sherwin White 1973, 76ff.; Bispham 2007, 101ff.; Laffi 2007). A prefecture was not so much a community as an administrative district, supervised by a prefect (*praefectus iure dicendo*—a delegate of the urban praetor), which could include small towns (*fora* and *conciliabula*—'markets' and 'meeting places'; see Frayn 1993) as well as villages (*pagi, vici*); a prefect could also be based in a colony or a municipality. Local magistrates in these communities had at their disposal the information from each census, which included tribal affiliations, wealth, family, and patrons (*Tab. Her.* 142–6; see *RS* 368), all of which was helpful to candidates soliciting influential backers. On prefectures, see Sherwin White 1973, 43ff., 74ff.; Knapp 1980; Linderski 1995, 143ff.; Tarpin 2002, 226ff.; Bispham 2007, 12. The importance of Italian voters, whose status was finally settled in the census of 70, remained topical in 64 (see **¶1 within a single, systematic form and in a logical order**).

even a single locality. 'Locality' (*locus*) can be included in formal expressions along with 'municipality' and 'colony' (e.g. in the *Lex de Gallia Cisalpina*, col. 2, line 40; see *RS* 465) and so is suitable here. Quintus is, in any case, straining himself in stressing Cicero's universal coverage of the electorate.

¶31 from every region. Every region of Italy. Quintus continues to focus on citizens outside the city of Rome.

candidates on your behalf. With this image Quintus indicates that Cicero's supporters throughout Italy will mobilize their influence on his behalf by employing, in their own communities, techniques similar to the ones recommended to Cicero in the *Brief Handbook*. However, Plut. *Cat. min.* 49.3 cites a senatorial decree, proposed by Cato in 52 when he was a candidate for the consulship, requiring each candidate to canvass in person and forbidding others to canvass on his behalf, an action which, if genuine, might suggest something exceptional about Quintus' advice here. But Plutarch's decree appears to be a muddled recollection of Cato's efforts against illegal electioneering during the elections of 63 (Cic. *Mur.* 71;

see Gruen 1974, 456 n. 27). On the use of surrogates in canvassing, see, further. §III.10.

in a manner that suits just this purpose. This manner is explained in what follows: Cicero should make himself familiar to his municipal supporters and reveal himself as keen to be helpful to them.

if they are simply known to us by name. See ¶28 **address them by name.** 'To us' probably refers not to the brothers Cicero but to members of the senatorial order, whose friendship even in its most attenuated form could only be desirable for anyone, not least men from the municipalities. Quintus' formulation here is not so condescending as it may at first glance appear: he goes on to insist that Cicero, unlike other senators and certainly unlike his rivals, will not settle for such superficial intimacy with men from municipalities, thereby advertising his extensive and genuine municipal connections (see ¶2 **your reputation**; ¶3 **municipalities that are devoted exclusively to you**).

protection for themselves. A blunt appraisal, but powerful friends were obviously worthwhile acquisitions. This was especially true for Roman citizens inhabiting the countryside, which, after the Social War, was often a dangerous place, and one where the senatorial order was itself often a menacing presence (see Frier 1985, 52ff.; Stewart 1995, 74f.; Paterson 2006, 614ff.). Quintus will later make the point that mere familiarity will not win over supporters unless they can be sure there is also a practical advantage in Cicero's friendship (¶32). That Cicero could offer protection to others (and of course had already done so extensively) is emphasized in the *Brief Handbook*'s previous expansion on Cicero's eloquence (see ¶2 **your fame as an orator**; ¶3 **municipalities that are devoted exclusively to you**) and reprised in Quintus' advice here.

Other candidates…who these men are. A bold, if somewhat narrow, claim: Cicero, Quintus asserts, excels his fellow senators insofar as the genuineness of his municipal attachments is concerned. The point is put in hyperbolic terms but Cicero truly was very familiar with large segments of the Italian aristocracy (see ¶3 **municipalities that are devoted exclusively to you**).

¶32 a friend of genuine value. Cicero can be a good friend (*amicus… bonus*) only if his relationships combine familiarity and utility. Once more, Cicero's utilitarian friendships, required in canvassing, are accorded a loftier stature by the *Brief Handbook*; see ¶16 **the definition of the word 'friend'.**

slave with a good head for names. That is, a *nomenclator* (see ¶28 **address them by name**). Knowing the name of a man, although it is something, is not enough to make him one's friend.

To sum up. Quintus identifies two types of supporter: ambitious men possessing influence (*gratia*) in their tribes, which reprises ¶¶18–19 above; and men whose usefulness derives from their connections in smaller administrative units, reprising ¶¶29–30. He can now turn to the crucial category of the knights.

¶33 **Now.** Quintus recurs to the knights (see ¶3 **the equestrian order**), the solicitation of whom, together with senators, he urged at ¶29. In this way, Quintus brings closure to this final segment of his treatment of 'gaining the support of friends' (¶16). Here it appears that Quintus concentrates on young knights who are members of the eighteen equestrian centuries (see next note), a group exemplifying the intimacy between the equestrian and senatorial orders: sons of senators were enrolled in the eighteen centuries; so, too, were sons of knights possessing a public horse. At ¶6, Quintus singled out the importance of young nobles (see ¶6 **young nobles**), who, if they were sons of senators (and all or nearly all will have been), also belong to the group Quintus emphasizes here under the rubric of young equestrians.

This is a difficult, even problematic, section of the *Brief Handbook*. Here Quintus adduces, in rapid succession: (i) the centuries of the knights (viz. the eighteen centuries of knights possessing a public horse); (ii) knights *simpliciter*, the reference for which ordinarily extends beyond knights possessing a public horse (see ¶3 **the equestrian order**); (iii) young equestrians; and (iv) the whole of the equestrian order, the *ordo equester*, which is here understood in terms of its centuries and so apparently refers again to the eighteen centuries. Quintus' lack of exactitude here, noted and objected to by Mommsen (*StR* 3.484 n. 3), led Mommsen to disbelieve in the authenticity of the *Brief Handbook* as a late republican document. This passage continues to stimulate scholarly commentary (e.g. Nicolet 1966, 77ff.; Nardo 1970, 97f.; Wiseman 1987, 64f.; Tatum 2002).

Quintus' detail is distinctive. At ¶3, he singled out the *publicani* (see ¶3 **publicans**) before evoking Cicero's broad equestrian support; at ¶29, he stressed the importance of the knights but without further elaboration. Here he expatiates on young equestrians, who are inclined to respect the disposition of their seniors within the centuries. If the reader understands all Quintus' references to knights in this section in terms of the eighteen centuries (the words that actually open Quintus' treatment here: *iam equitum centuriae*), then Quintus' terminology appears less muddled (see Nicolet 1966, 77; Wiseman 1987, 65; one may accept this point without accepting every point urged by Nicolet or Wiseman).

Still, this section presents further difficulties. Quintus offers no explicit transition from his introduction of the equestrian centuries to the young men within them. The discontinuity is severe, not least in a work replete with fulsome transitions (see Buecheler 1869, 6). The best explanation for this anomaly is to posit a hiatus in the text (Baehrens 1878, 30; Tatum 2002). But how extensive? At the very least, we should expect to find Quintus, after stressing the importance of soliciting the equestrian centuries, making an explicit turn to the value of winning over young equestrians—a sequence perhaps replicating his advice at ¶¶5–6 (where his introduction of the nobles is followed promptly by his underlining the value of attracting the enthusiasm of young nobles). Perhaps, then, the original was something like the following: *primum <oportet> cognosci equites (pauci enim sunt), deinde appeti adulescentes (multo enim facilius illa adulescentulorum ad amicitiam aetas adiungitur)*, or, 'First you must get to know the knights (for they are few). Then make a point of visiting the young knights personally, for young men are at an age when it is very easy to win their friendship.' The lacuna may have been longer, of course, but the addition of *adulescentes* (or something along that line, though *adulescentes* is a natural means of referring to young equestrians: e.g. Sall. *Cat.* 14.5; see ¶3 **young men**; ¶6 **young nobles**) suffices to render the sequence of thought less jarring and more compatible with Quintus' exposition elsewhere. For a fuller discussion, see Tatum 2002.

centuries of the knights. There were eighteen centuries of knights, whose votes were especially important in the centuriate assembly (see §II.3).

even more easily. Presumably because this is Cicero's natural constituency, emphasized already by Quintus (see ¶¶3, 8, 13, 29); and in fact his identification with the order was a hallmark of Cicero's political career (see, further, ¶3 **the equestrian order**).

for they are few. The eighteen centuries had a nominal membership of 2400 (or, less likely, 1800) men. This figure's uncertainty is due to inconsistencies between Cicero and Livy, our most important sources, and to textual problems afflicting the relevant passages (see Liv. 1.36.7; 1.43.8–9; Cic. *Rep.* 2.36; Ogilvie 1965, 152; Zetzel 1995, 191). On the overall problem of the number of knights in the eighteen centuries, see Nicolet 1966, 113ff.

young men. The minimum age for enrolment in the eighteen centuries was 17 (Liv. 27.11.15; see Nicolet 1966, 73ff.). In referring to young knights here, Quintus uses the word *adulescentuli*, the same word he employed for referring to young nobles (see ¶6 **young nobles**), not accidentally inasmuch as young nobles were enrolled as knights in the eighteen centuries (see above **Now**). On the jarring transition from 'the knights' to 'young men', which is the result of a lacuna in the text, see above **Now**.

the best of our youth. *Iuventus* ('youth') was often used in reference to the sons of senators, and especially the sons of the nobility, enrolled in the eighteen centuries—all the more so after 129, when knights entering the senate were obliged to surrender their public horse and remove them-selves from the eighteen centuries (Cic. *Rep.* 4.2; Plut. *Pomp.* 22; *contra* Lintott 1994, 75, suggesting that the measure was aimed at abolishing the institution of the public horse; see Hackl 1989 and esp. Giovannini 2010, arguing that even after surrendering his public horse a senator continued to vote in the eighteen centuries). And each of the men Cicero describes as 'a leading figure of the youth' (*princeps iuventutis*) is noble (*Verr.* 1.139 (L. Domitius Ahenobarbus); *Sull.* 34 (L. Manlius Torquatus); *Vat.* 24 (C. Scribonius Curio); *Fam.* 3.11.2 (M. Brutus)). Moreover, it was to nobles Cicero returned when soliciting equestrian support for his preferred candidates: Decimus Brutus on behalf of Lucius Lamia (Cic. *Fam.* 11.16.3); Scribonius Curio on behalf of Milo (Cic. *Fam.* 2.6.3; see Shackleton Bailey 1989, 72). Thus Quintus' focus here is on the sons of the nobility who are members of the eighteen centuries (see previous note) and not on the equestrian order as a whole or even on the majority of the equestrians in the eighteen centuries (see Corte 1924; Hellegouarc'h 1963, 468ff.; see also ¶6 **young nobles**, where, as here, Cicero has already won them over).

At *Fam.* 2.6.3, Cicero includes among Milo's assets in his campaign for the consulship of 52, 'the zealous support of the young, who are influential in the six centuries owing to his extraordinary influence with them and his assiduousness in cultivating them' (*iuventutis et gratiosorum in suffragiis studia propter excellentem in eo genere vel gratiam vel diligentiam*); on the meaning of *suffragiis* here, see Shackleton Bailey 1989, 72.

Instead of the more common *princeps* (see above), Quintus here uses *optimus* (*ex iuventute optimum*), the closest republican parallel for which is Ennius' *Annales* 563Sk: *optima cum pulchris animis Romana iuventus* ('the best Roman youth, marked by handsome courage') (see Val. Max. 3.2.9; on the use of *princeps* with reference to the equestrian order as a whole or to other sections of the order, see Hellegouarc'h 1963, 456f.). Does Quintus here allude to Ennius (after all, he immediately stresses the high culture of these young men)?

high culture. Quintus' word is *humanitas*, which often (as here) signals erudition, literary taste, and wit—especially when exhibited in aristo-cratic conversation (e.g. Cic. *Rosc. Am.* 121; *Verr.* 2.4.98; *Cael.* 54; *Pis.* 68; *Arch.* 3: *De or.* 1.27; *Att.* 1.5.1; *Fam.* 16.21.3; *Q. Fr.* 2.9.1–2; Varro *Rust.* 2.174; Gell. *NA* 13.17; see Hellegouarc'h 1963, 267ff.; Leeman and Pinkster 1981, 80ff.; Mitchell 1991, 37f.; Moatti 1997, 293ff.; Gildenhard 2011, 201ff.) Indeed, *humanitas* was a core aristocratic value during the late republic

(Hall 1998, 101ff.; Hall 2005). At ¶3, 'large numbers of young men' are said to be attached to Cicero on account of his eloquence; here his appeal derives from his charm and culture (Cicero was, in fact, a very witty man: Cic. *Fam.* 7.32.1–2; 9.16.4; 15.21.2; *Planc.* 35; *Quint.* 6.3.2–100; Plut. *Cic.* 5.6; 5.25–7). Quintus thus compliments both his brother and the young aristocrats whose support Cicero seeks.

the authority of their order. On authority (*auctoritas*), see ¶55 **authority.** The collective authority of the equestrian order is not often invoked (Cic. *Verr.* 2.3.61; Florus 2.1; cf. Plin. *NH* 33.32.2). References to the order's prestige (*dignitas*) are far more common (Nicolet 1966, 236ff.; Bleicken 1995, 59f.). Young knights, including young nobles, will be influenced both by their deference to the equestrian order as a whole and by its devotion to Cicero. An instance of young voters consulting their elders during a consular election is reported at Liv. 26.22.10–11.

¶34 attendance. Quintus now turns to the central and most conspicuous rituals of canvassing, which he reviews in ¶¶34–7 under the rubric of attendance (*adsectio*). These are the morning greeting (*salutatio*), the candidate's parade from his house to the forum (*deductio*), and his procession through the forum (*prensatio*, or glad-handing) (see §III.5). For most Romans, it was these activities that constituted canvassing (*petitio*), and it is these rituals that lie behind Quintus' tripartite definition of attendance. Although Quintus makes clear the public significance of these practices, they are treated relatively briefly and largely in terms of the candidate's relationship not with the people generally but rather with his various attendants, an emphasis underlined by Quintus' decision to discuss them under the heading of 'gaining the support of friends' (¶16) instead of 'dealing with the people' (¶41). Still, Quintus does not fail to recognize the importance of these rituals for registering a candidate's influence with the public (see below **sheer scale**). Quintus recurs to these practices at ¶¶49–50, and they lie behind his comments on pageantry at ¶52. These same three canvassing rituals are also discussed by Cicero at *Mur.* 44–5, 70–1; and *Planc.* 21, 66, instances in which the orator is advancing his views on correct and incorrect canvassing (see Cic. *De or.* 1.200; 1.239; 3.133; *Att.* 1.18.1). On the nature and significance of these campaign rituals, see, further, Hellegouarc'h 1963, 160ff.; Nicolet 1980, 356ff.; Vanderbroeck 1987, 83ff.; Flower 1996, 217ff.; Deniaux 1997; Yakobson 1999, 72ff.; Mouritsen 2001, 109ff.; Flaig 2003, 17ff.; Winterling 2009, 34ff.; Goldbeck 2010, 229ff.; Feig Vishnia 2012, 112ff.; Rollinger 2014, 134ff.

At the end of his discussion, Quintus leaves his candidate glad-handing in the forum. What of his return home? Neither the *Brief Handbook* nor any other source comments on that. Accompanying a prominent Roman to his house (an action usually indicated by some variant of *domum deducere* or *domum reducere*) was a courtesy that signalled respect, gratitude, or even fellow feeling (e.g. Cic. *Q. Fr.* 2.8.2; *Brut.* 86; *Sen.* 63; Val. Max. 7.5.4). It was a special honour for a public figure to be seen home by a crowd after a successful or rousing performance in the senate or the courts, or a speech before the people (e.g. Cic. *Amic.* 12; *Phil.* 14.12; Liv. 38.51.11–12; Gell. *NA* 13.29.1). Relevant to a candidate's aspirations was the custom of seeing magistrates-designate to their houses on the day of their election (e.g. Varro *Rust.* 3.2.1; Cic. *Verr.* 1.1.18; *Att.* 1.16.5; Liv. 4.24.7; 23.23.8–9), and, in the case of consuls, at the end of their first day in office a crowd accompanied them on their return home (Ov. *Pont.* 4.4.41; see Pina Polo 2011, 17f.). Unlike the morning greeting or even transiting to the forum in the company of a retinue, a celebratory homecoming was *not* a routine facet of an aristocrat's public presentation. Such a homecoming remained a truly special occasion, which took men out of their way at an awkward time of the day (hence its significance as a mark of honour). The silence of our sources is almost certainly to be explained by the reality that a well-attended homecoming was not a feature of canvassing.

supporters of every sort, of every rank, of every age. A hyperbolic triad designed to emphasize the inclusive following Cicero is instructed to gather. That it is not meant to be literal becomes clear at ¶37, where Quintus introduces the topic of men too old to participate in attendance. But Quintus' basic point is that Cicero should accumulate every available attendant because it is principally the *scale* of his following that matters, not the census category of the bulk of his followers. In electing to discuss attendance under the general heading of 'gaining the support of friends' instead of 'gaining the goodwill of the people' (see ¶16), where it perhaps fits more naturally, Quintus clearly stretches even his elastic definition of 'friend' (see ¶16 **the meaning of the word 'friend'**), and he concedes that some of Cicero's attendants will be there only as a courtesy to a third party and not owing to any direct association with Cicero (¶37). Still, including attendance here underscores Cicero's personal obligations to his followers and so emphasizes the candidate's active role in acquiring a notable retinue: a good candidate possesses a large following because he is a reliable and respected friend.

sheer scale. The primary objective for a candidate was to enjoy attendance by an enormous throng (Cic. *Mur.* 44–5, 70–1; *Planc.* 21; *De or.* 1.200; see ¶50; §III.5), which is why, when he was a candidate, Cicero took special pains never to refuse anyone an audience (Cic. *Planc.* 66). But what, precisely, does Quintus expect Cicero or any other observer to infer from the scale of his attendance? Presumably he could estimate the number of citizens who are likely to vote for him. But Quintus does not assume everyone in Cicero's attendance is present owing to a personal commitment to Cicero himself: some, at least, attend him owing to their obligations to other men who are in Cicero's debt (¶37). The crowd following Cicero, then, signals the extent of his *gratia* (see ¶4 **express their gratitude**) and for this reason exerts an influence on all likely voters: because the public sought political leaders who commanded the respect of all segments of the population, a candidate possessing the right kind of influence over the public, including especially the lower orders, was attractive to voters in every order, including the top classes (see, further, §III.5). Put differently, the right kind of popularity with the masses was helpful in attracting the votes of the elite. Quintus emphasizes the impression made on the public by displays of this sort when he concludes his advice on 'dealing with the people'; see ¶52 **full of pageantry**.

election day. Quintus writes *campus* ('field'), that is, the Campus Martius, where the centuriate assembly convened to elect consuls (§II.3). Cicero cites the use of *campus* as a metonymy for 'elections' as an effective and fine rhetorical ornamentation (Cic. *De or.* 3.167), which means that Quintus is aiming at effect here. See also ¶36 **escort you**.

attendance . . . can be separated into three parts. In keeping with his didactic approach, Quintus divides attendance into three parts. Instead of discussing the basic canvassing rituals (*salutatio, deductio, prensatio*), he divides the phenomenon of attendance into three kinds of followers: *salutatores* ('morning greeters'), *deductores* ('escorts'), and *adsectatores* ('constant attendants'). His principal concern is Cicero's relationship with the men involved in attending him. Consequently Quintus has little to say about the physical circumstances or the specific symbolism of these rituals apart from their role in signalling Cicero's prestige. Furthermore, because his focus is on the attendants themselves, he does not draw a clear division between *deductio* and *prensatio*, but instead distinguishes escorts who accompany the candidate *only* during his *deductio* from attendants who can remain with the candidate throughout his procession through the forum (¶37 **third element**).

[when they come to your home]. Orelli 1829, followed by most editors, rightly deleted this phrase as an interpolation: it is an unnecessary expansion that spoils the tight shape of this concise sentence. Sjögren 1913, however, defends the phrase, and Constans 1940 preserves it in his text. In any case, the house in question was not Cicero's famous house on the Palatine but his house, inherited from his father, on the Carinae (Plut. *Cic.* 8.3; Cic. *Q. Fr.* 2. 3. 7; *Har. resp.* 31).

throughout the day. Not the whole of the day in a modern sense. Business was carried on from the third hour through the fifth (Balsdon 1969, 24) and this is probably the period Quintus has in mind here. After the fifth hour, most men resorted to lunch or, during the summer, a siesta.

¶35 morning greeters. The formal reception of morning greeters (*salutatio*) was a recurring and essential feature of life for elite Romans, especially members of Rome's political aristocracy, whether or not they were candidates for office. A crowded house at the *salutatio* was a sign of prominence and power, just as a poorly attended *salutatio* signalled political and social inadequacy (Cic. *Mur.* 70; *Sull.* 73; *Pis.* 64; *Att.* 2.22.3; *Q. Fr.* 2.4.6). Morning receptions typically occupied the first two hours of the day (Iuv. 1.127–8; Mart. 4.8.1–2; see Goldbeck 2010, 106f.), although, when he was staying at his house in Formiae, Cicero's morning audiences went on to the fourth hour (*Att.* 2.14.2). Visitors waited in the vestibule or atrium (benches were sometimes provided: Gell. *NA* 16.5.8; Dio 58.5) until given an opportunity to approach the master of the house, usually seated in a distinct reception area (*tablinum*) and assisted by a *nomenclator*, who helped him to identify his guests (Plin. *NH* 29.12; see fig. 2). Guests might solicit favours and in any case exhibited respect for their host, who (ideally) reciprocated his guests' courtesy.

The *salutatio* was a natural environment for clients to meet their patrons, but not all morning visitors were clients in any technical sense, and in this discussion Quintus does not mention clients at all (on patronage, see §III.3; ¶17 **clients**). Instead, the *salutatio* enabled aristocrats to meet their moral obligation to be accessible and helpful to friends and dependants of any kind (see ¶42 **recognize people by name**), offered the needy a means of securing vital assistance, and by way of this social exchange implicated everyone, not least the poor, in the maintenance of Rome's hierarchy,

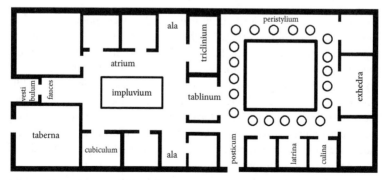

Fig. 2. Plan of a typical domus.

notwithstanding Rome's stark economic inequalities. So central was *salutatio* to the aristocracy that Romans believed the mansions of the rich (*domus*) were designed around this institution (Vitr. *De arch.* 6.5.1–2). An aristocrat's *domus*, both for its grandeur and its exhibition of his family's trophies and honours, was certainly recognized as a manifestation of his status and clout; consequently, the domestic setting for morning greetings emphasized the exalted position of the greeters' aristocratic hosts. On the *salutatio*, see, further, Friedländer 1907, 1.207ff.; Hug 1920; Rouland 1979, 484ff.; Flower 1996, 217ff.; Goldbeck 2010, esp. 235ff.; Feig Vishnia 2012, 105ff. On the importance of the *domus*, see Wallace-Hadrill 1994; Treggiari 2002, 74ff.; Beck 2009; Potter 2011; Clark 2014.

The importance of the *salutatio* in communicating the influence (*gratia*) of a Roman grandee can hardly be exaggerated. Hence its fundamental role in canvassing, when it was crucial for candidates to convey the extent of their popularity. And the size of a candidate's *salutatio* was considered a useful measure of his electoral prospects (Cic. *Mur.* 44–5; see ¶34). A poorly attended *salutatio* was an embarrassment and a sign that a campaign was in difficulty (Cic. *Att.* 4.3.5; *Fam.* 8.3.1). Quintus returns to the importance of morning greetings several times in ¶¶47–50. The *salutatio* also provided each candidate with an opportunity for soliciting his supporters and for exchanging valuable information, an environment in which the candidate could learn about his standing with various sections of the public, and supporters could learn how their candidate wished his public profile to be advanced or defended (Laurence 1994, 64ff.; Goldbeck 2010, 52ff.). It is also likely that candidates at least occasionally used their morning receptions to address their supporters with a speech, making the *salutatio* into something like a rally (Tatum 2013, 146ff.; Tatum forthcoming b). In his maturity, Cicero boasted of his accessibility when he stood for office (*Planc.* 66) and remained proud of his crowded morning receptions (*Att.* 1.18.1; 2.22.3; *Fam.* 7.24.2; 9.20.3).

common folk. The majority of morning callers were poor men seeking the acquaintance and assistance of the mighty (e.g. Cic. *De or.* 3.133; Hor. *Epist.* 1.5.56–7; 2.1.103–17; Iuv. 5.14–23; Mart. 2.18). In the imperial period, it was customary for a morning greeter to be presented with a gift of food or money, called a *sportula* ('little basket') (see Friedländer 1907, 4.77ff.; Goldbeck 2010, 174ff.). There is no evidence, however, for this practice during the republic (Le Gall 1966). Still, we can be certain that many morning callers expected material assistance from the grandees whose audiences they attended, even if this generosity had not yet been reduced into a more or less uniform system.

The circumstances of a political campaign supplied modest greeters with greater than usual social leverage, a situation that urged candidates to be complaisant (see ¶¶41–53, esp. ¶¶44–9). That candidates and their morning greeters had different agendas—the poor sought vital material aid, candidates sought high office—goes unaddressed by Quintus, who here prefers to depict morning callers purely as political supporters (his perspective changes when he turns to 'dealing with the people' at ¶41).

Not all morning greeters were lowly figures. It was also essential for members of the elite to pay morning calls on one another, during which visits their special status was observed (e.g. Sen. *Ben.* 6.34.3–4; Plin. *NH* 15.38; Dio 76.5). Such visits were especially important for young men (Polyb. 31.29.8; Cic. *Cael.* 18; Val. Max. 3.1.2; Plut. *Cat. min.* 3.2–4). In one of his letters, Cicero expresses pride in the elite quality of his morning callers (*Fam.* 9.20.3). Mouritsen 2001, 109, doubts whether many morning greeters were in fact poor, notwithstanding this explicit statement in the *Brief Handbook*.

modern custom of visiting several houses. Modern and in this instance dubious—from an elite perspective (but see ¶14 **in the fashion of recent years; ¶18 in recent years, men eager for advancement**). Still, the necessity of making multiple morning calls was one of the poor's many unpleasant and yet routine burdens (Iuv. 1.222; Mart. 9.92; 12.8.5; see Brunt 1988, 398f.; Saller 1989, 49ff.; Goldbeck 2010, 97ff.). It is not this common practice that Quintus has in mind here, however, but rather what was perceived by the political class as an unwillingness on the part of large sections of the public, especially the poor, to make a firm commitment to a single candidate. At *Mur.* 44–5, Cicero suggests that voters visit the houses of several candidates in order to decide who has the widest following and exudes the greatest confidence, because they prefer to support a likely winner (see Cic. *Mil.* 42, stressing how quickly public opinion can turn against a candidate; Yakobson 1999, 71ff.). Neither Quintus nor Cicero concedes that it was natural, during a political campaign, for humble Romans to seize from candidates whatever benefactions they could: hence their attendance on more than one candidate. Nor do they address the reality that, because there were multiple candidates for multiple magistracies, many modest citizens may have been over-extended in their obligations to appear at morning receptions: Quintus writes as if Cicero's contest for the consulship were the only race in Rome.

very simple duty. Attendance on the part of morning greeters, if undertaken owing to a previous favour on Cicero's part, can fairly be described, as Quintus does here, as an *officium* (see ¶4 **See to it that … express their gratitude; ¶16 favours and reciprocation of favours**). Quintus deploys the word here in order to register the proper moral bond between a candidate and his supporters, in contrast to the modern and unscrupulous habit (from Quintus' perspective) of voters' playing the field. Morning attendance can be described as a 'very simple duty' only from the perspective of the elite. During the summer months, when canvassing took place, the first hour of the day commenced as early as 4.30 a.m., and visitors, most of whom must stand until recognized, were expected to assemble earlier than that. Even for men of relatively high social distinction, attendance at morning receptions could be demanding: in an inscription of 166, ambassadors from Teos to Rome included their constant circulation at morning *salutationes* among the 'mental and bodily distress' they suffered on their city's behalf (*SIG*³ 656; see Sherk 1984, 25f.).

Give unmistakable signs. The literature of the empire, especially the poetry of Juvenal and Martial, teems with references to rude and insensitive patrons (see Friedländer 1907, 198ff.). Even Cicero, when he was a senior statesman, composed a letter in the midst of his morning reception (*Ad Brut.* 4 (2.4).1). For the candidate, however, amassing a crowd was his central concern, and for this it was necessary for him to exhibit extraordinary courtesy to his supporters.

one of them pay greater attention to their services. Voters are not won over by policies or platforms, it is indicated here, but instead by the personal attentions of candidates, notwithstanding the relatively superficial nature of such attention.

devote themselves to that one candidate. There was no obvious reason to do so, inasmuch as voters almost certainly cast votes for two candidates for the consulship (see §II.3). And it was often the case that more than a single candidate had claims on a voter's support. During the consular campaigning for 53, for example, Cicero supported M. Valerius Messalla (cos. 53) and did favours for Cn. Domitius Calvinus (cos. 53), and also lent assistance to C. Memmius (pr. 58) and M. Aemilius Scaurus (pr. 58). Each man was a candidate. This was a pattern of comprehensive helpfulness that Cicero clearly deemed prudent (Cic. *Q. Fr.* 3.1.16; cf. *Att.* 4.17.3).

instead of sham ones. The adjective here translated 'sham' is *fucosus*, derived from *fucus*, dye or cheap make-up, and, by extension, a disguise or pretence. Quintus recurs to the same vivid image a few lines later: 'playing you false' is *fucum facere*. This latter expression, though not widely attested, was probably common enough: it occurs at Ter. *Eun.* 589. And Cicero reports (*Att.* 1.1.1), with some glee, how his rival for the consulship, P. Sulpicius Galba, despite his efforts at winning supporters, suffered rebuffs that were *sine fuco ac fallaciis* ('unvarnished and unmistakable').

pretend that you have not heard it. To do otherwise would deprive Cicero of the presence of false supporters, whose numbers (whatever their true intentions when it came to voting) helped to swell his attendance and therefore enhance his prospects. He would also lose the opportunity to discover the schemes of his unreliable supporters. This kind of pretence (*dissimulatio*) on the part of a candidate differs from the pretence (*simulatio*) that is (possibly) invoked at ¶1 (see ¶1 **Although… nature… pretence is able to defeat nature**). *Dissimulatio* could be viewed as a political virtue and was certainly deemed politically prudent (see Syme 1958, 429f.).

cannot be your friend. Quintus continues to employ 'friend' in the sense appropriate to canvassing (see ¶16 **the definition of the word 'friend'**). Although candidates were expected to scrutinize their supporters closely (Cic. *Mil.* 42), it was generally recognized that open suspicion could undermine the confidence and integrity of the lower orders: Caesar gives Curio a speech in which he makes what is essentially the same point about rank and file soldiers (Caes. *B.Civ.* 2.31.4–5).

¶36 escort you. It was a routine practice for any important figure, after his *salutatio*, to receive an escort to the forum (*deductio*) (e.g. Cic. *Att.* 1.18.1; *Fam.* 10.12.2; *Phil.* 2.15; Asc. 22C; Dio 58.11.1). It was a clear and recognizable mark of honour. A *deductio* could mark a special moment even in the lives of humble citizens, who sometimes sought distinguished persons as escorts (Cic. *Mur.* 69). A grand *deductio* indicated strong political support and so naturally became a hallmark of candidature: 'as for me, I want a candidate, especially a candidate for the consulship, to be escorted (*deduci*) to the forum and the Campus Martius—with great hopes, great spirit, and a great crowd' (Cic. *Mur.* 44; cf. Cic. *Att.* 2.1.5; *Mur.* 49; Plin. *Ep.* 4.17.6; Plut. *Aem.* 38; *Cat. min.* 27). On political escorting (*deductio*), see further Leonhard 1901; Rouland 1979, 485ff.; Nicolet 1980, 356ff.; Deniaux 1997; Morstein-Marx 1998, 270ff.; Bell 2004, 214ff.; Goldbeck 2010, 117f.; O'Sullivan 2011, 54ff.; Östenberg 2015.

This ritual was particularly identified with candidature, even providing poets with a natural image for electoral competition (Cat. 112; Hor. *Carm.* 3.1.10–11). Transit to the forum during canvassing anticipated the candidate's final procession to the Campus Martius on the day of the elections: hence the frequent appearance of some variation on *in campum descendere*, an expression whose martial overtones—it can be used to describe the commencement of battle (e.g. *B.Afr.* 61.6; *B.Hisp.* 26.4; Caes. *B.Civ.* 2.40.3; Cic. *Mur.* 52; Liv. 10.27.2; see Oakley 2005a, 159)—underscored the intensely competitive atmosphere of Roman elections (Nisbet and Rudd 2004, 11; Fantham 2013, 146). The spectacles of *deductio* and *prensatio* were perhaps enhanced by the candidate's *toga candida*, his toga whitened by chalk (Isid. *Etym.* 4.24.6), a garment that unmistakably marked him off from his entourage (see §III.5).

their service to you is greater. Accompanying a candidate could be even more inconvenient for the lower orders than attendance at the morning greeting, because it might take men out of their neighbourhoods and away from their shops during the working day, thereby entailing real sacrifice. This doubtless is why escorts remaining with the candidate for an extended period were expected to be very poor, often unemployed, citizens (Cic. *Mur.* 70–1; see ¶37 **steady supply**; ¶37 **a great crowd at all times**). The *deductio* mattered more than the *salutatio* because, although a citizen might attend more than one morning greeting in a day (¶35 **modern custom of visiting several houses**; see Cic. *Mur.* 44), he could escort only one candidate to the forum and so this action represented a deeper level of support. This was true whatever his social status.

Neither Quintus' comment here nor his stress on punctuality below will support the view that *most* of the men escorting the candidate to the forum were distinguished, or even that elite members of the candidate's entourage are Quintus' focus here (*pace* Taylor 1949, 43; Vanderbroeck 1987, 83; Morstein-Marx 1998, 271f.; Mouritsen 2001, 109). Quintus distinguishes attendants who follow the candidate only during his *deductio* from those who can follow him longer (¶37 **steady supply**), but the latter category consists mostly of the unemployed (Cic. *Mur.* 70–1). Modest citizens were able to participate in the *deductio*, and, because bulk was highly desirable, were welcome. It is of course true that the presence of a senator or Roman knight was a precious and notable display of esteem in any phase of attendance (e.g. Cic. *Mur.* 70; *De or.* 1.239; Plin. *Ep.* 4.17.6), but the candidate sought 'a large crowd' (see below **a large crowd**). Even taking into consideration the numbers added by the retinue every distinguished attendant doubtless had in tow, that was possible only if the *deductio* included men from the lower orders. Nor was this a bad strategy: Scipio Aemilianus, when a candidate for the censorship of 142, descended to the forum with a crowd that included so many freedmen and low-born men that his rival thought he saw a good opening for ridicule and insult, but it was he who subsequently lost the election (Plut. *Aem.* 38.3; see Astin 1967, 112). And, at least according to Plutarch, voters were upset by Coriolanus' exclusively elite entourage during his canvass for the consulship (Plut. *Cor.* 15.2–3).

you appreciate them even more. Men were ordinarily *asked* to serve as escorts (Cic. *Mur.* 69), an action which itself played a part in the candidate's exchange of favours. Even when he was not a candidate for office, Cicero found the demands of making the right impression on his escorts oppressive (Cic. *Att.* 1.18.1).

at fixed times. The *salutatio* normally consumed the first two hours of the day, after which business in the forum began (Iuv. 1.127–8; Mart. 4.8.1–2;

see Goldbeck 2010, 106f.), so it was important that the candidate descend to the forum before the third hour commenced. At the height of summer, the first hour began around 4.30 a.m. (Balsdon 1969, 16). Notwithstanding the presence of sundials and water-clocks in the city (Balsdon 1969, 17ff.), punctuality was doubtless a challenge but remained a necessity nonetheless: elite Romans were busy men, as were Rome's shopkeepers and tradesmen, so there was always a danger they might stray from the fold if kept waiting too long.

a large crowd. A large retinue naturally impressed, and a small one could be embarrassing (e.g. Hor. *Sat.* 1.6.107–9). One cannot, however, be certain of the scale imagined by Quintus or his readers. At the height of his influence, we are told, Tiberius Gracchus was escorted by three or four thousand followers (Gell. *NA* 2.13.4 = Sempronius Asellio, fr. 7, *FRHist*; see Plut. *T. Gracch.* 20.2), while Plutarch reports that Cicero, when threatened with exile by Clodius, enjoyed sympathetic escort by 20,000 men (Plut. *Cic.* 31.1), an incredible figure that appears to misinterpret Cic. *Red. pop.* 8 (so Lintott 2013, 178). What mattered most, of course, was the size of one's escort in comparison with one's rivals', since the purpose of the procession was to signal the candidate's popularity. Inasmuch as all candidates for all offices were canvassing during the same weeks, the number of attendants who were available, from any social level, was necessarily divided, a reality that must have limited the size of any candidate's entourage. Even so, there must occasionally have been some uncomfortable crowding when multiple retinues shared the same streets or competed for space in the forum itself. It is perhaps best to imagine robust attendance but not a multitude like Tiberius Gracchus' remarkable following. Still, crowds were large enough that there were attempts, on the part of the elite, to limit them (see ¶37 **a great crowd at all times**).

¶37 third element. The third element is the candidate's circulation through the forum, denominated *ambitio* ('walking about') or *prensatio* ('glad-handing'). This activity was the most conspicuous aspect of any candidate's self-abasement during a political campaign, when he was most exposed to humiliating rejections or canvass-obliterating gaffes (see §III.4). Perhaps for these reasons, Quintus is here uninterested in the candidate's exertions in soliciting goodwill in the forum, but focuses rather on the positive impression made by his entourage and on his relationship with the members of his entourage. Even in Quintus' account, however, the candidate must remain unrelenting in his exhibition of gratitude, but at least this behaviour does not descend here to the degrading solicitations of *prensatio*. When Quintus returns to these displays under the heading of 'dealing with the people' (¶¶41–53), he again emphasizes only their positive side (see ¶52 **full of pageantry**).

Cicero makes it clear how welcome it was for a distinguished supporter to remain with a candidate during the *prensatio* and suggests that it was rare (*Mur.* 70). And yet the *prensatio* was an important opportunity for distinguished men to display their support for favoured candidates, an act of endorsement that came to be known as *suffragatio* (e.g. Cic. *Mur.* 38; *Planc.* 15; *Fam.* 2.6.3; Sall. *Iug.* 65.5; Liv. 10.13.13; the basic discussion remains Levick 1967). C. Fannius was elevated to the consulship of 122 not least owing to the attendance of Gaius Gracchus, who 'was seen leading Gaius Fannius into the Campus Martius and canvassed on his behalf along with Fannius' friends' (Plut. *C. Gracch.* 8.2). At *Planc.* 24–5, Cicero describes his efforts on behalf of Cn. Plancius (aed. 54), and at *Planc.* 85 he reminds his audience how he deployed his wit in skewering Plancius' rival, doubtless a common feature of canvassing on the part of anyone who could manage it (see Stroh 1975, 44); at *Mur.* 7 Cicero makes passing mention of his dutifulness to Ser. Sulpicius Rufus (cos. 51). One of the meritorious acts of Augustus was his habit of accompanying candidates on their rounds and appealing to voters on their behalf *more sollemni*, in the traditional and hallowed manner of the republic (Suet. *Aug.* 56.1). Quintus clearly expects the men whom Cicero has defended in court to show themselves (see ¶38). Personal appearances of this sort doubtless lie behind our notices of vigorous electoral support on the part of specified individuals (e.g. Liv. 22.34.2 (Q. Baebius Herennius for C. Terentius Varro); Liv. 35.10.5 (Scipio Africanus and Flamininus on behalf of their brothers); Liv. 39.32.10 (the consul Ap. Claudius Pulcher, having dismissed his lictors, accompanying his brother, P. Claudius Pulcher, on his rounds through the forum); Cic. *Amic.* 73 (Scipio Aemilianus for P. Rupilius; see Cic. *Tusc.* 4.40; Plin. *NH* 7.122); Plut. *C. Gracch.* 8.2; 11.2–3 (Gracchus for C. Fannius); Plut. *Sul.* 10.2–4 (Sulla for P. Servilius Vatia and Nonnius); Cic. *Att.* 1.16.2 (Pompeius for L. Afranius; see Dio 37.49.1); Cic. *Fam.* 8.14.1 (Caelius Rufus and Scribonius Curio for Mark Antony); Cic. *De or.* 2.247 (M. Sempronius for his brother A. Sempronius)).

steady supply. Persistent attention (*adsiduitas*: here Quintus speaks of *adsidua adsectatorum copia*) was a hallmark of devoted friendship (e.g. Cic. *Sest.* 7; *Planc.* 67; *Q. Fr.* 1.3.8). When crowds exhibited such devotion, even outside election campaigns, it was a mark of prestige (*dignitas*; see Cic. *Planc.* 21). This was the most demanding aspect of attendance, which is why it was a duty that fell, for the most part, to the poor or unemployed (Cic. *Mur.* 70–1).

voluntarily. A candidate who was doing well could expect to attract fresh supporters who were attracted by the candidate's momentum and its bandwagon effect. Indeed, a candidate must hope to do so if he expected to surpass his rivals. Hence the instruction that Cicero must find a way to express even more than his usual degree of gratefulness.

this service. In exchange for past favours. On the further implications of 'service' (*munus*), see ¶20.

neither age nor business is an impediment. The reference to business is realistic (see Cic. *Mur.* 71), and the infirmities of age obviously could prevent some Romans from meeting their obligations to Cicero. Quintus has in mind anyone indebted to Cicero, humble or exalted: either they or one of their connections must be required to perform this service.

appoint their personal connections. In this circumstance, which Quintus does not suggest would be unusual (quite the reverse, or why should he mention it at all?), the attendant would be performing a service not to Cicero but to his encumbered relation—another instance of political support that depends on intermediaries (see ¶31 **candidates on your behalf**). It is not suggested here that these surrogate attendants will, in the end, vote for Cicero, which was hardly the point. Their contribution to the bulk of Cicero's retinue was the essential thing.

a great crowd at all times. Attendance by large crowds could also attract suspicion, at least on the part of the governing class. The *lex Calpurnia* of 67 (sources assembled at *MRR* 2.142f.), a measure against illegal electioneering (*ambitus*; see ¶55 **bribery**), included a ban on hiring escorts during political campaigns (Cic. *Mur.* 67). The number of attendants in a man's entourage was limited by a *lex Fabia* as well as a decree of the senate passed in 64 (Cic. *Mur.* 71). It is probably, though not certainly, the case, that these two measures dealt solely with candidates for office, but nothing more is known about either of them. It is not obvious why a candidate's entourage should be limited, unless there were worries about congestion in the forum owing to the presence of numerous candidates and their followers, or anxiety about political violence or intimidation. In any case, it is far from clear how any candidate could stop his fellow citizens from following him about. Kinsey 1965 suggests that these measures exposed followers to prosecution for political violence if their numbers became so great as to be threatening, but that must remain nothing more than a guess.

The *lex Fabia* cannot be securely dated. Obviously, it was passed before Cicero's speech in 63, and because Cicero mentions it in tandem with a senatorial decree of 64, it is often concluded that the law was passed in that year (although the decree could have been a clarification or an affirmation of an earlier law). Neither the law nor the decree is mentioned in the *Brief Handbook*: on that basis, Niccolini 1934, 266, attributed the *lex Fabia* to an otherwise unknown Fabius who was tribune in 64 and carried his law some time after the dramatic date of the *Brief Handbook* (see ¶1 lasting but a few months); this is the origin of the queried Fabius at *MRR* 2.164. But none of this is compelling. Nor is the argument by Lange 1876, 566, and Lange 1879, 224, that the law was carried in 66 by the tribune M. Fabius Hadrianus: there is no evidence that Lange's Hadrianus was ever a tribune at any time (Münzer 1909, 1771), though it is of course possible (it is also *possible* that the law was carried at that time by some other unknown tribunician Fabius). Still, Lange is right in suggesting that the *lex Fabia* need not be dated to 64. Indeed, it could be a much older law (Ferrary 2002, 172). On the *lex Fabia*, see further Kinsey 1965; Kinsey 1966; Bauerle 1990, 61ff.; Ferrary 2002, 169ff.; Rosillio López 2010, 60f. If this *lex Fabia* is the work of the same (unknown) Fabius responsible for the *lex Fabia de plagio* ('the Fabian law concerning kidnapping and enslaving citizens and stealing slaves'), then perhaps it should be dated to the mid-60s (see *RS* 755; Kantor 2013).

Cicero claims that the *lex Fabia* and the senate's decree were unpopular with the public. His remarks also suggest that these measures were largely disregarded in practice. In fact, Cicero represents it as yet another oddity of Murena's prosecutor, the younger Cato, that he does not appreciate the social value of a candidate's attracting crowds (*Mur.* 70–1). This is a perspective that perhaps helps to explain why Quintus does not merely ignore the *lex Fabia* but also exhibits no awareness whatsoever of any social or political anxiety about a candidate's attracting too large a following: quite the reverse. It may be that he simply dismisses this issue because nearly everyone else did so, just as nearly everyone else ignored the ban on *nomenclatores*, which the younger Cato insisted on observing (Plut. *Cat. min.* 8.2, but see Cic. *Mur.* 77; see ¶28 address them by name).

¶38 at no cost to themselves. On the *lex Cincia*, which prohibited orators from accepting fees or gifts from their clients, see **¶2 deemed worthy of being patron.** Here the *Brief Handbook* advertises Cicero's probity.

their property. In what follows, Quintus elaborates what was apparently a familiar refrain regarding a client's debt to his forensic patron. At *Fam.* 7.29, M'. Curius, a Roman businessman defended by Cicero, asserts that he owes the orator 'what I am, what I possess, what men think of me'.

their standing as citizens. The basic reference of *salus*, the word used here, is to one's physical safety. But it was also commonly used to refer to a Roman's civil liberty and his standing within the republic (see *OLD* 1684; Hellegouarc'h 1963, 411f.). To lose one's *salus* meant, in practice, to be sent into exile. Which is why a successful advocate could be described as the defender or restorer of one's *salus* (Cic. *Mil.* 39; *Sen.* 3).

the whole of their fortunes. Fortune (*fortuna*) refers at once to wealth and social standing, predictably enough in a timocratic society like Rome (compare the strongly abusive term *perditus*, 'bankrupt', on which see Hellegouarc'h 1963, 532ff.). It is commonly paired (as here) with *salus* (Cic. *Verr.* 2.2.118; *Cat.* 4.3; *Red. sen.* 34; *Fam.* 2.6.3; 6.9.2; *Q. Fr.* 1.1.13; *Off.* 2.33). An alternative translation, taking *omnis* (here translated as 'the whole') as a nominative, recapitulating the 'some... others... others' of the previous clauses, is: 'still others their standing as citizens and all of them their fortunes' (so, e.g., Fedeli 1987; Duplá et al. 1990; see Cic. *Balb.* 62; *Sest.* 35).

¶39 deceit, treachery, and faithlessness. In this rapid crescendo of moral failings (*fraus, insidiae, perfidia*), Quintus emphasizes a recognized danger to any Roman's network of friends: a lack of trustworthiness (*fides*). *Fides*, like personal affection, was fundamental to friendship (Cic. *Amic.* 65; Brunt 1988, 355; Konstan 1997, 130f.; see ¶16 **the definition of the word 'friend'**; on *fides* generally, see Freyburger 1986); so, too, was truthfulness (*veritas*: Cic. *Quinct.* 26). Anxiety over the perils of false friendship appears early on in Latin literature and remains pervasive thereafter (e.g. Plaut. *Merc.* 839, bemoaning the impossibility of distinguishing true friends, *amici*, from false ones, *infideles*—on the recurring theme of unreliable friendship in Plautus, see Burton 2004; *Rhet. Her.* 4.25, citing the faithless friend as a natural trope in rhetoric; Sall. *Cat.* 10.5, complaining that political ambition makes men into false friends). Cicero, later in his career, complains of the harm done him by false friends (e.g. Cic. *Dom.* 29; cf. *Att.* 1.19.6; 1.20.3; 2.17; *Fam.* 1.9.5). Cicero, too, was accused by others of failing in his duties as a friend (Cic. *Mur.* 7, Cicero defends himself against the complaint that he was not a loyal friend to Ser. Sulpicius Rufus during the consular elections in 63; *Fam.* 3.10.7–8, Cicero insists that he has never been a false friend; *Phil.* 2.3–10, Cicero defends himself against Mark Antony's complaint that Cicero has been a false friend).

eternal debate. The topic was indeed old, originating in Greek philosophical discussions and concentrating mostly on the problem of distinguishing flatterers from friends (see Cic. *Amic.* 91–9, with Powell 1990, 114ff.; Konstan 1997, 98ff.). Still, philosophical fretting over treachery was also a long-standing concern: e.g. 'when you do a favour, scrutinize the recipient lest he be false and repay with evil instead of good' (Democritus 68B93 (DK); see, further, Griffin 2013, 17ff.).

a warning only. At *Att.* 1.19.8, Cicero informs Atticus that he is following the advice of Epicharmus (see below **Epicharmus**) by remaining watchful even of his friends. But this, Cicero later claims in another letter to Atticus, is not his natural condition:

Pompeius loves me and holds me dear. "Do you believe him?", you ask. I do…
Men of affairs, in their histories, precepts, even in their poetry, tell us to be
wary and forbid our trusting others. I follow their advice in one respect—
I am wary—but not in the other. I simply cannot be untrusting. (Cic. *Att.*
2.20.1)

As for Quintus, he was criticized by his brother for being too trusting of
others (Cic. *Q. Fr.* 1.1.12; 1.2.9).

to envy you. Envy, though incompatible with true friendship (see ¶13
closely attached to you in friendship), was not alien to its everyday variety, nor did envy inevitably result in enmity (see Brunt 1988, 369 and his
discussion there).

apophthegm of Epicharmus. Here Quintus employs Greek. Doing so was
a familiar feature of aristocratic correspondence in Rome, one effect of
which is to underline the correspondents' shared cultural background
(see Adams 2003, 316ff.).

Epicharmus. A Sicilian comic poet of the early fifth century. His dramatic
works survive only in fragments. He was also credited, though probably
mistakenly, with philosophical works; see Pickard-Cambridge 1962, 230ff.;
Kassel and Austin 2001, 8ff.; Olson 2007, 6ff. At *Tusc.* 1.15, Cicero describes
Epicharmus as intelligent and witty.

sinews and bone. This was a popular quotation in antiquity. In full it runs:
'stay sober and remember not to trust your neighbour: these are the
sinews of good sense' (fr. 218, Kassel and Austin 2001). Polybius cites it
twice (Polyb. 18.40; 31.13), and Cicero quotes it in Greek at *Att.* 1.19.8.
Proverbial expressions were deemed charming when introduced into
correspondence (Demetr. *Eloc.* 230, 235). Thus Quintus softens a censorious
sentiment that could, if poorly handled, strike a reader as reproachful.
Instead, so Quintus hopes, his disarmed reader will think himself sufficiently
worldly to nod in agreement.

¶40 detractors and enemies. Quintus' choice of words here—*obtrectatores*
and *adversarii*—avoids the much harsher expression *inimicus* ('bitter
enemy'), but their reference comes very close nevertheless (Hellegouarc'h
1963, 190f.). Here the men hostile to Cicero are animated by motives
depicted as natural but superficial and therefore potentially surmountable
by the orator.

when speaking against them. It is obvious how a prosecution could incur
enmity (Gruen 1974, 260ff.; Epstein 1987 90ff.; David 1992, 497ff.). Defending
a man's interests in private suits or public cases could do likewise. Plaintiffs

naturally resented any opposition to their material interests, and all speeches for the defence, because they, too, entailed aggression and invective, could offend. Which is why Roman orators ordinarily strove, when it was possible, to treat their aristocratic adversaries with a degree of courtesy (see, e.g., Craig 1981; Gotoff 1986; May 1988, 58ff.). Quintus may also have in mind men who are hostile to Cicero on account of his support of Pompeius: on that dimension of Cicero's campaign, and on enmity in Roman politics, see further **¶14 angry with you...cases you have pleaded.**

obligations of friendship. Although Cicero often adduces friendship as a motive for defending his client's interests (e.g. *Quinct*. 77; *Rosc. Am.* 4, citing Cicero's friendship with Roscius' associates; *Mur*. 5; *Sull*. 26, 48; *Arch*. 13; *Sest*. 4; *Cael*. 9; *Balb*. 1; *Planc*. 3; *Mil*. 100; see David 1992, 195ff.), the act of advocacy did not, in and of itself, register friendship (see **¶2 your fame as an orator;** §III.2; the essays in Powell and Paterson 2004). Which is why the matter of Cicero's accepting or rejecting cases is dealt with at **¶¶44–8,** under the rubric of 'dealing with the people' (**¶41**). Quintus' advice here, however, falls under the heading of 'gaining the support of friends' (**¶16**), and so it is to that aspect of legal representation that he urges Cicero to appeal in justifying himself to detractors. Cicero seeks to be, not their enemy or even a matter of indifference to them, but rather their friend.

friendship with your rivals. Rivalry or even hostility against an individual did not necessarily entail hostility against his friends and associates, and in Rome it is obvious that a man could be on good terms with men who were enemies to one another (Brunt 1988, 371ff.). And so a friend of one of Cicero's competitors need not, for that reason alone, be opposed to Cicero's candidature. In practice, Romans, at least occasionally, cast their two votes for men who were enemies: the election of Caesar and M. Calpurnius Bibulus, who detested one another, to consulships for 59 could only have come about because this was the case. And in 64 many voters cast ballots both for Cicero and Antonius, in some cases even for Cicero and Catilina, despite the forceful competition between them (see §VII.5).

well disposed towards your rivals. This should not have been difficult in case of rivals other than Antonius and Catilina (see **¶7 Publius Galba; ¶7 Lucius Cassius;** §VII.5). But what of Antonius and Catilina in view of the *Brief Handbook*'s vituperation at **¶¶8–12?** One wonders whether Quintus has them in mind here. Furthermore, at **¶52** Quintus advises Cicero to 'see to it that each of your competitors is traduced by a smear fitting his character'. Plainly Quintus relies on his readers' recognizing and accepting the conventional nature of electoral invective (see, further, **¶8 But, you will say...Quite the contrary; ¶54 escape animosity, gossip.**

¶41 **dealing with the people.** The second of Quintus' two divisions in his definition of canvassing (see ¶16 **a campaign for high office**) is the cultivation of 'the goodwill of the people' (*popularis voluntas*; see ¶16 **goodwill of the people**). Here Quintus turns to the correct means for achieving this, which he designates as 'dealing with the people' (*popularis ratio*). This expression routinely refers to public estimation (Cic. *Dom.* 88; *Fam.* 1.2.4) and that is its sense here. *Popularis ratio* also denotes the activities of a *popularis* politician (*Sest.* 101, 114; *Prov.* 39; *Brut.* 103; see ¶5 **champions of popular rights**), but that is clearly not the meaning Quintus has in mind. Although Quintus devotes far more space in the *Brief Handbook* to the topic of gaining friends, even friends from the lower orders, than he does to winning over the larger public, it remains unmistakable that he regards cultivating popular goodwill as equally essential (Morstein-Marx 1998, 263).

This requires. At *Off.* 2.31–8, in a discussion of *gloria* ('fame'; see ¶2 **your fame as an orator**), Cicero lists and discusses the most honourable means of winning popular favour. Both treatments emphasize the importance of a sound reputation, of generosity, of easy accessibility, and of industry, but Cicero's list is longer and incorporates abstract issues, like wisdom and justice, which Quintus omits here. Quintus reduces winning over the general public to just six elements: recognizing people by name (*nomenclatio*), an ingratiating manner (*blanditia*), constant effort (*adsiduitas*), generosity (*benignitas*), publicity (*rumor*), and civic pageantry (*species in re publica*). Some of the practices adduced by Quintus here are attributed by Plutarch to M. Crassus (cos. I 70) in his explanation of that man's popularity and influence: he was conspicuous for making himself constantly accessible, he routinely lent money without interest, he held private banquets at which even members of the public were present, and in his encounters with the masses he was easy-going and familiar (Plut. *Crass.* 3.1–3).

civic pageantry. The manuscripts read *spem in re publica* ('political promise'). Watt, like many editors, prefers Lambinus' emendation to *speciem in republica* ('civic pageantry'), a correction based on Quintus' treatment of that topic at ¶52, where it is signalled as the final item (*postremo*) in his discussion of dealing with the people. The reading of the manuscripts, however, is preferred by, i.a., Buecheler 1869, Tyrrell and Purser 1904, Constans 1940, Duplá et al.1990, and Broderson 2013. Shackleton Bailey 2002 prints <*speciem*> *et spem in re publica*, thereby collecting Quintus' later reference to civic pageantry at ¶52 as well as his emphasis on *spes rei publicae bona de te* ('the republic reposes high hopes in you') at ¶53; the translation of Shackleton Bailey's text reads: 'This requires recognizing people by name, an ingratiating manner, constant effort, generosity, publicity, civic pageantry, and political promise.' Shackleton Bailey's suggestion, although inviting, appears to trip over Quintus' *postremo* ('finally') at ¶52. It is probably better to regard Quintus' discussion of political promise (*spes rei publicae bona*) as a continuation of his commentary on civic pageantry and as part of his summing up of the discussion of dealing with the people (see ¶53).

¶42 recognize people by name. At ¶41, Quintus designates this skill as *nomenclatio* and its importance, in the context of winning friends, is discussed at ¶28 (see, further, **¶28 address them by name**). When canvassing, candidates were obliged to take the initiative in approaching citizens of every class (see §III.4), and it is obvious how an ordinary Roman would be delighted at being addressed by name. In accomplishing this feat, however, candidates often employed the services of an assistant (*nomenclator*; see **¶28 address them by name**; §III.5), and it was impossible for anyone to know the names of the bulk of Roman voters. Which is why Quintus here emphasizes the credit a candidate receives from making an effort, during his daily rounds (see §III.5), at improving his familiarity with the names of the citizens he meets: doing so signalled a welcome interest in winning popular goodwill.

what you lack by nature. Quintus now turns, very gradually, to the topic of 'an ingratiating manner' (*blanditia*). Ingratiation (*blanditiae*) had a place in the intimate communications of children with their parents (e.g. Lucr. 5.1018) and of lovers (e.g. Tib. 1.1.72; Prop. 1.16.16). In other settings, however, *blanditia* was unattractive and certainly un-senatorial (Quintus describes it below as 'base and sordid'). For the Romans, *blanditia* was nearly synonymous with flattery (Cic. *Amic.* 91; *Clu.* 36; *Att.* 12.3.1; 13.5c; see Arist. *Eth. Nic.* 1127a7–10) and the fawning characteristic of a parasite (Cic. *Amic.* 93; see Damon 1997, 80ff., 177ff.; and see below **expression and looks and conversation must be adapted**). It could even be linked with the dangerous wooing of the masses associated with demagoguery (Cic. *Amic.* 95–6; see Morstein-Marx 2004, 244ff.). Why should Quintus introduce so unwelcome a concept here? There were, after all, other means of expressing the idea that an aristocrat should behave in a pleasing manner in dealing with members of the lower orders (see, e.g., Cic. *Off.* 2.32, on *mansuetudo* ('gentleness') and *facilitas* ('an accommodating nature'; see **¶16 an accommodating and agreeable nature**); and see below **affability**). It is because an aggressively ingratiating manner was deemed essential to canvassing (Cic. *De or.* 1.112, '[canvassing] must be done very ingratiatingly [*blandius*]'; *Mur.* 44; *Planc.* 10; and see below **when canvassing**). Instead of occluding it altogether or resorting to euphemism, however, Quintus addresses the matter directly. In doing so, he concedes both its necessity and its tastelessness—and he endeavours to offer the practice at least some degree of moral cover (see below **someone becomes friendlier to you**).

Cicero must be urged to be ingratiating because this un-senatorial behaviour is unnatural for him. But it was conceded even in philosophical contexts that, for the sake of the republic, certain actions, even shameful ones, might be necessary (e.g. Cic. *Inv. rhet.* 2.176; *Off.* 1.159; 3.92–5; see Woolf 2007, 339), and excessive philosophical rigour in the matter of canvassing was prey to public censure (Cic. *Mur.* 60–6, 75–7; Val. Max. 7.5.1; Plut. *Cat. min.* 50.2). Every candidate found himself in this situation— *blanditia* was one of the indignities of canvassing that aristocrats loathed (see above; and §III.4)—and so this insistence on Quintus' part contributes to his depiction of Cicero as an ideal candidate who operates along suitably conventional aristocratic lines (see ¶2 **new man**; §III.4; §IV.5). Which is not to say Quintus is attempting to justify Cicero's behaviour as a candidate but rather that he seeks to depict Cicero as the right kind of candidate, one who resists the social and even moral compromises entailed by canvassing but at the same time is responsible enough to make them in order to win office under the inescapable circumstances of popular elections (see, further, ¶45 **The next lesson**; ¶46 **a Platonist like yourself**; Nardo 1970, 101ff.; Bruggisser 1984, 121ff.; Tatum 2007, 122ff.).

simulate. It is possible that this sentence was followed by: 'Although the strength of nature is indeed powerful, still, in an undertaking lasting but a few months, it seems clear that pretence is able to defeat nature' (¶1) (see, further, ¶1 **Although...nature...pretence is able to defeat nature**).

affability. This is *comitas*, the dignified accessibility characteristic of an aristocrat, who generously allows himself to be approached by others. *Comitas* was an asset in elections (Plin. *NH* 35.23). But *comitas* alone, Quintus insists, is inadequate (see above **what you lack by nature**). On *comitas*, see further Heuer 1941; Hellegouarc'h 1963, 215ff.; Deniaux 1993, 264f.; Hall 1996, 103f.

when canvassing. Ingratiation is permissible *only* when canvassing. The extraordinary circumstances of canvassing for office require and legitimize actions that would normally be deemed exceptionable (Cic. *De or.* 1.112; §III.4; Tatum 2007), a point emphasized more than once in the *Brief Handbook* (see ¶12 **required by your present situation**; ¶16 **the definition of the word 'friend'**; ¶25 **you can honourably do**). Still, Quintus will go on to depict Cicero's brand of ingratiation as something creditable.

through flattery. See above **what you lack by nature** for ingratiation's association with flattery.

someone becomes friendlier to you. Flattery, or ingratiation, is wrong because it is disgraceful and harmful (see above **what you lack by nature**), not least in that it undermines any possibility for true friendship (Cic. *Amic.* 91). Quintus can do nothing about the embarrassing aspects of ingratiation, but here he suggests that, at least when it is Cicero who is behaving in an ingratiating manner, or presumably any other candidate made of the right stuff, it is not harmful. Although a flatterer is a dishonest and unstable exploiter of others (e.g. Cic. *Amic.* 92), it is obvious, in the world of the *Brief Handbook*, that Cicero's is a consistent character (see ¶54 **continue to be one and the same man even as he adapts himself**) and that his friendship is an undeniably good thing (a central theme of ¶¶16–40). If, then, ingratiation results in friendship, or something approaching friendship, with Cicero, the outcome must be judged a positive one for all concerned. This is thin stuff, to be sure, but it is clear that in this section Quintus seeks to lend at least some moral shine to the ingratiation that no candidate can escape. His purpose is not to justify Cicero's canvassing to others but instead to reassure the political class that a behaviour which they all must share is not a wholly objectionable one.

expression and looks and conversation must be adapted. Accommodating one's manner in order to please another was characteristic of a parasite (e.g. Ter. *Eun.* 252–54; Cic. *Amic.* 93–4; Iuv. 3.100–8; see Damon 1997, 80ff.) or a slave (e.g. Plaut. *Amph.* 958–61). Certainly an opportunist (Cic. *Q. Fr.* 1.1.15). For an aristocrat, such behaviour was objectionable; see Cic. *Off.* 2.43: 'For men who suppose they can win unshakable glory by pretence and an empty show—by dissembling both in what they say and how they look—they are very much mistaken.' The candidate must accommodate 'everyone he meets'. Again, the reality of cultivating the masses involves social humiliation for an aristocratic candidate (see above; and §III.4. On the importance of one's facial expression in dealing with the people, see ¶44 **the look on your face.**

¶43 constant effort. Quintus' word here is *adsiduitas*, part of the network of exhortations to hard work that characterizes the *Brief Handbook* (see ¶1 **assiduousness**). Constant and visible exertions on behalf of others was a recognized means of winning popularity (e.g. Cic. *Off.* 2.36), and Quintus has already dismissed some of Cicero's rivals on account of their lack of industry (¶7 **because they lack vigour**).

being present in Rome. The city is where canvassing takes place during its final phase (see §III.5), and the city is where, according to Cicero, a political figure was likeliest to win public esteem (Cic. *Planc.* 13, 64–7 (employing the term *adsiduitas*); *Ad Brut.* 1.5.3; *Fam.* 2.12.2). At *Mur.* 42, however, Cicero adduces some of the advantages accruing to a candidate who has devoted himself to provincial service. At the time of an election, however, Rome was truly central: unless granted an exemption by the senate or the people, a candidate was required to be in Rome (Plut. *Mar.* 12; see Linderski 1995, 91ff.; see also §II.2). Quintus has already attacked Antonius for leaving Rome instead of canvassing (¶8 sleazy foreign mission), and here he underlines Cicero's constant canvassing of the people.

¶44 Generosity. Quintus here selects the word *benignitas*, which is more or less synonymous with *liberalitas* in Roman discussions of generosity (e.g. Cic. *Mur.* 77; *Off.* 1.20, 42–60; 2.52; see ¶50 *benignum ac liberalem* ('generous and munificent'); see Hellegouarc'h 1963, 217ff.). The philosophical view insisted that generosity be indifferent to advancing one's self-interest (e.g. Cic. *Amic.* 30–1; *Off.* 3.118; Sen. *Ben.* 1.1.3; 1.2.3; 2.33.3; 3.15.1–4; 4.3.3; Plin. *Ep.* 9.30), but in practice the acquisition of gratitude by way of generosity was one of the foundations of aristocratic power in Rome and was vital to success in elections (Cic. *Mur.* 77; *Off.* 2.21–6; 2.29–32; 2.52–64; see ¶4, with commentary). Generosity was expected of the rich in Rome and was absolutely required of any candidate for office (e.g. Polyb. 10.5.6; Cic. *Mur.* 73; see Yakobson 1999, 26ff.; Feig Vishnia 2012, 137ff.; see §II.2–3; §II.6; §II.12; ¶55 bribery). On generosity in Roman society, see Manning 1985; Griffin 2013, esp. 46ff.; Coffee 2016.

covers a wide field. At *Off.* 2.52–68, Cicero surveys and assesses various forms of aristocratic generosity, including making gifts of money and supplying other financial assistance (Cic. *Off.* 2.52; 2.56); providing public banquets (*Off.* 2.55; 2.58), gifts of meat (*Off.* 2.55), games and shows, including aedilician games (*Off.* 2.55; 2.57–8), gifts of grain (*Off.* 2.58); sponsoring public building (*Off.* 2.60); exhibiting generous behaviour in one's personal business affairs (*Off.* 2.64); showing hospitality (*Off.* 2.64); supplying personal services to others, especially advocacy in the courts (*Off.* 2.65–6) but also legal advice, as well as helping someone to find legal advice, acting as a character witness, and supporting someone who is canvassing for an office (*Off.* 2.66). Quintus, although he refers in passing to the advantage of enjoying a reputation for personal generosity, limits his discussion to two traditional expressions of generosity that were possible during the final weeks of a political campaign: offering public banquets and agreeing to act as an advocate.

one's private affairs. In his discussion of generosity in one's private dealings (Cic. *Off.* 2.64), Cicero cites liberality in enforcing one's property rights, avoiding litigation even when it is not unreasonable to press one's claim, and hospitality. He could have added the provision of financial succour for friends in need (e.g. Cic. *Att.* 3.22.1; 4.2.7; *Rab. Post.* 43). And simple gifts. Quintus does not elaborate because here he is concerned mainly with the effect of one's private generosity on his reputation with the masses.

praised by your friends. On the importance of a candidate's reputation, including aspects of his private life, see ¶17 **gossip** and ¶50 below.

banquets. Candidates were expected to supply public banquets for their fellow tribesmen, generosity that was especially important in winning the gratitude of the poor (Cic. *Mur.* 72–3; *Off.* 2.55; Liv. 23.4.2; Plin. *NH* 10.10; Tac. *Ann.* 3.55; see Deniaux 1987; Linderski 2007, 326ff.; Schnurbusch 2011, 240ff.; Rosillo López 2017, 72; see §III.6; ¶55 **bribery**). If imperial evidence is any guide to republican practices, the costs could be significant (see Duncan-Jones 1982, 138ff.). A cheap banquet could ruin a man's prospects (Cic. *Mur.* 75). Private banquets also had potential political significance: voters rejected an unknown candidate for the praetorship, it was alleged, because he served stork at a private banquet (Porphory ad Hor. *Serm.* 2.2.50; see Courtney 1993, 472f.). Restrictions were imposed on the scale of candidates' banquets by a *lex Orchia* of 182 (Macr. 3.17.2–3; see *MRR* 1.382); by way of comparison, see the restrictions on candidates' expenses, including banquets, stipulated by the *lex Coloniae Genetivae* (a Caesarian municipal charter drafted in 44) in section 132 (*RS* 416f. = *CIL* 2.5439).

for all and sundry and for individual tribes. A candidate for office could offer banquets only to members of his own tribe. His friends, however, provided they were not candidates themselves, were unrestricted, and it was expected that friends would aid one's candidature by offering banquets. But they had to do so at their own and not the candidate's expense, a distinction that was difficult for the general public to discern or for peers to police (see ¶55 **bribery**). Quintus draws attention to the correct approach to banqueting: they should be supplied 'by you and by your friends'. The presumption is that Cicero's friends act on his behalf out of gratitude (see, e.g., ¶31 **candidates on your behalf**; §II.3; §II.10). A *lex Antia* of 68 (Gell. *NA* 2.24.13; Macrob. *Sat.* 3.17.13; see *MRR* 2.139), among other provisions, regulated the attendance at banquets by candidates: the purpose, it has sensibly been proposed, was to prevent their taking undue credit for the generosity of surrogate hosts (Lintott 1990, 5f.; Ferrary 2002, 163f.). According to Macrobius, the law was routinely flouted.

especially through services to others. Cicero (*Off.* 2.52–3) insists that generosity in the form of services is superior to giving gifts to others, because services are manifestations of a man's personal excellence (*virtus*) and hard work (*industria*), on which qualities see ¶1 **assiduousness.**

Of course, Cicero was better equipped to supply his services than he was to dispense large quantities of money (note Cicero's comment at *Off.* 2.59; on Cicero's wealth, see Shatzman 1975, 403ff.). Doubtless reflecting this view and this reality, Quintus' focus, in his treatment of generosity, is on providing services to others, specifically on Cicero's capacity to take on legal cases for members of the public who require his aid. Cicero, at least according to Cicero, was constitutionally incapable of refusing requests for aid (*Planc.* 84).

means of approaching you. At *Att.* 6.2.5, Cicero recalls how hard he worked as a candidate to make himself accessible to others. Accessibility— and a gentle nature in dealing with others—were, unsurprisingly, key factors in an aristocrat's personal popularity and were essential for success in elections (e.g. Cic. *Off.* 2.32; for more extensive discussions of aristo- cratic accessibility in Rome, see ¶16 **an accommodating and agreeable nature**; ¶35 **morning greeters**; ¶42 **affability**; §II.4).

the entrance to your house. See ¶35 **morning greeters**.

the look on your face. Here Quintus does not advise Cicero to adjust his looks solely in order to please others, as he does above in ¶42, where Cicero's ingratiation must entail unpleasant social inversions (see ¶42 **expression and looks and conversation must be adapted**). It is taken for granted in this section that Cicero truly wants to be generous. Here he is warned against diminishing the effectiveness of his generosity by failing to exhibit his enthusiasm. That an aristocrat should convey his goodwill by way of his expression remained a topical piece of advice even during the empire (e.g. Sen. *Ben.* 2.2.2; see Arist. *Eth. Nic.* 4.1.1120a26–7), and Romans were well aware how easily an aristocrat could spoil his kindly gestures by way of sour looks (Sen. *Ben.* 1.1.5; 2.3.1; cf. Cic. *Amic.* 66; Plin. *Ep.* 4.3.2).

¶45 The next lesson. This lesson occupies Quintus' attention through ¶48, an expansion that renders it the most conspicuous aspect of dealing with the people in the *Brief Handbook*. Here Quintus, in a highly qualified way (see below), encourages Cicero to agree to offer his services to the public whether or not he believes he can, in the end, provide the service he has promised. This is an obvious moral compromise, which Quintus justifies by way of reference to the special circumstances of a political campaign (¶¶45, 46), by suggesting that members of the public would rather be lied to than refused on the spot (¶46), by adducing a distinguished historical exemplar of this practice (¶47), by observing that it is rarely the case in practice that anyone who receives a questionable promise is actually harmed or angered by that questionable promise (¶48), and by a clumsy attempt at attenuating the immorality of the action by insisting that Cicero, in attempting to gratify all comers, never violate his honour or duty (¶¶45, 47). Furthermore, Quintus emphatically distinguishes this method of dealing with the masses from his previous advice on sustaining the support of friends (¶49). Quintus, then, devotes a good deal of effort towards justifying this piece of advice. It is possible to view this section of the *Brief Handbook* as a specimen of the work's cynicism (e.g. Alexander 2009; see §V.4). It is probably better, however, to view Quintus' exertions here as another attempt to give a degree of social and moral cover to a recognized and indispensable facet of electioneering that aristocrats found embarrassing and disturbing (see ¶12 **required by your present situation**; ¶42 **what you lack by nature**; §III.4; see Nardo 1970, 101ff.; Tatum 2007, esp. 127ff.). Again, the purpose is not to justify Cicero's practices or Quintus' advice, but to remind readers how much they share in every proper aristocrat's discomfort with the obligatory compromises entailed by canvassing for office.

to your situation. Again Quintus underlines how necessary it is for Cicero to react to his specific situation (*tempus*) as a candidate for office, even if his predicament as an office seeker is at odds with the finer qualities of his nature (see, further, ¶12 **required by your present situation**; ¶42 **what you lack by nature**; previous note).

do *not* say no. We get a glimpse of the correct decorum for refusing to take on a case at Cic. *Att.* 8.4.2: there we learn that a straightforward refusal is offensive, even in the case of humble petitioners; instead, when one cannot actually take on a case, the proper procedure is to accept it but only provisionally, adding 'if I can' (*si potero*) or 'if I'm not hindered by a case I have already accepted' (*si ante suscepta causa non impediar*), transparent subterfuges that everyone was expected to respect; after all, it was recognized that, although a man may be willing to be helpful, doing so may well lie beyond his resources (Cic. *Off.* 2.32). In other words, no sophisticated Roman would ordinarily give a petitioner an unvarnished *no*, and once again Quintus' advice is conventional (see Hall 2009, 111f.). Care was necessary during these exchanges because refusing to take a case could be viewed as evidence of arrogance or cruelty (Cic. *Mur.* 10). This was especially true for a candidate, who was expected to make any promise he was asked to give, as Cicero observes in a public oration (Cic. *Planc.* 16). Still, below, Quintus will go on to address the moral difficulty that lies behind these Roman manners.

But Quintus may not have put it just this way. A hiatus in our text makes it impossible to know his precise wording, although his general sense is clear enough from the arguments of ¶¶46–8. Watt's emendation (<*neges aut etiam non> neges*), or something very similar to it, is generally accepted. But Buecheler 1869, 55, proposed 'you must manage to be agreeable in saying no or you must be very insincere in making promises [*aut adeo simultate promittas*]', a less neat but more truly stark choice for Cicero to make. A restoration along the lines of Buecheler's must remain a possibility.

without doing damage to our honour. Quintus makes it clear that Cicero will not under any circumstances, even when he is a candidate for office, take a case that is dishonourable.

declined graciously. At least once during his campaign, Cicero found himself in just this situation and he explained himself just as Quintus recommends here (Cic. *Att.* 1.1.3–4). It did not go well: see below **depart as your enemies.**

¶46 a Platonist like yourself. Cicero frequently identifies himself as an adherent of Academic scepticism and so, in that sense, a Platonist (e.g. *Acad. Pr.* 10–13; *Luc.* 99; *Nat. D.* 1.10–13; *Div.* 2.150; *Off.* 2.7–8; cf. Plut. *Cic.* 4.3); on Cicero's discussions of Plato, see DeGraff 1940. The range and complexity of Cicero's philosophical references and writings have combined to make the question of his philosophical allegiance a complicated one (see Griffin and Barnes 1989; Powell 1995a). Here Quintus emphasizes his brother's famous erudition. At the same time, because he expects his readers to identify with Cicero's moral qualms, he allows them a share in the same brand of erudition, if they want it (Nardo 1970, 63). Is there more to unpack from Quintus' expression here? After all, misleading the masses for the sake of sound government (viz. the election of Cicero as consul) could hardly, in principle, offend a Platonist in view of the centrality of the 'noble lie' in Plato's *Republic* (*Rep.* 3.414b–415d). See, also, Prost 2017, 80ff.

the alternative option. That is, Cicero's not refusing a case even when it is unlikely or impossible that he will be able to take it up.

Others…depart as your enemies. The possibility of giving offence, even when an orator had creditable reasons for rejecting a request, was very real (Cic. *Off.* 2.68). Two illustrations. (i) In 52, Cicero agreed to represent Phamea, a wealthy and influential figure from Sardinia; when, however, the day was set for hearing Phamea's case, it conflicted with Cicero's existing obligation to be present at the trial of his friend P. Sestius (pr. 54). When Cicero drew Phamea's attention to this, the man was furious—and Phamea and his relations were still upset with Cicero as late as 45, when their continued resentment posed Cicero worrisome social difficulties (Cic. *Att.* 13.49; *Fam.* 7.24.2). (ii) When canvassing for the consulship,

Cicero was asked by Atticus' uncle to appear as a witness in his suit against a certain Caninius Satyrus; Cicero had to decline because Satyrus was actively supporting his candidature and because he was a close connection of L. Domitius Ahenobarbus (cos. 54), Cicero's friend and chief noble supporter (see ¶3 **young men**; §VII *passim*). Atticus' uncle took it badly and attempted to enlist Atticus in acquiring Cicero's services, all of which put Cicero in an awkward bind (Cic. *Att.* 1.1.3–4). These examples suffice to demonstrate the complex network of personal connections involved in nearly every request for his services that Cicero received, and the abundant opportunities for putting someone's nose out of joint.

it would have been better had you lied to them. Put this way, Quintus appears to suggest that members of the public, if given the choice, would prefer being lied to rather than refused. The evidence of Cicero cited above (see ¶45 **do *not* say no**) perhaps confirms this claim in its basic terms, but Quintus is not here discussing the difference between a yes-that-everyone-knows-is-a-no and a straightforward refusal: he is urging Cicero to give his petitioners the impression that he will indeed take their case, and he later concedes that disappointed petitioners will be angry over Cicero's behaviour (¶¶47–8).

¶47 Gaius Cotta. C. Aurelius Cotta, described by Sallust as 'from the very centre of the ruling nobility' (*ex factione media*: Sall. *Hist.* 34.8 (McGushin)), was consul in 75 (the year of Cicero's quaestorship). As consul, he sponsored legislation restoring to the tribunes their right, removed by Sulla, to stand for higher offices. The senate awarded him a triumph for his achievements while governor of Cisalpine Gaul, but he died, in late 74 or early 73, before he could celebrate it. Cotta, an orator and intellectual, was much admired by Cicero (see Blom 2010, 227, 256, 260, 268). He is an interlocutor in *De oratore*, his speeches are admired in the *Brutus* (Cic. *Brut.* 305, 317), and in *De natura deorum* it is Cotta who represent the views of the Academy. Cotta, then, was remembered as an orator and a Platonist, like Cicero in the *Brief Handbook*. (See *MRR* 2.96,103, 111, 466; 3.31.)

master in the art of canvassing. In appealing to the precedent of Cotta, Quintus argues, in traditional Roman fashion, by way of *exempla*, that is, by way of examples from the Romans' past, in this instance the recent past. The habits of great men were deemed good habits, and looking to these men as models for imitation (*exempla maiorum*) was considered the best means of preserving traditional Roman virtues (*mos maiorum*). Hence the authority of exemplarity in Roman reasoning (see Roller 2004; Blom 2010; Hölkeskamp 2010, 66f.; Roller 2011). For Quintus, the noble Cotta is *in ambitione artifex* and is the *Brief Handbook*'s sole *exemplum* for correct

canvassing. And he was well chosen. In addition to Cotta's stature as a
noble and his success as a politician—and his attraction for Cicero owing
to his oratorical and intellectual qualities (see previous note)—his family
were, between the restoration of the republic by Sulla in 79 and the elections taking place in 64, unexcelled in their acquisition of consulships
(on the Aurelii Cottae, see Badian 1964, 64). In sum, he was the right kind
of winner. And his presence here gives Quintus' advice powerful moral
cover (see, further, Nardo 1970, 102ff.; Tatum 2007, 127f.; Prost 2017, 76ff.).

Or does it? In his *Historiae*, Sallust portrays Cotta as willing, on occasion, to support popular causes (e.g. *Hist.* 2.44 (McGushin)), and, in recognition of his political sharp practice in the *Historiae*, Syme concluded
that Sallust's version of Cotta 'was a master of intrigue' (Syme 1964, 200).
In addition, Cotta's role in restoring the tribunate (see previous note) was also
a popular measure which was against the wishes of the nobility (Asc. 66C).
On this basis, Michael Alexander has argued that, in the *Brief Handbook*,
Cotta is not a positive but a negative *exemplum* introduced in order to
lend irony to the discussion of electoral practices in this section (Alexander
2009, 53ff., 393ff.). This is one part of a larger argument by Alexander that
the *Brief Handbook* is a satire composed during the imperial period (see,
further, §V.4). Alexander, it must be noted, does not ignore Cicero's treatment of Cotta in his rhetorical and philosophical works, but in the end he
discounts Cicero's compliments on the grounds that they are 'lukewarm and
guarded' (Alexander 2009, 56). Readers must decide for themselves how
to view Cicero's treatment of Cotta. Cotta's restoration of the tribunician
rights, it must be observed, did not make him unpopular with the senatorial elite (Lewis 2006, 274, with further bibliography), who subsequently
were willing to award Cotta a triumph (see previous note). On the complexities of popular politics in Rome, see ¶5 **champions of popular rights.**

his duty. By introducing Cotta's respect for his *officium* ('duty'), Quintus
again attempts to signal the fundamentally moral approach to taking
cases adopted by the man; he makes a similar move in advising Cicero
(see ¶45 **The next lesson**). On *officium*, see ¶4 **See to it that…express
their gratitude.**

he explained. Perhaps this advice was actually associated with Cotta's
memory, but it is equally possible that here Quintus is putting words in his
mouth in order to add Cotta's authority to his advice to Cicero.

to fill his house. See ¶35 **morning greeters.**

The worst thing. The word employed is *extremum*, which here is regularly
taken in a temporal sense: e.g. 'the anger of the man to whom you lied
would be the last in the series' (Shackleton Bailey 2002). But Quintus

addresses this very point immediately in the next section (¶48: 'this man's anger... happens later'). It is more likely, then, that *extremum* refers to the worst possible outcome of Cotta's strategy (see *OLD* 662, definition 4), the point being that, whereas scrupulously saying no, early on, will offend many and spoil one's reputation for accessibility and helpfulness, always agreeing to accept a case can at worst result in the anger only of a few isolated individuals (and at a later date). Quintus perhaps quarantines this calculating advice by attributing it to Cotta, but he expects Cicero and all his readers to accept it as a normal and acceptable practice.

¶48 happens later. Presumably, insofar as Cicero's interests are concerned, after elections have taken place.

how much he would like to keep his promise. Once more Quintus tries to depict his advice as fundamentally decent: the circumstance in which Cicero, even Cicero the candidate, would let someone down, he suggests here, would be the kind of circumstance in which he could not represent someone owing to prior and respectable commitments (see ¶45: 'anything that we cannot do without doing damage to our honour or our interests').

¶49 departed from my own system of classification. See ¶16: 'Now, a campaign for high office divides itself into assiduousness of two types, one directed at gaining the support of friends, the other at gaining the good-will of the people'. Little in the previous sections, however, suggests that Quintus has violated this organizational principle: only his introduction of a candidate's need to have his house filled by morning greeters (¶47: 'to fill his house'), a need also cited in this section ('so that your house may be filled before dawn'), which is a matter Quintus discussed in his treatment of gaining the support of friends (see ¶35 **morning greeters**). Hence his concession that the two divisions 'are not entirely unrelated'.

But the essential reason Quintus introduces his system of classification here is to punctuate the point that, when he administers advice that encourages Cicero to compromise himself by making promises he may not be able to keep, he is not talking about Cicero's relations with his peers but instead is concentrating solely on how Cicero can 'win over the masses'. Elite readers are expected to be sympathetic with Cicero's predicament as a candidate and with Quintus' advice. Members of the elite certainly expected a political figure to be capable of winning over the masses: doing so was crucial to his public authority (see §II.1; §III.4–5; ¶5 **champions of popular rights**; ¶¶34–8; and the description of the ideal candidate at ¶53).

¶50 publicity. Quintus now turns to *rumor*, which is publicity for good or for ill, though here Quintus has in mind Cicero's industry in spreading abroad his good reputation. This was sensible advice, inasmuch as damaging publicity was a recurring feature of Roman society, especially for political figures (see, e.g. *Rhet. Her.* 2.12; see Pina Polo 2010; §III.6; ¶17 **gossip**, with further bibliography on the influence of rumour).

slavishly devoted. On the employment of servile language in describing canvassing, see §III.1; §III.4.

everything discussed so far. Instead of offering an abstract discussion focused on publicity (*rumor*), Quintus makes the point that every aspect of Cicero's campaign has been an exercise in winning the right kind of publicity. Consequently, this section becomes a summing up of the contents of much of the *Brief Handbook*, and through its references it shatters the distinction between dealing with friends and dealing with the public that Quintus establishes at ¶16 and emphasizes in ¶49:

'your reputation for eloquence': see ¶2 **your fame as an orator.**

'the devotion of the publicans and the equestrian order': see ¶3 **publicans;** ¶3 **the equestrian order;** ¶33 **centuries of the knights.**

'the goodwill of the nobles': see ¶4 **the goodwill of the nobles.**

'attendance by constant crowds of young men': see ¶3 **young men;** ¶6 **young nobles;** ¶33 **the best of our youth.**

'those whom you have defended in court': see ¶19 *passim*; ¶38 **at no cost to themselves.**

'multitudes from the municipalities': see ¶3 **municipalities that are devoted exclusively to you;** ¶24 **men who are influential in their neighbourhoods and municipalities;** ¶30 **municipality, colony, prefecture.**

'you are familiar with the public': see, e.g., ¶17 *passim*; ¶28 **address them by name;** ¶42 **recognize people by name.**

'you canvass constantly and assiduously': see, e.g., ¶4 **forceful reminders and solicitations;** ¶5 **solicited assiduously.**

'you are generous and munificent': see the discussion at ¶¶44–8

'your house is filled long before dawn': see ¶35 **morning greeters.**

'you are attended by a crowd drawn from every sort': see ¶3 **the number and variety of your friends;** ¶29 **many freedmen;** ¶30 **all the clubs, the boroughs, and the neighbourhoods;** ¶34 **attendance;** ¶35 **common folk;** ¶37 **a great crowd at all times.**

'you satisfy all in what you say, many in what you actually do': see ¶45 **The next lesson;** ¶¶45–8 *passim*.

'industry, skill, and assiduousness': see ¶1 **assiduousness;** ¶43 **constant effort.**

One might expect the work to conclude here, but it does not. This structural punctuation serves instead to emphasize the coda that follows, which draws the reader's attention to Cicero's relationship with Pompeius, an aspect of Cicero's efforts at publicity that is unmistakably singled out (¶51).

¶51 won over the urban masses. Here Quintus reprises matters he has already discussed at ¶5, although there he is at pains to stress that Cicero is not a demagogue but instead a politician who has supported popular issues in order to win Pompeius as a friend. Here, however, he asserts that Cicero has won over the public owing to his support of Pompeius. The two claims are not mutually exclusive: a collateral advantage of Pompeius' friendship is popularity with the public, and this popularity should not be construed as dangerous (see below **the goodwill of the distinguished classes**). See, further, **¶5 champions of popular rights; ¶5 any speech that appeared to support popular rights.**

men who dominate public meetings. A *contio* ('public meeting') was an assembly called by a magistrate or priest who possessed the legal authority to do so (*ius contionandi*). This assembly was addressed by the man who summoned it or by anyone he invited to speak. Anyone, even a non-citizen, was permitted to attend, and, although the crowd present was free to cheer, jeer, or walk away, no decisions were taken at a *contio* (and therefore those in attendance were not organized by tribe or century). The *contio* was a crucial medium for political communication in republican Rome and an important element in Rome's political theatre. The audience at any *contio* was relatively small, but was addressed by speakers and construed by politicians favourable to its proceedings as if it were the embodiment of the Roman people (e.g. Cic. *Verr.* 1.45; *Leg. Man.* 60; *Leg. agr.* 2.45; *Red. pop.* 6;. *Phil.* 4.15). Anyone who objected to the proceedings of a *contio*, however, dismissed its audience as infiltrated by foreigners or merely a sampling of the dregs of society (e.g. Cic. *Verr.* 2.1.151; *Sest.* 126; *Flacc.* 17, 66–7, 96–7). And it is clear that, with sufficient notice, the crowd at a *contio* could be stacked with adherents or opponents of a speaker. Quintus' language here avoids judgmental terms. But who were the men likely to populate a *contio*? The standard view is that most were denizens of the locality at which a *contio* was held (*contiones* were typically held in the forum), and therefore were largely members of the lower classes. Mouritsen, however, has argued that the audience at a *contio* was composed mostly of members of the prosperous classes (Mouritsen 2001, 38ff.), which is unlikely in light of the rhetoric of the *contio*, to the degree we can recover it, and Cicero's neutral assessments of the public at public assemblies (e.g. *Amic.* 95; *Brut.* 223; *Q. Fr.* 2.3.4). Still, audiences at *contiones* will almost certainly have varied from meeting to meeting, inasmuch as only different men on different days will have had motivation enough to prompt them to take the trouble to leave their work or even their leisure to listen to news or to a political harangue. On the operations and importance of the *contio*, see Pina Polo 1996; Millar 1998; Mouritsen 2001, 38ff.; Morstein-Marx 2004; the essays in Steel and Blom 2013.

you have glorified Pompeius. That is, in his speech *Pro lege Manilia* (*On the Manilian Law*), delivered in early 66, Cicero's first political speech to the Roman people (see §VII.3; see also ¶5 **Gnaeus Pompeius**).

taken up the case of Manilius. C. Manilius (tr. pl. 66) carried a law distributing Roman freedmen throughout all the tribes, but this measure was subsequently annulled by the senate; he then proposed a measure that put Pompeius in command of the Romans' war against Mithridates, a bill that Cicero publicly supported (*MRR* 2.153; 3.134). Unpopular with the senatorial elite, he was prosecuted when he laid down his tribunate, first for extortion (*repetundae*) and finally for treason (*maiestas*), on which charge he was ultimately condemned (Alexander 1990, 103, 105). Cicero at the very least offered to defend Manilius and certainly published a speech in support of the man—all actions taken on behalf of Pompeius. For a fuller discussion, with detailed references, see §VII.3.

defended Cornelius. On C. Cornelius (tr. pl. 67) and Cicero's defence of the man, see the detailed discussion at §VII.4; ¶19 **Gaius Cornelius**; see, also, ¶5 **champion of popular rights**; ¶5 **any speech that appeared to support popular rights**.

the goodwill of the distinguished classes. Popularity was essential to political authority and consequently even members of the elite sought as their leaders men who could command public respect and deference. Indeed, they could not sensibly support a candidate who was incompetent in his dealings with the masses. At the same time, they could not tolerate a demagogue. It is this brand of popularity that Quintus has in mind when he refers to 'that popularity which to this day no one has ever enjoyed if he lacked the goodwill of the distinguished classes'. See the detailed discussion of the importance of sound popularity in winning elite support at §III.5. A different perspective, however, is offered by Prost 2017, 36f. He emends the manuscripts' *nemo quin* to *nemo qui*, in which case the relevent section of this passage must be translated 'that popularity which no one has ever enjoyed who also possessed the goodwill of the distinguished classes'. In Prost's view, then, Quintus is here claiming for Cicero an unprecedentedly comprehensive popularity. But there is no obvious historical or philological reason to alter the text here.

Pompeius' goodwill towards you. Emphasized by its appearance in the immediate aftermath of the summary of the *Brief Handbook* offered at

¶50, and it is clear how Cicero's relationship with Pompeius is to the fore throughout the *Brief Handbook* (see ¶5 **Gnaeus Pompeius**; ¶14 **increasing the glory of Gnaeus Pompeius**). Notwithstanding Quintus' claim here that Pompeius is an ardent supporter of Cicero, Cicero, when he was a candidate, had his doubts (Cic. *Att.* 1.1.2; 1.2.2).

¶52 **full of pageantry.** The final item in Quintus' account of dealing with the people is pageantry (*pompa*). Rome was a culture marked by public spectacle and ritual, in which profound impressions were made on the populace through the theatricality of political performances (see, further, the discussion at §III.5). His principal reference here is to the daily canvassing rituals covered by Quintus at ¶34–8 (under the heading of gaining the support of friends): *salutatio* (the morning greeting), *deductio* (the parade from the candidate's house to the forum), and *prensatio* (gladhanding while circulating through the forum); see the commentary on ¶¶34–8 and the discussion of canvassing rituals at §III.5.

traduced by a smear. Quintus associates political invective with the pageantry of canvassing: negative campaigning is a part of the show expected by the public. On political invective and its conventional quality, see ¶8 **But, you will say ... Quite the contrary**; ¶54 **escape animosity, gossip.**

bribery. Quintus uses the word *largitio*, a loose and non-technical synonym for illegal electoral bribery (*ambitus*), a topic he will discuss at ¶¶55–7, again employing the term *largitio* (see esp. ¶55 **bribery**). Quintus has already smeared Cicero's principal rivals with accusations of wickedness and lust (see ¶¶8–10). Here he anticipates the theme of the third and final division of the *Brief Handbook*, where Quintus imputes this kind of illicit electioneering to Cicero's rivals. This smear was an important element in Cicero's campaign strategy (see §VII.5).

¶53 **the republic reposes high hopes in you.** Quintus' formulation here, *spes rei publicae*, routinely refers to the hope for good government and concern for the future well-being of the republic (e.g. Cic. *Leg. Man.* 62; *Sest.* 93; *Att.* 1.13.2; 8.3.2; *Fam.* 10.1.1; 10.8.1; 12.9.2).

avoid matters of state. It was not out of the question to introduce matters of policy during a political campaign, but it was not a common feature of canvassing (see §III.11).

let these be your aims. What follows is Quintus' description of the ideal candidate. He must be a figure who is deemed to be responsive to the concerns of the whole of the Roman people, who are here viewed in explicitly hierarchical terms (viz. the senate, the prosperous, the masses). During Roman elections, it is clear, the general public were affected by the views of the elite (see §III.2), and in any case no one could be elected to a consulship without the support of wealthy voters (see §II.3); at the same time, the prosperous classes could not prefer a candidate who was unattractive to the masses (see §III.5; ¶51 **the goodwill of the distinguished classes**). The concord embodied in Quintus' ideal candidate represents the objective of good government in Rome.

a guardian of its authority. The authority of the senate (*senatus auctoritas*) was the basis of its political primacy in Rome and a fundamental principle of the Romans' constitutional thinking (see, e.g., Bonnefond-Coudry 1989, 11ff.; Lintott 1999a, 86ff., 196ff.; see, further, §III.1). On the Roman concept of *auctoritas*, see ¶55 **authority**. Cicero was also a defender of the *auctoritas* of the equestrians (see ¶33 **the authority of their order**).

tranquillity and stability. See Cicero's claim at *Leg. agr.* 1.23: 'nothing is so popular as peace [*pax*], as social harmony [*concordia*], as tranquillity [*otium*]'.

at least. Quintus once again qualifies the extent of Cicero's enthusiasm for popular rights; see ¶5 **champions of popular rights**.

favourably disposed to their entitlements. A conspicious, if legendary, instance of failure in this regard is Coriolanus, who, despite his acknowledged virtues, lost the consulship because the public believed he was hostile to their interests (Dion. Hal. *Ant. Rom.* 7.2.1–2; Plut. *Cor.* 15.4).

¶54 So much, then. Quintus arrives at the third division in his tripartite organization of the *Brief Handbook*, corresponding to the third of Cicero's daily self-reminders: 'This is Rome' (¶2).

morning lessons … when going down to the forum. Quintus refers to his advice at ¶2: 'Almost every day, as you go down to the forum, you must say to yourself, "I am a new man. I seek the consulship. This is Rome."' His specific formulation here—morning lessons (*commentationibusmatutinis*)—recalls the diligent daily exercises practised by leading orators (e.g. Cic. *Brut.* 249; *De or.* 1.154), thus anticipating and contributing to the central message of what follows, which is that Cicero's excellence *as an orator* will suffice to shield him from the illegal tactics of his rivals (¶55). In this way, the third section of the *Brief Handbook* incorporates an essential point of the first (¶¶2–15)—namely, that Cicero's standing and success derive from his eloquence.

'This is Rome'—a state formed of a confluence of nations. Quintus reprises his formulation in ¶2, where he advises Cicero to 'consider what state this is' and provides as his answer, 'This is Rome'. The crescendo effect at ¶2 of 'new man', 'the consulship', and 'Rome' may have led Quintus' readers to anticipate, when the topic of Rome was reached, an evocation of the grandeur residing in the symbolic and ideological associations of the city's topography, an aspect of civic society that was important for public figures in Rome (see Vasaly 1993; Edwards 1996; Hölkeskamp 2004, 137ff.; Hölkeskamp 2011; Flower 2014). Instead, Quintus concentrates not on Rome but rather Rome's citizenry—and the unattractive quality of its inclinations during political campaigns.

Hence Quintus' description of Rome as a *civitas* ('state') 'formed of a confluence of nations'. The observation was, ostensibly, a neutral one (Noy 2000, 33). After all, the Romans' own traditions emphasized the complexities of their ethnic origins (Dench 2005; Gruen 2006; Gruen 2013), and Rome's early rise entailed the annexation and assimilation of neighbouring peoples (Cic. *Off.* 1.35; see Sherwin White 1973; Bispham 2007, 53ff.). Furthermore, the city's citizenry was constantly augmented by the addition of freed slaves, men who were imported from throughout the Mediterranean but became Romans upon manumission (Treggiari 1969, 11ff.; Mouritsen 2011, 66ff.). So natural, from the Roman perspective, was this diversity that Cicero could ridicule Greek claims of ethnic purity (Cic. *Rep.* 3.25).

And yet Quintus' remark prefaces a list of vices plaguing Rome, which gives it a derogatory connotation and perhaps insinuates that the unattractive tendencies about to be described are somehow un-Roman, at least in origin (see Tac. *Ann.* 15.44, describing Rome as a city 'where all things anywhere that are ghastly or shameful commingle and win favour' (*cuncta undique atrocia aut pudenda confluunt celebranturque*)). Now Romans, notwithstanding their frequent deployment of unflattering ethnic stereotypes (e.g. Cic. *Flacc.* 15–18, 65–6; *Font.* 14, 21, 26–33; *Scaur.* 14–16, 18–22; see Balsdon 1979; Coşkun 2005; Lintott 2008, 101ff.), were not markedly xenophobic (e.g. Cic. *Q. Fr.* 1.1.27–8; *Nat. D.* 2.8; see Noy 2000, 31ff.; Gruen 2006; Gruen 2013), and the city lay open to resident aliens, who apparently came to Rome in significant numbers (Purcell 1994, 653; Noy 2000, 53ff.). Cicero goes so far as to denounce any attempts at debarring foreigners from the city as inhuman aberrations (Cic. *Off.* 3.47). Nonetheless, as recently as 65, the tribune C. Papius had passed legislation temporarily expelling aliens originating outside Italy and establishing a permanent court for trying non-Italians alleged to be falsely claiming Roman citizenship (sources assembled in *MRR* 2.158; see Noy 2000, 38f., but a different view of this law and its circumstances is advanced by Hardy 1924, 43ff., followed by Gruen 1974, 410f.). This measure has plausibly been associated with electoral improprieties (Balsdon 1979, 100), and perhaps Quintus hopes here to evoke something of this brand of anxiety in his account of electoral corruption, thereby emphasizing its alien and objectionable quality.

Quintus employs this truism about Roman diversity as his point of departure for an unexpectedly unelevated account of the personality of the Roman electorate, a catalogue of vice and viciousness that underlines the importance of the candidate's character and moral stature. Quintus' representation of the voting public (and its unreliable proclivities) does not differ greatly from other unflattering portraits (e.g. Cic. *Mur.* 35–6; *Planc.* 7–8, 11; *Mil.* 42; *Brut.* 166; Plut. *Cat. min.* 49.5–6; 50.3; Dio 40.58.3), but whereas in other texts there is stress on the candidate's vulnerability to the unsavoury or unpredictable aspects of canvassing, here the unreliable and potentially venal public serve as foil to Cicero's steadfast integrity and his masterly authority.

The pessimism of this section of the *Brief Handbook* evokes the recurring complaint, so familiar by the first century that it bordered on cliché, that Rome suffered from a moral decline. In his public letter to Quintus on provincial administration, Cicero also bemoans the morality of contemporary Rome (Cic. *Q. Fr.* 1.1.19, 22). The complaint that one's native city could be a den of iniquity was, of course, an old one: as early as the third century, Plautus could put on the stage a young man turning his back on Athens because it was a place 'where immorality increases every day, where it is impossible to distinguish friends from the faithless…where, even with the gift of a throne, the citizens (*civitas*) are impossible to love' (Plaut. *Merc.* 837–40), sentiments that were plainly hackneyed at the time, inasmuch as Plautus can put them to comic effect (see Dunsch 2001, 316ff.). Although Roman writers disputed the origins of their moral decline, they agreed that its chief causes were extravagance and unrestrained political contention (Earl 1961, 41ff.; Lintott 1972, each assembling ancient sources; see Polyb. 6.57, with Walbank 1957, 744). This perspective furnishes the moralizing atmosphere for ¶¶55–7, where illegal electioneering on the part of Cicero's rivals is advanced as a threat to Cicero's candidature.

treachery. See ¶39, where Quintus warns against the treacherous behaviour of false friends, a specific specimen of this passage's more comprehensive complaint. Quintus' generalized treachery (*insidiae*) here may also evoke the hidden and dangerous ambitions attributed to Catilina at ¶11 and to Catilina and Antonius alike in *Tog. cand.* (Asc. 87C, 92–93C).

arrogance. Arrogance (*superbia*) is a failing frequently associated with the nobility (Hellegouarc'h 1963, 439ff.), but that is not the obvious reference here, where Quintus complains of the arrogance 'of many'.

tiresomeness. The Latin word is *odium*, but here the sense seems to be not so much 'hatred' as 'tedious disagreeableness' (see Fraenkel 1957, 263). Canvassing, it appears, is exhausting in its demands for disagreeable hobnobbing, a common and unexceptionable view on the part of aristocratic candidates (see §III.4). And of course there was always a danger that the public might weary of a candidate's solicitations.

how wise and skilful a man has to be. Negotiating the vices of the public requires a candidate equipped with wisdom (*consilium*) and skill (*ars*), that is, a candidate who is adept in the methods and practices explained in the *Brief Handbook*: native virtue is not enough, nor is inherited splendour. It is obvious to the reader that Cicero is the kind of man Quintus has in mind here.

At *Planc.* 62, Cicero employs similar language in making a different point. There the prosecution, in making its case that Plancius resorted to bribery in the aedilician elections of 55, complained that Plancius had been elected despite his oratorical deficiencies, an allegedly suspicious result. Deflecting this charge, Cicero responded, 'what we seek in candidates are merit, uprightness, honesty—not clever speech, not skill [*ars*], not learning'. Plainly Cicero is talking about Plancius' substandard oratory and not the brand of skilfulness Quintus refers to here.

escape animosity, gossip. Invective against a figure like Cicero, it is suggested, is likely to prove ineffectual, whereas men wanting wisdom and skill—men like Cicero's rivals—may well fall prey to such tactics. Put differently, employing invective is not objectionable (see ¶8 **cut-throats since their childhood**; 52 **traduced by a smear**) but succumbing to it exhibits one's failure as a candidate.

continue to be one and the same man even as he adapts himself. This is an important claim: the ideal candidate, as prescribed by the *Brief Handbook* and therefore embodied in Cicero, though he must exhibit versatility, is able to respond to the multifarious and sometimes socially awkward requirements of canvassing, even vicious fickleness on the part of the public at its worst, without abandoning true aristocratic constancy or violating his native integrity (see §III.4; ¶42 **what you lack by nature**; Tatum 2007, esp. 124f.).

¶55 through oratory. The centrality of oratory in aristocratic life has already been underlined (see ¶2 **your fame as an orator**). Here Quintus refers to oratory's crucial role in political affairs from the perspective of the elite: persuasion was the means by which the unstable passions of the masses were managed by their aristocratic betters (see Cic. *De or.* 1.30–4; *Inv. rhet.* 1.3–5; for analysis both of this idea and its application, see Leeman and Pinkster 1981, 102ff.; Morstein-Marx 2004, 62ff.; Steel 2013a; the essays included in Steel and Blom 2013; Morstein-Marx 2015). The idea was traditional and uncontroversial, and it reached back to Homeric representations of the ideal (heroic) leader (e.g. *Il.* 1.274; 3.216–24; 9.440–3; *Od.* 8.169–73). Its inclusion here, where Cicero the candidate is urged to deploy his eloquence in restraining the worst impulses of the electorate, draws attention to the importance of oratory in furnishing a consul with authority (e.g. Cic. *Mur.* 24; see, further, Pina Polo 2011, 83ff.).

to hamper or harm you. Quintus elides from the orator as ideal magistrate to the orator as formidable candidate. Here Quintus begins to lay out, for Cicero's rivals and readers, the orator's capacity for protecting his interests.

bribery. The Latin word is *largitio*, which can refer to any sort of largess but is frequently used in reference to bribery and so, in the context of canvassing, can register illegal electioneering or *ambitus* (Hellegouarc'h 1963, 219ff.) Although generosity was expected of every candidate (see ¶44), custom regulated its exercise in order to restrict the advantages of the richest candidates and thereby sustain what the aristocracy regarded as fair competition for office (see §III.5). Codification of these traditional limitations began early (e.g. Liv. 7.15.12–13; cf. Liv. 4.25.13–14) and remained sporadic and piecemeal until the late republic, when it became increasingly frequent and severe, especially after a permanent tribunal was established for hearing cases of *ambitus* (certainly by 116: see Brennan 2000, 366, providing testimonia and further bibliography). The various laws that defined *ambitus* are poorly known, and the Romans' fitful reclassification of familiar practices from objectionable to criminal continually expanded its scope (see Mommsen 1899, 865ff.; Bauerle 1990; Lintott 1990; Jehne 1995; Linderski 1995, 107ff., 638–9; Nadig 1997; Yakobson 1999, 22ff.; Riggsby 1999, 21ff.; Mouritsen 2001, 109ff.; Ferrary 2002; Alexander 2002, 119ff.; Linderski 2007, 613–14; Rosillo López 2010, 49ff.; Feig Vishnia 2012, 134ff.; Kleinman 2012; Beck 2016).

It is clear enough that a candidate was expected to restrict certain acts of generosity—seats at games, spectacles, or banquets, or outright gifts— to members of his own tribe. Friends and supporters were permitted to act as his surrogates in their own tribes (¶31), but a candidate was forbidden from assisting his surrogates by providing them with funds of his own (Cic. *Mur.* 67, 72; Dio 54.16.1). And there were other restrictions: the employment of *nomenclatores* (¶32) was illegal (Plut. *Cat. min.* 8), nor was a candidate permitted to pay a crowd to attend him (Cic. *Mur.* 67, 71). Still, the boundary between *ambitus* and appropriate generosity was not always entirely clear to everyone (Cic. *De or.* 2.105).

In the canvassing of 64, Cicero made *ambitus* an election issue through which he could impugn the integrity of Antonius and Catilina (see §VII.5). The issue had resonance: recent controversy over *ambitus* had led in 67 to the passage of the *lex Calpurnia* (*MRR* 2.142–3) and, in the next year, the consuls-designate, P. Cornelius Sulla and P. Autronius Paetus, were convicted of its violation and deprived of their office and membership in the senate (*MRR* 2.167). It is possible that at some point in 64 a *lex Fabia* was carried regulating the practice of attendance (see ¶37) and it is certain that, during the final stages of Cicero's canvassing, there was an effort by a majority in the senate to allow the promulgation and passage of a fresh law on *ambitus* (see §VII.5). By introducing *ambitus* here, Quintus contributes to Cicero's overall campaign strategy. The tactic was bold, not least because the Romans appear to have felt that a new man, or at least someone from outside the nobility, was more likely than a noble to rely on *ambitus* in order to win elections (Adamietz 1986, 111; Alexander 2002, 124f., 140ff.), an anxiety that was believed to go back to the early republic (Liv. 7.15.12–3 with Oakley 1998, 175–6).

It has long been suggested, on the basis of a puzzling remark at Cic. *Q. Fr.* 1.3.9, that, during his canvass for the aedileship in 66, Quintus was falsely associated with an epigram 'on the Aurelian law' (*de lege Aurelia*), believed by some to have been an otherwise unattested law on *ambitus* carried either by C. Aurelius Cotta (cos. 75) or by L. Aurelius Cotta (pr. 70) (Bauerle 1990, 50ff., with further bibliography). Canvassing in that year was rife with bribery (as evidenced by the convictions of the consuls-elect for 65: *MRR* 2.157), so the proposition is not unreasonable (if Quintus could be associated with lax attitudes toward *ambitus*, his enemies will have believed, that ought to damage his electoral prospects; hence the false attribution). If this explanation is correct, Quintus would have had practical and painful experience of the tactic of smearing rival candidates through the imputation of illicit electioneering. But this proposition is no more than guesswork. Most scholars prefer the view that the *lex Aurelia* referred to by Cicero is the law of 70 that organized juries into panels of senators, equestrians, and *tribuni aerarii* (sources assembled at *MRR* 2.127: see Tyrrell 1885, 362, followed by Shackleton Bailey 1980, 168), although this explanation is equally speculative and in any case does little to elucidate Cicero's remark. Cicero's letter to his brother was penned in 58, when the orator was in exile and worried that Quintus would be prosecuted. But he does not tell us what the offending epigram actually said or how it could count against Quintus in 66 or 58. His comment to Quintus, then, must remain obscure.

merit and prestige. On merit (*virtus*), see ¶7; on prestige (*dignitas*), see ¶2. Romans agreed that *ambitus* violated custom as well as law and was therefore an abhorrent practice: elections were meant to be decided on the basis of honest *gratia*, earned by way of merit and prestige and not *ambitus* (Cic. *Att.* 4.15.7–8; *Q. Fr.* 2.15.4; cf. *Off.* 2.22; [Sall.] *Ep.* 2.8.2). And yet *ambitus* remained commonplace: candidates routinely found the means to circumvent its prohibitions or to evade its detection, and bribery remained an effective means of motivating supporters. As for members of the public, although they felt obliged to disapprove of *ambitus* (legislation expanding the definition of *ambitus* or increasing the severity of punishing it was normally carried in the assemblies), they nonetheless welcomed the illicit benefactions they received (otherwise the tactic would have been pointless) and at least privately resented attempts to reduce or eliminate them (Cic. *Planc.* 45; *Mur.* 72; App. *B.Civ.* 2.24–7). This appears to have been the case for voters of all classes. Even under the empire, *ambitus* persisted in municipal elections (*lex coloniae Genitivae* 132, see *RS* 416f.; *Dig.* 48.14.1 pr. and 1). It is obvious that *ambitus* sometimes entailed considerable costs (though perhaps not in every instance: see Jehne 1995, 63–4; see Plin. *NH* 35.162).

who it is you are. Not a reference to Cicero's *novitas* (see ¶2 **consider what...what...who**) but rather to Cicero's impressive powers as an orator and candidate. In what follows, Quintus delivers a concise but very forceful definition of Cicero's public identity, which is characterized by his assiduousness (*diligentia*; see ¶1 **assiduousness**), authority (*auctoritas*; see below), eloquence (¶2 **your fame as an orator**), and the depth of his support by the equestrian order (¶3 **the equestrian order**). This is Quintus' final representation of Cicero in the *Brief Handbook*.

they are being watched and monitored. It is unsurprising that Cicero is urged to monitor the machinations of his rivals, but this admonition strikes an attractive moral note as well: Romans were deeply censorious by nature, and spying out faults in others was deemed a virtuous practice (see Pöschl 1961; Veyne 1983; Kaster 2005, 84ff.). Previously in the *Brief Handbook* Cicero has been advised to keep a close watch on his supporters: ¶¶22, 24, 35.

authority. Although in this section he reprises earlier themes, this is Quintus' first reference to Cicero's authority (*auctoritas*): he has previously referred to Cicero as a champion of the *auctoritas* of the equestrian order (¶33) and the senatorial order (¶53). *Auctoritas* refers to what was a core value in Roman society: the capacity to initiate, execute, and guarantee vital social exchanges, a concept that ranged from assuring a sale to acting as a guardian, from acting as a responsible patron to affecting the deliberations and decisions of the people and senate. In public life, an individual's *auctoritas*—his capacity to influence events by asserting his personal authority—derived above all from his possession of high office (e.g. Cic. *Leg. Man.* 2) and his influence among his peers and the wider public; it was, then, also a key constituent in political persuasion and therefore naturally associated with eloquence (see, further, Heinze 1925 (fundamental); Balsdon 1960; Hellegouarc'h 1963, 295ff., 330ff.; Galinsky 1996, 10ff.; Morstein-Marx 2004, 63ff.; Hölkeskamp 2013, 23ff.; Jehne 2013a; Arena 2015). All of the qualities in Cicero's depiction in this section combine in a consistent and complimentary manner: in adducing Cicero's *auctoritas* here, near the conclusion of the *Brief Handbook*, Quintus underlines his claim that Cicero is the ideal candidate because he possesses the traditional qualifications for leadership in Rome.

Cicero's possession of *auctoritas*, introduced at this moment, also highlights his capacity to deal with adversaries. Thus the *Brief Handbook* depicts Cicero comprehensively as a figure capable of helping his friends and, if need be, harming his enemies—or, from a different perspective, capable of protecting Roman tradition and Roman law from subversion.

the equestrian order's devotion to you. Once again Quintus stresses Cicero's close relationship with the equestrian order (see ¶¶3, 33). Here, because this remark forms part of his oblique warning to Cicero's rivals, Quintus also flatters the order by calling attention to its clout.

¶56 already planning to prosecute them. Conducting or even preparing a prosecution against a rival candidate was a risky matter. The elder Cato disgraced himself during his unsuccessful campaign for the censorship of 189 by joining in the prosecution of his rival, Acilius Glabrio (Liv. 37.57.9–58.2). At *Mur.* 43–6, admittedly for tactical reasons, Cicero dilates on the foolishness of wasting time and damaging one's image in preparing a case for *ambitus* against a rival (see Tatum 2013, 139ff.; Fantham 2013, 144ff.): in Cicero's view, doing so leads the voters to believe that one has given up any hope of winning the election and, as a consequence voters look for another candidate to support (see also Cic. *Mur.* 51, 57, 61; cf. Plut. *Cat. min.* 21). When he was a candidate for the aedileship, Cicero undertook his very first prosecution, winning celebrity through his sensational prosecution of Verres (Tatum 2013, 138ff.; see §VII.2). But Verres was not a rival for office and so Cicero's action could not be discredited as self-serving or a symptom of defeatism. This exhortation on Quintus' part allows Cicero's campaign in effect to threaten prosecutions even as it insists that it is not threatening prosecutions (the threat recurs: see ¶57 **if we remain vigilant...the possibility of a prosecution**). Quintilian knew of a public letter, attributed to Antonius and distributed during his campaign for the consulship, in which Antonius insisted: 'I do not fear him [Cicero] as a prosecutor, because I am innocent' (Quint. 9.3.94; the letter was probably composed by an ally of Antonius: Asc. 94C). Antonius' reaction perhaps suggests that Cicero's tactic of imputing dishonesty to his rivals was effective.

to whom they have strong ties. These are Cicero's *necessarii*, voters attached to Cicero through *necessitudo* (see ¶16 **any other close tie**. By distinguishing these men from voters of the venal sort, Quintus compliments his readers (Laser 2001, 188).

¶57 if we remain vigilant . . . the possibility of a prosecution. Once again Quintus identifies himself with Cicero's canvass ('we remain'; see ¶5 **our political opinions**). Into this admonition that Cicero remain alert to the peril of *ambitus*, Quintus inserts the requirement that Cicero sustain the enthusiasm and correct deployment of his followers, reprising especially ¶¶3–6 and ¶¶16–41 (vigilance is stressed at ¶22, 24, and 35, as well as ¶56 above; the deployment of friends is emphasized at ¶20), thereby pointedly contrasting Cicero's model canvass with the corrupt behaviour attributed here to his rivals. On the quality of the threat implicit in reminding Cicero's competitors of 'the possibility of a prosecution', see above ¶56 **already planning to prosecute them.**

dishonest electioneers . . . bribery agents. Bribery agents (*divisores*) were men who, on behalf of a busy candidate, distributed entirely respectable donatives to members of that candidate's tribe. It is a plausible, but far from certain, suggestion that the men who acted as *divisores* were often tribal officials and therefore well placed to act on a candidate's behalf; consequently these men could at once earn a profit and also enhance their local prestige (Adamietz 1989, 195, with further bibliography; Yakobson 1999, 40). The same term was applied to agents (doubtless the same men, by and large) who, on behalf of a candidate, supplied illicit donatives to voters outside the candidate's tribe (see ¶55 **bribery**) (Liebenam 1905; Deniaux 1987, 290–97; Cosi 1998). In order to shield any direct connection between candidate and *divisor* when the latter was engaged to make illegal distributions, further intermediaries were employed: these were 'dishonest electioneers', or *sequestres*, though sometimes the term *interpres* was used instead of *sequester* (e.g. Cic. *Verr.* 1.36); the word simply indicates the responsible recipient of a deposit (see Kaser 1971, 389; cf. Lintott 1990, 8). In his *In toga candida*, Cicero accuses Antonius and Catilina of holding a nocturnal meeting with dishonest electioneers at the house of an unnamed Roman noble (Asc. 83C), another instance of the careful coordination of talking points in Cicero's canvass (see §III.7–10; §IV.5; §VII.5). The activities of *divisores* and *sequestres* were often managed by societies described as fraternities (*sodalitates*) (see ¶16 **religious fraternity**).

Divisores could be put to varying uses. In the aedilician elections for 69, Verres, although he was not a candidate, paid *divisores* to work against Cicero's election to the office: he had hoped to operate secretly, but one of the *divisores* was affiliated with Cicero and divulged Verres' scheme (Cic. *Verr.* 1.22.3; 2.1.19). Despite the necessity of their dealing with *divisores*, aristocrats often disparaged the job (Cic. *Att.* 1.16.2; 1.18.4; *Verr.* 2.3.161; *Planc.* 48; *De or.* 2.257).

a means of intimidating. It was not until legislation carried in 55 that agents of electoral corruption became liable for prosecution (the *lex Licinia de sodaliciis*, *MRR* 2.215; an attempt to extend legal penalties to bribery agents in 67 by the tribune C. Cornelius failed, on which episode see Griffin 1973, 197). Quintus, then, is suggesting that by conducting a model canvass Cicero will conjure such widespread support that unethical *divisores* will be overawed. When threatened, *divisores* could respond forcefully, even violently (see Asc. 75C: they pushed back hard against Cornelius' proposed legislation on *ambitus*), a reality that lends an impressive degree of confidence to Quintus' assertion here, assurance that is underlined by Quintus' claim that Cicero is capable of so neutralizing *ambitus* on the part of his rivals in this election that, in the end, it can have no bearing on the result.

¶58 Here, then. Quintus draws the *Brief Handbook* to a close by reprising ideas and expressions central to ¶¶1–2, an enveloping structure that lends an impression of unity to the work as a whole.

I understand better than you. For the sentiment, see ¶1 Although… I nonetheless; ¶1 anything new.

I am better able. On the contrast between Quintus' leisure and Cicero's preoccupation with canvassing, see ¶2 lasting but a few months.

into a single account. This expression, *unum in locum*, recollects 'within a single work' (*sub uno aspectu*) from ¶1.

does not pertain to everyone. Despite its posture as a didactic epistle and despite its normative claims, the *Brief Handbook* is not universal in its application (see, further, §IV.5).

revision. It was normal practice in Rome for aristocratic writers to solicit suggestions for revision from their peers, an action that signalled an interest in high standards and an operation that helped to mark friendship and intellectual community (Starr 1987, esp. 213f.; Gurd 2011, esp. 51ff.). Cicero frequently sought literary advice (e.g. Cic. *Att.* 1.13.5; 13.26.2; *Fam.* 6.7.6; 16.17.1; *Q. Fr.* 2.8.1; 3.5.1–2; see, further, Gurd 2011, 70ff.). So, too, did

Quintus (Cic. *Att.* 2.16.4; *Q. Fr.* 2.16.3–4; 3.1.13; 3.5.7; 3.7.6). Revision or rewriting were especially to be expected from any work designating itself a *commentarius*; on the ostensibly provisional character of *commentarii*, see §IV.3. Requests for correction are also a characteristic of didactic writing (e.g. Cic. *Inv. rhet.* 2.9; see Peter 1901, 257f.). Consequently, there is no reason to see in Quintus' request for Cicero's revision any sign that the *Brief Handbook* was never put before the public (which is the view of Bruhn 1908, 262f.; Clift 1945, 102f.; Richardson 1971, 439).

brief handbook on canvassing. Here Quintus describes his letter to Cicero as a *commentariolum petitionis*. In this way, Quintus emphasizes the work's practical and traditional qualities: on the cultural significance of the *Brief Handbook*'s association with the genre of *commentarii*, see, further, §IV.3. On the modern employment of this expression as the work's title, see **A Brief Handbook on Canvassing for Office**.

perfect in every respect. Quintus' closing formulation here (*omni ratione perfectum*) harks back to the central purpose of his work, described in ¶1 as arranging the particulars of canvassing 'within a single, systematic form and in a logical order' (*ratione et distributione*) (see, further, ¶1 **within a single, systematic form and in a logical order**).

Bibliography

Adamietz, J. 1986. 'Ciceros Verfahren in den Ambitus-Prozessen gegen Murena und Plancius', *Gymnasium* 93: 102–17.

Adamietz. J. 1989. *Marcus Tullius Cicero: Pro Murena, mit einem Kommentar*. Darmstadt.

Adams, J.N. 1978. 'Conventions of Naming in Cicero', *CQ* 28: 145–66.

Adams. J.N. 2003. *Bilingualism and the Latin Language*. Cambridge.

Alexander, M.C. 1990. *Trials in the Late Roman Republic, 149 BC to 50 BC*. Toronto.

Alexander, M.C. 2002. *The Case for the Prosecution in the Ciceronian Era*. Ann Arbor.

Alexander, M.C. 2007. 'Oratory, Rhetoric, and the Politics of the Republic', in W. Dominik and J. Hall (eds.), *A Companion to Roman Rhetoric*. Oxford, 98–108.

Alexander, M.C. 2009. 'The *Commentariolum petitionis* as an Attack on Election Campaigns', *Athenaeum* 97: 31–57; 369–95.

Alföldi, A. 1956. 'The Main Aspects of Political Propaganda in the Coinage of the Roman Republic', in R.A.G. Carson and C.H.V. Sutherland (eds.), *Essays in Roman Coinage Presented to Harold Mattingly*. Oxford, 63–95.

Allély, A. 2003. 'La confiscation des biens des *hostes* dans le cadre des déclarations d'*hostis* sous la République romaine', in M.-C. Ferriès and F. Delrieux (eds.), *Spolier et confisquer dans les mondes grec et romain*. Chambéry, 147–62.

Allen, Jr., W. 1938. 'On the Importance of Young Men in Ciceronian Politics', *CJ* 33: 357–9.

Allen, Jr., W. 1955. 'The British Epics of Quintus and Marcus Cicero', *TAPhA* 86: 143–59.

Andreau, J. 1999. *Banking and Business in the Roman World*. Cambridge.

Arena, V. 2007. 'Roman Oratorical Invective', in W. Dominik and J. Hall (eds.), *A Companion to Roman Rhetoric*. Oxford, 149–60.

Arena, V. 2015. 'Informal Norms, Values, and Social Control in the Roman Participatory Context', in D. Hammer (ed.), *A Companion to Greek Democracy and the Roman Republic*. Oxford, 217–38.

Astin, A.E. 1958. *The Lex Annalis before Sulla*. Brussels.

Astin, A.E. 1967. *Scipio Aemilianus*. Oxford.

Astin, A.E. 1978. *Cato the Censor*. Oxford.

Astin, A.E. 1985. 'Censorships in the Late Republic', *Historia* 34: 175–90.

Astin, A.E. 1988. '*Regimen morum*', *JRS* 78: 14–34.

Atkins, J.W. 2013. *Cicero on Politics and the Limits of Practical Reason: The Republic and the Laws*. Cambridge.

Ausbüttel, F.M. 1982. *Untersuchungen zu den Vereinen im Westen des römischen Reiches*. Kallmünz.

Badian, E. 1958. *Foreign clientelae (264–70 B.C.)*. Oxford.

Badian, E. 1964. *Studies in Greek and Roman History*. New York.

Badian, E. 1972. *Publicans and Sinners: Private Enterprise in the Service of the Roman Republic*. Ithaca.

Badian, E. 1988. 'The Clever and the Wise: Two Roman *Cognomina* in Context', in N. Horsfall (ed.), *Vir bonus discendi peritus: Studies in Celebration of Otto Skutsch's Eightieth Birthday*. London, 6–12.

Badian, E. 1989. 'The *scribae* of the Roman Republic', *Klio* 71: 582–603.

Badian, E. 1990. 'The Consuls, 179–49 BC', *Chiron* 29: 371–413.

Badian, E. 1998. 'Two Numismatic Phantoms: The False Priest and the Spurious Son', *Arctos* 32: 45–60.

Baehrens, E. 1878. *Miscellanea critica*. Groningen.

Baird, J.A., and Taylor, C. (eds.), 2011. *Ancient Graffiti in Context*. London.

Baiter, I.G., and Kayser, C.L. 1866. *Ciceronis opera quae supersunt omnia*. Leipzig.

Balsdon, J.P.V.D. 1960. 'Auctoritas, dignitas, otium', *CQ* 10: 43–50.

Balsdon, J.P.V.D. 1963. 'The *Commentariolum petitionis*', *CQ* 13: 242–50.

Balsdon, J.P.V.D. 1969. *Life and Leisure in Ancient Rome*. London.

Balsdon, J.P.V.D. 1979. *Romans and Aliens*. London.

Bannon, C.J. 1997. *The Brothers of Romulus: Fraternal Pietas in Roman Law, Literature, and Society*. Princeton.

Baraz, Y. 2012. *A Written Republic: Cicero's Philosophical Politics*. Princeton.

Batstone, W.W., and Damon, C. 2006. *Caesar's Civil War*. Oxford.

Bauerle, E.A. 1990. *Procuring an Election: Ambitus in the Roman Republic*. Ann Arbor.

Beard, M. 2008. *Pompeii: The Life of a Roman Town*. London.

Beard, M. 2015. *Laughter in Ancient Rome*. Berkeley and Los Angeles.

Beck, H. 2005. *Karriere und Hierarchie: Die römische Aristokratie und die Anfänge des cursus honorum in der mittleren Republic*. Berlin.

Beck, H. 2009. 'From Poplicola to Augustus: Senatorial Houses in Roman Political Culture', *Phoenix* 63: 361–84.

Beck, H. 2016. 'Money, Power, and Class Coherence: The *ambitus* Legislation of the 180s B.C.', in H. Beck, M. Jehne, and J. Serrati (eds.), *Money and Power in the Roman Republic*. Brussels, 188–207.

Beck, H., Duplá, A., Jehne, M., and Pina Polo, F. (eds.), 2011. *Consuls and the res publica*. Cambridge.

Bell, A. 2004. *Spectacular Power in the Greek and Roman City*. Oxford.

Beltrami, A. 1892. 'De Commentariolo petitionis Q. Tullio Ciceroni vindicando', *Ann. Sc. Norm. Sup. Pisa* 9: 3–75.

Bernard, J.-E. 2013. *La sociabilité épistolaire chez Cicéron*. Paris.

Berry, D.H. 1996. *Cicero, Pro P. Sulla Oratio*. Cambridge.

Berry, D.H. 2003. '*Equester ordo tuus est*: Did Cicero Win his Cases because of his Support for the *equites*?', *CQ* 53: 222–34.

Berry, D. 2004. 'The Publication of Cicero's *Pro Roscio Amerino*', *Mnemosyne* 57: 80–7.

Bispham, E. 2007. *From Asculum to Actium: The Municipalization of Italy from the Social War to Augustus*. Oxford.

Biundo, R. 2003. 'La propaganda elettorale a Pompei: La funzione e il valore dei programmata nell'organizzazione della campagna', *Athenaeum* 91: 53–119.

Bleicken, J. 1955. *Das Volkstribunat der klassischen Republik*. Munich.

Bleicken, J. 1995. *Cicero und die Ritter*. Göttingen.

Blom, H. van der. 2010. *Cicero's Role Models: The Political Strategy of a Newcomer*. Oxford.

Blom, H. van der. 2016. *Oratory and Political Career in the Late Roman Republic*. Oxford.

Blösel, W. 2011. 'Die Demilitarisierung der römischen Nobilität von Sulla bis Caesar', in W. Blösel and K.-J. Hölkeskamp (eds.), *Von der 'militia equestris' zur 'militia urbana': Prominenzrollen und Karrierefelder im antiken Rom*. Stuttgart, 55–80.

Bollmann, B. 1998. *Römische Vereinhauser: Untersuchungen zu den Scholae der römischen Berufs-, Kult- und Augustalen-Kollegien in Italien*. Mainz.

Bömer, F. 1953. 'Der Commentarius: Zur Vorgeschichte und literarischen Form der Schriften Caesars', *Hermes* 81: 210–50.

Bonnefond-Coudry, M. 1989. *Le sénat de la République romaine de la guerre d'Hannibal à Auguste*. Paris.

Bonner, S.F. 1977. *Education in Ancient Rome from the Elder Cato to the Younger Pliny*. Berkeley and Los Angeles.

Boriaud, J.-Y. 1992. *Quintus Cicéron: Petit manuel de campagne électorale, suivi de l'art de gouverner une province de Marcus Cicéron*. Arles.

Boscherini, S. 2000. 'La dottrina medica communicata *per epistulam*: Struttura e storia de un genere', in A. Pigeaud and J. Pigeaud (eds.), *Les textes médicaux latins comme littérature*. Nantes, 1–11.

Bradley, K.R. 1984. *Slaves and Masters in the Roman Empire*. Oxford.

Bradley, K.R. 1994. *Slavery and Society at Rome*. Cambridge.

Brennan, T.C. 2000. *The Praetorship in the Roman Republic*. Oxford.

Brennan, T.C. 2014. 'Power and Process under the Republican "Constitution"', in H. Flower (ed.), *The Cambridge Companion to the Roman Republic*, 2nd edn. Cambridge, 19–53.

Brink, C.O. 1971. *Horace on Poetry: The 'Ars Poetica'*. Cambridge.

Briscoe, J. 1992. 'Political Groupings in the Middle Republic: A Restatement', in C. Deroux (ed.), *Studies in Latin Literature and Roman History*, vol. 6. Brussels, 70–83.

Briscoe, J. 2008. *A Commentary on Livy, Books 38–40*. Oxford.

Broderson, K. 2013. *Q. Tullius Cicero: Tipps für einen erfolgreichen Wahlkampf*. Stuttgart.

Broughton, T.R.S. 1991. *Candidates Defeated in Roman Elections: Some Ancient Roman 'Also-Rans'*. Philadelphia.

Brown, L. 2014. 'Why is Aristotle's Virtue of Character a Mean? Taking Aristotle at his Word (*NE* ii 6)', in R. Polanksy (ed.), *A Cambridge Companion to Aristotle's Nicomachean Ethics*. Cambridge, 64–80.

Brown, M. 2012. *A Political History of John Toland*. London.

Bruggisser, P. 1984. 'Le *Commentariolum petitionis*, acte électoral?', *Les Études Classiques* 52: 115–30.

Bruhn, E. 1908. 'Q. Ciceros Handbüchlein für Wahlbewerber', *Neue Jahrbücher für das klassische Altertum* 21: 254–69.

Brunt, P.A. 1971. *Italian Manpower, 225 B.C.–A.D. 14*. Oxford.

Brunt, P.A. 1982. 'Nobilitas and novitas', *JRS* 72: 1–18.

Brunt, P.A. 1988. *The Fall of the Roman Republic and Related Essays*. Oxford.

Buckland, W.W. 1937. 'Civil Proceedings against Ex-magistrates in the Republic', *JRS* 27: 37–47.

Buecheler, F. 1869. *Quinti Ciceronis reliquae*. Leipzig.

Buller, J.L. 1987. 'The Case of the Missing Greek: *Cum homine Graeco* in *Commentariolum petitionis* 8', *CB* 63: 119–23.

Buongiorno, P. 2006. 'Gaio Antonio (cos. 63) e l'appellativo «Hybrida»', in G. Traina (ed.), *Studi sull'età de Marco Antonio*. Lecce, 297–309.

Burckhardt, L. 1990. 'The Political Elite of the Roman Republic: Comments on Recent Discussions of the Concepts *nobilitas* and *homo novus*', *Historia* 39: 77–99.

Burton, P.J. 2004. '*Amicitia* in Plautus: A Study of Roman Friendship Processes', *AJPh* 125: 209–43.

Capogrossi Colognesi, L. 2002. '*Pagi, vici* e *fundi* nell'Italia Romana', *Athenaeum* 90: 5–48.

Capogrossi Colognesi, L. 2014. *Law and Power in the Making of the Roman Commonwealth*. Cambridge.

Carandini, A. 2017. *The Atlas of Ancient Rome*. Princeton.

Carlsen, J. 2006. *The Rise and Fall of a Roman Noble Family: The Domitii Ahenobarbi 196 BC–AD 68*. Odense.

Castrén, P. 1975. *Ordo populusque Pompeianus: Polity and Society in Roman Pompeii*. Rome.

Ceccarelli, P. 2013. *Ancient Greek Letter Writing: A Cultural History (600 BC–150 BC)*. Oxford.

Christes, J. 2003. 'Texte im Elementarunterricht als Träger sittlicher Werter in republikanischer Zeit', in A. Haltenhoff, A. Heil, and F.-H. Mutschler (eds.), *O tempora, o mores! Römische Werte und römische Literatur in den letzten Jahrzehnten der Republik*. Leipzig, 51–70.

Ciaceri, E. 1939. *Cicerone e i suoi tempi*, 2nd edn. Milan.

Citroni Marchetti, S. 2000. *Amicizia e potere nella lettere di Cicerone e nelle elegie ovidiane dall'esilio*. Florence.

Clark, A.J. 2007. *Divine Qualities: Cult and Community in Republican Rome*. Oxford.

Clark, J.R. 2014. '*Domus*/Single Family House', in R.B. Ulrich and C.K. Quenemoen (eds.), *A Companion to Roman Architecture*. Oxford, 343–62.

Clemente, G. 1972. 'Il patronato nei collegia dell'impero romano', *Studi classici e orientali* 21: 142–229.

Clift, E.H. 1945. *Latin Pseudepigrapha*. Baltimore.

Cloud, D. 1994. 'The Constitution and Public Criminal Law', in A. Crook, A. Lintott, and E. Rawson (eds.), *The Cambridge Ancient History*, 2nd edn., vol. 9. Cambridge, 505–30.

Coarelli, F. 1982. 'Su alcuni proconsoli d'Asia tra le fine del II e gli inizi del I secolo A.C. e sulla politica di Mario in oriente', *Tituli* 4: 435–51.

Coffee, N. 2016. *Gift and Gain: How Money Transformed Ancient Rome*. Oxford.

Constans, L.A. 1940. *Cicéron, Correspondance*, vol. 1. Paris.

Cooley, M.G.L, Murrell, J., Taylor, D.W., and Thorpe, M.A. 2009. *Cicero's Consulship Campaign: A Selection of Sources Relating to Cicero's Election as Consul for 63 BC, including 'A Short Guide to Electioneering'*. London.

Corbeill, A. 2002. 'Ciceronian Invective', in J. May (ed.), *Brill's Companion to Cicero: Oratory and Rhetoric*. Leiden, 197–218.

Cornell, T.J. 1995. *The Beginnings of Rome: Italy and Rome from the Bronze Age to the Punic Wars, c.1000–263 BC*. London.

Corte, M. della. 1924. *Iuventus*. Arpino.

Cosi, R. 1998. 'La degenerazione politiche tardorepubblicane: i "divisores"', *Annali della Facoltà di Lettere e Filosofia dell'Università de Bari* 41: 335–49.

Cosi, R. 2002. *Le solidarietà politiche nella repubblica romana*. Bari.

Coşkun, A. 2005. 'Inklusion und Exklusion von Fremden in den Gerichtsreden Ciceros', in S. Harwardt and J. Schwind (eds.), *Corona coronaria: Festschrift für Hans-Otto Kröner zum 75. Geburtstag*. Hildesheim, 77–98.

Cottier, M., Crawford, M.H., Crowther, C.V., Ferrary, J.-L, Levick, B.M., Salomies, O., and Wörrle, M. (eds.). 2008. *The Customs Law of Asia*. Oxford.

Couhade-Beyneix, C. 2003. 'La confiscation des biens dans le cadre de la procédure *de maiestate*', in M.-C. Ferriès and F. Delrieux (eds.), *Spolier et confisquer dans les mondes grec et romain*. Chambéry, 163–78.

Courtney, E. 1993 *The Fragmentary Latin Poets*. Oxford.

Craig. C.P. 1981. 'The *accusatus* as *amicus*: An Original Roman Tactic of Ethical Argumentation', *TAPhA* 111: 31–7.

Craig, C.P. 2004. 'Audience Expectations, Invective, and Proof', in J. Powell and J. Paterson (eds.), *Cicero the Advocate*. Oxford, 187–214.

Crawford, J.W. 1984. *M. Tullius Cicero: The Lost and Unpublished Orations*. Göttingen.

Crawford, J.W. 1994. *M. Tullius Cicero: The Fragmentary Speeches*, 2nd edn. Atlanta.

Crawford, M.H. 1968. 'The Edict of M. Marius Gratidianus', *PCPhS* 14: 1–4.

Crook, J.A. 1967. *Law and Life of Rome*. Ithaca.

Crook, J.A. 1986. 'Lex "Rivalicia" (*FIRA* 1, no. 5)', *Athenaeum* 64: 45–53.

Crook, J.A. 1995. *Legal Advocacy in the Roman World*. Ithaca.

Cugusi, P. 1970a. *Epistolographi Latini minores*, vol. 1. Turin.

Cugusi, P. 1970b.'Un letterato della tarda repubblica: Q. Tullio Cicerone', *Annali della Facoltà di Lettere e Filosofia dell'Università di Cagliari* 33: 5–34.

Cugusi P. 1979. *Epistolographi Latini minores*, vol. 2. Turin.

Cugusi P. 1983. *Evoluzione e forme dell'epistolografia latina nella tarda repubblica e nei primi due secoli dell'imperio con cenni sull'epistolografia preciceroniana*. Rome.

Dahlmann, H. 1963. *Studien zu Varro De poetis*. Darmstadt.

Damon, C. 1993. 'Comm. pet. 10', *HSCPh* 95: 281–8.

Damon, C. 1997. *The Mask of the Parasite: A Pathology of Roman Patronage*. Ann Arbor.

Damon, C., and Mackay, C.S. 1995. 'On the Prosecution of C. Antonius in 76 B.C.', *Historia* 44: 37–55.

D'Arms, J.H. 1981. *Commerce and Social Standing in Ancient Rome*. Cambridge, Mass.

D'Arms, J.H. 1984. 'Upper-Class Attitudes Towards *viri municipales* and their Towns in the Early Roman Empire', *Athenaeum* 82: 440–67.

David, J.-M. 1992. *Le patronat judiciaire au dernier siècle de la République romaine*. Rome.

David, J.-M. 2006. 'Rhetoric and Public Life', in N. Rosenstein and R. Morstein-Marx (eds.), *A Companion to the Roman Republic*. Oxford, 421–38.

David, J.-M., Démougin, S., Deniaux, E., Ferey, E., Flambard, J.-M., and Nicolet, C. 1973. 'Le 'Commentariolum petitionis' de Quintus Cicéron: État de la question et étude prosopographique', *ANRW* 1. 3: 239–77.

Degl'Innocenti Pierini, R. 2000. 'Orgoglio di esule: Su due frammenti di un'epistola di Q. Cecilio Metello Numido', *Maia* 52: 249–58.

DeGraff, T.B. 1940. 'Plato in Cicero', *CPh* 35: 143–53.

Dehon, P.-J. 2000. 'Quintus Cicéron et Lucrèce: Aux sources du fragment transmis par Ausone', *Museum Helveticum* 57: 265–9.

De Ligt, L. 2000. 'Governmental Attitudes toward Markets and Collegia', in E. Lo Casico (ed.), *Mercati permanenti e mercati periodici nel mondo romano*. Bari, 242–52.

De Marino, A. 1965. *Quinto Cicerone, Manualetto del candidato*. Naples.

Dench, E. 2005. *Romulus' Asylum: Roman Identities from the Age of Alexander to the Age of Hadrian*. Oxford.

Dench, E. 2013. 'Cicero and Roman Identity', in C. Steel (ed.), *A Cambridge Companion to Cicero*. Cambridge, 122–40.

Deniaux, É. 1987. 'De l'*ambitio* à l'*ambitus*: Les lieux de la propagande et de la corruption électorale à la fin de la République', in *L'urbs: Espace urbain et histoire (Ier siècle av. J.-C. – IIIe siècle ap. J.-C.)*. Rome, 279–304.

Deniaux, É. 1993. *Clientèles et pouvoir à l'époque de Cicéron*. Paris and Rome.

Deniaux, É. 1997. 'La rue et l'opinion publique à Rome et en Italie (1er siècle avant J.-C.): Cortèges et popularité', in A. Leménorel (ed.), *La rue, lieu de sociabilité? Rencontres de la rue*. Rouen, 207–13.

Deniaux, É. 2003. 'La *toga candida* et les élections à Rome sous la République', in F. Chausson and H. Inglebert (eds.), *Costume et société dans l'Antiquité et le haut Moyen Âge*. Paris, 49–55.

Deniaux, É. 2006. 'Patronage', in N. Rosenstein and R. Morstein-Marx (eds.), *A Companion to the Roman Republic*. Oxford, 401–20.

Deniaux, É. 2016. 'The Money and Power of Friends and Clients: Successful Aediles in Rome', in H. Beck, M. Jehne, and J. Serrati (eds.), *Money and Power in the Roman Republic*. Brussels, 178–87.

Develin, R. 1979. *Patterns of Office-Holding, 366–49 B.C.* Brussels.

Dickey, E. 2002. *Latin Forms of Address from Plautus to Apuleius*. Oxford.

DiLuzio, M.J. 2016. *A Place at the Altar: Priestesses in Republican Rome*. Princeton.

Dixon, S. 1992. *The Roman Family*. Baltimore.

Dixon, S. 2007. *Cornelia: Mother of the Gracchi*. London.

Dondin-Payne, M. 1981. '*Homo novus*: Un slogan de Caton à Cesar', *Historia* 30: 22–81.

Drexler, H. 1966. '*Dignitas*', in R. Klein (ed.), *Das Staatsdenken der Römer*. Darmstadt, 231–54.

Drumann, K.W., and Groebe, P. 1899. *Geschichte Roms in seinem Übergang von der republikanischen zur monarchischen Verfassung*, vol. 1. Berlin.

Drumann, K.W., and Groebe, P. 1929. *Geschichte Roms in seinem Übergang von der republikanischen zur monarchischen Verfassung*, vol. 6. Berlin.

Drummond, A. 1989a. 'Early Roman *clientes*', in A. Wallace-Hadrill (ed.), *Patronage in Ancient Society*. London, 89–115.

Drummond, A. 1989b. 'Rome in the Fifth Century II: The Citizen Community', in F.W. Walbank, A.E. Astin, M.W. Fredericksen, R.M. Oglivie, and A. Drummond (eds.), *The Cambridge Ancient History*, 2nd edn., vol. 7, pt 2. Cambridge, 172–242.

Dufallo, B. 2001. 'Appius' Indignation: Gossip, Tradition, and Performance in Republican Rome', *TAPhA* 131: 119–42.

Dugan, J. 2005. *Making a New Man: Ciceronian Self-Fashioning in the Rhetorical Works*. Oxford.

Duncan-Jones, R. 1982. *The Economy of the Roman Empire*, 2nd edn. Cambridge.

Dunsch, B. 2001. *Plautus' Mercator: A Commentary*. St Andrews.

Duplá, A. 1988. '*Novus sum, consulatum peto, Roma est*: El *Commentariolum petitionis* de Quinto Ciceron', *Studia Historica: Historia Antigua* 6: 107–16.

Duplá, A., Fatás, G., and Pina Polo, F. 1990. *El Manual del candidato de Quinto Cicerón (El Commentariolum petitionis)*. Erandio.

Dutoit, E. 1969. '"Vicinus, vicinitas", ou Les rapports de voisinage dans l'Antiquité romaine', *REL* 47: 25–6.

Dyck, A.R. 1996. *A Commentary on Cicero, De officiis*. Ann Arbor.

Dyck, A.R. 2004. *A Commentary on Cicero, De legibus*. Ann Arbor.

Dyck, A.R. 2008. *Cicero, Catilinarians*. Cambridge.

Dyck, A.R. 2010. *Cicero, Pro Sexto Roscio*. Cambridge.

Dyck, A.R. 2012. *Marcus Tullius Cicero, Speeches on Behalf of Marcus Fonteius and Marcus Aemilius Scaurus*. Oxford.

Earl, D.C. 1961. *The Political Thought of Sallust*. Cambridge.

Earl, D.C. 1967. *The Moral and Political Tradition of Rome*. Ithaca.

East, K. 2013. *Cicero Illustratus: John Toland and Ciceronian Scholarship in the Early Enlightenment*. London.

Eckert, A. 2016. *Lucius Cornelius Sulla in der antiken Erinnerung: Jener Mörder, der sich Felix nannte*. Berlin.

Edmondson, J. 2008. 'Public Dress and Social Control in Late Republican and Early Imperial Rome', in J. Edmondson and A. Keith (eds.), *Roman Dress and the Fabrics of Roman Culture*. Toronto, 21–46.

Edwards, C. 1993. *The Politics of Immorality in Ancient Rome*. Cambridge.

Edwards, C. 1996. *Writing Rome: Textual Approaches to the City*. Cambridge.

Eilers, C. 2002. *Roman Patrons of Greek Cities*. Oxford.

Epstein, D.F. 1987. *Personal Enmity in Roman Politics, 218–49 BC*. London.

Erdkamp, P. 1992. 'Polybius, Livy and the Fabian Strategy', *Ancient Society* 22: 127–47.

Eussner, A. 1872. *Commentariolum petitionis examinatum atque emendatum*. Würzburg.

Evans, R.J. 1987. 'Norbani Flacci: The Consuls of 38 and 24 BC', *Historia* 36: 121–8

Evans-Grubbs, J. 1993. '"Marriage More Shameful than Adultery": Slave-Mistress Relationships, "Mixed Marriages", and Late Roman Law', *Phoenix* 47: 125–54.

Eyben, E. 1972. 'Youth and Politics during the Roman Republic', *RBPh* 50: 44–69.

Eyben, E. 1993. *Restless Youth in Ancient Rome*, trans. P. Daly. London.

Facciolati, J. 1732. *Commentariolum petitionis ad Marcum fratrem, cum adnotationibus et italica interpretatione*. Padua.

Fantham, E. 1991. '*Stuprum*: Public Attitudes and Penalties for Sexual Offences in Republican Rome', *Échos du Monde Classique/Classical Views* 35: 267–91.

Fantham, E. 2013. *Cicero's Pro L. Murena oratio*. Oxford.

Farney, G.D. 2004. 'Some More Roman Republican "Also Rans"', *Historia* 53: 246–50.

Farney, G.D. 2007. *Ethnic Identity and Aristocratic Competition in Republican Rome*. Cambridge.

Fedeli, P. 1987. *Manualetto di campagna elettorale (Commentariolum petitionis)*. Rome.

Feig Vishnia, R. 2012. *Roman Elections in the Age of Cicero: Society, Government, and Voting*. London.

Ferrary, J.-F. 2002. 'La législation de ambitu, de Sulla à Auguste', in C. Russo Ruggieri (ed.), *Iuris Vincula: Studi in onore de Mario Talamanca*. Naples, 161–98.

Ferriès, M.-C. 2007. *Les partisans d'Antoine: Des orphelins de César aux complices de Cléopâtre*. Bordeaux.

Ferriès, M.-C. 2016. 'Les confiscations durant les guerres civiles: Une arme supplémentaire ou un mal nécessaire?', in C. Chillet, M.-C. Ferriès, and Y. Rivière (eds.), *Les confiscations: Le pouvoir et Rome de la fin de la République à la mort de Néron*. Bordeaux, 139–64.

Ferriès, M.-C., and Delrieux, F. (eds). 2014. *Spolier et confisquer dans les mondes grec et romain*. Chambéry.

Fezzi, L. 2007. 'Il *Commentariolum petitonis*: Sguardi dale democrazie contemporanee'. *Historia* 56: 14–26.

Flaig, E. 2003. *Ritualisierte Politik: Zeichen, Gesten und Herrschaft in alten Rom*. Göttingen.

Flaig, E. 2013. *Die Mehrheitsentscheidung: Enstehung und kulturelle Dynamik*. Paderborn.

Flambard, J.-M. 1981. 'Collegia compitalicia: Phénomène associatif, cadres territoriaux et cadres civiques dans le monde romain à l'époque républicaine'. *Ktema* 6: 143–66.

Flower, H.I. 1996. *Ancestor Masks and Aristocratic Power in Roman Culture*. Oxford.

Flower, H.I. 2014. 'Spectacle and Political Culture in Rome', in H. Flower (ed.), *The Cambridge Companion to the Roman Republic*, 2nd edn. Cambridge, 377–98.

Fögen, T. 2009. *Wissen, Kommunikation und Selbstdarstellung: Zur Struktur und Charakteristik römischer Fachtexte der frühen Kaiserzeit*. Munich.

Forbis, E. 1996. *Municipal Virtues in the Roman Empire*. Stuttgart.

Formisano, M. 2001. *Tecnica e scrittura: Le letterature tecnico-scientifiche nello spazio letterario tardolatina*. Rome.

Forni, G. 1966. '"Doppia tribù" di cittadini romani e cambiamenti di tribù romane', in *Tetraonyma: Miscellanea Graeco-Romana*. Genoa, 139–55.

Fortenbaugh, W.W. 1993. 'Theophrastus on Law, Virtue, and the Particular Situation', in R.M. Rosen and J. Farrell (eds.), *Nomodeiktes: Greek Studies in Honor of Martin Ostwald*. Ann Arbor, 447–55.

Fortenbaugh, W.W., and Schütrumpf, E. 2000. *Demetrius of Phalerum: Text, Translation and Discussion*. New Brunswick.

Fox, M. 2007. *Cicero's Philosophy of History*. Oxford.

Fox, M. 2009. 'Translatio Ciceronis', in W. Kolfer, F. Schaffenrath, and K. Töchterle (eds.), *Pontes V: Übersetzung als Vermittlerin antiker Literatur*. Innsbrück, 245–56.

Fraenkel, E. 1957. *Horace*. Oxford.

Franklin Jr., J.L. 1980. *Pompeii: The Electoral Programmata, Campaigns and Politics*, A.D. 71–79. Rome.

Fraschetti, A. 1990. *Roma e il principe*. Rome.

Frayn, J.F. 1993. *Markets and Fairs in Roman Italy: Their Importance from the Second Century BC to the Third Century AD*. Oxford.

Frazel, T.D. 2009. *The Rhetoric of Cicero's In Verrem*. Göttingen.

Frederiksen, M.W. 1966. 'Caesar, Cicero, and the Problem of Debt', *JRS* 56: 128–41.

Freeman, P. 2012. *How to Win an Election: An Ancient Guide for Modern Politicians*. Princeton.

Freyburger, G. 1986. *Fides: Étude sémantique et religieuse depuis les origines jusqu'à l'époque augustéenne*. Paris.

Friedländer, L. 1907. *Roman Life and Manners under the Early Empire*, vol. 1. London.

Frier, B. 1985. *The Rise of the Roman Jurists: Studies in Cicero's Pro Caecina*. Princeton.

Fuhrmann, M. 1960. *Das Systematische Lehrbuch: Ein Beitrag zur Geschichte der Wissenschaftlichen in der Antike*. Göttingen.

Galinsky, K. 1996. *Augustan Culture*. Princeton.

Gallia, A.B. 2015. 'Vestal Virgins and their Families', *ClAnt* 34: 74–120.

García Morcillo, M. 2008. 'Staging Power and Authority at Roman Auctions', *Ancient Society* 38: 153–81.

Garnsey, P. 1970. *Social Status and Legal Privilege in the Roman Empire*. Oxford.

Gee, E. 2007. 'Quintus Cicero's Astronomy?', *CQ* 57: 565–85.

Gelzer, M. 1912. *Die Nobilität der römischen Republik*. Leipzig.

Gelzer, M. 1969a. *Cicero: Ein biographischer Versuch*. Wiesbaden.

Gelzer, M. 1969b. *The Roman Nobility*, trans. R. Seager. Oxford.

George, M. 2001. 'A Roman Funerary Monument with a Mother and a Daughter', in S. Dixon (ed.), *Childhood, Class and Kin in the Roman World*. London, 178–89.

Gibson, R.K. 1997. 'Didactic Poetry as "Popular" Form: A Study of Imperatival Expressions in Latin Didactic Verse and Prose', in C. Atherton (ed.), *Form and Content in Didactic Poetry*. Bari, 67–98.

Gildenhard, I. 2011. *Creative Eloquence: The Construction of Reality in Cicero's Speeches*. Oxford.

Gill, C. 2003. 'The School in the Roman Imperial Period', in B. Inwood (ed.), *The Cambridge Companion to the Stoics*. Cambridge, 33–58.

Giovannini, A. 2010. 'Cheval public et ordre équestre à la fin de la République', *Athenaeum* 98: 353–64.

Goldbeck, F. 2010. *Salutationes: Die Morgenbegrüßungen in Rom in der Republik und der frühen Kaiserzeit*. Berlin.

Gotoff, H. 1986. 'Cicero's Analysis of the Prosecution Speeches in the Pro Caelio', *CPh* 81: 122–32.

Green, P. 1990. *Alexander to Actium: The Historical Evolution of the Hellenistic Age*. Berkeley and Los Angeles.

Greenidge, A.H.J. 1901. *The Legal Procedure of Cicero's Time*. Oxford.

Grieve, L. 1985. 'The Reform of the *Comitia Centuriata*', *Historia* 34: 278–309.

Griffin, M.T. 1973. 'The Tribune C. Cornelius', *JRS* 63: 196–213.

Griffin, M.T. 1995. 'Philosophical Badinage in Cicero's Letters to his Friends', in J.G.F. Powell (ed.), *Cicero the Philosopher*. Oxford, 325–46.

Griffin, M.T. 2013. *Seneca on Society: A Guide to De beneficiis*. Oxford.

Griffin, M.T., and Barnes, J. (eds.). 1989. *Philosophia togata I: Essays on Philosophy and Roman Society*. Oxford.

Grillo, L. 2012. *The Art of Caesar's Bellum civile: Literature, Ideology and Community*. Cambridge.

Gruen, E.S. 1974. *The Last Generation of the Roman Republic*. Berkeley and Los Angeles.

Gruen, E.S. 2006. 'Romans and Others', in N. Rosenstein and R. Morstein-Marx (eds.), *A Companion to the Roman Republic*. Oxford, 459–77.

Gruen, E.S. 2013. 'Did Romans Have an Ethnic Identity?', *Antichthon* 47: 1–17.

Gruter, J. 1618. *Opera Ciceronis*. Hamburg.

Gurd, S.A. 2011. *Work in Progress: Literary Revision as Social Practice in Ancient Rome*. Oxford.

Guthrie, W.K.C. 1969. *A History of Greek Philosophy*, vol. 3. Cambridge.

Hackl, U. 1989. 'Eques Romanus equo publico: Ein Beitrag zur Definition des römischen Ritterstandes während der Zeit der Republik', in W. Dahlheim, W. Schuller, and J. von Ungen-Sternberg (eds.), *Festschrift Robert Werner zu seinem 65. Geburtstag dargebracht von Freunden, Kollegen und Schülern*. Freiburg, 107–15.

Hahm, D.E. 1963. 'Roman Nobility and the Three Major Priesthoods, 216–167 BC', *TAPhA* 94: 73–85.

Haimson Lushkov, A. 2015. *Magistracy and Historiography of the Roman Republic: Politics in Prose*. Cambridge.

Hall, J. 1996. 'Social Evasion and Aristocratic Manners in Cicero's *De Oratore*', *AJPh* 117: 95–120.

Hall, J. 1998. 'The Deference-Greeting in Roman Society', *Maia* 50: 413–26.

Hall, J. 2005. 'Roman Politeness, and the Socialization of Marcus Cicero the Younger', in. K. Welch and T.W. Hillard (eds.), *Roman Crossings: Theory and Practice in the Roman Republic*. Swansea, 259–78.

Hall, J. 2009. *Politeness and Politics in Cicero's Letters*. Oxford.

Hall, J. 2014. *Cicero's Use of Judicial Theater*. Ann Arbor.

Hall, U. 1964. 'Voting Procedure in Roman Assemblies', *Historia* 13: 267–306.

Hammar, I. 2013. *Making Enemies: The Logic of Immorality in Ciceronian Oratory*. Lund.

Harders, A.-C. 2017. 'Familienbande(n): Die politische Bedeutung von Verwandtschaft in der römischen Republik', in M. Haake and C.-A. Harders (eds.), *Politische Kultur und soziale Struktur der römischen Republik: Bilanzen und Perspektiven*. Stuttgart, 197–214.

Hardie, P. 2012. *Rumour and Renown: Representations of 'Fama' in Western Literature*. Cambridge.

Hardy, E.G. 1924. *Some Problems in Roman History*. Oxford.

Harries, J. 2006. *Cicero and the Jurists*. London.

Harries, J. 2007. *Law and Crime in the Roman World*. Cambridge.

Harris, W.V. 1971. *Rome in Etruria and Umbria*. Oxford.

Harris, W.V. 1979. *War and Imperialism in Republican Rome 327–70 BC*. Oxford.

Harvey, P. 1980. 'Rev. of Shackleton Bailey, *Two Studies in Roman Nomenclature*', *AJPh* 101: 114–20.

Heinze, R. 1925. 'Auctoritas', *Hermes* 60: 348–66.

Hellegouarc'h, J. 1963. *Le vocabulaire latin des relations et des partis politiques sous la république*. Paris.

Henderson, M.I. 1950. 'De Commentariolo petitionis', *JRS* 40: 8–21.

Henderson, M.I. 1972. '[Quintus Cicero], Handbook of Electioneering', in W.G. Williams, M. Cary, and M. Henderson, *Cicero: The Letters to his Brother Quintus, The Letters to Brutus, Handbook of Electioneering, Letter to Octavian*. Cambridge, Mass.: 739–91.

Hendrickson, G.L. 1892. 'On the Authenticity of the Commentariolum petitionis of Quintus Cicero', *AJPh* 13: 200–12.

Hendrickson, G.L. 1904. 'The Commentariolum petitionis Attributed to Quintus Cicero', *Decennial Publications of the University of Chicago* 6: 69–93.

Heuer, K.H. 1941. *Comitas–facilitas–liberalitas*. Münster.

Hinard, F. 1985. *Les proscriptions de la Rome républicaine*. Rome.

Hinard, F. 2011. *Rome, la dernière République: Recueil d'articles*. Paris.

Hine, H.M. 2011. '"Discite ... Agricolae": Modes of Instruction in Latin Prose Agricultural Writing from Cato to Pliny the Elder', *CQ* 61: 624–54.

Hirzl, R. 1895. *Der Dialog: Ein literarhistorischer Versuch*. Leipzig.

Hölkeskamp, K.-J. 2001. 'Fact(ions) or Fiction? Friedrich Münzer and the Aristocracy of the Roman Republic', *International Journal of the Classical Tradition* 8: 92–105.

Hölkeskamp, K.-J. 2004. *Senatus populusque Romanus: Die politische Kultur der Republik—Dimensionen und Deutungen*. Munich.

Hölkeskamp, K.-J. 2006. 'Rituali e cerimonie "Alla romana": Nuove prospettive sulla cultura politica dell'età repubblicana', *Studi storici* 47: 319–63.

Hölkeskamp, K.-J. 2010. *Reconstructing the Roman Republic: An Ancient Political Culture and Modern Research*. Princeton.

Hölkeskamp, K.-J. 2011a. *Die Entstehung der Nobilität: Studien zur sozialen und politischen Geschicthe der römischen Republik im 4. Jh. v. Chr.*, 2nd edn. Stuttgart.

Hölkeskamp, K.-J. 2011b. 'The Roman Republic as Theatre of Power: The Consuls as Leading Actors', in H. Beck, A. Duplá, M. Jehne, and F. Pina Polo (eds.), *Consuls and the Res Publica: Holding High Office in the Roman Republic*. Cambridge, 161–81.

Hölkeskamp, K.-J. 2011c. 'Self-Serving Sermons: Oratory and the Self-Construction of the Republican Aristocrat', in C. Smith and R. Covino (eds.), *Praise and Blame in Roman Republican Rhetoric*. Swansea, 17–34.

Hölkeskamp, K.-J. 2013. 'Friends, Romans, Countrymen: Addressing the Roman People and the Rhetoric of Inclusion', in C. Steel and H. van der Blom (eds.), *Community and Communication: Oratory and Politics in Republican Rome*. Oxford, 11–28.

Hölkeskamp, K.-J. 2014. 'Under Roman Roofs: Family, House, and Household', in H. Flower (ed.), *The Cambridge Companion to the Roman Republic*, 2nd edn. Cambridge, 101–26.

Hollis, A.S. 2007. *Fragments of Roman Poetry, c.60 BC–AD 20*. Oxford.

Hopkins, K., and Burton, G. 1983. 'Political Succession in the Late Republic (259–50 BC)', in K. Hopkins, *Death and Renewal*. Cambridge, 31–119.

Horsfall, N. 1987. 'The "Letter of Cornelia": Yet More Problems', *Athenaeum* 65: 231–4.

Horster, M., and Reitz, C. (eds.). 2003. *Antike Fachschriftsteller: Literarischer Diskurs und sozialer Kontext*. Stuttgart.

Hübner, W. 2005. 'Die Rezeption der Phainomena Arats in der lateinischen Literatur', in M. Horster and C. Reitz (eds.), *Wissensvermittlung in dichter-ischer Gestalt*. Stuttgart, 133–54.

Hug, A. 1920. 'Salutatio', *RE* 1A.2. Stuttgart, 2060–72.

Humm, M. 2011. 'The Curiate Law and the Religious Nature of the Power of Roman Magistrates', in O.E. Tellegen-Couperus (ed.), *Law and Religion in the Roman Republic*. Leiden, 57–84.

Hutchinson, G.O. 1998. *Cicero's Correspondence: A Literary Study*. Oxford.

Hutchinson, G.O. 2009. 'Read the Instructions: Didactic Poetry and Didactic Prose', *CQ* 59: 196–211.

Iddeng, J.W. 2006. 'Publica aut peri! The Releasing and Distribution of Roman Books', *Symbolae Osloenses* 81: 58–84.

Innes, D.C. 1995. 'Demetrius On Style', in S. Halliwell, W.H. Fyfe, D. Russell, D.C. Innes, and W.R. Roberts, *Aristotle, Poetics; Longinus, On the Sublime; Demetrius, On Style*. Cambridge, Mass., 309–525.

Instinsky, H.U. 1971. 'Zur Echtheitsfrage der Brieffragmente der Cornelia, Mutter der Gracchen', *Chiron* 1: 177–89.

Inwood, B. 2007. 'The Importance of Form in Seneca's Philosophical Letters', in R. Morello and A.D. Morrison (eds.), *Ancient Letters*. Oxford, 133–48.

Ioannatou, M. 2006. *Affaires d'argent dans la correspondance de Cicéron: L'aristocratie sénatoriale face à ses dettes*. Paris.

Isayev, E. 2007. 'Unruly Youth? The Myth of Generation Conflict in Late Republican Rome', *Historia* 56: 1–13.

Jacotot, M. 2013. *Question d'honneur: Les notions d'honos, honestum et honestas dans la République romaine antique*. Rome.

Janson, T. 1964. *Latin Prose Prefaces: Studies in Literary Conventions*. Stockholm.

Jehne, M. 1995. 'Die Beeinflussung von Entscheidungen durch "Bestechung": Zur Funktion des Ambitus in der römischen Republik', in M. Jehne (ed.), *Demokratie in Rom? Zur Rolle des Volkes in der Politik der römischen Republik*. Stuttgart, 51–76.

Jehne, M. 2000. 'Rednertätigkeit und Statusdissonanzen in der späten römischen Republik', in C. Neumeister and W. Raeck (eds.), *Rede und Redner: Bewertung und Darstellung in den antiken Kulturen*. Möhnesee.

Jehne, M. 2006. 'Who Attended Roman Assemblies? Some Remarks on Political Participation in Rome', in F. Marco Simón, F. Pina Polo, and J. Remesal Rodríguez (eds.), *Repúblicas y ciudadanos: Modelos de participación cívica en el mundo antiguo*. Barcelona, 221–34.

Jehne, M. 2009. 'Le système electoral des Romains et le désespoir des candidats', *Revue Historique de Droit Français et Étranger* 87: 495–513.

Jehne, M. 2010. 'Die Dominanz des Vorgangs über den Ausgang: Struktur und Verlauf der Wahlen in der römischen Republik', in C. Dartmann, G. Wassilowsky, and T. Weller (eds.), *Technik und Symbolik vormoderner Wahlverfahren*. Munich, 17–34.

Jehne, M. 2011a. 'Blaming the People in Front of the People: Restraint and Outbursts of Orators in Roman Contiones', in C. Smith and R. Covino (eds.), *Praise and Blame in Roman Republican Rhetoric*. Swansea, 111–26.

Jehne, M. 2011b. 'The Rise of the Consular as a Social Type in the Third and Second Centuries B.C.', in H. Beck, A. Duplá, M. Jehne, and F. Pina Polo (eds.), *Consuls and the Res Publica: Holding High Office in the Roman Republic*. Cambridge, 211–31.

Jehne, M. 2013a. 'Feeding the *plebs* with Words: The Significance of Senatorial Public Oratory in the Small World of Roman Politics', in C. Steel and H. van der Blom (eds.), *Community and Communication: Oratory and Politics in Republican Rome*. Oxford, 49–62.

Jehne, M. 2013b. 'Konsensfiktionen in römischen Volksversammlungen: Überlegungen zur frührepublikanischen Curienversammlung und zu den kaiserzeitlichen Destinationscenturien', in E. Flaig and E. Müller-Luckner (eds.), *Genesis und Dynamiken der Mehrheitsentscheidung*. Munich, 129–52.

Jehne, M. 2016. 'The Senatorial Economics of Status in the Late Republic', in H. Beck, M. Jehne, and J. Serrati (eds.), *Money and Power in the Roman Republic*. Brussels, 188–207.

Johnston, D. 1999. *Roman Law in Context*. Cambridge.

Kantor, G. 2013. 'SEG LV 1482, ll. 32–34, and the Crime of *plagium* in the Late Republic', *ZPE* 184: 219–24.

Kaser, M. 1971. *Das römische Privatrecht*. Munich.

Kassel, R., and Austin, C. 2001. *Poetae comici Graeci*, vol. 1. Berlin.

Kaster, R.A. 1988. *Guardians of Language: The Grammarian and Society in Late Antiquity*. Berkeley and Los Angeles.

Kaster, R.A. 2005. *Emotion, Restraint, and Community in Ancient Rome*. Oxford.

Kaster, R.A. 2006. *Cicero: Speech on Behalf of Publius Sestius*. Oxford.

Kay, P. 2014. *Rome's Economic Revolution*. Oxford.

Keaveney, A. 2005. *Sulla: The Last Republican*, 2nd edn. London.

Keegan, P. 2014. *Graffiti in Antiquity*. London.

Kelly, G.P. 2006. *A History of Exile in the Roman Republic*. Cambridge.

Kelly, J.M. 1966. *Roman Litigation*. Oxford.

Kenney, E.J. 1982. 'Books and Readers in the Roman World', in E.J. Kenney and W.V. Clausen (eds.), *The Cambridge History of Classical Literature*, vol. 2, pt 1. Cambridge, 3–50.

Kerferd, G.B. 1981. *The Sophistic Movement*. Cambridge.

Kidd, D. 1998. *Aratus: Phaenomena*. Cambridge.

Kierdorf, W. 1966. 'Comm. pet. 9 und die Bedeutung von *corroboratus*', *Hermes* 94: 443–9.

Kinsey, T.E. 1965. 'Cicero «Pro Murena» 71', *Revue Belge de Philologie* 43: 57–9.

Kinsey, T.E. 1966. 'A *senatus consultum* in the Pro Murena', *Mnemosyne* 19: 272–73.

Kirby, J.T. 1990. *The Rhetoric of Cicero's Pro Cluentio*. Amsterdam.

Klebs, E. 1894. 'C. Antonius', *RE* 1.2. Stuttgart, 2577–82.

Kleinman, B.H. 2012. *Ambitus in the Late Roman Republic (80–50 b.c.)*. Montreal.

Knapp, P.C. 1980. 'Festus 262L and *praefecturae* in Italy', *Athenaeum* 58: 14–38.

Kolendo, J. 1989. *Nomenclator: Memoria del suo padrone o del suo patrone*. Faenza.

Konrad, C.F. 2006. 'From the Gracchi to the First Civil War (133–70)', in N. Rosenstein and R. Morstein-Marx (eds.), *A Companion to the Roman Republic*. Oxford, 167–89.

Konrad, C.F. 1996. 'Notes of Roman Also-Rans', in J. Linderski (ed.), *Imperium sine fine: T. Robert S. Broughton and the Roman Republic*. Stuttgart, 103–43.

Konstan, D. 1997. *Friendship in the Classical World*. Cambridge.

Konstan, D. 2010. 'Are Fellow Citizens Friends? Aristotle versus Cicero on *philia, amiticia*, and Social Solidarity', in R.M. Rosen and I. Sluiter (eds.), *Valuing Others in Classical Antiquity*. Leiden, 233–48.

Koskenniemi, H. 1956. *Studien zur Idee und Phraseologie des griechischen Briefes bis 400 n. Chr.* Helsinki.

Kroll, W. 1933. *Die Kultur der ciceronischen Zeit.* Leipzig.

Laffi, U. 2007. *Colonie e municipi nello stato romano.* Rome.

Lange, L. 1876. *Römische Alterthümer*, 3rd edn., vol. 1. Berlin.

Lange, L. 1879. *Römische Alterthümer*, 3rd edn., vol. 2. Berlin.

Langlands, R. 2006. *Sexual Morality in Ancient Rome.* Cambridge.

Langlands. R. 2011. 'Roman *exempla* and Situation Ethics: Valerius Maximus and Cicero *De officiis*', *JRS* 101: 100–22.

Langslow, D. 2007. 'The *epistula* in Ancient Scientific and Technical Literature, with Special Reference to Medicine', in R. Morello and D.A. Morrison (eds.), *Ancient Letters.* Oxford, 211–34.

Laser, G. 2001. *Q. Tullius Cicero: Commentariolum petitionis.* Darmstadt.

Lau, D. 1975. *Der lateinische Begriff 'Labor'.* Munich.

Laurence, L.R. 1994. 'Rumour and Communication in Roman Politics', *G&R* 41: 62–74.

Lausberg, H. 1990. *Handbuch der literarischen Rhetorik*, 3rd edn. Stuttgart.

Lebek, W.D. 1991. 'Das SC der Tabula Larinas: Rittermusterung und andere Probleme', *ZPE* 85: 41–70.

Leeman, A.D., and Pinkster, H. 1981. *M. Tullius Cicero De oratore libri III*, vol. 1 (1.1–165). Heidelberg.

Leeman, A.D., Pinkster, H., and Rabbie, E. 1989. *M. Tullius Cicero De oratore libri III*, vol. 3 (2.99–290). Heidelberg.

Le Gall, J. 1966. 'La nouvelle plèbe et la sportule quotidienne', in R. Chevallier (ed.), *Mélanges d'archéologie et d'histoire offerts à André Piganiol.* Paris, 1449–53.

Lendon, J.E. 1997. *Empire of Honour: The Art of Government in the Roman World.* Oxford.

Leo, F. 1895. 'Die Publication von Ciceros Briefen an Atticus', *NGG*: 447–50.

Leonhard, R. 1901. 'Deductio', *RE* 4.2. Stuttgart, 2364–5.

Leunissen, P.M.M. 1993. 'Conventions of Patronage in Senatorial Careers under the Principate', *Chiron* 23: 101–20.

Levick, B.M. 1967. 'Imperial Control of the Elections under the Early Principate: Commendatio, suffragatio, and "nominatio"', *ZPE* 16: 207–30.

Levick, B.M. 1981. '*Professio*', *Athenaeum* 59: 378–88.

Levick, B.M. 2015. *Catiline.* London.

Lewis, A.-M. 1992. 'The Popularity of the Phaenomena of Aratus: A Reevaluation', *Studies in Latin Literature and Roman History* 6: 94–118.

Lewis, R.G. 2006. *Asconius: Commentaries on Speeches by Cicero.* Oxford.

Licandro, O. 1997. 'Candidature e accusa criminale: Strumenti giuridici e lotta politica nella tarda repubblica', *Index* 25: 447–71.

Liebenam, W. 1905. 'Divisor', *RE* 5. Stuttgart, 1237–8.

Linderski, J. 1995. *Roman Questions: Selected Papers.* Stuttgart.

Linderski, J. 2007. *Roman Questions II: Selected Papers.* Stuttgart.

Lintott, A.W. 1972. 'Imperial Expansion and Moral Decline in the Roman Republic', *Historia* 21: 626–38.

Lintott, A.W. 1990. 'Electoral Bribery in the Roman Republic', *JRS* 90: 1–16.

Lintott, A.W. 1992. *Judicial Reform and Land Reform in the Roman Republic.* Cambridge.

Lintott, A.W. 1993. *Imperium Romanum: Politics and Administration.* London.

Lintott, A.W. 1994. 'Political History, 146–95 B.C', in J.A. Crook, A. Lintott, and E. Rawson (eds.), *The Cambridge Ancient History*, 2nd edn., vol. 9. Cambridge, 40–103.

Lintott. A.W. 1999a. *The Constitution of the Roman Republic.* Oxford.

Lintott, A.W. 1999b. *Violence in Republican Rome*, 2nd edn. Oxford.

Lintott, A.W. 2004. 'Legal Procedure in Cicero's Time', in J. Powell and J. Paterson (eds.), *Cicero the Advocate.* Oxford, 61–78.

Lintott, A.W. 2008. *Cicero as Evidence: A Historian's Companion.* Oxford.

Lintott, A.W. 2013. *Plutarch: Demosthenes and Cicero.* Oxford.

Lobur, J.A. 2008. *Consensus, Concordia and the Formation of Roman Imperial Ideology.* London.

Lomas, K. 2004. 'A Volscian Mafia? Cicero and his Italian Clients in the Forensic Speeches', in J. Powell and J. Paterson (eds.), *Cicero the Advocate.* Oxford, 97–116.

Lomas, K. 2012. 'The Weakest Link: Elite Social Networks in Republican Italy', in S.T. Roselaar (ed.), *Processes of Integration and Identity Formation in the Roman Republic.* Leiden, 197–213.

Long, A.A. 1995. 'Cicero's Politics in De officiis', in A. Laks and M. Schofield (eds.), *Justice and Generosity: Studies in Hellenistic Social and Political Philosophy.* Cambridge, 213–40.

Lott, J.B. 2004. *The Neighborhoods of Augustan Rome.* Cambridge.

Lucrezi, F. 1998. 'Commentariolum petitionis', *Studia et Documenta Historiae et Iuris* 64: 413–39.

Lucrezi, F. 2001. *Quinto Tullio Cicerone, Manualetto per la campagna elettorale.* Naples.

McConnell, S. 2014. *Philosophical Life in Cicero's Letters.* Cambridge.

McCoy, M.B. 1987. 'Quintus Cicero, the Commentariolum petitionis, and the Political Aspirations of the Ciceros', *AnW* 15: 99–104.

McDermott, W.C. 1970. 'Commentariolum petitionis 2', *Historia* 19: 384–5.

McDermott, W.C. 1971. 'Q. Cicero', *Historia* 20: 702–17.

McDonnell, M. 2006. *Roman Manliness: Virtus and Republican Rome.* Cambridge.

MacDowell, D.M. 2009. *Demosthenes the Orator.* Oxford.

MacMullen, R. 1980. 'How Many Romans Voted?', *Athenaeum* 58: 454–7.

MacMullen, R. 1986. 'Personal Power in the Roman Empire', *AJPh* 107: 512–24.

Malherbe, A.J. 1988. *Ancient Epistolary Theorists.* Atlanta.

Mamoojee, A.H. 1977. *Quintus Tullius Cicero: A Monograph on his Life and Work*. Ottawa.

Mankin, D. 2011. *Cicero, De oratore, Book III*. Cambridge.

Manning, C.E. 1985. 'Liberalitas: The Decline and Rehabilitation of a Virtue', *G&R* 32: 73–83.

Marco Simón, F., and Pina Polo, F. 2000. 'Mario Gratidiano, los *compita* y la religiosidad popular a fines de la república', *Klio* 82: 154–70.

Marshall, B.A. 1985a. 'Catilina and the Execution of M. Marius Gratidianus', *CQ* 35: 124–33.

Marshall, B.A. 1985b. *A Historical Commentary on Asconius*. Columbia.

May, J.M. 1988. *Trials of Character: The Eloquence of Ciceronian Ethos*. Chapel Hill.

May, J.M. 2007. 'Cicero as Rhetorician', in W. Dominik and J. Hall (eds.), *A Companion to Roman Rhetoric*. Oxford, 250–63.

Mayer, E. 2012. *The Ancient Middle Classes: Urban Life and Aesthetics in the Roman Empire, 100 BCE–250 CE*. Cambridge, Mass.

Mayer, R.G. 2005. 'The Impracticality of Latin "Kunstprosa"', in T. Reinhardt, M. Lapidge, and J.N. Adams (eds.), *Aspects of the Language of Latin Prose*. Oxford, 195–210.

Meier, C. 1965. 'Populares', *RE* Suppl. 10. Stuttgart, 549–615.

Meier, C. 1980. *Res Publica Amissa: Eine Studie zu Verfassung und Geschichte der späten römischen Republik*, 2nd edn. Wiesbaden.

Merguet, H. 1884. *Lexikon zu den Reden des Cicero*, 4 vols. Jena.

Merguet, H. 1894. *Lexikon zu den philosophischen Schriften*, 3 vols. Jena.

Michaels, A.K. 1967. *Calendar of the Roman Republic*. Princeton.

Mignone, L.M. 2016. *The Republican Aventine and Rome's Social Order*. Ann Arbor.

Millar, F. 1998. *The Crowd in Rome in the Late Republic*. Ann Arbor.

Millar, F. 2002. *Rome, the Greek East, and the East*, vol. 1: *The Roman Republic and the Augustan Revolution*. Chapel Hill.

Mitchell, T.N. 1979. *Cicero: The Ascending Years*. New Haven.

Mitchell, T.N. 1991. *Cicero: The Senior Statesman*. New Haven.

Mitsis, P. 1993. 'Committing Philosophy in the Reader: Didactic Coercion and Reader Autonomy in *De rerum natura*', in A. Sciesaro, P. Mitsis, and J. Strauss Clay (eds.), *Mega nepios: Il destinatario nell'epos didascalico. The Addressee in Didactic Epic*. Pisa, 111–28.

Moatti, C. 1997. *La raison de Rome: Naissance de l'esprit critique à la fin de la République (IIe–Ier siècle avant J.-C.)*. Paris.

Mommsen, T. 1899. *Römisches Strafrecht*. Leipzig.

Moreau, P. 1990. 'Adfinitas: La parenté par alliance dans la société romaine (Ier siècle av. J.-C.–Ier siècle ap. J.-C.)', in *Parenté et stratégies familiales dans l'Antiquité romaine*. Paris, 3–26.

Morello, R. 2013. 'Writer and Addressee in Cicero's Letters', in C. Steel (ed.), *The Cambridge Companion to Cicero*. Cambridge, 196–215.

Morgan, M.G. 1971. 'The Portico of Metellus: A Reconsideration', *Hermes* 99: 480–505.

Morgan, M.G. 1973. 'Villa Publica and Magna Mater', *Klio* 55: 215–46.

Morley, N. 1996. *Metropolis and Hinterland: The City of Rome and the Italian Economy*. Cambridge.

Morrison, A.D. 2007. 'Didacticism and Epistolarity in Horace's Epistles 1', in R. Morello and A.D. Morrison (eds.), *Ancient Letters*. Oxford, 107–32.

Morstein-Marx, R. 1998. 'Publicity, Popularity and Patronage in the *Commentariolum petitionis*', *ClAnt* 17: 259–88.

Morstein-Marx, R. 2004. *Mass Oratory and Political Power in the Late Roman Republic*. Cambridge.

Morstein-Marx, R. 2012. 'Political Graffiti in the Late Roman Republic: Hidden Transcripts and Common Knowledge', in C. Kuhn (ed.), *Politische Kommunikation und öffentliche Meinung in der Antiken Welt*. Stuttgart, 191–217.

Morstein-Marx, R. 2015. 'Persuading the People in the Roman Participatory Context', in D. Hammer (ed.), *A Companion to Greek Democracy and the Roman Republic*. Oxford, 294–309.

Mouritsen, H. 1988. *Elections, Magistrates and Municipal Élite: Studies in Pompeian Epigraphy*. Rome.

Mouritsen, H. 1998. *Italian Unification: A Study in Ancient and Modern Historiography*. London.

Mouritsen, H. 2001. *Plebs and Politics in the Late Roman Republic*. Cambridge.

Mouritsen, H. 2011. *The Freedman in the Roman World*. Cambridge.

Mouritsen, H. 2017a. 'Cicero's *familia urbana* and the Social Structure of Late Republican Rome', in M. Haake and C.-A. Harders (eds.), *Politische Kultur und soziale Struktur der römischen Republik: Bilanzen und Perspektiven*. Stuttgart, 215–30.

Mouritsen, H. 2017b. *Politics in the Roman Republic*. Cambridge.

Moussy, C. 1966. *Gratia et sa famille*. Paris.

Muecke, F. 2016. 'Biondo Flavio on the Roman Elections', *PBSR* 84: 275–97.

Münzer, F. 1897. 'L. Cassius Longinus', *RE* 3. Stuttgart, 1738–9.

Münzer, F. 1901. 'Vargula', *RE* 8A. Stuttgart, 2392.

Münzer, F. 1909. 'M. Fabius Hadrianus', *RE* 6.2. Stuttgart, 1771.

Münzer, F. 1920. 'M'. Sabidius, M'. f', *RE* 1A.2. Stuttgart, 1570.

Münzer, F. 1923a. 'A. Sempronius Musca', 1923. *RE* 2A. Stuttgart, 1435.

Münzer, F. 1923b. 'T. Sempronius Musca', 1923. *RE* 2A. Stuttgart, 1435.

Münzer, F. 1930. 'M. Marius Gratidianus', *RE* 14.2. Stuttgart, 1825–7.

Münzer, F. 1948. 'Q. Tullius Cicero', *RE* 7A.2. Stuttgart, 1286–306.

Nadig, P. 1997. *Ardet ambitus: Untersuchungen zum Phänomen der Wahlbestechungen in der römischen Republik*. Frankfurt am Main.

Nardo, D. 1970. *Il 'Commentariolum petitionis': La propaganda elettorale nella 'Ars' di Quinto Cicerone*. Padua.

Nardo, D. 1972. Q. *Ciceronis Commentariolum petitionis*. Florence.

Niccolini, G. 1934. *I fasti dei tribuni della plebe*. Milan.

Nicolet, C. 1964. 'Les noms des chevaliers victims de Catilina dans le *Commentariolum petitionis*', in *Mélanges d'histoire ancienne offerts à William Seston*. Paris, 381–95.

Nicolet, C. 1966. *L'ordre équestre a l'époque républicaine (312–43 av. J.-C.)*, vol. 1. Paris.

Nicolet, C. 1972. 'Amicissimi Catilinae (À propos du *Commentariolum petitionis*)', *REL* 50: 163–86.

Nicolet, C. 1974. *L'ordre équestre a l'époque républicaine (312–43 av. J.-C.)*, vol. 2. Paris.

Nicolet, C. 1980. *The World of the Citizen in Republican Rome*. Berkeley and Los Angeles.

Nicolet, C. 1996. 'Les littératures techniques dans le monde romain', in C. Nicolet (ed.), *Les littératures techniques dans l'Antiquité romaine: Statut, public et destination, tradition*. Geneva, 1–17.

Nippel, W. 1988. *Aufruhr und Polizei in der römischen Republik*. Stuttgart.

Nippel, W. 1995. *Public Order in Ancient Rome*. Cambridge.

Nisbet, R.G.M. 1961a. *Cicero: In L. Calpurnium Pisonem oratio*. Oxford.

Nisbet, R.G.M. 1961b. 'The *Commentariolum petitionis*: Some Arguments against Authenticity', *JRS* 51: 84–7.

Nisbet, R.G.M. 1990. 'Cola and Clausulae in Cicero's Speeches', in E.M. Craik (ed.), *'Owls to Athens': Essays on Classical Subjects Presented to Sir Kenneth Dover*. Oxford, 349–59.

Nisbet, R.G.M., and Rudd, N. 2004. *A Commentary on Horace, Odes, Book III*. Oxford.

Nixon, C.E.V., and Rodgers, B.S., 1994. *In Praise of Later Roman Emperors: The Panegyrici Latini*. Berkeley and Los Angeles.

Norden, E. 1966. *Kleine Schriften zum klassischen Altertum*. Berlin.

Notomi, N. 1999. *The Unity of Plato's Sophist: Between the Sophist and the Philosopher*. Cambridge.

Noy, D. 2000. *Foreigners at Rome: Citizens and Strangers*. Swansea.

Núñez González, J.M. 1999. 'En torno al estilo del *Commentariolum petitionis*', in *Corona Spicea: In Memoriam Cristóbal Rodríguez Alonso*. Oviedo, 233–42.

Oakley, S.P. 1997. *A Commentary on Livy, Books 6–10*, vol. 1. Oxford.

Oakley, S.P. 1998. *A Commentary on Livy, Books 6–10*, vol. 2. Oxford.

Oakely, S.P. 2005a. *A Commentary on Livy, Books 6–10*, vol. 3. Oxford.

Oakley, S.P. 2005b. *A Commentary on Livy, Books 6–10*, vol. 4. Oxford.

Ober, J. 1989. *Mass and Elite in Democratic Athens*. Princeton.

Ogilvie, R.M. 1965. *A Commentary on Livy, Books 1–5*. Oxford.

Olson, K. 2008. 'The Appearance of the Young Roman Girl', in J. Edmondson and A. Keith (eds.), *Roman Dress and the Fabrics of Roman Culture*. Toronto, 139–57.

Olson, S.D. 2007. *Broken Laughter: Select Fragments of Greek Comedy*. Oxford.

O'Neill, P. 2003. 'Going Round in Circles: Popular Speech in Ancient Rome', *ClAnt* 22: 135–66.

Opelt, I. 1965. *Die lateinischen Schimpfwörter und verwandte sprachliche Erscheinungen: Eine Typologie*. Heidelberg.

Orelli, J.C. 1829. *Ciceronis opera quae supersunt omnia*, vol. 3.1. Zürich.

Östenberg, I. 2015. 'Power Walks: Aristocratic Escorted Movements in Republican Rome', in I. Östenberg, S. Malmberg, and J. Bjørnebye (eds.), *The Moving City: Processions, Passages and Promenades in Ancient Rome*. London, 13–22.

O'Sullivan, L. 2009. *The Regime of Demetrius of Phalerum in Athens, 317–307 BCE: A Philosopher in Politics*. Leiden.

O'Sullivan, T.M. 2011. *Walking in Roman Culture*. Cambridge.

Palermus, V. 1583. *In M. Tulli Ciceronis De philosophia volumen secundum Aldi Mannuccii commentarius, in Q. Ciceronis de petitione consulatus ad M. Tullium fratrem librum Valerii Palermi Veronensis commentarius*. Venice.

Palma, A. 1988. *Iura Vicinitatis: Solidarietà e limitazioni nel rapporto di vicinato in diritto romano dell'età classica*. Turin.

Palmer, R.E.A. 1971. 'Tre lettere in cerca di storico', *RFIC* 99: 385–409.

Panciera, S. 1980. 'Catilina e Catone su due coppette romane', in M.J. Fontan, M.T. Piraino, and R.P. Rizzo (eds.), *Φιλίας χάριν: Miscellanea di studi classici in onore de Eugenio Manni*. Rome, 1635–51.

Pani, M. 2007. 'Il modello dell'obbligazione sociale nel Commentariolum petitionis', in E. Lo Cascio and G.D. Merola (eds.), *Forme di aggregazione nel mondo romano*. Bari, 303–12.

Pani, M. 2010. *La repubblica romana*. Bologna.

Pasoli, L.E. 1975. 'Sul testo e l'interpretazione del §1 del *Commentariolum petitionis*', *Vichiana* 4: 256–60.

Paterson, J. 1985. 'Politics in the Late Republic', in T.P. Wiseman (ed.), *Roman Political Life, 90 BC–AD 69*. Exeter, 21–43.

Paterson, J. 2006. 'Rome and Italy', in N. Rosenstein and R. Morstein-Marx (eds.), *A Companion to the Roman Republic*. Oxford, 606–24.

Patimo, V.M. 2009. *La Pro Cluentio di Cicerone: Introduzione e commento dei §§1–81*. Herzberg.

Peirano, L. 2012. *The Rhetoric of the Roman Fake: Latin Pseudepigrapha in Context*. Cambridge.

Pelling, C. 2000. *Literary Texts and the Greek Historian*. London.

Pelling, C. 2011. *Plutarch, Caesar*. Oxford.

Peter, H. 1901. *Der Brief in der römischen Literatur*. Leipzig.

Petersson, T. 1920. *Cicero: A Biography*. Berkeley and Los Angeles.

Pfeilschifter, R. 2005. *Titus Quinctius Flamininus: Untersuchungen zur römischen Griechenlandpolitik*. Göttingen.

Phillips, D.A. 2004. 'Voter Turnout in Consular Elections', *AHB* 18: 48–60.

Phillips, E.J. 1970. 'Cicero and the Prosecution of C. Manilius', *Latomus* 29: 595–607.

Pickard-Cambridge, A.W. 1962. *Dithyramb, Tragedy and Comedy*, 2nd edn., rev. T.B.L. Webster. Oxford.

Pina Polo, F. 1996. *Contra arma verbis: Der Redner vor dem Volk in der späten römischen Republik*. Stuttgart.

Pina Polo, F. 2010. '*Frigidus rumor*: The Creation of a (Negative) Public Image in Rome', in A.J. Turner, K.O. Chong Gossard, and F.J. Vervaet (eds.), *Public and Private Lies: The Discourse of Despotism and Deceit in the Graeco-Roman World*. Leiden: 75–90.

Pina Polo, F. 2011. *The Consul at Rome: The Civil Functions of the Consuls in the Roman Republic*. Cambridge.

Pina Polo, F. 2012. '*Veteres candidati*: Losers in the elections in republican Rome', in F. Marco Simón, F. Pina Polo, and J. Remesal Rodríguez (eds.), *Vae Victis! Perdedores en el mundo antiguo*. Barcelona, 63–82.

Pina Polo, F. 2016. '*Cupiditas pecuniae*: Wealth and Power in Cicero', in H. Beck, M. Jehne, and J. Serrati (eds.), *Money and Power in Republican Rome*. Brussels, 165–77.

Pöschl, V. 1961. 'Invidia nelle orazione di Cicerone', *Atti del 1 congresso internazionale de studi Ciceroniani*, vol. 2. Rome, 119–25.

Potter, D. 2011. 'Holding Court in Republican Rome (105–44)', *AJPh* 132: 59–80.

Powell, J.G.F. 1988. *Cicero, Cato maior de Senectute*. Cambridge.

Powell, J.G.F. 1990. *Cicero, Laelius, On Friendship and The Dream of Scipio*. Warminster.

Powell, J.G.F. (ed.). 1995a. *Cicero the Philosopher*. Oxford.

Powell, J.G.F. 1995b. 'Friendship and its Problems in Greek and Roman Thought', in D. Innes, H. Hine, and C. Pelling (eds.), *Ethics and Rhetoric: Classical Essays for Donald Russell on his Seventy-Fifth Birthday*. Oxford, 31–45.

Powell, J.G.F., and Paterson, J. (eds.). 2004. *Cicero the Advocate*. Oxford.

Premerstein, A. von. 1900. 'Commentarii', *RE* 4.1. Stuttgart, 726–59.

Prost, F. 2017. *Quintus Cicéron, Petit manuel de la campagne électorale, & Marcus Cicéron, Lettres a son frère Quintus I, 1 et 2*. Paris.

Purcell, N. 1994. 'The City of Rome and the *plebs urbana* in the Late Republic', in A. Crook, A. Lintott, and E. Rawson (eds.), *The Cambridge Ancient History*, 2nd edn., vol. 9. Cambridge, 644–88.

Ramsey, J. 1980a. 'The Prosecution of C. Manilius in 66 B.C. and Cicero's *Pro Manilio*', *Phoenix* 34: 323–36.

Ramsey, J. 1980b. 'A Reconstruction of Q. Gallius' Trial for *ambitus*: One Less Reason for Doubting the Authenticity of the *Commentariolum petitionis*', *Historia* 29: 402–21.

Rawson, E. 1985. *Intellectual Life in the Late Roman Republic*. Baltimore.

Rawson, E. 1991. *Roman Culture and Society: Collected Papers*. Oxford.

Reinhardt, T. 2003. *Marcus Tullius Cicero, Topica*. Oxford.

Reynolds, L.D. (ed.). 1983. *Texts and Transmissions: A Survey of Latin Classics*. Oxford.

Richardson, J.S. 1971. 'The *Commentariolum petitionis*', *Historia* 20: 436–42.

Richardson, Jr., L. 1992. *A New Topographical Dictionary of Ancient Rome*. Baltimore.

Riggsby, A.M. 1999. *Crime and Community in Ciceronian Rome*. Austin.

Riggsby, A.M. 2006. *Caesar in Gaul and Rome: War in Words*. Austin.

Rilinger, R. 1976. *Der Einfluss des Wahlleiters bei den römischen Konsulwahlen von 366 bis 50 v. Chr.* Munich.

Rilinger, R. 2007. *Ordo und dignitas: Beiträge zur römischen Verfassungs- und Sozialgeschichte*. Stuttgart.

Robb, M.A. 2010. *Beyond* populares *and* optimates: *Political Language in the Late Republic*. Stuttgart.

Robertis, F.M. de. 1938. *Il diritto associativo romano, dai collegi della repubblica alle corporazioni del basso impero*. Bari.

Roller, M.B. 2004. 'Exemplarity in Roman Culture: The Cases of Horatius Cocles and Cloelia', *CPh* 99: 1–56.

Roller, M.B. 2011. 'The Consul(ar) as Exemplum: Fabius *Cunctator*'s Paradoxical Glory', in H. Beck, A. Duplá, M. Jehne, and F. Pina Polo (eds.), *Consuls and res publica: Holding High Office in the Roman Republic*. Cambridge, 182–210.

Rollinger, C. 2014. *Amicitia sanctissime colenda: Freundschaft und soziale Netzwerke in der späten Republik*. Trier.

Romano, D. 1961–2. 'Sul Commentariolum petitionis di Quinto Cicerone', *Atti Acad. Sc. Lett. Arti Palermo*: 133–90.

Rosenmeyer, P.A. 2001. *Ancient Epistolary Fictions: The Letter in Greek Literature*. Cambridge.

Rosenstein, N. 1990. *Imperatores victi: Military Defeat and Aristocratic Competition in the Middle and Late Roman Republic*. Berkeley and Los Angeles.

Rosenstein, N. 1993. 'Competition and Crisis in Mid-Republican Rome', *Phoenix* 47: 313–38.

Rosenstein, N. 2006. 'Aristocratic Values', in N. Rosenstein and R. Morstein-Marx (eds.), *A Companion to the Roman Republic*. Oxford, 365–82.

Rosillo López, C. 2010. *La corruption à la fin de la république romaine (IIe–Ier s. av. J.-C.)*. Stuttgart.

Rosillo López, C. 2013. 'The Common (*mediocris*) Orator of the Late Republic: The Scribonii Curiones', in C. Steel and H. van der Blom (eds.), *Community and Communication: Oratory and Politics in Republican Rome*. Oxford, 287–98.

Rosillo López, C. 2016. 'The Workings of Public Opinion in the Late Roman Republic: The Case Study of Corruption', *Klio* 98: 203–27.

Rosillo López, C. 2017. *Public Opinion and Politics in the Late Roman Republic*. Cambridge.

Rosokoki, A. 1995. *Die Erigone des Eratosthenes: Eine kommentierte Ausgabe der Fragmente*. Heidelberg.

Rostovtzeff, M. 1941. *The Social and Economic History of the Hellenistic World.* Oxford.

Rotondi, G. 1912. *Leges publicae populi romani.* Milan.

Rouland, N. 1979. *Pouvoir politique et dépendance personnelle dans l'Antiquité romaine: Genèse et rôle des rapports de clientèle.* Brussels.

Rowland, R.J. 1970. 'Cicero's *necessarii*', *CJ* 65: 193–8.

Rüpke, J. 1992. 'Wer las Caesars *Bella* als *Commentarii*?', *Gymnasium* 99: 201–26.

Rüpke, J. 2011. *The Roman Calendar from Numa to Constantine: Time, History, and the Fasti.* Oxford.

Russell, A. 2016. *The Politics of Public Space in Republican Rome.* Cambridge.

Ryan, F.X. 1995. 'Two Senators in 73 BC', *ZPE* 108: 306–8.

Salerno, F. 1990. *Dalla consecratio alla publicatio bonorum.* Naples.

Saller, R. 1982. *Personal Patronage under the Early Empire.* Cambridge.

Saller, R. 1989. 'Patronage and Friendship in Early Imperial Rome: Drawing the Distinction', in A. Wallace-Hadrill (ed.), *Patronage in Ancient Society.* London, 49–62.

Saller, R. 1994. *Patriarchy, Property and Death in the Roman Family.* Cambridge.

Salway, B. 1994. 'What's in a Name? A Survey of Roman Onomastic Practice from c. 700 B.C. to A.D. 700', *JRS* 84: 124–45.

Santangelo, F. 2007. *Sulla, the Elites and the Empire: A Study of Roman Policies in Italy and the Greek East.* Leiden.

Suerbaum, W. 2002. *Die archaische Literatur von den Anfängen bis Sullas Tod: Die vorliterarische Periode und die Zeit von 240 bis 78 v. Chr.* Munich.

Savunen, L. 1997. *Women in the Urban Texture of Pompeii.* Helsinki.

Schanz, M., and Hosius, C. 1928. *Geschichte der römischen Litteratur bis zum Gesetzgebungswerk des Kaisers Justinian.* Munich.

Schmidt, P.L. 1972. 'Catos Epistula ad M. filium und die Anfänge der römischen Briefliteratur', *Hermes* 100: 568–76.

Schnurbusch, D. 2011. *Convivium: Form und Bedeutung aristokratischer Geselligkeit in der römsichen Antike.* Stuttgart.

Scholz, P. 2011. *Den Vätern folgen: Sozialisation und Erziehung der republikanischen Senatsaristokratie.* Berlin.

Scholz, U.W. 1963. *Der Redner M. Antonius.* Erlangen.

Schulz, F. 1951. *Classical Roman Law.* Oxford.

Schulze, W. 1904. *Zur Geschichte lateinischer Eigennamen.* Berlin.

Schwarz, C.G. 1720. *Commentariolum de petitione consulatus ad Marcum fratrem.* Altdorf.

Schwarz, C.G., and Hummel, B.F. 1791. *Commentariolum de petitione consulatus ad Marcum fratrem.* Nuremberg.

Sciarrino, E. 2011. *Cato the Censor and the Beginnings of Latin Prose.* Columbus.

Scullard, H.H. 1973. *Roman Politics, 220–150 B.C.*, 2nd edn. Oxford.

Scullard, H.H. 1981. *Festivals and Ceremonies of the Roman Republic*. Ithaca.

Seager, R. 1964. 'The First Catilinarian Conspiracy', *Historia* 13: 338–47.

Seager, R. 1972a. 'Cicero and the Word *Popularis*', *CQ* 22: 328–38.

Seager, R. 1972b. '*Factio*: Some Observations', *JRS* 62: 53–8.

Seager, R. 1994. 'Sulla', in J.A. Crook, A. Lintott, and E. Rawson (eds.), *The Cambridge Ancient History*, 2nd edn., vol. 9. Cambridge, 165–207.

Seager, R. 1997. '*Repetundae, maiestas* and Cruelty in Cicero's *Verrines*', *Ancient History: Resources for Teachers* 27: 1–7.

Seager, R. 2001. '*Maiestas* in the Late Republic: Some Observations', in J.W. Cairns and O.F. Robinson (eds.), *Critical Studies in Ancient Law, Comparative Law and Legal History*. Portland, 392–400.

Seager, R. 2002. *Pompey the Great*, 2nd edn. Oxford.

Sedley, D. 1989. 'Philosophical Allegiance in the Greco-Roman World', in M. Griffin and J. Barnes (eds.), *Philosophia Togata I: Essays on Philosophy and Roman Society*. Oxford, 97–119.

Seel, O. 1968. *Bellum Gallicum*, 2nd edn. Leipzig.

Shackleton Bailey, D.R. 1965. *Cicero's Letters to Atticus*, vol. 1. Cambridge.

Shackleton Bailey, D.R. 1966. *Cicero's Letters to Atticus*, vol. 5. Cambridge.

Shackleton Bailey, D.R. 1971. *Cicero*. London.

Shackleton Bailey, D.R. 1976. *Two Studies in Roman Nomenclature*. New York.

Shackleton Bailey, D.R. 1977. *Cicero: Epistulae ad Familiares*, vol. 1. Cambridge.

Shackleton Bailey, D.R. 1980. *Cicero: Epistulae ad Quintum fratrem et M. Brutum*. Cambridge.

Shackleton Bailey, D.R. 1986. '*Nobiles* and *novi* reconsidered', *AJPh* 107: 255–60.

Shackleton Bailey, D.R. 1988. *M. Tullius Cicero: Epistulae ad Quintum fratrem, Epistulae ad M. Brutum accedunt Commentariolum petitionis, fragmenta epistularum*. Stuttgart.

Shackleton Bailey, D.R. 1989. 'Two Passages in Cicero's Letters', *AJAH* 14: 70–2.

Shackleton Bailey, D.R. 1994. '*Com. pet.* 10', *HSCPh* 96: 197–9.

Shackleton Bailey, D.R. 1995. *Onomasticon to Cicero's Letters*. Stuttgart.

Shackleton Bailey, D.R. 2002. *Cicero: Letter to Quintus and Brutus, Letter Fragments, Letter to Octavian, Invectives, Handbook of Electioneering*. Cambridge, Mass.

Shatzman, I. 1975. *Senatorial Wealth and Roman Politics*. Brussels.

Sherk, R.K. 1984. *Rome and the Greek East to the Death of Augustus*. Cambridge.

Sherwin White, A.N. 1973. *The Roman Citizenship*, 2nd edn. Oxford.

Shorey, P. 1909. 'Φύσις, μελέτη, ἐπιστήμη', *TAPhA* 40, 185–201.

Sillett, A. 2016. 'Quintus Cicero's *Commentariolum*: A Philosophical Approach to Roman Elections', in E.P. Cueva and J. Martinez (eds.), *Splendide mendax: Rethinking Fakes and Forgeries in Classical, Late Antique, and Early Christian Literature*. Groningen, 177–91.

Sjögren, H. 1913. 'Tulliana III', *Eranos* 13: 111–46.

Skinner, M.B. 2005. *Sexuality in Greek and Roman Culture*. Oxford.

Smith, C.J. 2006. *The Roman Clans: The Gens from Ancient Ideology to Modern Anthropology*. Cambridge.

Smith, C.J., and Covino, R. (eds.), 2011. *Praise and Blame in Roman Republican Oratory*. Swansea.

Solin, H., and Salomies, O. 1988. *Repertorium nominum gentilium et cognominum Latinorum*. Hildesheim.

Solmsen, F. 1968. 'Dialectic without the Forms', in G.E.L. Owen (ed.), *Aristotle on Dialectic: The Topics*. Oxford, 49–68.

Spielvogel, J. 1993. *Amicitia und res publica*. Stuttgart.

Spina, L. 1996. 'Ricordo "elettorale" di un assassino (Q. Cic. *Comm. Pet.* 10)', in G. Germano (ed.), *Classicità, medioevo e umanesimo: Studi in onore di Salvatore Monti*. Naples, 57–62.

Starr, R.J. 1987. 'The Circulation of Literary Texts in the Roman World', *CQ* 37: 213–23.

Staveley, E.S. 1972. *Greek and Roman Voting and Elections*. Ithaca.

Steck, U. 2009. *Der Zeugenbeweis in den Gerichtsreden Ciceros*. Frankfurt am Main.

Steel, C. 2001. *Cicero, Rhetoric, and Empire*. Oxford.

Steel, C. 2006. *Roman Oratory*. Cambridge.

Steel, C. 2011. 'Cicero's Oratory of Praise and Blame and the Practice of Elections in the Late Roman Republic', in C. Smith and R. Covino (eds.), *Praise and Blame in Roman Republican Rhetoric*. Swansea, 35–48.

Steel, C. 2013a. 'Cicero, Oratory, and Public Life', in C. Steel (ed.), *The Cambridge Companion to Cicero*. Cambridge, 160–70.

Steel, C. 2013b. *The End of the Roman Republic, 146 to 44 BC*. Edinburgh.

Steel, C. 2014. 'Rethinking Sulla: The Case of the Roman Senate', *CQ* 64: 657–68.

Steel, C., and Blom, H. van der (eds.). 2013. *Community and Communication: Oratory and Politics in Republican Rome*. Oxford.

Stewart, R. 1995. 'Catiline and the Crisis of 63–60 BC', *Latomus* 54: 62–78.

Stirewalt, Jr., M.L. 1993. *Studies in Ancient Greek Epistolography*. Atlanta.

Stowers, S.K. 1986. *Letter Writing in Greco-Roman Antiquity*. Philadelphia.

Strasburger, H. 1939. 'Optimates', *RE* 18.1. Munich, 773–98.

Stroh, W. 1986. *Taxis und Taktik: De advokatische Dispositionskunst in Ciceros Gerechtsreden*. Stuttgart.

Stroup, S.C. 2010. *Catullus, Cicero, and a Society of Patrons: The Generation of the Text*. Cambridge.

Sumi, G.S. 2005. *Ceremony and Power: Performing Politics in Rome between Republic and Empire*. Ann Arbor.

Sumner, G.V. 1973. *The Orators in Cicero's Brutus: Prosopography and Chronology*. Toronto.

Sykutris, J. 1931. 'Epistolographie', *RE* Suppl. 5. Stuttgart, 185–220.

Syme, R. 1939. *The Roman Revolution*. Oxford.

Syme, R. 1958. *Tacitus*, 2 vols. Oxford.

Syme, R. 1964. *Sallust*. Berkeley and Los Angeles.

Syme, R. 1979. *Roman Papers*, 2 vols. Oxford.

Syme, R. 2016. *Approaching the Roman Revolution: Papers in Republican History*, ed. F. Santangelo. Oxford.

Tarpin, M. 2002. *Vici et pagi dans l'Occident romain*. Rome.

Tatum, W.J. 1988. 'The Epitaph of Publius Scipio Reconsidered', *CQ* 38: 253–8.

Tatum, W.J. 1990. 'The *Lex Clodia de censoria notione*', *CPh* 85: 34–43.

Tatum, W.J. 1991a. 'Cicero, the Elder Curio, and the Titinia Case', *Mnemosyne* 44: 364–71.

Tatum, W.J. 1991b. 'Military Defeat and Electoral Success in Rome', *AHB* 5: 149–52.

Tatum, W.J. 1997. 'Friendship, Politics and Literature in Catullus: Poems 1, 65 and 66, 116', *CQ* 47: 482–500.

Tatum, W.J. 1999. *The Patrician Tribune: Publius Clodius Pulcher*. Chapel Hill.

Tatum, W.J. 2001. 'The Consular Elections for 190 B.C.', *Klio* 83: 388–401.

Tatum, W.J. 2002. Q. 'Cicero, *Commentariolum petitionis* 33', *CQ* 52: 394–8.

Tatum, W.J. 2003–4. 'Elections in Rome', *CJ* 99: 203–16.

Tatum, W.J. 2007. '*Alterum est tamen boni viri, alterum boni petitoris*: The Good Man Canvasses', *Phoenix* 61: 109–35.

Tatum, W.J. 2009a. 'The *Plebiscitum Atinium* Once More', in H. Kowalski and P. Modejski (eds.), *Terra, mare et homines II: Studies in Memory of Tadeusz Łoposzko*. Lublin, 189–208.

Tatum, W.J. 2009b. 'Roman Democracy?, in R.K. Balot (ed.), *A Companion to Greek and Roman Political Thought*. Oxford, 214–28.

Tatum, W.J. 2011. 'The Late Republic: Autobiographies and Memoirs in the Age of the Civil Wars', in G. Marasco (ed.), *Political Autobiography and Memoirs in Antiquity: A Brill Companion*. Leiden, 161–87.

Tatum, W.J. 2013. 'Campaign Rhetoric', in C. Steel and H. van der Blom (eds.), *Community and Communication: Oratory and Politics in Republican Rome*. Oxford, 133–50.

Tatum, W.J. 2015. 'The Practice of Politics and the Unpredictable Dynamics of Clout in the Roman Republic', in D. Hammer (ed.), *A Companion to Greek Democracy and the Roman Republic*. Oxford, 257–73.

Tatum, W.J. 2017. 'Intermediaries in Political Communication: *Adlegatio* and its Uses', in C. Rosillo López (ed.), *Political Communication in the Roman World*. Leiden, 55–80.

Tatum, W.J. forthcoming a. ''88', in A. Valentina and J. Prag (eds.), *A Companion to Roman Political Culture*. Oxford.

Tatum, W.J. forthcoming b. 'Contio domestica', *Parola del Passato* 70.

Taub, L.C., and Doody, A. (eds.) 2009. *Authorial Voices in Greco-Roman Technical Writing*. Trier.

Taylor, L.R. 1939. 'Cicero's Aedileship', *AJPh* 60: 194–202.

Taylor, L.R. 1949. *Party Politics in the Age of Caesar*. Berkeley and Los Angeles.

Taylor, L.R. 1957. 'The Centuriate Assembly before and after the Reform', *AJPh* 78: 337–54.

Taylor, L.R. 1960. *The Voting Districts of the Roman Empire*. Rome.

Taylor, L.R. 1966. *Roman Voting Assemblies from the Hannibalic War to the Dictatorship of Caesar*. Ann Arbor.

Tempest, K. 2011. *Cicero: Politics and Persuasion in Ancient Rome*. London.

Thommen, L. 1989. *Das Volkstribunat der späten römischen Republik*. Stuttgart.

Thraede, K. 1970. *Grundzüge griechisch-römischer Brieftopik*. Munich.

Tibiletti, G. 1949. 'Il funzionamento dei comizi centuriati alla luce della Tavola Hebana', *Athenaeum* 27: 210–45.

Till, R. 1962. 'Ciceros Bewerbung ums Konsular (ein Beitrag zum Commentariolum petitionis)', *Historia* 11: 315–38.

Toland, J. 1714. *The Art of Canvassing at Elections, Perfect in all Respects*. London.

Trapp, M. 2003. *Greek and Latin Letters*. Cambridge.

Treggiari, S. 1969. *Roman Freedmen during the Late Republic*. Oxford.

Treggiari, S. 1991. *Roman Marriage: Iusti coniuges from the Time of Cicero to the Time of Ulpian*. Oxford.

Treggiari, S. 2002. *Roman Social History*. London.

Treggiari, S. 2007. *Terentia, Tullia and Publilia: The Women of Cicero's Family*. London.

Tydeman, J.W. 1838. *In Q. Tulli Ciceronis de petitione consulatus librum adnotatio*. Leiden.

Tyrrell, R.Y. 1885. *The Correspondence of M. Tullius Cicero*, 2nd edn., vol. 1. Dublin.

Tyrrell, R.Y. 1877. 'The Letters of Quintus Cicero', *Hermathena* 5: 40–59.

Tyrrell, R.Y., and Purser, L.C. 1904. *The Correspondence of M. Tullius Cicero*, 3rd edn., vol. 1. Dublin.

Vanderbroeck, P.J.J. 1986. 'Homo novus Again', *Chiron* 16: 239–42.

Vanderbroeck, P.J.J. 1987. *Popular Leadership and Collective Behavior in the Late Roman Republic (ca. 80–50 B.C.)*. Amsterdam.

Vasaly, A. 1993. *Representations: Images of the World in Ciceronian Oratory*. Berkeley and Los Angeles.

Vasaly, A. 2009. 'Domestic Politics, and the First Action of the Verrines', *ClAnt* 28: 101–37.

Vasaly, A. 2013. 'The Political Impact of Cicero's Speeches', in C. Steel (ed.), *The Cambridge Companion to Cicero*. Cambridge, 141–59.

Verboven, K. 1994. 'The Monetary Enactments of M. Marius Gratidianus', in C. Deroux (ed.), *Studies in Latin Literature and Roman History*, vol. 7. Brussels, 117–31.

Verboven, K. 2002. *The Economy of Friends: Economic Aspects of Amicitia and Patronage in the Late Republic*. Brussels.

Verboven, K. 2007. 'The Associative Order: Status and Ethos among Roman Businessmen in Late Republic and Early Empire', *Athenaeum* 95: 861–94.

Veyne, P. 1983. 'La folklore à Rome et les droits de la conscience publique sur la conduite individuelle', *Latomus* 42: 3–30.

Vlastos, G. 1991. *Socrates: Ironist and Moral Philosopher*. Cambridge.

Vogt, J. 1978. 'Nomenclator: Vom Lautsprecher zum Namenverarbeiter', *Gymnasium* 85: 327–38.

Waibel, L. 1969. *Das Commentariolum petitionis: Untersuchunger zur Frage der Echtheit*. Munich.

Walbank, F.W. 1957. *A Historical Commentary on Polybius*, vol. 1. Oxford.

Walbank, F.W. 1967. *A Historical Commentary on Polybius*, vol. 2. Oxford.

Walbank, F.W. 1985. *Selected Papers: Studies in Greek and Roman History and Historiography*. Cambridge.

Wallace-Hadrill, A. 1982. 'Civilis princeps: Between Citizen and King', *JRS* 72: 32–48.

Wallace-Hadrill, A. 1990. 'Roman Arches and Greek Honours: The Language of Power at Rome', *PCPhS* 37: 143–81.

Wallace-Hadrill, A. 1994. *Houses and Society in Pompeii and Herculaneum*. Princeton.

Wallace-Hadrill, A. 1997. '*Mutatis morum*: The Idea of a Cultural Revolution', in T. Habinek and A. Schiesaro (eds.), *The Roman Cultural Revolution*. Cambridge, 3–22.

Wallace-Hadrill, A. 2008. *Rome's Cultural Revolution*. Cambridge.

Walters, J. 1997. 'Invading the Roman Body: Manliness and Interpenetrability in Roman Thought', in J.P. Hallett and M.B. Skinner (eds.), *Roman Sexualities*. Princeton, 29–46.

Waltzing, J.-P. 1895–1900. *Étude historique sur les corporations professionnelles chez les romains depuis les origines jusqu'à la chute de l'empire d'occident*, 4 vols. Louvain.

Warrior, V. M. 1990. 'A Technical Meaning of *ducere* in Roman Elections? Livy's Account of the Elections of the Consuls for 189 B.C.', *Hermes* 133: 144–57.

Watson, G.R. 1969. *The Roman Soldier*. Ithaca.

Watt, W.S. 1958a. *M. Tulli Ciceronis Epistulae*, vol. 3. Oxford.

Watt, W.S. 1958b. 'Notes on the text of the *Commentariolum petitionis*', *CQ* 52: 32–44.

Weeber, K.-W. 2011. *Fièvre électorale à Pompéi*. Paris.

Wegehaupt, H. 1932. *Die Bedeutung und Anwendung von dignitas*. Breslau.

Weische, A. 1966. *Studien zur politische Sprache der römischen Republik*. Münster.

Welch, K. 1996. 'T. Pomponius Atticus: A Banker in Politics', *Historia* 19: 414–36.

Wesenberg, A.S. 1872. *Ciceronis Epistolae*. Leipzig.

White, N.P. 1978. 'Two Notes on Stoic Terminology', *AJPh* 99: 111–19.

White, P. 2010. *Cicero in Letters: Epistolary Relations of the Late Republic*. Oxford.

Wiedemann, T. 1992. *Gladiators and Emperors*. London.

Wiemer, W. 1930. *Quintus Tullius Cicero*. Halle.

Wikarjak, J. 1966. *Brochure électorale de Quintus Cicéron*. Wrocław.

Wilcox, A. 2012. *The Gift of Correspondence in Classical Rome: Friendship in Cicero's Ad Familiares and Seneca's Moral Epistles*. Madison.

Wildfang, R.L. 2006. *Rome's Vestal Virgins: A Study of Rome's Vestal Priestesses in the Late Republic and Early Empire*. London.

Williams, C.A. 2010. *Roman Homosexuality: Ideologies of Masculinity in Classical Antiquity*, 2nd edn. Oxford.

Williams, J.H.C. 2001. *Beyond the Rubicon: Romans and Gauls in Roman Italy*. Oxford.

Winterling, A. 2009. *Politics and Society in Imperial Rome*. Oxford.

Wirszubski, C. 1961. 'Audaces: A Study in Political Phraseology', *JRS* 51: 12–22.

Wiseman, T.P. 1971. *New Men in the Roman Senate, 139 B.C.–A.D. 14*. Oxford.

Wiseman, T.P. 1974. *Cinna the Poet and Other Roman Essays*. Leicester.

Wiseman, T.P. 1987. *Roman Studies*. Liverpool.

Wiseman, T.P. 1994. 'The Senate and the *populares*, 69–60 B.C.', in J.A. Crook, A. Lintott, and E. Rawson (eds.), *The Cambridge Ancient History*, 2nd edn., vol. 9. Cambridge, 327–67.

Wiseman, T.P. 2009. *Remembering the Roman People: Essays on Late Republican Politics and Literature*. Oxford.

Wisse, J. 2013. 'The Bad Orator: Between Clumsy Delivery and Political Danger', in C. Steel and H. van der Blom (eds.), *Community and Communication: Oratory and Politics in Republican Rome*. Oxford, 163–94.

Witcher, R. 2005. 'The Extended Metropolis: *Urbs, suburbium* and Population', *JRA* 18: 120–38.

Woolf, R. 2007. 'Particularism, Promises, and Persons in Cicero's *De officiis*', *OSAP* 23: 317–46.

Wooten, C. 1997. 'Cicero and Quintilian on the Style of Demosthenes', *Rhetorica* 15: 177–92.

Worthington, I. 2013. *Demosthenes of Athens and the Fall of Classical Greece*. Oxford.

Yakobson, A. 1999. *Elections and Electioneering in Rome*. Stuttgart.

Yakobson, A. 2014. 'Marius Speaks to the People: "New Man", Roman Nobility and Roman Political Culture', *SCI* 33: 283–300.

Yakobson, A. 2017. 'Consuls, Consulars, Aristocratic Competition and the People's Judgment', in M. Haake and A.-C. Harders (eds.), *Politische Kultur und soziale Struktur der römischen Republik: Bilanzen und Perspektiven*. Stuttgart, 497–516.

Zetzel, J.E.G. 1995. *Cicero: De re publica*. Cambridge.

Zmeskal, K. 2009. *Adfinitas: Die Verwandtschaften der senatorischen Führungsschicht der römischen Republik von 218–31 v. Chr.* Passau.

Zumpt, A.W. 1871. *Der Kriminal-Prozess der römischen Republik*. Leipzig.

Index

This index does not repeat guidance offered by the table of contents. Nor does it cover the continuous Latin text of the *Brief Handbook* furnished in this volume. References to ancient writers are supplied only when they are material to the discussion in which they are located.

glory 7, 123, 131, 158, 238–9;
  see also fame
good luck 185, 212, 237
goodwill 23, 24, 25, 28, 92, 125, 127, 129,
  149, 234
goodwill of the nobles 149, 180–1;
  see also goodwill
goodwill of the people 83 n. 441, 92, 123,
  218–19, 220–1, 229, 264;
  see also goodwill; popular favour
gossip, *see* rumour
Gracchus, Gaius, *see* Sempronius
  Gracchus, Gaius
grafitti 38
gratia 6, 8, 21, 23, 27, 29, 30, 34, 36,
  40, 43–4, 64, 97, 98, 168, 171,
  178, 179–80, 186, 214, 240, 244,
  250, 252, 285–6; *see also* gratitude;
  influence
Gratidia 202–3
Gratidius, Marcus 83 n. 446, 202–3
gratiosus 179–80
gratitude 6, 28, 39–40, 83, 85, 86, 91, 92,
  104–5, 115, 125, 127, 131, 137, 139, 169,
  179–80, 231–3, 235, 249, 268–9; see
  also *gratia*
gratuita comitia 44, 180
Greek subjects of Rome 70 n. 356, 117

Hannibal 44
hendiadys 161
Helvius Sabinus, Gnaeus 39
Herennius, Marcus (cos. 93) 213
Herodotus 51
high birth, *see* aristocracy; family; nobility
high culture 83, 87, 121, 135, 247–8, 273,
  283, 289–90; *see also* erudition as
  cultural capital
hill 241–2
Hirtius, Aulus (cos. 43) 106
homoeoptoton 50 n. 252
homoeoteleuton 50 n. 252
honor 5, 29
honour, *see* dignity; *dignitas*
hope 135; *see also* political promise
Horace 29 n. 138, 30
Hortensius Hortalus, Quintus (cos. 69)
  84, 86–7, 91 n. 497, 95
hospitality 268–9
hospites 21
Hostilius Mancinus, Lucius (cos. 145) 46
house 117, 125, 137, 143, 145, 147, 165, 222,
  225, 248–50, 251–3, 270, 274–5; see
  also *domus*

household 225
humanitas 247–8; *see also* high culture

imperatives 62
imperium 7
in campum descendere 255
incest 198; *see also* sexual immorality
industria, see assiduousness; industry
industry 123, 125, 129, 133, 141, 143, 147,
  149, 157, 166, 178, 185, 189, 240, 264,
  267, 269, 280; see also *cura*;
  assiduousness
infamia 206
infamis 191
influence 21, 23, 25, 26, 28, 91, 125, 127,
  129, 133, 166, 168, 178, 179, 223–4,
  230, 231–2, 236, 240–1, 244;
  see also *gratia*
ingenium 157, 161, 166, 210, 214;
  see also talent
ingratiation 30, 37, 70, 71, 141, 221,
  264–70; see also *blanditia*
ingratitude, *see* gratitude
innocens, see blameless
insidiae 261, 282; *see also* treachery
integrity 77, 102; *see also* candidates,
  personal morality
intelligence 20, 25, 83
intermediaries in canvassing 28, 29, 32,
  39–40, 42–3, 115, 131, 133, 135, 137,
  143, 182, 226, 227, 240–4, 259;
  see also recommendations,
  supporters
interpres 288
interrex 13 n. 52
invective 70, 74, 101, 104, 167, 186–8, 190,
  191, 193, 196, 263, 279, 283;
  see also negative campaigning
invidia 166, 216, 228; *see also* envy
irony 72–3, 97, 162, 274
Isocrates 52, 57
Italy 64, 133, 160, 174, 225–6, 227, 231,
  242–3
iuventus 177, 247

Jugurthine War 44
Julius Caesar, Gaius (cos. I 59) 23 n. 106,
  40 n. 191, 49, 53–5, 55, 57 n. 292, 58,
  59, 78, 79, 80, 189, 192, 199, 200, 208,
  209, 221, 224
Julius Caesar, Lucius (cos. 90) 205
Julius Caesar, Lucius (cos. 64) 55, 89–90
Julius Caesar Augustus, Gaius (cos. I 43)
  11, 106, 258